JOY DAVID'S

Hotels, Inns, Restaurants, Places to Visit

WALES
Central England & East Anglia

Potted History County by County
Exciting Attractions and Places to Visit
Great Venues, Great Food
and Comfort, Great Value

THE PERFECT COMPANION FOR
LOCALS & VISITORS
WHICH YOU CANNOT AFFORD TO BE WITHOUT

Copyright Joy David
First Published 1996
ISBN 1-899311-30-0
All rights reserved

British Library Catalogue-In-Publication Data
Catalogue Data is available from the British Library

All information is included in good faith and is believed to be correct at the time of going to press. No responsibility can be accepted for error.

The book is sold subject to the condition that it shall not by way of trade or otherwise be lent, re-sold, hired out, or otherwise circulated without the publisher's prior consent in any form of binding or cover other than that in which it is published and without similar condition including this condition being imposed on the subsequent purchaser.

Typesetting, film and scanning by: Typestyle, Ivybridge, Devon
Printed and Bound in Great Britain by BPC Wheaton, Exeter, Devon

DON'T DELAY

SEND FOR YOUR

JOY DAVID
ADVANTAGE CARD

TODAY

MEMBERSHIP IS ABSOLUTELY
FREE
TO PURCHASERS OF THIS BOOK

THE ADVANTAGE CARD..
..enables members to take advantage of the many special offers;
Discounted Accommodation, Entrance Fees, Food and Wines - a more enjoyable time for less outlay.

Save yourselves £££ whenever you visit participating venues featured in this book as well as receiving a chatty newsletter and an up date on special offers three times a year.

HOTELS, INNS, RESTAURANTS AND COUNTRY HOUSES

INTRODUCTIONS

CONTENTS INCLUDE:

Chapter 1 **WALES NORTH AND SOUTH**
*Things to do, places to stay, all the rich
and wonder of Wales for you to explore*   p.4

Chapter 2 **THE HEARTLAND OF ENGLAND**
including Hereford & Worcester, Staffordshire   p.88
Shropshire, Warwickshire, The West Midlands
*Sights to see and places to visit Venues in which
to lunch, dine, stay and visit From Stratford-upon-Avon
and Shakespeare to the Potteries*

Chapter 3 **THE MID-SHIRES**
Northampton, Derbyshire   p.154
*Sights to see, places to visit, venues in which to lunch
dine and stay from Robin Hood country to the tiniest
county of all, Rutland*

Chapter 4 **THE COTSWOLDS**
including Gloucestershire, Oxfordshire   p.187
*Sights to see and places to visit in which to lunch,
dine, stay and visit The glorious beauty of the
Cotswolds and the magic of Oxford*

Chapter 5 **BUCKINGHAMSHIRE, BERKSHIRE,
BEDFORDSHIRE & HERTFORDSHIRE**
Sights to see and places to visit   p.212
*Venues in which to lunch, dine, stay and
visit including Windsor Castle*

Chapter 6 **EAST ANGLIA**
including Norfolk, Suffolk, Cambridgeshire &   p.225
Lincolnshire
*Sights to see and places to visit Venues in which to
lunch, dine, stay and visit Wonderful coast and
countryside, historic cities and the University town
of Cambridge*

Guide to Short Breaks   p.274
Guide to Where to eat & Drink   p.278
Guide to Conference Venues   p.296
Guide to Places to Visit   p.300
A-Z Index   p.385
Maps   p.396
Glossary of Welsh pronunciation   p.401

ales has always held an awed fascination for me with its rugged beauty, its determined independence and its doughty people. There is so much to see and do and I have to admit that you really have to spend time in the Principality to really begin to understand the ethos and appreciate the scenic splendour. North Wales for example has long been the playground of travellers from the great western conurbations and with improvements to the A55 coast road, day visits no longer consist of hastily snatched hours of pleasure between wearisome car journeys. Yet always there is the choice between the sea and land, because perhaps nowhere in Britain is there such a diversity of breathtaking scenery, with so many leisure activities to be indulged in. Driving south-west along the A487 from Machynlleth will immediately transport you into an area with an astonishingly rich history which will be new to many. Then there is the opportunity to explore the Pembrokeshire Coast to the south of Cardigan Bay - the area now known as Dyfed - taking in most of the coast in a great sweep from Aberaeron right round to Carmarthen. South West Wales is totally different but with so much to offer the visitor. A wonderful, exciting country.

The Heartland of England covers the excitement of Skakespeare country and the extraordinary history of The Pottery Towns as well as introducing you to unusual and unknown parts of Birmingham which may well have escaped your notice. In the Midshires there is the man-made masterpiece Rutland Water and the fairytale Sherwood Forest whilst the chapter on the Cotswolds unveils all the magical beauty of this most treasured part of England. East Anglia has been a happy stomping ground to me for years - indeed I lived there at one time - and so it is always a pleasure to include it knowing that it will delight every visitor who goes there whether it is inland and the stunning
villages like Lavenham, the coastline facing out to the North Sea, the flower town of Spalding in Lincolnshire or the majesty of Cambridge with its ancient university buildings.

Everytime I write a book I find out more and more about the British Isles and wish that I had spent more time travelling its length and breadth in my younger days rather than seeking out other countries. We miss so much if we do not discover our own treasures. Do remember to apply for your ADVANTAGE CARD - it offers you so many benefits and a chatty magazine full of information and up-date news on your favourite establishments. The form is at the back of the book.

INTRODUCTIONS

Slightly different from my usual books both in format and content, the objective has been to provide a compact and comprehensive volume which encompasses everything the visitor may wish for in the areas covered. Giving such a variation of Visitor Attractions has left me short of space in which to write about the counties covered in each chapter but I hope it is enough to whet your appetites and lead you on to discover more.

You may wonder why I have decided to include Wales alongside the counties stretching across to East Anglia. Basically it is because I could not get the whole of the British Isles into one book and so the decision was reached to make this the first in a series of four books covering the whole of these islands. This has also been subject to change because the forerunner to this book is Joy David's Choice - England.

HOTELS, INNS, RESTAURANTS AND COUNTRY HOUSES

WALES

Includes

Preswyla Guest House	Aberdovey	p.47
Three Salmons Inn	Abergavenny	p.48
Fron Heulog Country House	Betswy-y-Coed	p.49
Rhiw Goch Inn	Bronaker	p.50
White Horse Hotel	Builth Wells	p.51
Tafarn Pantydderwen	Carmarthen	p.52
Gwern Borter Manor	Rowen Nr. Conwy	p.53
Hawk & Buckle	Denbigh	p.54
Penmaenuchaf Hall Hotel	Dolgellau	p.55
The Ivy House	Dolgellau	P.56
The Maesllwch Country Hotel	Glasbury	p.57
The Old Rectory	Glan Conwy	p.58
Llwyndu Farmhouse	Llanaber	p.59
Guidfa House	Llandrindod Wells	p.60
Hundred House Inn	Llandrindod Wells	p.61
Llanerch 16th Century Inn	Llandrindod Wells	p.62
Bryn-y-Bia Lodge	Llandudno	p.63
Southcliffe Hotel	Llandudno	p.64
Queens Hotel	Llandudno Junction	p.65
Lake Country House	Llangammarch Wells	p.66
Penrhos Golf & Country Club	Llanrhystud	p.67
Dolbrodmaeth Inn	Machynlleth	p.68
Golden Lion	Newport	p.69
Lower New Inn	Pontypool	p.70
Egerton Grey Country House	Porthkerry	p.71
Portmeirion	Portmeirion	p.72
Holt Lodge	Rossett	p.73
The Alyn	Rossett	p.74
Ye Old Anchor Inn	Ruthin	p.75
The Old Mill	St Clears	p.76
St Non's Hotel	St Davids	p.77
Ramsey House	St Davids	p.78
New Inn	Talgarth	p.79
Maes-y-Nevadd Hotel	Talsaenau	p.80
The Ysgethin Inn	Talybont	p.81
Castle Coaching Inn	Trecastle	p.82
Barratts Restaurant	Tyn Rhyl	p.83
Peppers Restaurant	Welshpool	p.84
Golfa Hotel	Welshpool	p.85
Erdig	Wrexham	p.86
Llwyn Onn Hall	Wrexham	p.87

HOTELS, INNS, RESTAURANTS AND COUNTRY HOUSES

o attempt to describe Wales in a chapter, albeit a lengthy one, is ludicrous. To do it justice in a large volume would still bedifficult but as this option is not open to me I hope you will find the tales of my journeying an appetiser encouraging you to delve into, and enjoy the beauty, the splendour, the warmth and the people of this wonderful Principality.

I decided to start by embracing Anglesey, Snowdonia and the Lleyn Peninsula which allows me a choice between the sea and land, with a breathtaking diversity of scenery and activities. Firstly, I used **Bangor** as a base. Here is a city of impressive religious and historic heritage. A place in which to enjoy the natural beauty of the area and to be drawn to the many old buildings which have been carefully maintained or restored. **The cathedral** was founded by St Deiniol in 575Ad - 70 years before Canterbury - and is built on one of the oldest Christian sites in Britain. Its turbulent history has included sacking by the Vikings and destruction by King John's forces when they burnt Bangor in 1210, and it is the resting place of Prince Owain of Gwynedd. Work was begun on the present Cathedral in the mid 13th Century, and was finished with the completion of the Central Tower in 1967.

The City of Bangor is dominated by the academic towers of the **University of Wales** - the 'college on the hill' - which celebrated its centenary in 1984. Apart from good shopping in pedestrianised streets I wandered down to the waterfront intent on visiting the Pier. It stretches a full 1500feet into the Menaï Straits, and has recently been restored to its Victorian splendour.

As I moved away from the coast and drove into the mountains the scenery became truly spectacular. Dyffryn Ogwen - the Ogwen Valley - delights artists and photographers. My route took me through **Bethesda**, a village with a Hebrew name which means 'a house of mercy', and along the shores of Llyn Ogwen. The landscaped was dominated by the mountain ranges of Carnedd Llywelyn, Carnedd Dafydd, Tryfan, Glyder Fach and Glyder Fawr. Salmon and sea-trout ascend the River Ogwen as far as the falls below Llyn Ogwen, and many of the lakes in the area - Ogwen, Bochlwyd, Ffynnon Lloer - provide excellent sea-trout fishing, for which permits are available locally.

And so to **Llanberis**. With a history going back to the Iron Age, the town is one of the oldest settlements in Wales and a bastion of the Welsh language and tradition. Old Roman forts lie to the east and west, and the uplands behind Llanberis are reputed to be linked to the legends of King Arthur. Although perhaps best known as the lower terminus of the **Snowdon Mountain railway**, Llanberis is also renowned as a centre for climbers.

The views across the twin lakes to the mountains are stunning, and from here their grandeur contrasts sharply with the softness of lush green meadows and the beauty of the lower wooded slopes. You may well opt for the Mountain Railway, as I did, as the favoured way of reaching Snowdon's summit - climbing up tracks is no longer for me! The Mountain Railway is Britain's only public rack and pinion railway. It was opened in 1896 and climbs more than 3,000 feet, the journey lasting approximately an hour. Views on the way up are spectacular, and from the summit, on clear days, you can see the Isle of Anglesey, the Wicklow mountains in Ireland, and the Isle of Man. First train of the day is usually at 9am from Llanberis - much depends on the weather.

Two places to visit in Llanberis - **The Piggery Pottery** and **The Snowdon Honey Farm** which are right in the centre of town. **The National Museum of Wales** has its Northern branch in Llanberis, and the Power of Wales Exhibition is particularly well-presented.

To most people, at least since 1969, **Caernarfon** means ' castle'. It was then that the Investiture of HRH Prince Charles as Prince of Wales took place, although what is not quite such common knowledge is that Caernarfon was also the scene for the Investiture of Prince Edward in 1911 - later to be Edward VIII and then Duke of Windsor, after his abdication. The setting of the castle is superb. The King's Gate is said to be the mightiest in the land; the Eagle Tower houses an exhibition and audio visual programme; the Royal Welch Fusiliers have their museum in the Queen's Tower; the Prince of Wales' exhibition is in the North-East Tower; and in the Chamberlain Tower there is an exhibition of the Castles of Edward I.

But Caernarfon is much more than a magnificent castle. In the past the landscape artist, Turner, came here, and marvelled at the quality of the light and sunsets. At the turn of the century so many famous newspaper men had connections with the town that it was known as the Fleet Street of Wales. The River Seiont flows past the castle walls into the Menai Strait. There can surely be no finer way of viewing both town and castle than from a boat on one of the regular trips run from the quayside.

The lovely, quiet part of Britain that is the Lleyn Peninsula is full of rare, natural treasures, whether it is the Peninsula's own breed of sheep, the abundant wild flowers, the hedgerows abounding in honeysuckle, rosehips and blackberries, or the overwhelming sense of history. It is a very Welsh heartland.

The journey down the Peninsula is dominated by the two peaks of Yr Eifl (The Rivals) mountains, proof surely that nowhere in North Wales can you ever be far from high ground! Going along the B4417 one comes to **Nefyn**, a coastal resort which was once a halt for pilgrims on their way to **Bardsey Island** (Ynys Enlli - the island of tides, where 20,000 saints are said to be buried.) Now, the village's church of St Mary houses a maritime museum, and if you have time to pause take a look at the fine, sweeping bay formed by Nefyn, Morfa Nefyn and Porth Dinllaen. The 'Whistling Sands' at **Porthoer** is one of the area's outstanding beaches, an ideal spot to take the folding chairs out of the car boot and relax for a while. It is fact that the golden sands whistle mysteriously as one picks one's way across the picturesque bay.

Churches in the Lleyn Peninsula are among the most attractive in Wales. There is a stunningly simple example at **Llangwnnadl**, which lies to the north-east of Porthoer, and a mile or so inland at **Bryncroes** is St Marys on the site of St Mary's Well, an important watering place on the Pilgrim's Route. By taking a minor road across country I came to **Llangian** where, in the churchyard of St Gian's, one of the earliest known doctors from the 16th century is buried.

The final point of interest on the southernmost tip of the Lleyn Peninsula is **Aberdaron**, which was always the last port of call for pilgrims on their way to Bardsey. The place is steeped in history. At least one Prince of Wales has sheltered in the 6th-century church of St Hywyn which nestles on the seashore, as have Cromwell's soldiers. It is said that the marks still visible on the door pillars were made by those same soldiers as they sharpened their swords.

Next to **Abersoch**. This is best done by taking the A499, which together with the A497, is a most attractive road following the southern coastline of the Peninsula as far as Porthmadog. This section of the coast is stunningly beautiful and has the weather to match. It is a mecca for sailing enthusiasts and sometimes referred to as ' Cowes of the North'. Ideal conditions mean that Abersoch and nearby Pwllheli are frequent locations for major British, European and World sailing championships, and for the casual sailor the waters offer some of the very best sheltered sailing facilities in Britain.

Until the earlier part of this century **Porthmadog** was a bustling shipping port. It served the international Welsh slate trade which was brought down from **Blaenau Ffestiniog** by the Ffestiniog Railway, now a major tourist attraction. The full round trip takes about 2 hours, and is well worth taking because of the wonderful scenery. Much of the town is flat - it is recognised as a model of 18th century town planning.

Whatever you do, do not leave this beautiful coast without visiting **Portmeirion**. This unique village was created by Sir Clough Williams-Ellis between 1925 and 1972 in what he calls his 'light opera approach'. It is located on a secluded peninsula which juts out into Traeth Bach. It consists of fifty buildings arranged around a central Piazza, all predominantly Italianate in style, and is surrounded by the sub-tropical woodlands of Y Gwyllt.

I love the place for its beauty, its escapism and the totally peaceful atmosphere. To stay here either in self-catering accommodation in one of the villas or houses or to enjoy the superb hotel is a never to be forgotten experience. It is equally pleasureable for day visitors to wander round the village, have a meal in one of the restaurants, sit a while on the Piazza and dream dreams. Portmeirion Pottery is available in the shop - seconds in the Portmeirion shop and others in one of the delightful little shops.

Leaving the Lleyn Peninsula I took the A498 which led me to the A4085 and a spectacular, if slightly tortuous journey through the Snowdon mountain range to **Beddgelert**. There is a tradition here, and romantic legend, which suggests that the village's name (Geldert's Grave) comes from Prince Llywelyn's heroic dog Gelert, slain by the Prince who mistakenly thought the dog had killed his son. Later the prince realised a dead wolf was to blame, and the blood-spattered dog had been killed defending the boy.

The village which won the Queen Mother's Birthday Award 1992 - Keep Wales Tidy Campaign, is vastly different from those I visited on the Lleyn Peninsula. There the sea was always evident, the small hamlets bright and airy, a feeling of space all around. In the Aberglaslyn Valley lushness prevails. Paths close by lead to Snowdon, Moel Hebog, Moelwyn and the Cnicht, and the Rivers Glaswyn and Colwyn merge to flow through the glorious beauty of the Aberglaslyn Pass. Other beauty spots not to be missed include the Nant Gwynant Pass, and Cwm Pennant, where the River Dwyfor flows through one of Britain's most lyrical valleys.

Conwy is, literally, a fortress city by the sea. As you swoop down from the Sychnant Pass you will see that it is dominated by the castle built by Edward I as part of his master plan to subdue the Welsh. That was between 1283 and 1289 and today the castle is perhaps the most picturesque in Wales, the town walls with 22 towers and 3 original gateways the most complete of any in Europe. To make room for his castle, Edward moved Cistercianmonks from their Abbey to Maenan in the Conwy Valley. Of the Abbey all that remains is the Abbey church which is still in use after seven centuries - a haven of peace in the very centre of the busy town.

Thomas Telford's graceful suspension bridge is one of three crossing the river Conwy. It was opened in 1826 and in use until the modern road bridge was completed in 1958. As you drive east out of Conwy you will see alongside both bridges the tubular railway bridge, built by Robert Stephenson in 1846. A superb technical achievment, it is still a vital link on the railway line between Chester and Holyhead. Odd, how even in those days, care was taken in building the mock-medieval towers so that they harmonised with the castle. We are surely wrong to believe that our generation is the first to care about the environment!

HOTELS, INNS, RESTAURANTS AND COUNTRY HOUSES

From **Llandudno Junction** the A470 goes through another area famed for its scenery. The Vale of Conwy is more usually referred to locally as the **Conwy Valley**, and the road winds up the eastern bank of the river. This really is a lovely area to explore, and I suggest a drive as far as **Betws-y-Coed** where you can cross the river by bridge and so return to Conwy.

Llanrwst is an old market town and famed for its bridge built by Inigo Jones in 1636. Pont Fawr is narrow and humped, and until traffic lights were installed it was frequently the scene of heated arguments as drivers claimed right of way! If you walk to the centre of the bridge you will see a group of standing stones on the far bank. These are the Gorsedd Stones, and they are closely connected with the ceremonies associated with the bards who attend the National Eisteddfodau. At Llanrwst the stones are frequently marooned when the River Conwy breaks its banks during the winter months.

Betws-y-Coed is four miles further on. It is just 50 feet above sea level and entirely surrounded by hills of an average height of 1,000 feet. 'Y Coed' is the Welsh for 'the wood', and as you drive in over Telford's cast-iron Waterloo Bridge you must becaptivated by the surrounding woodlands - native hardwoods, and many species of conifer. This famous little village has four churches, of which St Michael's is the most venerable. The old part of the building dates back to the 14th century, while the large transept at the northern end and the vestry at the south-east were added in 1843.

Three rivers - the Conwy, the Lledr and the Llugwy - pass through or very close to Betws-y-Coed. This means there are several old bridges in the area. The Waterloo bridge I have mentioned already, and the other one that attracts tourists is Pont-y-Pair - the Bridge of the Cauldron. The River Llugwy passes beneath it, cascading out of the foaming waters of the upstream 'cauldron' formed by masses of black rock.

That water has already had a tumultous passage before it reaches Pont-y-Pair. The Swallow Falls are the most famous of several in the area, and these are found but a short drive up the A5. Steps lead down to the water's edge, and during the rainy season they are a truly spectacular sight as the waters of the Llugwy thunder down the rocky gorge, drenching the unwary.

High up in the hills there are the most beautiful lakes you could imagine, at altitudes ranging from 600 feet to almost 1500 feet. Lead pollution from old mines means that there are no fish in Llyn Gerionwydd, but it is a superb sailing and water-skiing venue. Llyn-y-Parc is shallow and also dead, but it is reachable from Pont-y-Pair and can be exceedingly beautiful, particularly when bracken and larches change colour in the autumn. There are gentle river walks along the banks of the Llugwy from Pont-y-Pair.

You will probably know of **Harlech** for its castle, again the work of Edward I, and from hearing those magnificent Welsh male voice choirs singing the rousing 'Men of Harlech'. The Castle does dominate the town. It was the stronghold of Owain Glyndwr, and was the last castle to fall in the Wars of the Roses. The town is charming with narrow streets and a wonderful golf course at Royal St Davids with International Class facilities. If you are a walker you will delight in the Rhinog range of mountains which form a grand backdrop to all these coastal towns and villages. You can reach them through the valleys of Cwm Bychan and Cwm Nantcol.

Barmouth is famed for its two miles of golden sands and is hard to beat for a family seaside holiday in Wales. You simply cannot get away from the sight of sleek sailing boats in this part of the world, and at Barmouth they look a picture.

Moving inland from Barmouth on the A496 which hugs the wooded banks of the Afon Mawddach is no hardship. The route is one followed by the art critic Ruskin and the poet Manley Hopkins. Wordsworth too loved this magnificent walking country.

At **Bontddu** is **The Clogau Gold Mine** - the Old Clogau - situated in a fold eight hundred feet up in the hills alongside the Hirgwm stream which tumbles downhill to Mawddach. It sounds extraordinary to those who do not know the story, but it is one of many in the area - so many that a ring round the Rhinog mountains has been called 'the Dolgellau Gold Belt'. Princess Margaret, the Princess Royal and the Princess of Wales all wear wedding rings fashioned from Clogau's Welsh gold.

15th-century **Dolgellau** was the Welsh Parliament capital of Owain Glyndwr. It is built of Welsh granite and roofed with grey-blue Welsh slate, yet what might be an unremittingly bleak scene is overwhelmed by the majesty of Cader Idris range of mountains, and further relieved by the softer beauty of the Mawddach Estuary.

Penmaenpool is on the south bank of the river at the point where the Mawddach estuary opens out. An ideal place to watch a wide variety of birds in their natural habitat from the RSPB Observatory and afterwards to call at **Penmaenuchaf Hall** for one of their famous afternoon teas. The Hall was built as a summer house for the Leigh-Taylor family in 1860, a Lancashire family with cotton connections, and has since housed two High Sheriffs of Meirionnydd. A delightful spot.

Bala, a pleasantly flat, market town makes a wonderful base for a holiday. Here there is a lake which when the water is low may allow you to see the remains of Pentre Celyn, the tiny village which was flooded to create what is now a reservoir supplying water for Liverpool. It seems always that progress has its down side, doesn't it? Yet filled with crystal-clear water from the mountains, stocked with lake trout and perch, this man-made lake is beautiful, hides its secrets well, and serves many useful purposes.

The town is best known as an international centre for watersports, with the five mile long Llyn Tegid judged by many to be the finest sailing lake in Britain. So you will head hereif you are a yachtsman, and turn to the River Tryweryn if you are keen to hone your canoe slalom skills or try the wild white waters that make the river one of Europe's finest venues for canoeists. Llyn Tegid will also attract you if you intend to pit your wits against the perch, pike and roach. The deep water gwyniad fish has been unique to the lake since the Ice Ages.

Bala is famous too for its Sheepdog Trials. They began here and the town has been associated with television's 'One Man and his Dog'.

Finally in this section, **Anglesey**. You cross one of the two bridges over the Menai Strait. The Menai Suspension Bridge was built by Telford in 1826, with graceful arches of Pemmon limestone and a central span suspended high above the water by massive chains. The nearby Britannia Bridge was once a tubular structure built by Stephenson, but while his similarly constructed bridge at Conwy is still in use in its original state, this one was destroyed by fire in 1970. It has since been remodelled, and is now a twin road and rail link with its new road deck carrying the A5. You cannot fail to notice that each bridge carries a large sign which reads 'Mon Man Cymru'. It is the Welsh for 'Anglesey, Mother of Wales'. For centuries this island's mild climate and rich farmland has made it the provider of grain for the harsher highlands of the Welsh interior. So you will find windmills here too, Llynnon Mill at **Llanddeusant** near Holyhead was built in 1775 and has recently been restored.

Anglesey is wonderful. It has a tremendous sense of freedom. Gone are the immensity of the mountain ranges, so much a part of this journey and instead there are gently rolling hills, low white cottages, and skies which seem endless. The whole of the island is criss-crossed with enticing small roads although there are two or three excellent A roads. I made for **Menai Bridge** with the intention of making my way up the east coast.

You will reach **Beaumaris** along a delightful wooded section of the A545 which follows the coast past the landscaped gardens of elegant Victorian mansions. The town was Edward I's 13th-century English garrison borough, which later became a busy seaport and fashionable Victorian resort. There is a castle, of course, andthe one at Beaumaris was the last and largest of those Edward built to contain the Welsh.

Llansadwrn off the B5109 has a gem of a Victorian church which is home for the oldest memorial stone in Wales. It is dedicated to St Saturnius and his wife, and you will find it set into the wall of the chancel.

Anglesey is famed for its sheltered beaches. **Red Wharf Bay** is a snug cove that reveals fifteen square miles of sand at low tide. Bathing only advisable on the incoming tide - the soft sands can be a trap for the unwary. Charles Dickens came here to report on the wreck and called in at The Panton Arms at **Pentraeth** for refreshment. At **Moelfre** you will be able to take a headland walk to the site of the 'Royal Charter' shipwreck in 1859. There are so many ancient sites on Anglesey, it is impossible to mention them all. At **Din Lligwy** between Moelfre and Amlwch, for example, there are the remains of six foot thick hut walls that were once part of an iron age village.

Llaneilian has a 15th-century church with Norman tower - passageways link the church to an old chapel with well-preserved carvings and decorative features. To the east of **Llangadrig** lies the site of an oratory or chapel established by a female recluse in the 7th century. At **Valley** I rejoined the A5. This wonderful old London to Holyhead road has been with us since the time of Elizabeth I - England's link with Ireland. A causeway carries it across from the mainland of Anglesey to Holy Island, and after a mile or so it reaches **Holyhead** and swings sharply right towards the inner harbour.

Holyhead was founded in the 3rd century AD, when the Romans built a fortress. St Cybi's Church is named after a Celtic saint who settled here in the 6th century, and dates from the 13th century to the 17th century. Holyhead mountain is a modest 220 metres high, but Celtic warriors once stood watch on the ramparts of the Iron Age hillfort, and Roman soldiers lit beacons from a watchtower.

From these heights if you look down and a little way to the west you will see South Stack, a lump of rock joined to Holy Island by a precarious suspension bridge. Unfortunately the bridge is closed to the public. Nevertheless there is a fine view of the lighthouse, built in 1909 and now automatic. This is where wildlife really flourishes. The RSPB confidently expect about 3,000 guillemots, 400 razorbills and 100 puffins each year. The best time to come is during the breeding season in late May or June.

If the weather is fine and sunny there is no finer spot to spend an hour or so than **Trearddur Bay**. Slip down to one of the rocky coves and inlets for a quiet picnic, or if you want to stay, there is plenty of excellent holiday accommodation ranging from simple caravans to the finest hotels.

The journey back across the island along the A5 will take you through **Gwalchmai** where the Anglesey Agricultural Show is held each August. Electricity there now comes from the national grid, which is no doubt an improvement on the supply - the first on Anglesey - which was once generated by a watermill.

No one should miss **Plas Newydd**. This elegant 18th-century house by James Wyatt, is the home of the Marquess of Anglesey, and is set in a landscaped garden on the banks of the Menai Strait. It contains an exhibition devoted to the work of Rex Whistler, and a military museum with relics of the Battle of Waterloo. You will find it open from April to late September, and it will be one of the fond memories you take with you as you retrace your route across the Britannia Bridge.

My next adventure took me to the north-east coast and to **Llandudno**. This elegant 19th-century purpose built holiday resort retains its character and the local council lays down strict guidelines which ensure that the many hotels on the sea front perpetuate the old world charm. The curved promenade stretches for two miles between Great Orme to the west and the slightly less impressive bulk of the Little Orme to the east. A visit to Llandudno must always include a trip to the summit of the Great Orme, and there are two excellent ways of getting there. The Great

Orme Tramway was opened in 1902, and is the longest cable-hauled tramway in Britain. From Victoria Station in Church Walks the climb is at first steep, the views spectacular. Yet, even that experience is surpassed by the breathtaking exhilaration afforded by the alternative route - The Cable Car. This, too, is reputed to be the longest in Britain.

The Great Orme has a history dating back some 300 million years. The newest tourist attraction in this designated Country Park, the Great Ore Copper Mine, is also of a great age, and is opening the eyes of visitors and experts alike.

Over recent years the discovery of rib and thigh bones which once served as scrapers and picks suggest that mining was carried out here more than 4000 years ago. Now it is possible to go on a short guided tour through candlelit Bronze Age tunnels, and one can only marvel at the work that was done by native Britons in a mining complex that went out of business 2000 years ago!

From **Llandudno Junction** it is easy to pay a visit to **Glanwydden** where **The Queen's Head** in the capable hands of Robert Cureton has won many awards for its imaginative food. The A55 will take you to **Rhos-on-Sea**. Here lie the dried-up beds of three long-dead creeks that once carried small timber ships inland from the coast. But for many years now Rhos-on-Sea has been a delightful backwater where holidays proceed at a leisurely pace.

Colwyn Bay next. The Welsh mountains form an impressive backdrop to the wonderful crescent of golden sands. The whole stretch of coastline is a combination of its Victorian ancestry and modern times. The town's Victorian architecture delights the historian, while Theatr Colwyn will provide for the lover of music and drama, a programme of productions that has included a visit by the Welsh National Opera.

The arrow straight road into **Abergele** will take you past Gwyrch Castle, a romantic 19th-century folly which was built to a medieval design by Lloyd Bamford Hesketh. Nestling against wooded hills the castle looks in excellent condition, yet closer examination will reveal broken windows and other signs of neglect. Many ambitious plans for its use have been mooted, sadly, none so far has reached fruition.

Abergele is an historic market town, with some splendid walking country in the hills behind the excellent golf course. Nearby **Pensarn** is its seafront suburb. As well as fine sandy beaches there are long walks here too, along grassy dunes which afford an alternative view of Gwrych Castle.

There is a landmark familiar to all regular visitors to this area; the graceful spire of St Margaret's Church, **Bodelwyddan**. You can reach this wonderful building - popularly known as the Marble Church - by taking the A55 out of Abergele until you reach the first exit. The foundation stone was laid in 1856, and the church was built of native limestone to a design by John Gibson. There is a marvellous hammer-beam roof with arched principals and collars and cusped spandrils together with beautiful stained glass windows by Burne-Jones, T.F. Curtis and

WALES

The Parish Church of St Giles was built in the late 15th and early 16th centuries, and is one of the 'Seven Wonders of Wales'. Incidentally all seven are mentioned in the 19th century rhyme which goes:

> Pistyll Rhaeadr and Wrexham Steeple,
> Snowdon;s Mountain without its people,
> Overton Yew Trees, St Winefride's Well,
> Llangollen Bridge and Gresford Bells.

You reach the church by strolling through Church Walks, a gentle little backwater with quaint half-timbered buildings. The church is at least the third to be built on the site - there was one already standing in 1220. It is a church full ofinterest and one or two surprises.

Before I set off to explore the border country starting at Chirk,I went to **Holt** taking the A534 out of Wrexham. Apart from its beautiful Norman church,Holt is so closely linked with **Farndon** that you proceed from one to the other without noticing the difference. There is the ancient, narrow bridge crossing the River Dee, a brief wait if the traffic lights are against you, but no matter which direction you are taking, if the prominent signs are ignored then, logically, there should be nothing at all to say that one town has been left behind and another entered. Yet, each town has its own, distinctive character and charm. Each has developed quite differently - and the reason is that Holt and Farndon, not only straddle the beautiful River Dee, but also the border between England and Wales.

I love **Bangor-on-Dee** (Bangor-is-y-Coed) with its superb medieval bridge spanning the River. Racegoers will already know of the racecourse which provides an excellent mix of steeplechasing, hurdle races, and the occasional National Hunt Flat Race. South east of Bangor lies the village of **Hanmer** - you can reach it by taking the A525 and the A539 - where in the 15th century the legendary Welsh leader Owain Glydwr married Margaret Hanmer. Close by is **Penley**, which is believed to be the only thatched school in Britain. **Overton** is a mile or so further on. In St Mary's Churchyard you will find the glorious yew trees mentioned as one of the 'Seven Wonders of Wales.'

Chirk from the south is the Gateway to Wales and for many years it was a bottleneck on Thomas Telford's London to Holyhead A5 road. Thankfully, the heavy traffic now bypasses the town, and conditions are much improved for residents and visitors.

Chirk Castle has been continuously occupied since it was built by a Marcher Lord, Roger Mortimer, in the early 14th-century, and the elegant staterooms with Adam-style furniture, tapestries and portraits bear testimony to the loving care bestowed on it over the years. On a more sombre note, there is also a nightmare dungeon which reminds us all of the violence and cruelty that once ravaged the Welsh Marches. Now looked after by the National Trust, the castle is located one and a half miles west of the town, set in beautiful gardens amid fine parkland. Offa's

Dyke traverses the grounds. In the 12th century St Mary's Church you will see monuments to the Myddleton family occupiers of Chirk Castle for almost 400 years.

Two immense structures are famous landmarks hereabouts: a wonderful viaduct constructed in 1848 to carry the former Great Western Railway, and running alongside and below it Telfords Shropshire Union Canal aqueduct, built in 1801. Both of these arebest viewed on foot - and you will be able to see a quarter mile long canal tunnel, which lies immediately to the north.

Along the A5 and within a few miles you will pass close to yet another spectacular aqueduct, this one an iron trough, 1006 feet long which soars 121 feet above the River Dee between Froncasyllte and Trevor. It is the Pontcysyllte Aqueduct, again the work of Thomas Telford.

If you remain on the A5 you can easily pass through **Llangollen** and feel that you have not missed a great deal. That would be a pity. You must turn right at the traffic lights and proceed down Castle Street, and at once you will see that this is a little town of great character. There is a large car park, and you will find that many of the attractions here are within easy walking distance. Trevor Bridge is one of the ' seven wonders' dating back to the 14th century. Beneath it the waters of the River Dee tumble wildly over black rocks. Here, white water canoeing championships have been held, on a testing and hazardous course.

A handsomely converted Baptist Chapel in Castle Street is now the European Centre for traditional and Regional Cultures, and reflects Llangollen's stature as the home of the International Music Eisteddfod.

The Llangollen Steam Railway is of standard gauge and was restored by volunteers. It will enthrall steam buffs, while others will simply sit back and enjoy the five and a half mile trip through beautiful countryside. Along the route there are stations, halts and restored workshops, all open to visitors throughout the year. The trips start from Trevor Bridge, and continue up the Dee Valley as far as **Glyndyfrydwy**.

Plas Newydd must be seen although it is a bit of a climb up Hill Street. This is a wonderful half-timbered building with ornate woodwork and a lovely interior filled with rare medieval oak carvings. Inside and out it is beautiful. It was the home of Lady Eleanor Ponsonby and Miss Sarah Butler, two Irishwomen who eloped from Waterford in 1778 and became known as the 'Ladies ofLlangollen. In Sarah's words, the area is 'the beautifullest countie in the world.'

You can view Llangollen Canal by taking a more gentle climb up Wharf Hill. There is an information museum for canal enthusiasts, and wonderfully relaxing trips on horse-drawn barges. Many of the local walks are very strenuous but keen walkers will delight in the views from the Panorama Walk - another section of the Offa's Dyke National Trail - Llantysilio Mountain, and Geraint's Hill.

From Llangollen you will have a drive of no more than fifteen or sixteen miles to **Ruthin** which has been a seat of administrative and commercial importance for more than 700 years, and recent discoveries suggest a Roman connection. It has St Peter's Square in a lovely elevated position with splendid old buildings put to excellent modern use. The half-timbered old Courthouse of 1401 is now the National Westminster Bank. Exmewe Hall is now in the hands of Barclays. Outside its doors is the Maen Huail Stone, said to be where King Arthur had a rival beheaded. As you wander across the Square your eyes will be drawn to the Myddleton Arms, which is at it should be. For gazing back at you will be the 'Eyes of Ruthin', an extraordinary multi-dormer roof in the Dutch style whose seven windows flash in the bright sun. It was built in the 16th century. In Castle Street is Nantclwyd House, a fine Elizabethan town house built around an earlier medieval structure. A little further along is the pillared entrance to a long, shaded drive which will bring you to Ruthin Castle. Now a gracious hotel, it was built between 1277 and 1282 by Edward I.

During the Civil War the garrison at Ruthin capitulated to Cromwell's forces after a severe bombardment, and in 1646 the castle was demolished. The ruins and land were owned by the Myddleton family from 1677, and remained in a sorry state until 1826, when a castellated, two storey, double block of limestone was built on the south-east corner of the ruined site. Then, in 1849, part of that building too was demolished, and the present building designed by Henry Clutton, was erected on the same site.

Eight miles north-west of Ruthin along the A525 is **Denbigh**, also set on a hill, with a castle that dominates the town. Denbigh has ample free parking, most of it close to the town centre. This is important, because although High Street itself is well elevated, there is a stiff walk to the castle - and it is best approached on foot.

You will reach it through the impressive Burgess Gate, or by passing Leicester's Church (intended to supplant St Asaph Cathedral) and St Hilary's Church tower, which will bring you to the green where the medieval Denbigh once stood. This is another of the strongholds Edward I built as part of his plans for subjugating Wales. Construction under the direction of Henry de Lacy was begun in 1282 - and there is a strong gatehouse with a trio of towers. The town walls are almost complete. The castle is sited on a limestone bluff, and there are splendid views. The town is delightful with an exceptionally wide High street flanked by colonnades. If you are here on any Wednesday you will be able to wander among the stalls in the small but lively street market. If perchance your visit includes Boxing Day you will see a strange happening - a barrel race that takes place on a straw-lined course up and down the High Street.

Having travelled through Anglesey, Denbighshire and Caernarvonshire, and touched on Merioneth. Now for Montgomeryshire and a final tour of the southern part of Merioneth.

There is a wonderful scenic route out of Dolgellau, up a steep, winding road past Cader Idris, which at almost 3,000 feet is an attraction to both walkers and climbers.

HOTELS, INNS, RESTAURANTS AND COUNTRY HOUSES

Charles Darwin once said that 'Old Cader is a grand fellow' but my own recent memories of that road are of descending it and experiencing some shock as an RAF jet came screaming up towards me from somewhere far below!

Eventually the road begins to tumble down towards less giddy heights, and before taking the B4405 towards **Trwyn** it's worth going on the couple of miles into **Corris**. You will first pass through **Corris Uchaf**, along a stretch of road lined with pine, beach and oak, and picturesque cottages once used by quarry workers. The craft centre at Corris is open all year. In summer you will appreciate the splendid picnic area, while in winter the warmth of the restaurant will beckon after you have watched various craftspeople at work.

Almost as soon as you turn onto the B4405 you are on the shores of Lake Tal-y-Llyn. For a mile or so the southern bank of a stretch of water is breathtakingly beautiful, and especially popular with fishermen in season.

At **Abergynolwyn** there is a small slate museum and here too is the inland terminus of the Tallyn railway. This 'Great Little train of Wales' - there are eight of them altogether - was bought and rescued in 1951, and now travels the six miles or so from Tywyn through wild hills and thick woodland around **Nant Gwernol** and Abergynolwyn. On the way it passes close to the rushing waters of Dolgoch Falls.

Tywyn is a popular seaside resort which has six miles of firm sands. At the right time of the year the conditions are perfect for swimming, sailing and windsurfing.

Before you drive into **Aberdovey** on the A493 you will see on the right the lush greens of Aberdovey's championship golf course, whose two mile long links occupy an enviable position twixt hills and sea. Aberdovey is almost Mediterranean in character, with the proximity of the Gulf Stream ensuring that temperatures are always higher than further inland.

Its pleasures are unashamedly of the sea, with fishing, windsurfing and waterskiing favoured sports, and private yachts of all sizes making splashes of bright colour in the waters of the pretty harbour. Many of its fine hotels and guesthouses were built during the Edwardian era when it was at the height of its popularity.

The drive inland towards **Machynlleth** is along an exceptionally pretty stretch of the A493 that hugs the cliffs as it takes one through an area of the Dovey Estuary rich in rhododendrons. The town has an impressive broad main street and a wonderful old clock tower with needle sharp spire and arched openings.

In 1991 Machynlleth celebrated the 700th anniversary of its market charter. It was granted in 1291 by Edward I to Owen de la Pole, Prince of Powys, and enabled two fairs in Spring and Autumn and a weekly street market ' to be held in perpetuity'. The midweek market has been held ever since, and has grown to become one of the largest and liveliest street markets in Wales.

It would be strange to visit any part of Wales without hearing mention of Owain Glyndwr, and Machynlleth does not disappoint. The great man held a Welsh parliament here in 1404. An old stone building in Maengwyn Street is now the Owain Glyndwr Centre, and home to an absorbing heritage exhibition that displays his campaigns and charts his contribution to Welsh history.

Newtown is the commercial capital of Montgomeryshire, and like Machynlleth it has a well-known street market held on Tuesdays with one in the Market Hall on the same day. The town has a delightful situation in a loop of the River Severn, and as the home of the Welsh flannel industry it was at one time known as the 'Busy Leeds of Wales'. One of the original hand-loom weaving factories is now the Newtown Textile Museum on Commercial Road. You will find in Newtown a bewildering mixture of architecture with Tudor, Gothic, Jacobean, Georgian, Victorian and modern buildings standing cheek by jowl so that scarcely two blocks are alike. The Royal Welsh Warehouse is the tallest building in the town. It was built in 1861 by Sir Pryce-Pryce Jones. His mail order company was the world's first - so now you know where all those catalogues originated! Queen Victoria was one of the company's customers, and the warehouse is still open to the public to this day.

Montgomery, a delightful border town is a wonderland of Georgian architecture, perhaps the finest example of which is the imposing Town Hall with its white clock tower. The ruins of the old Montgomery Castle stand on a rocky promontory overlooking the town, a position which made it virtually impregnable until the Civil War. For once Edward I had no hand in it; it was built at the command of Henry III in 1223.

The garrison Parish Church of St Nicholas contains the chapel of the poet, George Herbert, and in the graveyard you will find an odd grave. John Davies was convicted of murder in 1821. Before he died he swore his innocence, and declared that as proof nothing would grown on his grave for one hundred years. When you visit the Robber's Grave you can judge for yourself whether he was innocent or not!

Not many people know that **Welshpool** was originally called Poole. It is built on the banks of the River Severn, and long ago the flatlands were criss-crossed by a network of creeks known as 'pills'. These were frequently devastated by flash floods from the river, hence the town's original name. But they have long since been drained, and the name of the town was eventually changed to Welshpool to distinguish it from the English town of Poole.

You will see a wide diversity of attractive buildings and as well as having the river close by, Welshpool is also a canal town. The Montgomery Canal passes through the town. It was part of a grand scheme to link the rivers Mersey and Severn. Work finished in 1821, and it was a busy inland waterway until long decline led to its closure in 1944. Volunteers are valiantly bringing it back to life, and at the Powysland Museum situated in a restored canalwarehouse you can see some important local collections covering the archaeology and social history of Montgomeryshire

Powys Castle stands on a dramatic, rocky outcrop one mile south of Welshpool. It was built by the medieval Princes of Upper Powys in the 13th century, and has been occupied continuously for 700 years. In 1587 it was bought by Sir Edward Herbert, and has been the family's ancestral home ever since. That family, and later the Clives - descendants of Clive of India - continually laboured to create a jewel of a building set in the most beautiful gardens.

These are thought to have been planted by William Wilde. Dating from the 17th-century, they are laid out in four formal terraces influenced by French and Italian styles. Those hanging, terraces are the most famous in the world. Each is 200 yards long, falling away towards the Severn Valley. In the 18th-century an informal wilderness was added. The extensive parklands were landscaped by Capability Brown in the 19th-century. The castle is full of atmosphere and crammed with treasures. In particular are those brought from India by Clive and his son, and on display in the Clive Museum since 1987: relics of Tipu, Sultan of Mysore, Moghul jades, textiles and ivories, and a wonderful array of Chinese and Indian bronzes.

Amongst the many wonderful sights to be seen there is one just eight miles or so from **Llangedwyn**. It is well off the beaten track but take the B4396 towards **Llanrhaedr-ym-Mochnant** onto a minor road into stunning countryside. Cadair Berwyn lies ahead of you as you approach the Berwyn Mountains beyond which lies Corwen and the Dee Valley. It is **Pistyll Rhaeadr** I wanted to see, one of the highest waterfalls in Britain, cascading over a narrow ledge with delicate trees on all sides. George Burrows found this an enchanting place, and said of Pistyll Rhaeadr 'I never saw water falling so gracefully, so much like thin beautiful threads, as here'. There is a legend which relates how giants were disturbed while building a bridge and dropped the huge rocks which now lie scattered at its base.

Driving south-west along the A487 from Machynlleth will immediately transport you into an area with an astonishingly rich history. I was not aware that the lands belonging to the Welsh once stretched as far north as Strathclyde in Scotland. They did and in 451 AD the chieftain Cunedda and his sons marched an army south to the area we know as Wales, where they succeeded infreeing those lands from seaborne invaders. A district known as Tyno Goch was awarded to Cunedda's son, Ceredig. Today Ceredigion - the land of Cerig - stretches from the Dovey Estuary to Cardigan in the south, with its inland boundary following a semi-circular path.

My route took me along the south side of the Dovey Estuary where I visited the Ynis-Hir Reserve run by the RSPB. The easiest way to find it is to follow the signposts from the village of **Eglwysfach**. The reserve attracts some 67 species of bird to its salt and fresh water marshes, reed beds, peat bogs, woodland and open hillside. If you are a keen bird-watcher you will be reaching for your field-glasses at the mere mention of the pied fly-catcher, wood warbler, blacktrap and treecreeper.

Borth has three miles of virtually unbroken sands. It also has an interesting legend. Stumps in the sand, which you will see if the tide is right, are said to be the vestigial remains of an ancient forest - the last reminder of the drowned Welsh lowlands of Cantre'r Gwaelod.

The last village before Aberystwyth is **Clarach**, where the fine beach is sheltered by steep shale cliffs along which there are magnificent coastal walks. This was my first visit to **Aberystwyth**. It is one of Wales' favourite seaside towns, and for the academic it provides unrivalled facilities with the University of Wales and the National Library of Wales on the one site off Penglais Road. There are three good beaches. Tanybwlch Beach to the south of the harbour, while North and South beaches are separated by the wind driven headland which is the site of Aberystwyth Castle. Its history has a familiar pattern. Built by Edward I in 1277, damaged and rebuilt in 1282, captured by Prince Owain Glyndwr in 1404. Uniquely coins from the local silver mine were minted here between 1637 and 1646. The castle was doomed to fall to the enemy soon after: Cromwell's army overcame its defences, and it was blown up in 1649.

An interesting and unusual attraction can be found on the 450foot summit of Constitution Hill which stands at the north end of North Beach. Equally unusual is the manner in which you can reach the apex. **The Aberystwyth Electric Cliff railway** is the longest in Great Britain. It dates back to Victorian times and once again demonstrates how much we owe to the people who lived and worked in that imaginative age.

The ride to the summit is nothing short of spectacular, and once there you will find, in a fascinating octagonal tower, the **Great Aberystwyth Camera Obscura**. The very name spells out that it was a popular Victorian amusement, and it consists of a massive 14 inch lens which focusses detailed views onto a screen in a darkened viewing gallery. The outside viewing balconies will reward you with a beautiful panorama.

The Vale of Rheidol Railway runs from Aberystwyth to **Devil's Bridge**. It is a narrow gauge steam railway and there are conflicting theories about why it came into being. One suggests that it was opened in 1902 to serve the lead traffic of the valley. Another says that it is the only one of the 'little trains' to have been built to satisfy the tourist trade. At any rate, now it is British Railway's last operational link with the 'age of steam' and is an exciting ride. the line clings to the hillside as it climbs towards Devil's Bridge, affording views of the broad river valley, thickly wooded hillsides, and the wonderful open moorland of Plynlimon. The train is pulled by the engines 'Owain Glyndwr', 'Llewlyn' or 'Prince of Wales' on a journey through a natural wonderland.

Devil's Bridge (Pontarfynach) is a village set amid scenery which needs to be explored at length on foot. There are three bridges over the River Mynach, built one on top of the other. The first dates back to the 11th century, probably built by Cistercian monks. The second bridge was built in 1708, the third in 1901. You can take an easy path to visit the bridges but it is an area of such charm that you will almost certainly opt to do some energetic scrambling. There are 94 steps of Jacob's Ladder to be descended, the 300 foot cascade where the Mynach tumbles through spectacular chasms carved in the rock to join the River Rheidol, and naturetrails and footpaths. Not suitable for the disabled or the infirm and please do wear sensible shoes.

You will get a different view of Devil's Bridge after turning right onto the A4120, but you must then turn smartly onto the B4343 which will take you south along a lovely, winding route to the village of **Pontrhydfendigaid**. The Cistercian Abbey of Strata Florida was founded in 1164 and by 1184 had acquired thye patronage of Rhys ap Gruffydd, the last independent native prince of South Wales. Here at Ystrad Fflur, in 1238, Llywelyn the Great called together the Welsh Princes to swear allegiance to his son, Dafydd. Later, hard on the trail of Owain Glyndwr (the last native prince of a fully-independent Wales),

Henry IV expelled the monks, and took the abbey as his headquarters. The building fell into disrepair after the Dissolution, but you can still see the magnificent Norman arch. In the abbey grounds are buried some of the princes and princesses of old Ceredigion, while Dafydd ap Gwilym, the amorous medieval Welsh poet - still popular to this day - is buried under the spreading yew tree in the adjacent churchyard. Once the Westminster of Wales, the Abbey's name means 'Vale of Flowers'.

Tregaron lies at the junction of several roads, in countryside which is now a Natural Nature Reserve and famous for the variety and numbers of wild birds. George Borrow was reminded of 'an Andalusian village overhung by its sierra', and the mile upon mile of heathered upland to the east was once the haunt of Twm Sion Cati, the Robin Hood of Wales.

Before leaving this stunningly beautiful area and making my way towards the coast, I continued along the B4343 as far as **Llanddewi Brefi**. Ceredigion was the birthplace of St David, Patron Saint of Wales, and the church at this tiny village is dedicated to his name.

In **Llandiloes** we are back in Montgomeryshire, and this bonny little town is the first the River Severn encounters as it flows down from its source in the high moorlands of Plimlumon. History here in full measure with a Market Charter granted in 1280 and a 16th-century Market Hall of black and white timber which is the only one in Wales to survive on its original site. The town owes much of its prosperity to the lead mining which took place in the surrounding hills. Relics of the woollen trade can still be seen in the neat row of weaver's cottages, and there is a fine, half-timbered merchant's house on Llangurug Road.

Natural and man made lakes abound in the Montgomeryshire countryside, and Llyn Clywedog, between Llandiloes and Machynlleth is one of the more recent of the latter. The dam was built in the 1960s, and is the tallest in Britain. From Llandiloes you can reach the lake by taking the B4518; it is a short and very pleasant drive. LLyn Clywedog is used to control flooding on the River Severn, but wherever there is an expanse of water you will find sailors of one kind or another. This is also ideal walking country in the green pastureland and sweeping open hills that surround it.

The three mile route of the Llyn Clywedog Scenic Trail has been carefully designed to reveal the best features of the reservoir and the wooded slopes flanking the deep valley. An alternative walk pays more attention to the engineering feats involved in the dam's construction. The Clywedog Gorge Trail is self-guided, and also takes in the abandoned lead mine.

There are two rivers of note as you travl south along the A470. One is the River Wye, and the other is the River Elan whose course follows another wonderful valley.

The gateway to the Elan Valley is **Rhayader**, a town dating back to the fifth century and the setting for one of the most important markets of the area. For a small town it also has an extraordinarily violent past: in Tudor times the assize judge was murdered and the town razed, the castle was destroyed during the Civil War, and more recently it was the scene of the Rebecca Riots which were protests against toll gates. Like Machynelleth, the town centre features a fine clock tower, and in Rhayader the main streets radiate from this focal point.

There are five reservoirs quite close by and no shortage of Information Centres for those wishing to explore this wonderland of lakes and hills. The main one to note is the Elan Valley Visitor Centre which is located on the B5418 south-west of Rhayader. Interesting to note that it was these dams Barnes Wallace used when trying out the famous bouncing bomb.

Although **Llandrindod Wells** is not an old town, the chalybeate springs there have been used from time immemorial. The first reference to the Saline Spring was in 1694. The town was built to fulfil the Victorian's increasing demand for healing waters. They came for sulphur for their complexions, magnesium to aid their digestion, chalybeate for the blood and saline for 'inner cleanliness' - all were available and still are at the restored Pump Room in Rock Park. There is a good leaflet available from the Memorial Gardens in Temple Street which proves to be an excellent guide around the town.

Hundred House Village has a splendid inn of the same name and it is possible that when the Shire was divided into 'hundreds' and courts were held, they might well have used the Inn as well as the Vicarage. The Hundred House Inn was used by cattle drovers, who, because of the distance between West Wales and London, would provide their cattle with shoes - and ducks and geese had their feet dipped in tar!

Builth Wells is another example of a town that grew up around a spa, although the saline and sulphur springs are no longer used. Ask a farming Welshman - there for the Monday sheep and cattle markets - about the town and he will immediately lift his head and tell you with pride of the Royal Welsh Agricultural Show which is held here each year. It is the biggest agricultural show in the country, and is held on a permanent site alongside the River Wye.

Llandovery is quite charming with Town Hall and Market Square and a feeling of history which comes from being a former cattle collection point for drovers about to make the long walk to the English cities. Stock markets are still held two or three times weekly, and market stalls make a splash of colour under the Town Hall each Friday.

I found the task of exploring the peninsula to the south of Cardigan Bay - the area now known as Dyfed - quite daunting. It takes in most of the coast in a great sweep from Aberaeron right round to Carmarthen plus a whole lot of inland areas of special interest.

Aberaeron does not immediately spring to mind as a place likely to attract lovers of history but how wrong can one be. I soon discovered that in this corner of Wales one house in every four in Aberaeron is designated of special architectural interest and it is one of Wales' first planned towns. August 1807 seems to be the recognised starting point of any study of the town's history.

On that date Royal Assent was given to an 'Act to enable the Reverend Alban Thomas Jones-Gwynne, his Heirs and Assigns, to repair and enlarge the Harbour and Port of Aberaeron...and to regulate the mooring of Ships and Vessels there'. The good Reverend carried out his task well providing money for design and construction which involved the eminent engineer John Rennie, and taking the advice of John Nash on the layout and design of the fledgling town.

The town is now a gracious, picturesque place, with well laid out streets and squares, and a charming, stone-walled harbour. It is very worthwhile spending some time here.

From Aberaeron to **Newquay** is just a short distance even on the minor roads. Establishing New Quay's origins is difficult, though an admiralty survey undertaken in 1748 does mention the name, albeit with a different spelling (New Key). It is a lovely little town, thoroughly deserving its reputation as the 'jewel of the Welsh Coast'. It is built on terraced slopes which fall steeply to a crescent of sand and a sheltered harbour, and is thought to be the town Dylan Thomas used as a model for Llareggrub in 'Under Milk Wood'. He spent some time in new Quay between 1944 and 1945.

Aberporth is another wonderful seaside gem with a snug little bay and a wedge of clean sand that will delight all children and many adults. Moderately high cliffs on either side make fine natural boundaries, a comforting situation. It is a place well known for its cliff-top walks and one in particular is very popular. It links Aberporth with the neighbouring village of **Tresaith** - no more than a mile to the east - and at low tide you can then go on to reach the golden beach at **Penbryn**. If you take that path you are moving back towards New Quay. Penbryn beach, once beloved by smugglers, can also be reached by road from **Sarnau** on the A487. The name Tresaith is said to derive from the landing of seven banished Irish princesses, who settled in the area and married local Welshmen. If you have no romance in you then you are more likely to believe that the name comes from the local river - the Saith!!

Llangrannog is a little further on in the same direction, another village bounded by rocky headlands. One of them, which I believe is known as Ynys-Lochtyn, is worth exploring more fully for it has the remains of a prehistoric fort.

The correct name for **Cardigan** is Aberteifi - the mouth of the Teifi - and the word Cardigan is a derivation from a word already familiar to us: Ceredigion, for which Aberteifi was once the county town. Today the town is of strategic importance to visitors, not invaders, for its position makes it an ideal base for those wishing to explore the spectacular Pembrokeshire countryside. Cardigan is famous for staging the very first competitive National Eisteddfod, which was held in the castle under the patronage of Rhys ap Gruffudd in 1176. That event was commemorated in 1976 when the Eisteddfod came back to the town to celebrate the eight hundredth anniversary of Rhy's original event.

Cilgeran an be found by driving a little way south of Cardigan, and on a crag overlooking a deep gorge of the River Teifi the two powerful towers of Cilgerran Castle dominate a romantic scene. The castle was begun in 1220 and was the subject of a well knwon painting by Richard Wilson. No finer setting could have been chosen for any fortress - both beautiful and unassailable - and in August each year it is all enhanced with the staging of the annual coracle races. A glance at any good map will show you that Cardigan is the start of the Pembrokeshire Coast Path which wriggles its tortuous way around the jagged coastline and is almost unbroken until it reaches distant Milford Haven.

Heading south from Cardigan you will find the village of **St Dogmaels** by taking the B4546 especially taking a look at the ruins of the Benedictine Abbey. The story is interesting. The Benedictine Abbey was founded by monks of the French order of Tiron in 1113. The Sagranus Stone now in the parish church dates from the 6th century, and the Latin inscriptions on its face provided the key to the interpretation of the ogham alphabet of the ancient Giodelic language.

The church at **Nevern** - quite hard to find, best off the A487 and B4582 - was founded by St Brynach. A dark avenue of yews leads to the church door and one of them exudes a blood-red stain from a sawn branch. This is the bleeding Yew. The ogham alphabet is again encountered on the Vitalianus Stone which stands beside the church porch: it commemorates a prominent man who died around 500 AD. This one I found absolutely charming: there is a carved cross some 13feet high standing in the churchyard, and from it, each year on April 7th (St Brynach's Day), the first cuckoo sings.

Another interesting church can be found at Eglwyswrw which lies on the A487. This one is an early foundation that may have been built within a pre-Christian earthwork. Roughly between Nevern and Eglwyswrw you will find Pentre Ifan, which was one of the finest burial chambers in the country. A massive capstone is supported by three tall pillars, and George Owen once described it as 'one of the wonders of Pembrokeshire'.

Newport is an Ancient Borough with its own Mayor, Burgesses and Court Leet. It lies on the slope of a hill beneath a Norman castle, and below the town the River Nevern meanders across a wide estuary to enter the sea in Newport Bay, the Welsh name for Newport is Tredraeth Edrywy, and it is said not only that the original settlement stood near the shore, but that it was 'swallowed by the sands, like another Peranzabuloe'.

Not far from the old trading quays there is a beautiful sandy beach, with the shallow surf of **Newport Sands** offering safe bathing for all. If you intend staying here for any length of time, you will find plenty to do, with sailing, pony-trekking and golf - on a pleasant, nine hole course adjoining Newport Sands.

Fishermen of all temperaments will find sport here. Salmon, sea trout and brown trout are found in the Nevern, and surf fishing from Newport Sands will often bring good catches of bass. During the season there is also salmon fishing from those same sands, using seine-nets.

In 1191 the Lord of Cemais, William Martin, was driven out of Nevern, and he established his stronghold at Newport where he built a castle. The castle was captured by Llywelyn the Great in 1215, and by Llywelyn the Last in 1257; during the revolt of Owain Glyndwr it suffered heavily, and was reckoned to be worth no more than £33!. By 1583 the castle had been in ruins for many years, and it was not until 1859 that the gatehouse was converted into a residence by Sir Thomas Lloyd, and the ruins substantially restored. You can still see what remains of the Hunter's Tower, the Kitchen Tower and the Great Tower, and the site on a spur standing over the estuary is most impressive.

Cwym-yr-Eglwys is tucked away at the eastern curve of Newport Bay, and this 'valley of the church' is one of the loveliest little bays in Wales. Most road atlases will show you Dinas Head, but only the larger Ordnance Survey maps will show the tiny peninsula bearing the name **Dinas Island**. In fact this small promontory was once cut off from the mainland by the Pwllgwaelod - Cwmyreglwys depression, and was once known as Ynys Fach Lyffan Gawr - ' the little island of Lyffan the Giant'. The Pembrokeshire Coastal Path leads around it, and there are twointeresting books by R.M. Lockley - Island Farmers and The Golden Year - which tell of the author's life on Dinas Island Farm.

I was eager to visit **Fishguard**. With its wonderful harbour and fascinating town, it demands attention, but beyond that it also holds a unique place in the history of our islands; it was the scene of the last invasion of Britain. In 1797, French troops led by Colonel William Tate, an American, landed in a rocky bay beneath Carresgwastad Point, with the intention of rousing the population against George III. Popular legend tells us that the attack ended when the troops mistook Welsh women wearing traditional red cloaks for British soldiers. They advanced no further than Goodwick Sands, where they laid down their arms. Today a stone marks their landing place at Carregwastad.

The eastern coast of Dyfed has several fair-sized islands of the kind which are always formed as exposed coastlines are gradually eroded by the hungry seas. Ramsey Island and Skomer Island are the two largest, and from Fishguard I took the A487, this time towards **St Davids**. I knew that it is quite easy to get from the town to the coastal path, from which Ramsey is clearly visible - but my main intention was to spend some time at St David's Bishop's Palace, which I had briefly visited once before. It was built largely by Henry de Gower (1328-47).

The richly decorative building stands within the Cathedral Close, among a group of buildings unique in Wales. The arcaded parapets of Bishop Henry extend along both main wings of the palace, and are decorated with some of the finest medieval sculptured heads and animal figures in Wales. The entrance to the Great Hall is also impressive, and the other great joy is the piscina in the Palace Chapel - a stone basin which carries away water used in rinsing chalices. Supposedly the presence of the Cathedral makes St David's the smallest city in Britain. The people of St Asaph will tell you differently!

Skomer Island can be rached by taking the A487 for six or seven miles in a south-westerly direction, then switching to a delightful minor road that hugs the coastal path. Skomer is included in the Marine Nature Reserve which takes in the islandand the coastline around the Marlowe Peninsula - the only one of its kind in Wales, and only the second in the UK. Over 150 seals are born regularly making it the second largest pupping site in South West Britain. In addition, it is home to the largest concentration of sea birds such as puffins, guillemots and 5 razor bills in England and Wales, and over half the world population of the Manx Shearwater.

To get to Pembroke I meandered, quite intentionally, and found the easiest way, having got quite lost en route, was to take the B4327 and follow that to **Haverfordwest**. This market town of narrow streets which overlooks the River Cleddau is attractive, and like many others all over Wales is overlooked by an ancient castle.

Built in 1100 it was part of a chain of fortifications erected across Pembrokeshire by English invaders to pen in the Welsh to the north. Later modifications strengthened the walls which are between six and twelve feet thick, and although Cromwell ordered the castle's destruction during the Civil War, much of it was left intact. It is now an appropriate site for the area's Information Centre, and it also houses a museum.

The road into Pembroke passes conveniently close to **Carew** with its castle built between 1280 and 1310, and considerably enlarged in the 15th century. It is particularly interesting because it has a long window and large galleries which illustrate the transition from the original stronghold to a charming Elizabethan country residence. Also in Carew there is a tidal mill - **Carew French Mill** - which is one of only three restored tidal mills in Britain, and the only one remaining intact in Wales. This grand, four-storey building dates back to 1558, and almost all its original machinery has been retained. Restoration of the huge south wheel has taken place in recent years.

Whilst there is no apparent direct route from Carew to **Upton**, although the distance is no more than a mile, it is somewhere worth seeking out. Upton Castle grounds offer hours of enjoyment. The 35 acres contain almost 200 different species of trees and shrubs. Woodland and formal gardens are thoughtfully provided with all weather footpaths. There is also an interesting 11th-century family chapel.

Pembroke did not begin its development until the late 11th century although there is ample evidence, with standing stones and burial mounds, of an earlier, prehistoric occupation. Not surprisingly the development was around the splendid castle, the oldest in West Wales. It is certainly one of the best preserved Norman castles in Britain. It was founded by the Montgomerys in 1093, and around the year 1200 work was started on the Great Tower.

This enormous structure is 75ft high and has walls at the base up to 19ft thick. Its circular shape is unusual, and it is also roofed, which was not common practice. Other claims to fame include the birth within the castle walls of the founder of the House of Tudor - Henry VII. It was held by both Royalists and Parliamentarians during the Civil War, and the siege that led to its final surrender was led by Cromwell himself. You may visit the castle on any day of the year except Christmas Day, Boxing Day and New Year's Day. From the end of May to the end of August guided tours are available.

The town experienced a period of decline until about 1814, when the Royal Naval Dockyard was moved from Milford Haven to Pembroke Dock, and brought prosperity with it. Since that date over 250 warships have been built at Pembroke Dock, as well as three Royal yachts for Queen Victoria. If nautical history interests you there are boat trips which will take you to see Warrior, the first iron-clad warship, which was launched in 1860 and is now at Pembroke Ferry. From there they continue the short distance to Milford Haven.

Milford Haven is both the name of the town and the stretch of water it overlooks, which was fittingly described by Nelson as ' one of the finest natural harbours in the world'. In fact the town was founded in 1793 - by Sir William Hamilton, husband of Nelson's mistress, Emma - and was a whaling port before becoming a dockyard. Milford Haven was used by Henry II to launch his invasion of Ireland in 1172, and Henry Tudor, Earl of Richmond landed there in 1485 on his was to defeating Richard III at the Battle of Bosworth Field. Since 1960 Milford Haven has gradually expanded to become a major oil port, its huge refineries fed by supertankers from all over the world.

Daniel Defoe described **Tenby** as ' the most agreeable town on all the south coast of Wales, except Pembroke', and since then thousands of visitors have echoed those words in one way or another. It is sheer delight, a compact little town with shops and houses almost touching across the narrow streets packed inside the town walls. Appropriately, the remains of a 13th-century Norman castle overlook the old fishing harbour, standing on the site occupied by a Welsh fort called Dinbych-y-Pysgod - Little Fort of the Fish. The town is also the birthplace of the portrait painter Augustus John, and of Robert Recorde, the mathematician who invented the $=$ sign.

In Tenby you cannot escape the wonderful beaches, four of which encircle the headland. But they can be boisterous or placid as the fancy takes you, with quiet picnic spots always available to those who will venture away from the crowds.

Carmarthen shares with **Caerleon** the title of the oldest town in Wales, and settlement in the area can be traced back almost 2,000 years. There are remains of a large hill fort at Abergwili, three miles to the east, and a local bastion of Roman rule that was built near the centre of the present town survives in the modern name: Moridunum (mor dinas, or sea fort) became Caer-mori-dunum, and then Carmarthen! A Roman ampitheatre that once seated 5,000 people was identified in the 1930s on a site at the east end of Priory Street, and saved for posterity by the quick thinking of a former Borough Engineer, George Ovens. The arena wall has been reconstructed, and adjacent gardens cover still more remains.

Life is nothing without legend to intrigue and inspire, and here Welsh folklore tells how King Arthur's wizard, Merlin, was born near the town in 480AD. The story is given further credence by the decayed stump of an oak that stood at the end of Priory Street and apparently carried his spell: 'When Merlin's oak shall tumble down, then shall fall Carmarthen town'. But a more likely story is that it was planted at Priory Street's junction with Oak Street to commemorate the accession of Charles II to the throne - and what is absolutely certain is that it was removed in the interests of road safety in 1978. Carmarthen is fascinating to explore and demands attention.

South West Wales has its own charm. I proceeded along the A40 in the direction of **Llandeilo** with the intention of branching off to view two nearby attractions. The first, **Dinefwr Castle**. This is not one of the country's better known ruins, yet for all that it has an air about it, a certain brooding presence that on gloomy days can set the imagination racing. It was built on the site of an older castle, and its position has a lot to do with its undoubted attraction, for it is poised on the edge of a precipice. Its moats were carved from the rock and, like the keep and parts of the curtain wall which are all that remain, were designed to keep out the enemy in the long struggles with the Anglo-Normans. From 877 AD it was the principal residence of the princes of South Wales. I'm told the castle can be reached by walking through Castle Woods, where there are fine nature trails and superb parkland landscaped by Capability Brown. The paths are waymarked, and easily followed, though if you are going to be brave enough to walk from Llandeilo, you have a long walk ahead of you. En route you will come across the church of Llandyfeisant, which is within the park and is reputed to be built on the site of a Roman temple. The second is **Paxton's Tower**, a mile or so south of Dinefwr Castle, and surely one of the finest follies ever. Designed by Samuel Pepys Cockerel, it is triangular and crenellated, and was apparently erected in honour of Lord Nelson. It dates from the 19th century, and affords magnificent views of the Tywi valley. National Trust owned, it is open all the year round, whereas Dinefwr Castle is open only on appointed days.

There is yet another castle a few miles further west. **Dryslwyn** is again in a magnificent position, and was the scene of a three week siege in 1287 at the beginning of a revolt led by Rhys ap Meredudd. Some among you may know that Sappers are soldiers in the Royal Engineers and that their name comes from work they once did which involved the 'digging of saps for the purpose of moving towards the enemy, being under cover at all times'. The reason I bring that up is because Dryslwyn Castle had its defences quite literally undermined when what must have been the distant forerunners of those Sappers dug tunnels under the walls, which led to their collapse. There is a car park and a picnic site at Dryslwyn.

Llandeilo is a pleasant market town, built on a hill, and you will notice that most of the buildings in the main part of the town are early Victorian. the bridge over the river was built in 1848 - a splendid structure. The restored Church is mainly Victorian but has an interesting 13th-century tower.

If you turn from the A40 onto the B4302, after a few miles you will reach the skeletal ruins of **Talley Abbey**. It dates back to the late 12th century when Rhys ap Gruffydd founded a House of Premonstratension Canons, which was severely handled in uprisings and revolts during the Middle Ages. Although once protected by Edward I it was again much abused, and after the rebellion of Owain Glyndwr there was little left of it. Nevertheless the site in the Carmarthenshire hills is a pretty one, and what is left is impressive - part of the central tower of the church has survived and there are two, high-pointed arches and several lancet windows.

If by now you have a nodding acquaintance with the Welsh language you will know that **Pumsaint** means 'five saints'. The name of this pleasant little village comes from the quintuplets born to Cynnyr Farfdrwch ap Gwron ap Cunedda. However my real reason for driving up the A482 was to visit the Roman gold mines at **Dolcaucothi**, which were actually worked as recently as 1938 - though not by the Romans! They were exploiting it almost 2000 years ago, and although you will now have difficulty interpreting the site on your own, there are self-guided trails which you can follow using the explanatory leaflets. As proof of the advanced techniques used so long ago, there is a fragment of a timber waterwheel - used to drain the galleries - in the National Museum at Cardiff.

Back tracking a bit along the A482 and then the A40 my intention was to seek out the village of **Bethlehem**. Not surprisingly this is a popular posting place for Christmas mail. Near it lie the ancient earthwork remains known as Carn Goch. This is well known as the largest Iron Age hill fort in Wales. It is enormous with its two forts spread over 800 metres. The views from here were breathtaking. Stay on the minor roads and you will see **Carreg Cennen**. This one outdoes most castles you will ever see! Its limestone eyrie must be seen to be believed - and if you intend taking a closer look you must be prepared for a stiff climb from the farmyard beneath its walls.

The remote, timeless air which pervades appealed to artists during the Romantic Revival, and it is not hard to understand why. The building dates back to the 13th and 14th centuries, but there was a castle on the site long before then. There is an inner ward with a fine gatehouse, and this is the earliest part of the castle. The arrow slits in the gatehouse walls are of the cross-slit variety, which apparently gave cross-bows more freedom of movement, and thus a greater arc of fire. The castle fell to Edward I in 1277 and seems to have remained in English hands from that date. Edward I gave it to John Gifford and another owner was John of Gaunt. Lancastrian supporters during the Wars of the Roses overcame the defence and the castle was demolished in 1462 to prevent its use as a robbers' refuge. That work was accomplished by 500 men armed with picks and crow bars - a task of monumental proportions!

You will certainly head towards **Trapp** when you leave Carreg Cennen. The latter is isolated and it is really hard to imagine why the village ever came about. There is a good Arts and Crafts Centre here with a charming tea-room. There is also a splendid working Welsh hill farm with a 17th century longhouse and a number of rare and unusual farm animals. Here too you can eat in the converted 18th-century barn. On the menu good home-made farmhouse cooking. Either before or after your meal you can enjoy walking along riverside or hill footpaths. and there is every chance that you will see many of Britain's rarest birds of prey.

Whilst I am aware that from here **Swansea** is close by, I want to leave it for now and tell you about the Gower Peninsula. Gower has long been an Area of Outstanding Natural Beauty, and most of it is protected by the National Trust and the Gower Society. It is a peninsula but its extreme isolation brought about by the flanking estuaries and the sandstone scarp at its eastern or inland border has enabled it to escape the industry that has mushroomed close by. There is just one major road (the A4118), a sparse network of byways - and that is it. The rest is sheer beauty, an area to explore until intoxicated.

The A4067 comes to an abrupt end just before Mumbles Head which marks the eastern end of the Gower. The name Mumbles actually refers to the two rounded rocks at the entrance to the bay, but has gradually come to cover the whole area from the pier to the shopping centre.

Mumbles is just five miles along the shore from Swansea, but it has established a unique reputation for itself while managing to retain a delightful village atmosphere. I knew Mumbles from details of the lifeboat tragedy, when the entire crew of the Mumbles lifeboat perished during rescues from the merchant ship Tampana. So the images I bore with me were of stormy seas and jagged rocks, and while those conditions do exist, Mumbles boasts wonderful sandy beaches, quaint coves just around the headland, and waters that are ideal for the staging of international yachting events.

Oystermouth is of interest for several reasons, not least the restored church which has a low tower often seen in this corner of Wales. The three bells came to the Mumbles from the burned cathedral of Santiago, Chile, and part of the aisle consists of fragments of Roman paving stones which were found nearby. Oystermouth Castle stands above the A4067; it was constructed in the late 13th century by the infamous Norman lord, de Breos, a member of a family noted for their villainous deeds. The drum towers that once flanked the main gateway leading to the single courtyard have long since disappeared, but there is doubt about Cromwell being instrumental in their destruction for the castle was not involved in the Civil Wars. Oystermouth Castle is full of interest. the keep has fine domestic apartments with beautiful windows, and there is a romantically named room - the White Lady's Chamber. The chapel adjoins the banqueting hall on the second floor, and here you can see a piscina, and more elaborate windows.

I like **Bishopston**. Such a tranquil place with a small church containing an interesting font, and earthwork remains on nearby Pwlldu Head. There are also delightful little coves nearby with firm, sandy beaches.

Oxwich National Nature Reserve and Centre is an area of dunes, marshes and woodlands above the sweeping curve of Oxwich Bay, and you will find here a wonderful concentration of wildlife. Information is readily available at the Centre, though opening times vary. But much of the Reserve is there for you to explore, and it is always open.

You will find **Oxwich** church on a rocky ledge near the sea. The Tudor Mansion known as Oxwich Castle is on a hill above the village. In the 16th century the Mansel family abandoned PenriceCastle to move into their new home, and there is still an impressive crested gateway leading into the courtyard. From Oxwich Bay you can see the medieval castle at **Penrice** that was abandoned in favour of Oxwich; as you would expect, it was built round about the 12th century, and is now in ruins.

Port Einon is just beyond Oxwich and is a fishing hamlet overlooking its own small bay. Tales of smuggling and piracy abound, and at the base of a reef known as Skysea you will come across the ruins of the Salthouse, which once had contrband wine stored in its cavernous vaults. The bay is often stormy, and evidence of this can be found in the churchyard where there is a statue commemorating a lifeboat hero. From Port Einon there is a wonderful cliff-top walk as far as **Rhossli**, but even keen and experienced walkers will need to take care on the rocky paths.

It is well worth the effort, for the caves here are large enough to be marked on maps; both Culver Hole and Paviland Cave can be reached, but it is difficult. Of the two it is Paviland (actually a number of caves) that has a tale to tell. The 'Red Lady of Paviland' was a red-stained, human skeleton - minus skull - that was discovered in the Goat's Hole in 1823. A hundred years later, research resulted in a change of sex, for the remains turned out to be those of a youth who had been buried some 18,000 years ago. The gory stains were red ochre.

If you are still full of energy you can continue walking beyond Rhossli, Rhossisli Downs are quite desolate but they have more than their fair share of secret places, and budding archaeologists will pick their way quite happily through the rough grass around two Neolithic chambered tombs. These are Sweyne's Houses (or Swine Houses'), and date from around 2500BC. Beneath the Downs there is probably the finest beach on the Gower, with sands stretching for three miles in a graceful curve between Worm's Head and Burry Holms, a tiny island with the remains of a ruined church and a teeming bird population.

Llandewi is where you will find the **Gower Farm Museum** in a cluster of old farm buildings in which the owners have recreated rural life as it was at the turn of the century. The farm courtyard is stocked with many animals - chickens and ducks, goats, even rare breeds such as Gloucester Old Spot pigs - and there is a pets corner where children can gently handle guineapigs and rabbits. The Gower Farm Museum is open May to September.

Another minor road off the A4118 would bring you to **Reynoldston**, which is considered to be the central point of the Gower. It is a pretty village with a green, and if you make the stiff walk to the summit of nearby Cefyn Bryn, a clear day will allow you to see across the Channel to South West England. It is worthwhile continuing your walk from there, for you will soon come across Arthur's Stone, a prominent landmark backed by interesting legends. It is actually four stones supporting a mighty capstone, and this is rumoured to have been split by Arthur.

There are conflicting historical details about **Weobley Castle** which you will find near **Cheriton**. It seems that all or part of this late medieval fortified house was built towards the end of the 13th century, probably by Henry Beaumont, Earl of Warwick. Later, it was occupied by the de la Bere family. Other sections were added in later centuries, and of the substantial remains perhaps the biggest difference you will notice between Weobley and other castles is the sheer variety of towers. Some have six or eight sides, some are square, yet all come together to form a complete square. If you visit on any day of the year you will be able to see the hall, kitchens and cellar, and an interesting exhibition on the history of the castle and of the Gower through the ages.

Llanrhidian is worth an hour of your time. Among the sights to be seen is St Rhidian's church, which has a curiously carved stone in the porch for which no-one can offer an explanation. As you stroll through the village you will see two standing stones on the green, and the old village stocks. Nearby Cil Ifor Top is the site of an Iron Age fort of considerable size, with terraces which can still be clearly seen.

Once upon a time you would have seen the cockle-women of **Penclawdd** in their bonnets and flannel dresses crossing the sand at low tide, their donkey carts ready to be loaded with the fresh harvest of shellfish. Things have changed but the sprawling village is still the centre of the cockle industry.

I left The Gower with reluctance but the history of **Kidwelly** beckoned me. It is a fine example of a town that has grown arounda Norman castle. The estuary location at the mouth of the river Gwendraeth again demonstrates how the rulers and military commanders of the day recognised the importance of access from the sea. The earthwork defences of Kidwelly date back to the reign of Henry I, when they were raised by Roger, Bishop of Salisbury. The semi-circular moat is early 12th century, the inner ward was constructed by Payn de Chaworth late in the 13th

century, and the cliffside chapel - it juts out over a scarp which formed a natural defence to the east - was added around 1300. In fact most of the existing building is the work of castle builders who were active in the 13th and 14th centuries.
Even before that period was reached, the castle had changed hands several times. One notable battle involved Maurice de Londres, Lord of Kidwelly, who in 1136 was faced by an army led by a woman - Gwenllian, the wife of Gruffydd ap Rhys. The Normans won the day in a fierce, bloody fight, and both Gwenllian and her son, Morgan, were beheaded.

Centuries later, Kidwelly Castle suffered severe damage in the Glyndwr rebellions. Concentric castles, of which Kidwelly is a fine example, had two rings of defences. The inner bailey or ward would have high walls with their own gateway. This would be encircled by the outer bailey protected by exterior walls with towers and - in Kidwelly's case - a massive gatehouse. You can see that three-storey structure to this day, and several of the towers are complete to their turrets. The old town of Kidwelly would have been completely walled; now, although it has lost its medieval buildings, the roads almost certainly follow their original lines and you can still see the early 14th-century town gate, which lies to the south.

If you continue on the A484 out of Kidwelly you will come to **Ferryside**, a little village with wonderful views and super sands with the sheltered waters of the estuary making it a lovely spot to spend a lazy afternoon.

Swansea makes a wonderful starting point from which to set out on the next stage of my travels, a remarkable journey which includes the two largest cities in Wales - one of which is the capital - and the astonishing contrast between vast urban industrial complexes and the breathtaking beauty of the Brecon Beacons. Cardiff may be the capital, but Swansea is justifiably proud to be the second largest city in Wales. Its name has buccaneering undertones, too, for it reached its present form from the original Sweyn's Ea (the island of Sweyn). Sweyn was a Viking pirate who used the site on the River Tawe as a base from which he could plunder the south coast. The docks at Swansea were established in 1306 for the purpose of ship building, but by the 18th century a change was underway as the exporting of Welsh coal, copper and iron ore became big business.

The city is full of interest with an excellent market on Oxford Street, an exciting Maritime Quarter which has a marina with berths for 600 craft, a waterfront village, restaurant, art gallery, theatre, sailing and sea angling schools, and an unusual floating restaurant. The centrepiece of the Maritime Quarter is the Maritime and Industrial Museum with Wales' largest collection of historic vessels; the lightship Helwick and steam tug Canning can be boarded.

The Glynn Vivian Art Gallery on Alexander Road should not be missed. Among its static displays is one of the largest collections of Swansea porcelain and an outstanding collection of European ceramic and glass. These and many other displays which are constantly changing bring to the people of Swansea and visitors, the best in art from around the world.

The Brangwyn Hall is a mile from the city centre and just off the A4067 as you head back towards Mumbles. It could actually be called two buildings in one, for it was built in 1934 as the Guildhall and now comprises Swansea's civic offices, and the Brangwyn Concert Hall. The latter was named after Sir Frank Brangwyn, who designed the murals of the British Empire which were intended for the House of Lords but now adorn the walls of this splendid building. They did not get there without some difficulty - the 18 panels are so big that in order to accommodate them adjustments had to be made to the building! Brangwyn Hall is the focal point for the Swansea Festival of Music which is held each Autumn. International orchestras and soloists perform there, while opera is staged at the Grand Theatre.

The Vale of Neath is renowned for its own natural beauty and a number of major attractions that draw visitors in their thousands. **Neath** town centre is fully-pedestrianised, and as in Swansea, there is a thriving Victorian covered market. The Neath Borough Museum is housed in a beautifully refurbished Grade II listed building. Neath has a castle too, which was built in 1284 on a promontory guarding the approach to the town. It is currently being restored. Neath Abbey was founded in 1130 by the Norman Baron Richard de Granville.

Today it can be found on the edge of the Tennant Canal in an industrial area just off the A465. It does not sound like the ideal position for an Abbey that became Cistercian in 1147, and was considered by the Tudor historian, John Leland to be, 'The fairest Abbey in all Wales.' In fact the site is still tranquil and haunting and now in the care of CADW: Welsh Historic Monuments. The substantial ruins are open all year.

Aberdulais Falls and Ironworks will interest people with disparate tastes. I was intrigued to learn the natural waterfalls are not just beautiful to behold: a new water wheel will soon harness the natural energy source to produce electricity in a wooded gorge that contains the remains of 400 years of industrial activity. There is an interesting exhibition which deals with history and displays works of art by famous painters, and guided tours are available at this important National Trust site.

On the A4109 you will find the Cefyn Coed Colliery Museum. So much of this part of the world is inextricably linked to the production of coal that a brush with the reality of the industry, however brief, is a must. The museum is located a little way south of **Crynant**, and is next to an operational mine. Most of the surface buildings remain from the former active colliery, and in the museum there are simulated underground workings, a huge steam winding engine, and massive boilers that once powered the pithead winding gear. There is also a good display of photographs which vividly trace the history of the workings, and round about there are lovely forest walks and picnic sites. An unusual and fascinating attraction.

On the same subject, it is worth going to Afon Argoed Country Park where there is the Welsh Miners Museum. Best reached by returning to Neath and taking the B4287 and then the A4107. You can look at this as confirmation that here the countryside and industry have always been uncomfortable bedfellows, or as an example of how two different natural resources complement each other - the one never complete without the other.

Afon Argoed Country Park has wonderful facilities on a beautiful steep sided valley that can be explore in several ways. Cycle tracks run along both banks of the River Afan (bikes can be hired), there are waymarked walks fanning out from the Countryside Centre, which is situated to the west of Cynonville, and landrover tours operate from the main car park during the summer season. My own reason for taking a look was to add to the coalmining information I had picked up at Cefyn Coed. Here, the story is by miners, from their point of view: there is a traditional miner's cottage scene, historic photographs, the story of children underground and a lot of mining equipment in realistic settings. Quite absorbing and always there is theknowledge that it can be tempered with the beauty of the Country Park waiting to embrace you when you tire of your research.

The Neath Canal deserves a mention. Some sections of it have recently been restored and now offer delightful diversions. Head for **Resolven** on the A465 where there is a tea room and gift shop in an 18th century cottage, and the 'Thomas Dadford' waiting to transport you along the placid waterways through idyllic scenery. Good towpath walks, too.

Porthcawl is regarded as the leading resort in South Wales - no doubt some would argue that it is not but what is certain is that it grew up as a coal port in the 19th century, and with the decline of that industry turned naturally to the holiday trade. Brochures will tell you of the seven beaches and coves of the district, in particular Sandy Bay which is overlooked by the massive Cony beach entertainment complex.

However, at the risk of being dubbed an old stick in the mud, I'd like to draw your attention to the dunes to the north west where the lost city of Kenfig lies buried by the sand. It was apparently engulfed in the Middle Ages, and today you may still see the ruins of Kenfig Castle poking through the sands. Kenfig Pool is also something of an oddity. Scarcely a mile from the sea, it is locked in by the dunes and is the county's largest freshwater lake.

Porthcawl is famous for golf. The Royal Porthcawl Club will be known to most people, if only by name, for it has hosted many international events including in recent years the Coral Classic. But there is also Pyle and Kenfig Club, the Southerndown Club and the Maesteg Club, the last two having wonderful views which could possibly result in ruined handicaps (or better handicaps, depending on how you view these things!) A word of warning - letters of introduction from your own club are usually required before you can tee off.

This is an outstanding stretch of coast for castles. The three main castles of Ogwr - all clustered around **Bridgend** - bear testimony to the ruthlessness of Prince Llywelyn, who partially destroyed them to prevent their being used by invaders. Ogmore Castle guarded a river crossing on the River Ewenny. It was constructed of undressed boulders, and probably dates back to the 12th century. Stepping stones lead across the river to the tiny village of **Merthyr-Mawr**, perhaps the most attractive in Ogwr. **New Castle**, paradoxically, controlled a ford on the River Ogmore.

The third castle is Coity, and this one can be traced back to the days of the Norman Lordships. Those of you who have read Thomas Hardy will recognise the name when I tell you that Coity Castle was held by the Turbevilles. Legend has it that the family acquired the castle through marriage, but certainly their descendants were one of Glamorgan's most powerful families. The castle was rebuilt in the 14th century, and added to in Tudor times.

Bridgend straddles the River Ogmore where three valleys meet - the Ogmore, Garw and Llynfi, and as well as being the traditional market town of the area it is now an industrial centre. The A48 from Bridgend will take you to **Cowbridge** whose origins lie in the first century AD and its location is on the important Roman road between Carmarthen and Caerleon. Modern thought also suggests that it is the sight of a missing Roman fort - Bomium - though nothing has been found to support the theory. It is now largely Georgian in character with many of the buildings listed. Charming place to be and full of interest.

The Vale of Glamorgan next with its plethora of places to see. **Llantwit Major** was once known as Llanilltud Fawr - 'Great Church of Illtud' - and as such was the first Christian College in Britain. It is also mentioned in the Guiness Book of Records as the site of the oldest school in Britain, and in legend St David, St Gilda and St Patrick are said to have been educated in this little town.

Barry or the old Port of Barry was first mentioned in 1276, and went on to flourish in the 16th and early 17th centuries. The larger, more modern town of Barry grew up as a port in the 1880s, like Porthcawl there to serve the needs of the South Wales coal industry. Now this bustling town is an excellent shopping centre, with good leisure facilities and a varied night life.

It is also the location of Glamorgan Borough Council's head office, a fact worth noting as they can supply a wealth of information on accommodation, and places to see in the Vale of Glamorgan. Barry Island is linked by road and rail, and is a flourishing holiday resort. Its situation is ideal, for as a peninsula it has sea on three sides and all road and rail communications in the centre. There are two very large sandy beaches, plenty of rock pools to explore, and promenades and landscaped gardens ideal forstrolling or lazing in the sun.

The B4267 is the road you need to take you towards Cardiff, and there are several interesting places to visit en route. Cosmeston Lakes Country Park has all the attractions you would expect, and in addition a Medieval Village which is not a reconstruction. Archaeologists are excavating and restoring, and a personal guide is there to introduce you to the history of Comeston Village.

Like Llandudno on the north coast, **Penarth** has a fine Victorian esplanade that provides a touch of old world charm. It is a pleasant resort on high ground to the west of Cardiff, which has been in turn fishing village and coal-exporting port. This is probably not the place for those who like sea swimming, for there are strong currents running off the shingle beach that is backed up by cliffs up to 100 feet high. There are, however, several swimming pools which make ideal alternatives. From Penarth pier you can embark on The Waverley, the world's last, sea-going paddle steamer. Five miles offshore - almost midway between Penarth and Weston-Super-Mare - Flat Holm island is reputed to be the burial place of the knights who murdered Thomas Becket.

We must go back to 75AD to learn of the first settlements where **Cardiff** stands today, for it was then the Romans built a fort by the River Taff to control Welsh tribesmen. It was extended in 300 AD, this time as a defence against pirates from across the Irish Sea. The town grew up around a fort built by Robert FitzHamon - which can still be seen in the grounds of Cardiff Castle -and it was given its first Royal Charter by Elizabeth I in 1581. Coal played a big part in the town's prosperity, leading to the construction of docks which in 1794 were linked by canal to Merthyr Tydfil.

Shirley Bassey fans will know of **Tiger Bay**, a region of sprawling quays to the east of the Taff where seamen frequented taverns with names such as The Bucket of Blood and the House of Blazes. A once tough area, now developed into a modern city suburb with up to date docks.

It is almost impossible to know where to start exploring Cardiff, and you will be guided by preferences. Sports fans are certain to head for Cardiff Arms park, others will go first to the waterfront, while the Castle will for many be the magnet that first attracts. **The National Museum of Wales** is located at Cathays Park. Permanent exhibitions here cover an enormous range of subjects such as geology, botany, zoology, archaeology -surely enough 'ologies' to keep Maureen Lipman happy for months! Other sections feature industry and art, and there are temporary exhibitions, holiday activities for children, lunchtime and evening concerts and regular lectures and readings.

The Welsh Industrial and Maritime Museum is on Bute Street and, appropriately, the site is adjacent to the Bute West Dock Basin. It was opened in 1977 so is comparatively new, but its comprehensive coverage of industrial and maritime matters in Wales over the past two centuries is staggering. This is very much an open air site too; the steam tug 'Sea Alarm', a pilot cutter and a canal boat, a number of cranes and industrial locomotives as well as a railway footbridge and a lifeboat, will have people from all walks of life enthralled.

The Welsh Folk Museum is some distance away at St Fagans - about five miles west of the city centre. This is a museum packed with fascinating exhibits, and I found it wonderful because it reflects everyday life in Wales, which of course is of interest to absolutely everybody. The setting is super - an Elizabethan mansion standing within the walls of a medieval castle.

Cardiff Castle is different in several respects from others we have seen. It is for a start, in the very centre of this capital city, and it is also the creation of a Victorian Architect. The castle was considerably extended in the 13th century, but the ornate 150 foot clock tower, the Guest Tower, the guest rooms and Octagonal Tower are all the work of William Burges, who rebuilt the castle in the 1870s to fulfil the dreams of John Patrick Crichton-Stuart, the third Marquess of Bute.

There are mixed opinions about this castle, some love it, some think it to be so lavishly decorated that it is vulgar in parts and yet the design and construction of other parts approaches perfection. The Entrance Hall has elegant stained glass windows showing the monarchs who have owned the castle. The Library also has lovely stained glass windows - this time with a Biblicaltheme.

St David's Hall is the National Concert and Conference Hall of Wales and was completed in 1982. I always associate it with that wonderful television programme 'Cardiff - Singer of the World' - which appears every two years and allows me to listen to truly wonderful voices every night for a week.

It is centrally located alongside the St David's Shopping Centre, and as well as an auditorium seating 2000 there are numerous meeting rooms and dressing rooms. Excellent bar facilities and an in-house catering department.

What can one say of Cardiff Arms Park? An ideal situation alongside the River Taff, minutes away from the town centre and Cardiff Central railway station, and of course known to millions of Rugby Union fans all over the world. If you are there on the day of an international - perhaps Wales versus England -the singing may well move you to tears.

Singing of a different kind can be heard at the New Theatre, which opened in 1906 and is Cardiff's sole surviving traditional theatre. The Royal Shakespeare Company, London Contemporary Dance Theatre and Sadlers Wells Royal Ballet have all appeared here, plus West End Musicals, and, of course, the Welsh National Opera for which the new Theatre provides a fitting home.

Probably one of my favourite locations in Wales is **The Brecon Beacons**. The scenery is stunning and varied as are the villages. Along the A470 for just five miles and you come to Castell Coch. This is the first fairy-tale castle

I have seen in Wales. A marvellous jumble of round towers and conical of a Victorian dream - and the same two people are responsible: William Burges, and John Patrick Crichton-Stuart. The work on Castell Coch ran in parallel with the work five miles down the road, and if anything Burges gave even freer rein to his imagination. All is lavishly decorated with murals, carvings, paintings and figures taken from Aesop's Fables and Greek mythology - yet there is a sombre note, too, for a flight of stone steps lead down to a gloomy dungeon.

I suggest the simplest way of tackling the Brecon Beacons National Park is to drive slowly through to **Brecon** and then pause to catch your breath and take stock. You are in exhilirating mountain country all the way and some six miles from Garwnant you will come abreast of the three peaks of the beacons: Pen-y-Fan (2907 ft), which is flanked by Cribyn (2608 ft) and Corn Du (2863 ft). They are the highest mountains in South Wales, and it is very easy to see why this daunting terrain is ideal training ground for elite army units, and the haunt of mountaineers.

Brecon is situated at the junction of the rivers Usk and Honddu, and is one of the oldest Welsh towns. It was granted its first charter in 1246 and a second granted in 1366 gave it the right to hold a fair. That right is never taken lightly in Wales, and pleasure fairs are still held in the Brecon streets for three days each May and November. The town has a bewildering mixture of architectural styles - Medieval, Georgian, Jacobean and Tudor, as well as excellent modern buildings. There was a castle, but all that remains now are a tower and battlemented wall.

If you are tired of driving yet determined to see more of this beautiful part of Wales, all is not lost. Brecon and Beyond is the name of a firm running luxury landrover tours, and they offer the ideal way to get off the beaten track without ruining the family car's suspension. Drovers' tracks criss-cross a 12,000 acre private estate, and there are super views, rugged mountains, waterfalls and limestone gorges.

It was a great disappointment to me to discover that **Caerphilly** cheese is mainly made in Somerset today and not in this small town where until 1910 there used to be a bustling cheese market. Caerphilly has experienced enormous changes, as have most towns and villages in this land with an unusually turbulent history. In the hills around the town the Welsh held out against the Norman invaders for 200 years after 1066. Later, around 1268, Gilbert de Clare, the Red Earl of Gloucester, began the construction of Caerphilly Castle, which is the largest in Wales and the second largest in Britain. It was destroyed just two years later by Llywelyn ap Gruffydd, Prince of Wales, when it was still only partially built. A second attempt at construction was begun - again by the Earl - in 1271, and this time it was successful. The site is right in the middle of the town and very impressive. The concentric ground plan and huge encircling moat rendered normal siege methods ineffective, and even in mopdern times it's easy to visualise the attackers' abortive attempts to break through. A magnificent sight!

One of the first things a visitor notices is a tower that leans almost 12 feet off the perpendicular, and not for the first time I came across conflicting stories when I tried to root out an explanation. The first suggests that during the Civil War - in 1646 - the Royalists attempted to blow up the castle to prevent the Roundheads from using it, and in so doing badly damaged the tower. The other theory is that the lean is caused by subsidence. The first appeals to me infinitely more than the second!

Caerphilly Castle has a ghost. Known as the Ghost of the Green Lady, it is said to be Alice of Angouleme, bride of Gilbert de Clare, who fell for a Welsh Prince called Griffith the Fair and was immediately banished to her home in France. Since then her spirit has looked out from the grey ramparts, waiting for the return of her prince....

The ruins of Newport Castle stand close to the bridge over the River Usk. It was built in the 15th century and has a wonderful Gothic arch on which can still be seen the grooves of the original portcullis. By the 16th-century Newport was already known for its excellent harbour; three hundred years later that came to good use when the Industrial Revolution brought coal pouring down from the Monmouthshire valleys. **Newport** is now the foremost shopping and commercial centre in Gwent, with a heritage dating back three thousand years and a character moulded by Celts, Romans, Saxons, Normans, Plantagenets and Tudors.

You will need to take the B4236 to reach old **Caerleon**, which today is an attractive village, of interest in its own right. Visitors flock to see Caerleon Isca, a fortress laid out beside the River Usk in about 74AD which became one of the three principal military bases in Roman Britain, headquarters of the 2nd Augustan Legion. The aerial photographs I had seen clearly show the shape of these wonderful remains, but actually walking through them left me with the uncanny sensation of having stepped a long way back in the past - obviously true, yet I felt it here stronger than anywhere else (except perhaps Canterbury Cathedral).

The Barracks at Caerleon are the only Roman legionary barracks on view anywhere in Europe. It is an extraordinary feeling to see the buildings that once housed 80 men, and realise you are walking down a Roman street. Broadway is the course of the Via Principalis, and a sign on a farm wall to the left marks the site of the soutwest gateway - Port Dextra. The Fortress Baths are if anything more impressive. They served as the main leisure centre for the soldiers, and the building once stood 60 feet high. There is an open air swimming pool - now displayed under cover - that was discovered as recently as 1964.

The Ampitheatre stands outside the fortress walls. It once seated 5,000 spectators - the whole garrison. Today it is still a superb setting for open-air theatrical events and festivals. All the separate parts of this wonderful site are brought together and thoroughly explained in the spacious Legionary Museum.

From Caerleon I had intended to go straight to Caldicot. But there is no M4 junction there so instead I took the A48, which allowed me to call at Penhow and Caerwent.

Penhow Castle is the home of the Seymour family, and the oldest lived-in castle in Wales. It was restored in 1973 by the owner, who still lives there. An interesting way of touring the building is provided: audio cassettes in handy 'walkman' players act as guides, providing an acommpaniment of authentic period music.

Caerwent is just a few miles further on, a peaceful village that is built on the site of the Roman walled town of Venta Silarum. Excavations here have revealed houses, shops and a temple, and in places the well-preserved walls stand 15 feet high. All of this interests me tremendously, because it is not something I have delved deeply into yet in the space of a few short miles I have come across a

Roman fortress, a Roman town, and a little further on is **Portskewett**, a tiny village close to the River Severn, which centuries ago was an important landing stage for the Romans when they first came to Wales. The landing point at Black Rock is now a delightful picnic site.

From Caerwent it is a short drive down a minor road to **Caldicot**, a lovely town which was mentioned in the Domesday Book in the 11th century. Rich in history - in particular that relating to the Roman occupation. At nearby Mount Ballan, Crick - home of showjumper David Broome - the Wales and the West Showjumping events are held.

Caldicot Castle was built in stages during the 12th and 14th centuries, but unlike others that were left to decay it was restored by a wealthy Victorian and converted into a family home. The castle is the focal point of a delightful country park and also renowned for its medieval banquets. Large parties must be booked but quite often there are tables available for smaller numbers.

Chepstow marks the western edge of my tour through Wales. It is delightfully situated in a loop of the River Wye and has streets that slope down to the river. There are many tea-houses, antique shops, galleries and craft shops on the way down to the riverbank which is the spectacular setting for, among other things, the fine new bandstand.

The castle dominates the town and is the earliest Norman stone castle in Wales. William Fitzosbern, Earl of Hereford, built it on limestone cliffs at the water's edge, and it was greatly enlarged in the 12th and 13th centuries. It is one of the few sites where it is possible to follow the many phases of castle building in Britain. It was considered impregnable until the walls were breached by Cromwell's guns during the Civil War. Several grand walks are waymarked from Chepstow. one of them beginning on the Welsh side of the river, is the Wye Valley walk, which starts at the castle and passes through glorious countryside. For the other you will need to cross to the English side; it is Offa's Dyke.

You must look out for the signs to the village of **Tintern**. This is an attractive hamlet with a south-facing hill overlooking the Abbey where Welsh table wines are produced from a fine vineyard. But it is Tintern Abbey that folk come to see and it really is a wonderful sight.

The original abbey was a Cistercian house founded by Henry I in 1131, but the existing remains are much larger, and date from the late 13th century. The setting is superb, with the river flowing through grassy banks dotted with white cottages, and all around thickly wooded hills. Wordsworth was impressed while on a walking tour, and indeed the abbey ruins are among the most beautiful and best preserved in Britain.

Monmouth is a splendid town. It stands at the confluence of the Wye, Monnow and Trothy rivers, and this former county town of Monmouthshire boasts many well-preserved Tudor and Georgian buildings. Agincourt Square is elegant, bordered by a cluster of fine inns and the Shire Hall and library, and a statue there is itself a tribute to a man who helped bring elegance to the motorindustry: Charles Stewart Rolls, co-founder of Rolls-Royce, who was born at nearby Rockfield.

I am sure you will be smitten by **Usk**. It is a wonderfully picturesque town that has several times been voted 'Best Kept Small Town in Wales'. It has also won the small town category in the 'Britain in Bloom' competition, and in the summer months you will find it ablaze with masses of flowers in beds, window boxes and hanging baskets. July and September are good months to visit Usk. The Usk Festival is held in midsummer, and in recent years jousting tournaments have been added to the traditional music and drama. The Usk Agricultural Show takes place at summers end, and is held in Trostrey on the outskirts of the town.

Abergavenny was my last port of call on this tour of Wales. If I were asked to name my favourite spot in this old market town then I would certainly plump for Castle Meadows alongside the River Usk. On a summer's day there can be no more idyllis place to be and a picnic beneath tall trees on the gently sloping banks is certainly my idea of heaven.

This has been a wonderful journey for me, and I hope you have found something along the way to inspire you and room in your heart to forgive my ommissions. Some have been deliberate, giving me the excuse to return.

PRESWYLFA GUEST HOUSE
Aberdovey
Gwynedd LL35 0LE
Tel: 01654 767239

It is the warmth and hospitality emanating from Marion and Jim Billingham, which takes Preswylfa Guest House into a class of its own. They both have the ability to make strangers into friends very quickly. Jim is a retired sea captain who spent many years in the Mediteranean and Carribean on luxury mega/motor yachts which taught him a great deal about caring for people at the very highest level. It is just over a year since Jim joined Marian permanently and together they have set about refurbishing thehouse and this year a new Dining room has been added on to the side of the house.

There are only three, beautifully appointed ensuite bedrooms, all recently refurbished, two of which which overlook the Dovey estuary and Cardigan Bay from a high position. The views are breathtaking. On entering Preswylfa there is a strong feeling of the style of the 20's and 30's due to the careful attention paid to decor and antiques. Jim is an enthusiastic pianist and he is known to be found at the splendid Grand piano, much to the enjoyment of guests. He also has a number of entertaining seafaring stories. Both he and Marian are always delighted if guests can play an instrument so that everyone can take pleasure in a musical evening. The garden is colourful and beautiful with abundant flowerbeds. The food is superb with the emphasis on good English fare with a hint of French. Casseroles are a speciality of the house, using local produce if at all possible. Currently Preswylfa is not licensed but you are welcome to bring your own wine. Children are welcome if well behaved and pets may visit by arrangement.

USEFUL INFORMATION

OPEN; All year
CHILDREN; Well behaved welcome
CREDIT CARDS; None taken
LICENSED; No
ACCOMMODATION; 3 ensuite rooms
PETS; By arrangement

RESTAURANT; Not applicable
BAR MEALS; Not applicable
VEGETARIAN; By arrangement
DISABLED ACCESS; No
GARDEN; Large with abundant flowers

THE THREE SALMONS INN,
Cross Ash, Abergavenny.
Tel: 01873 821297

A charming and efficient young woman, Jenny Wood, is the proud proprietor of The Three Salmons Inn at Cross Ash, Abergavenny. You will find the pub on the B4521, Ross-on-Wye to Abergavenny road, just outside the village. She has created a wonderful atmosphere in this house which is surrounded by much lovely countryside with the Welsh hill called The Graig behind it. The Graig is certainly worth making the effort to walk to the top because from here you can see five counties, Gwent, Mid-Glamorgan, Powys, Gloucestershire and Herefordshire. There is also the spectacular 3 Castles walk starting just down the road from The Three Salmons.

Running a pub and restaurant was a new departure for Jenny when she bought the Three Salmons but she took to it like the proverbial duck to water. The villagers have been coming here for generations and were delighted to welcome her to their local. It is a wonderfully relaxed atmosphere and one should never be surprised to see a tractor or even an odd chicken in the car park. At the bar too you will find a great mixture of people who enjoy this happy establishment whatever their backgrounds. The interesting and beautifully cooked food has become well known in the area - Jenny's mother cooks at the weekend. Wonderful vegetables and traditional puddings have their place on the menu. In addition to the main meals there are excellent hot snacks and super sandwiches. There is a Children's Menu and a three course set meal on Sunday lunchtimes. Booking is advisable especially at weekends.

USEFUL INFORMATION

OPEN; 12-2.30pm & 6-11pm
Closed Thursday lunchtime.
CHILDREN;;Children welcome at lunchtime.
VEGETARIAN;Several dishes
ACCOMMODATION; None

RESTAURANT; Interesting, beautifully cooked food
BAR FOOD; Wide Range
CREDIT CARDS; None taken

DISABLED ACCESS; Level entrance

FRON HEULOG COUNTRY HOUSE
Betws-y-Coed, LL24 0BL
Tel: 01690 710736

Jean and Peter Whittingham rescued this charming house from dereliction in 1988 and have spent the ensuing years restoring it to its original character with the help of local craftsmen. It is now a delightful, strictly non-smoking home into which they welcome guests. They welcome people from all over the world and because of their exceptional local knowledge - they have had their home in the area for 30 years - every guest has this additional benefit when planning what to see and do. Easily found, once in Betws-y-Coed centre, you cross the Pont-Y-Pair Bridge, turn left, go past the car park and up ahead along the river bank. Fron Heulog is on the right, 150 metres from the bridge, facing south in quiet, peaceful, wooded, riverside scenery.

Inside, this elegant Victorian stone-built house has comfortable decoration and furnishing co-ordinated overall with lots of original polished pine - and the warmth of full modern centralheating. The modern bedrooms have magazines, hairdryers, toiletries, hot water bottles, hospitality trays, full bathrooms ensuite, and colour television is available. The spacious lounges are comfortably furnished, ideal for meeting people, enjoying conversations, watching television or just curling up with a good book. The attractive dining room is where you will be served a satisfying Welsh breakfast and if you wish dine at night by arrangement. At the time of writing Fron Heulog is not licensed but you are most welcome to bring your own choice of wine. You may well find your hosts giving you a drink or wine as a gesture of hospitality. This is just one of the many touches like the bedroom flowers, the sweet bowl in the hall, the newspapers at breakfast, the variety of freshly-baked local bread and the choice of home-made marmalade and jams, that make it such a good place to stay. The Whittinghams thoroughly deserve their Welsh Tourist Board 3 Crowns Highly Commended grading. They are winners of the WTB Guest House Award. Short Breaks are a house speciality. Facilities for walkers are happily provided. Price Band 'B'.

USEFUL INFORMATION

OPEN; All year.
A Non-Smoking house
CHILDREN; By arrangement only
CREDIT CARDS; None taken
LICENSED; Not at present
ACCOMMODATION; 5 ensuite rms
PETS; Not allowed

RESTAURANT; Not applicable
BAR MEALS; Not applicable
VEGETARIAN; By arrangement
DISABLED ACCESS; Welcome but no special facilities
GARDEN; Yes & parking on private ground

THE WHITE HORSE
Builth Wells,
Powys,
Wales LDZ3DN
Tel: 01982 553171

Gary and Diane Cooper have been mine hosts in this charming inn for over 9 years during which time they have made several alterations but in such a sympathetic manner that the character of the White Horse has not changed. From the front one might suppose it to be small but go in and you will see how deceptive first impressions are. It was the first building built of brick 'by public subscription' after the Great Fire of Builth in 1690. Within the inn, it is the warmth and friendliness that make it special. The Coopers work hard to ensure that everyone who visits The White Horse, whether a regular or a stranger, is made to feel at home. In fact it has a true pub atmosphere. For anyone wanting to stay there are five comfortable ensuite bedrooms with Television and a bountiful tea/coffee tray.

At the back of the inn is the restaurant which serves some of the best steaks in Powys, each one cooked to order. The menu is not extensive but is delicious and well presented. From time to time the room is used for small functions especially for lively local Rugby and Archery parties. Bar meals are served daily and there are always 'Specials' which include many favourite dishes. From a simple, fresh, well filled sandwich to a main meal, the choice is excellent, sensibly priced and value for money.

USEFUL INFORMATION

OPEN: All year
CHILDREN; By arrangement
CREDIT CARDS;
All except Amex/Diners
LICENSED; Full
PETS; No
ACCOMMODATION; 5 ensuite rooms

RESTAURANT; Excellent steaks etc
BAR FOOD; Wide range. Daily Specials
VEGETARIAN; Catered for
DISABLED ACCESS; No
GARDEN; No. Large Car park

TAFARN PANTYDDERWEN
Llangain,
Carmarthen, Dyfed
Tel: 01267 241560

The Tafarn Pantydderwen attracts visitors from all over the world because of the all pervading warmth and friendliness it provides. The owners, Mr and Mrs Griffiths and their staff have made Pantydderwen the social and cultural centre of Llangain, in which the contented regulars are only too happy to extend their good humour to everyone who visits.

You will find the pub off the B3412, the main road from Carmarthen to Llanstephan. It is readily accessible and only four miles from the centre of Carmarthen. The village has grown in recent years with newcomers who have been welcomed and integrated into the life of the community. There is sailing on the Towy, the magnificent relics of Llanstephan Castle on a hill overlooking Carmarthen Bay and many points of interest within easy reach. There are attractive coastal walks, leisurely beach activities and a quiet round of golf or two for anyone who enjoys it.

Pantydderwen provides good ale, the meals served are of an exceptionally high standard and stand comparison with the best available in West Wales. Under the personal supervision of Dawn Griffiths, interesting menus are prepared and she readily caters to meet individual tastes and palates.

USEFUL INFORMATION

OPEN; 12-3pm & 6-11pm. Supper ext
CHILDREN; Yes. Pony paddock
CREDIT CARDS; Access
LICENSED; Full. Supper extension
ACCOMMODATION; Not applicable
GARDEN; Small beer garden with tables
RESTAURANT; Wide choice. Daily specials
BAR FOOD; Freshly cooked. Excellent value
VEGETARIAN; Choice of 5 dishes
DISABLED ACCESS; Ramp.

GWERN BORTER COUNTRY MANOR

Barker's Lane,
Rowen, Nr Conwy,
Gwynedd LL32 8YL
Tel: 01492 650360

Gary and Tracy Powell, the owners of Gwern Borter Country Manor, spent many years of their lives running at a busy city pace. They left this lifestyle with the aim of creating a perfect rural retreat. This they have achieved splendidly at Gwern Borter in the ten years they have been there. This handsome Country Manor House stands in 10 acres of landscaped grounds with beautiful ornamental gardens, organic kitchen garden, woodland, duck pond, pet's corner and many ancient cures can be found in the medicinal herb garden. The setting amongst the forest, rivers and lakes of Snowdonia, is superb. It lies at the foot of the Tal-Y-Fan mountain between the award winning village of Rowen and Conwy, the finest example of a medieval walled town in Wales, with its beautiful harbour and magnificent Edwardian castle. The Manor is full of 'Olde Worlde' charm with an oak entrance hall and impressive staircase. The magnificent oak fireplace in the dining room is something which delights the eyes of the diners and sets the room off perfectly for those about to enjoy a delicious four course evening meal, traditionally cooked with herbs and vegetables from the kitchen garden. The day starts with typically Welsh breakfasts. All the bedrooms are ensuite and have colour TV, radio alarms, hairdryers and tea/coffee making facilities. Excellent activity facilities are available. Gwern Borter offers a unique experience in Pony trekking with Gary tailoring a trail ride to your own ability reaching within 400ft of the peak of the Talyfan mountain. Everyone from beginner to expert can enjoy this excellent facility. 10 varied Golf courses, fishing in surrounding rivers and lakes, deep sea fishing from Conwy harbour, dry ski-slopes in Llandudno, and beautiful mountain walks are there for your enjoyment. Gwern Borter has its own gymnasium, Sauna and Pool/Snooker room. Gary may also treat you to a reading of Welsh legends after dinner. Children love the pet's corner with Jeeves and Worcester, the goats, Honey, Tessa, Legs and Georgie, the horses, Ike & Tina Turkey plus lots of chickens, ducks and geese. Short breaks are available throughout the year. AA Select 4 Q's. Welsh Tourist Board 3 Crown HighlyCommended.

USEFUL INFORMATION

OPEN; All year except Christmas
CHILDREN; Welcome
CREDIT CARDS; All except Amex/Diners
LICENSED; Yes
PETS; Well behaved dogs welcome
ACCOMMODATION;
4 ensuite + 8 Cottages

DINING ROOM; Not open to non-residents
BAR FOOD; Not applicable
VEGETARIAN; Catered for
DISABLED ACCESS; Yes. 2 cottages have facilities for partially disabled
GARDEN; Yes, glorious ten acres

THE HAWK AND BUCKLE INN

Llannefydd,
Denbigh, Clwyd LL16 5ED
Tel: 01745 540249 Fax: 01745 540316

Off the beaten track in the unspoilt village of Llannefydd, and sitting high in the hills overlooking the beautiful countryside of the Vale of Clwyd, the 17th century Hawk and Buckle is a delightful old coaching Inn on what was once the stagecoach route to Holyhead. Today there are no stagecoaches, no ostlers in the yard, no hustle and bustle but the inn still caters for the traveller and is situated in what is now a quiet country lane. Of course there have been alterations over the centuries but nothing has been done to take away the charm of the building, even the discreet modern extension to the Hawk and Buckle has not intruded on the authentic frontage of the inn.

Inside its welcoming walls, full central heating ensures warmth whilst the friendly landlords Bob and Barbara Pearson make sure that newcomers are as much at home as the regulars who frequent the bars. Ten attractively furnished en suite bedrooms with modern facilities mostly have superb views over the lovely surrounding countryside. The Hawk and Buckle is renowned for the excellence of its food both in the restaurant and bar, where extensive menus ensure there is something to tempt everyone's palate. Much use is made of local produce; lamb and salmon in season are a speciality. Vegetarian meals are always available.

The Hawk and Buckle is an ideal base. Guests can travel in any direction and be sure of finding something of beauty and interest. The walled city of Chester is within easy reach as is the seaside resort of Llandudno. There are no less than nine golf courses within thirty minutes drive and for the fisherman, salmon, trout and sea fishing are available locally. WTB 3 crowns highly commended, and talked about in Ashley Courtenay, Egon Ronay, Logis and Michelin, this is a hotel that is justifiably popular.

USEFUL INFORMATION

OPEN; All year
CHILDREN; Over 8 years not sharing
CREDIT CARDS; All major cards
LICENSED; Full Licence
PETS; No
ACCOMMODATION: 8dbl 2 twin all ensuite

RESTAURANT; Extensive menu,
BAR MEALS; Delicious, wide range
VEGETARIAN; Several dishes daily
DISABLED ACCESS; Not good
GARDEN; No. Residents car park
Bar car park opposite Inn

PENMAENUCHAF HALL HOTEL,
Penmaenpool, Dolgellau
Tel: 01341 422129

This wondrous and romantic pile of gables and half-dormers, built in ' the noble crystalline rock of Wales' with its 21 acres of grounds and even peacocks on the lawns, scarcely belongs to this century. It has the grace and elegance of the 19th century and the appointments of the one to come. Around it are birch-hung slopes and massed Rhododendrons, Cedars, Wellingtonias and Douglas in their prime. The topiary will enchant you, the sunken rose-garden will assail your nostrils and the soothing sound of a fountain tossing its feathery stream into the air will underline the immediate relaxation that partners, Lorraine Fielding and Mark Watson set out to achieve when they purchased Penmaenuchaf.

Inside, oak wainscotting greets you, broken only by a huge decorative fireplace. There are comfortable chairs and a profusion of flowers everywhere. The morning room has an Adam ceiling, and you lunch or dine in an oak-scented and wainscotted room. Then there is the fine library, a rod room where fishermen weigh their catches, after trying out the ten miles of fishing rights on the rivers Mawddach and Wnion. Ingeniously created and stunningly beautiful bedrooms delight visitors. Non-residents are very welcome to enjoy meals, take morning coffee or indulge in the delicious afternoon teas. The food and wine are like the rest of this wonderful place - incomparable.

USEFUL INFORMATION

OPEN; 8am- 11.30pm.
CHILDREN; Over 8.
CREDIT CARDS; All major cards
LICENSED; Residential & eating
ACCOMMODATION; 14 ensuite rooms
Conference facilities
PETS; By arrangement

RESTAURANT; Memorable food
BAR FOOD; Not applicable
VEGETARIAN; Several dishes daily
DISABLED ACCESS;; Yes + toilets
GARDEN; 21 acres, landscaped & woodland
Free trout & salmon fishing

THE IVY HOUSE
Finsbury Square,
Dolgellau, Gwynedd
Tel: 01341 422535

Dolgellau nestles happily at the foot of Cader Idris in the valley of the River Wnion. It is a contented country town built mostly of granite and local Welsh slate. Ivy House is just out of the main square on the Twywn Road. What an interesting house it is, proclaiming on the front that it was built in 1829, yet the focal point of the pretty dining room is a fine fireplace which is almost an inglenook and must show that part of the building is very much older. Every one of the six letting rooms is attractively furnished with every facility. Children are very welcome and highchairs are available. Everywhere is centrally heated and guests are encouraged to enjoy the comfort of the lounge and the fun of the cellar bar. Non-residents are very welcome at Ivy House for meals which are an enjoyable experience, cooked by Margaret Bamford, who with her husband James, owns the establishment. They have been here 10 years, gradually bringing the house to its present standard. With the exception of the ice-cream and sorbet everything on the menu is home-made and produced in Margaret's sparkling and well-planned kitchen. The range of dishes is certain to provide something to suite everyone no matter what the age. There are Vegetarian dishes and a Welsh Supper which is quite delicious.

USEFUL INFORMATION

OPEN; All year. Meals 5.30pm-9.30pm
CHILDREN; Welcome
CREDIT CARDS; Visa/Master/Euro
LICENSED; Residential & Residential
ACCOMMODATION; Comfortable rooms
GARDEN; Small garden for pre-dinner drinks. Open to non-residents
DINING ROOM; Delicious food. Everything Home-made except Icecream & sorbet
BAR FOOD; Not applicable
VEGETARIAN; Several dishes
DISABLED ACCESS; Level entrance

THE OLD RECTORY
Llansanffraid,
GlanConwy,
Nr Conwy, Gwynedd LL28 5LF
Tel: 01492 580611
Fax: 01492 584555

Michael and Wendy Vaughan have achieved outstanding success at their beautiful 16th Century Georgian style, Grade II Listed home, The Old Rectory, which they share with no more than twelve house guests ensuring the true feeling of a country house. Their reputation has travelled world wide and en route has earned them more accolades than one can mention here. For example, a Cesar award for 'Welsh Hospitality at its Best, Red Stars status by the AA and a coveted Blue Ribbon by the RAC for 'Outstanding Comfort, Welcome, Service and Food'. The review in Vogue Magazine stated: 'The torch for fine cooking on the North Wales coast is carried by Wendy Vaughan, faultless throughout'. Indeed gourmet dinners from this Michelin Red 'M' Chef will never be forgotten. So many accolades might in some ways frighten people into supposing that this was a very formal establishment. Not a bit of it, the Vaughans have created a calm, relaxing, unfussy atmosphere. Comfortable rooms, beautifully appointed, abound with paintings and antiques. House guests may either have dinner country house style and dine at the long, elegant, mahogany table with fellow guests, or dine separately, the choice is yours. You will be served aperitifs before dinner in the pine panelled drawing room. There, if you wish, you may meet the other house guests, half of whom are usually from overseas. A total ban on smoking inside the house enhances the enjoyment of food and wine.

The panoramic views from the gardens are reason enough for staying in this delightful house. Its hillside perch overlooks the grand sweep of Conwy Estuary, historic Conwy Castle and the Snowdonian mountains. Situated mid-way (forty minutes' drive) between Chester and Caernarfon, it is an ideal centre for touring North Wales, Bodnant Gardens, Betws-y-Coed, and the Victorian seaside spa of Llandudno. Three championship golf courses are all within three miles of the hotel. Michael's knowledge of Welsh history and all things Welsh helps with planning touring and adds the finishing touches to what will be a memorable stay. The Old Rectory is a member of the Wolsey Lodge consortium.

USEFUL INFORMATION

OPEN; Closed 20th Dec-1st Feb
CHILDREN; Over 5 years
CREDIT CARDS; Visa/Access/Diners/Amex
PETS; In coach house only
LICENSED; Yes. Outstanding wine list
ACCOMMODATION; 6 ensuite rooms
Smoking allowed only in 2 coach house rooms

DINING ROOM; Superb set menu
BAR MEALS; Not applicable
VEGETARIAN; By arrangement
DISABLED ACCESS;2 ground floor Rooms. No special facilities
GARDEN; 2 1/2 acres secluded grounds

THE MAESLLWCH COUNTRY HOTEL
Glasbury, Powys
Tel: 01497 847637

There are many hotels in Great Britain that come under the heading of Country Hotels but there can be few with a more certain right to this title than The Maesllwch Country Hotel. A building which has aged gracefully, has enchanting grounds, a fisherman's lodge and a moat house, it offers everything one could possibly want to enjoy a relaxing break. Robert and Carol Taylor own and run the hotel aided by a competent and very friendly staff. It is often said that the busiest people have the most time to spare for others and this is true of the Taylors who are not only welcoming and caring hosts but also find time to run an efficient and highly regarded outside catering facility. Every room is furnished with grace, warmth and elegance, fresh flowers, pretty drapes and fine pictures. The ensuite bedrooms have been appointed to encompass much more than just ordinary bedrooms. Complete with Colour TV and a hostess tray, they are light and spacious, warm in winter and cool in summer. The restaurant offers exceptionally good food with an innovative menu that incorporates not only traditional Welsh dishes but international touches as well. There is always emphasis on local and fresh vegetables. Fishing, gliding, walking and golf are all within easy reach of The Maesllwch which makes it an ideal base but it is equally good for those who just want to potter and take things easy.

USEFUL INFORMATION

OPEN;All year
CHILDREN;Well behaved welcome
CREDIT CARDS;All major cards
LICENSED;Full Licence
ACCOMMODATION;Delightful ensuite rooms

RESTAURANT;Innovative, traditional and international
BAR FOOD;Not applicable
DISABLED ACCESS;Yes
GARDEN;Lovely grounds

LLWYNDU FARMHOUSE
Llanaber,
Nr Barmouth LL42 1RR
Tel: 01341 280144 Fax: 01341 281236

This non-smoking house is steeped in history and every nook and crannie has a fascination, but most of all it is the relaxed, friendly, and informal atmosphere which has been built up over hundreds of years, which makes it a very special place. It was known for its great hospitality as far back as the 16th century and that tradition is carried on admirably by Peter and Paula Thompson. You will find Llwyndu Farmhouse overlooking the sea, nestling above Cardigan Bay, on the Snowdonian coastline, 2 miles north of Barmouth and 8 miles south of Harlech. Located some 300 yards east of the A496 Llwyndu is secluded with often just the sound of the waves breaking on the beach below. The house is only a few minutes drive from extensive sandy beaches and the nearby hills give a variety of good walks. Snowdon and the 'heart' of the Snowdonia National Park is only 45 minutes drive.

There are seven ensuite rooms for guests, three in the house and four in a splendidly converted barn. The Thompsons have cleverly kept a delightful blend of exposed timbers and stonework which they have married with attractive fabrics. All rooms are centrally heated, have beverage making facilities, TV's and radios. The dining room in what was the old parlour, is lit by candlelight and old lanterns and is a delightful setting for a perfect dinner. The food whether at dinner or breakfast is delicious and of a very high standard. In order that you may have a relaxed evening meal, younger children can be fed at 6pm. To complement the enjoyment of the meal there is a selection of good and moderately priced wines, beers, spirits and liquers. From the lounge after dinner you may be fortunate enough to catch one of the spectacular sunsets that are occasionally seen across the bay. Llwyndu is a haven of peace, tranquillity and conviviality.

USEFUL INFORMATION

OPEN; All year
CHILDREN; Welcome. Cots, Highchairs
CREDIT CARDS; None taken
LICENSED; Residential
ACCOMMODATION; 7 ensuite rooms
PETS; By arrangement

DINING ROOM; Excellent, home-fare
BAR MEALS; Not applicable
VEGETARIAN; Catered for
DISABLED ACCESS; No special facilities
GARDEN; Yes, vistas to Cardigan Bay

GUIDFA HOUSE

Crossgates,
Llandrindod Wells,
Powys LD16RF
Tel: 01597 851241
Fax: 01597 851875

Comfort, good food and a relaxing atmosphere are just three of the things you remember when you have stayed at the early 18th century Guidfa House near the beautiful Elan Valley. This elegant Georgian House is the home of Tony and Anne Millan and their aim is to offer their guests an enjoyable, value for money stay complimented by professional yet unobtrusive service. Situated just three miles north of the Spa Town of Llandrindod Wells, it is easily found in the centre of the village of Crossgates and offers plenty of private parking.

The individually furnished bedrooms are spacious and bright and include a ground floor room for less active guests. The rooms are all ensuite and central heating, colour television and tea/coffee making facilities are standard throughout. Anne Millan is a Cordon Bleu trained cook and adds flair and imagination in a combination of new and traditional recipes. Most dishes are based on the modern trend towards healthier eating but never fear, those wonderfully naughty puddings are not totally overlooked!! The well chosen wine list compliments the food and is amazing value for money. Coffee and tea are served afterwards in the pretty sitting room where Tony also dispenses drinks from the bar, if you so wish. On fine evenings you will probably be lured into the garden with its many unusual plants and trees. Set in the very heart of Wales, Guidfa House is an excellent base from which to explore the magical countryside. Walkers and bird-watchers alike will find plenty to interest them, including the local RSPB Red Kite feeding station. Golf, cycling and any trekking can be arranged together with quad trekking, hang-gliding or 4 wheel driving courses. Adjacent to Guidfa House is the former coach house, which has recently been converted into a delightful self-contained unit for 2/4 people. This is available for weekly lets.

USEFUL INFORMATION

OPEN; All year
CHILDREN; Over 10 years
CREDIT CARDS; All except Amex/Diners
PETS; Guide dogs only
LICENSED; Yes
ACCOMMODATION; 7 ensuite rooms

RESTAURANT; Cordon bleu menus - not open to non-residents
BAR MEALS; Not applicable
VEGETARIAN; Yes & all diets by arrangement
DISABLED ACCESS; Yes for less active
GARDEN; Yes

THE HUNDRED HOUSE INN,
Hundred House Village,
Llandrindod Wells,
Powys
Tel: 01982 570231

The village of Hundred House is quite unique. The name comes from the time when the county was divided into 'Hundreds' and courts were established in each hundred to try civil and criminal cases. It may be that the court was held at the Hundred House Inn. This attractive hostelry on the Welsh borders is surrounded by peaceful hills where sheep are more prolific than people. It is close to spectacular mountains and the road to the Hundred House village from Llandrindod Wells provides some of the finest scenic mountain views in Mid Wales. From the terrace of the inn you can watch the gently flowing River Edw, a tributary of the River Wye. From the pub you can follow a path through the richly beautiful hills down to the Wye. It is an area in which you can picnic and find constant places of interest including the famous Aberedw Rocks. The Hundred House has delightful country style accommodation, a fascinating 'Farmer's Bar', in which there are interesting mottos and newspaper cuttings but it is the colourful local customers who create the wonderful atmosphere. The china decked, cosy parlour has seating for 22 diners and the larger garden parlour overlooking the hills and the beer garden, seats 30. The menu is extensive, home-made and with a varied content to suit all tastes. This is a happy pub for all age groups.

USEFUL INFORMATION

OPEN; 11-3.30pm & 6.30-12am All day Bank holidays
CHILDREN; Welcome
CREDIT CARDS; None taken
LICENSED; Yes
ACCOMMODATION; Ensuite rooms
RESTAURANT; Super food
BAR FOOD; Good range
VEGETARIAN; Yes
DISABLED ACCESS; Yes
GARDEN; Yes

THE LLANERCH 16TH CENTURY INN,
Llanerch Lane,
Llandrindod Wells,
Powys
Tel: 01597 822086 Fax: 01597 824618.

This delightful 16th-century inn was here before the town itself. Once an old staging post it just oozes an atmospheric sense of the past. You will find it on the edge of Llandrindod Wells, a fascinating Victorian Spa town. It has a large garden and an orchard at the front with an open aspect at the rear and is within easy reach of the town centre. People who have stayed in the inn will tell you how comfortable the en-suite bedrooms are and how very welcome they were made. They will also tell you of the excellent breakfasts which were sufficient to keep them going all day long. Mini breaks are available here - 2 days half board; ideal for golfers, ramblers, fishermen and cyclists in particular, although it is equally attractive to people who just want to relax, enjoy the pub and spend time wandering round the town. The week before the August Bank Holiday is 'Victorian Week' when the townsfolk dress in appropriate costumes. It is good fun and well worth visiting. John Leach runs the pub with the occasional help of his father, who is the owner, but now semi retired. Over the last thirteen years the Leach family have built up a tremendous reputation for hospitality, well kept traditional ales and good food. You will find the dishes on offer are all home-made and Sunday lunch is an occasion. There are no rules and regulations at The Llanerch; just one instruction - relax!

USEFUL INFORMATION

OPEN; 11.30-2.30pm & 6-11pm.
CHILDREN; Welcome in the lounges
CREDIT CARDS; Access/Visa
LICENSED; Yes
ACCOMMODATION; 12 ensuite rooms
RESTAURANT; Good, home-cooked fare
BAR FOOD; Wide range, home-cooked
VEGETARIAN; Selection of dishes
DISABLED ACCESS: Reasonable
GARDEN; Beer Garden. Patio. Play area

BRYN-Y-BIA LODGE,
Craigside,
Llandudno,
Gwynedd LL303AS
Tel: 01492 549644/540459

Very much a part of the busy resort of Llandudno, Bryn-y-Bia Lodge is nonetheless a world apart where peace and relaxation hold pride of place. Built in the 1850's the elegant house stands in its own beautiful walled grounds overlooking the sea. An ideal place in which to recharge your batteries and at the same time take in some of the stunning scenery in Snowdonia National Park. The Great Orme tramway - a railway and cable car lift will take you to the summit of the Great Orme.
Owned and run by Geoffrey and Carol Grimwood, the house is furnished beautifully with a pleasing and very comfortable mixture of antiques and Chinese pieces. The thirteen ensuite guest rooms are attractive and well equipped. Each is different in size, shape and decor and has that blessing to the traveller, tea and coffee making facilities as well as colour television, central heating, radio and direct-dial telephone. The spacious lounge overlooks the gardens and the pleasant cocktail bar is the ideal place in which to meet your fellow guests. Dinner, served in the attractive, intimate dining room, is an eagerly awaited six course meal, with mainly English dishes but with Continental overtones. Frozen food is strictly taboo. Menus change daily and the emphasis is on fresh local produce. The dining room is open to non-residents at night. Breakfast is also a memorable meal, substantial and enough to keep one going all day. Children are welcome and dogs allowed by arrangement. Aptly described as 'The Country House on the Edge of Town', Bryn-y-Bia Lodge has won some well deserved accolades, AA 2 Star, Tourist Board 3 Crown Highly Commended and recognition from Ashley Courtenay and Michelin.

USEFUL INFORMATION

OPEN; All year except December
CHILDREN; Welcome
CREDIT CARDS; All major cards, not Diners
LICENSED; Residential & Restaurant
PETS; Dogs allowed by arangement
ACCOMMODATION; 13 ensuite rooms
PARKING; Guaranteed off road
DINING ROOM; Open to non residents
BAR MEALS; Not applicable
VEGETARIAN; By arrangement
DISABLED ACCESS; No Ground floor bedrooms
GARDEN; Yes.

SOUTHCLIFFE HOTEL
Hill Terrace,
Llandudno,
Gwynedd LL30 2LS
Tel: 01492 876277 Free Phone 0500 691 7833

Llandudno has many good hotels but few can have the individual and unique touches that you will find in the gracious Southcliffe Hotel based on the Alice in Wonderland Theme. It is south facing and commands superb views over the bay and surrounding mountains and has everything that one would expect from a hotel of this standard. Under the personal supervision of the owners, Ann and Des Goldsmith, the staff are friendly and attentive. Attractively and comfortably furnished, the atmosphere is enhanced by the fascinating collection of Pot Boots and Tea Pots and hundreds of thank you cards which are pinned up all around the hotel. The whole collection has been given to the Goldsmiths by guests who have stayed over the years, many of whom have become very good friends.

There are 32 ensuite bedrooms, each with its own character and complete with TV and tea/coffee making facilities. All the public rooms bear out the Alice in Wonderland Theme with the Alice Lounge, for entertainment and relaxation. The split level restaurant is known as Mad Hatters and is renowned for its excellent cuisine and extensive menus. The Rabbit Hole Bar is a fun place to be for a drink before or after dinner and the Looking Glass Lounge is a quiet room for the non-smoker and non-drinker, or simply somewhere to sit in comfort for an hour or two just reading. One of the favourite places is the Sun Terrace which faces south and overlooks the stunning bay. Three nights a week there is live music and once a week, a party night, bingo and quiz. Special breaks are offered between October and April and for those who have sampled Christmas at the Southcliffe, they will tell you it is never to be forgotten.

USEFUL INFORMATION

OPEN; All year
CHILDREN; Over 9 years
CREDIT CARDS; None taken
PETS; Small dogs
LICENSED; Full license
RESTAURANT; Excellent, home-cooked
BAR FOOD; Not applicable
VEGETARIAN; Catered for
DISABLED ACCESS; No
GARDEN; No
ACCOMMODATION; 32 ensuite rooms. 2 Star AA 3 Crowns WTB

THE QUEENS HEAD,
Glanwydden,
Llandudno Junction,
GWYNEDD
Tel: 01492 546570

People from far and wide make the pilgrimage to the very small village of Glanwydden, close to Llandudno, especially to eat at The Queens Head. This really is the most remarkable pub, not easy to find but so worth seeking out. Every evening and lunchtime you will find it full of people tucking into the feast of good food provided by Robert and Sally Cureton, the owners. This one time wheelwright's cottage has three times reached the national finals of Guinness'Pure Genuis pub food awards. Robert Cureton has a passion for the local ingredients that he uses. Imagine Conway salmon wrapped in filo pastry served with fennel sauce. The fennel grows wild in the country lane leading to the pub and the salmon is from the River Conway which flows into the sea at Conway. The pureed raspberries in the accompanying salad's vinaigrette are locally grown and even the butter will be Welsh. Fresh ingredients are a matter of great importance to Robert Cureton. He has known most of his suppliers for years and he likes to present dishes that use Welsh produce in an original way. One of his superb dishes is Glanwydden lamb with plum and port sauce, the loin spread with Welsh honey then roasted until just pink. During the winter season, Game is added to the menu. The Curetons use plenty of herbs and if they think a vegetable, a herb, a fruit and a cheese will marry, they give it a try. Something like a dozen home-made desserts are served and there is a plethora of old fashioned puds. The Queens Head is a wonderful experience.

USEFUL INFORMATION

OPEN; 11.30-3.30pm & 6.00-11.30pm
CHILDREN; Welcome over 7 years
CREDIT CARDS; Access/Visa/Master/Euro.
LICENSED; Fine wine list
ACCOMMODATION; None
RESTAURANT; Exceptional food
BAR FOOD; Award winning
VEGETARIAN; 5 dishes
DISABLED ACCESS; Not suitable
GARDEN; Outside seating. Car park

THE LAKE COUNTRY HOUSE
Lake Road,
Llangammarch Wells,
Powys LD4 4BS
Tel: 01591 620202 & 620474
Fax: 01591 620457

The Lake Country House is almost unique. It is a welcoming Welsh Country House set in its own 50 acres, with sweeping lawns, rhododendron lined pathways, riverside walks and a large well stocked trout lake. Everything about it is beautiful and elegant but without that sometimes off-putting formality that some establishments have. To reach it you take the A40 Abergavenny-Brecon road going through Brecon and turn left at the cathedral. Here you take the B4519 to Upper Chapel, then turn left for Llangammarch Wells. Drive across Mount Eppynt (6 miles), at the foot of the hill turn left at the crossroads and the house is one mile along this road on the right.

Inside the house is calm and comfort epitomised. The charming lounges are richly furnished with fine antiques, beautiful paintings and sumptuous sofas beside log fires. Fresh flowers are everywhere and the unobtrusive staff are there to cater for your every need. One might suppose one was staying in a country home rather than an hotel. The Welsh are renowned for their food and they excel in breads and cakes. Every afternoon traditional Welsh teas are served in the drawing room beside log fires and in the Summer teas are also served beneath the chestnut tree in the garden overlooking the river. The superbly appointed candlelit restaurant has an excellent menu which relies heavily on fresh produce and an array of herbs from the gardens. The resulting dishes combine delicacy and richness with imaginative presentation. There are over 300 wines on the outstanding wine list. Each comfortable bedroom has its own particular and character; with elegant fabrics, period furniture, pictures and books. Every room has a private bathroom, direct dial telephone and television. The suites have beautifully appointed sitting rooms.

This is a fisherman's paradise within easy reach of some of the best rivers in Wales. The grounds are a haven for wildlife and to help you appreciate the Welsh countryside hacking and trekking can be arranged. For golf enthusiasts there are four course in close proximity. Clay pigeon shoots within the grounds, tennis and billiards, beautiful walks and drives complete the range of activities.

USEFUL INFORMATION

OPEN; All year
CHILDREN; Welcome
CREDIT CARDS; All major cards
LICENSED; Full. Fine wines
ACCOMMODATION; Suites & ensuite, 50 rooms
GARDEN; 50 acres of superb grounds

RESTAURANT; Award winning. Imaginative menu
BAR MEALS; Not applicable
VEGETARIAN; Always a choice
DISABLED ACCESS; Yes, no special facilities

PENRHOS GOLF AND COUNTRY CLUB,
Llanrhystud, Dyfed
Tel: 01974 202999/202236/202254/202238.

Situated some nine miles South of Aberystwyth and seven miles North of Aberaeron on the A487. Look out for sign posts on entering Llanrhystud. Penrhos Golf Course nestles in the soft valleys of West Wales, totally tranquil yet it is easily accessible from North and South Wales, Liverpool, Manchester, Bristol and the Midlands. The 18 hole Championship length course recently constructed is maturing rapidly and is destined to become one of Wales premier venues. You will enjoy the challenging variety of holes and terrain set among some of the finest scenic views in the country. Serious golfer or modest beginner, a round at Penrhos will provide a most pleasant and memorable day. The Clubhouse facilities are excellent, offering visitors first class changing and shower amenities, a fully stocked professional's shop, along with bars and restaurant areas, including a 'Golfers only' spike bar. The Club professional is available for teaching on the separate golf practice range.

To add to your enjoyment of a visit to Penrhos the lecentre is at the disposal of you and your family. There is a beautiful fun indoor swimming pool, jacuzzi, solarium, steam room, sauna and well fitted gymnasium. Bar meals or full restaurant service is available as was a children's room and pool room. In conjunction with Penrhos Holiday Park, situated alongside the course, great value golfing holidays with luxury mobile home accommodation is on offer. Book one of the modelwide luxury mobile homes and you will not be disappointed. Each has two double bedrooms, bathroom with shower, fridge, colour television, equipped to the highest standard, a fully valeted home from home. Ring for further details.

USEFUL INFORMATION

OPEN: All year
RESTAURANT; First class fare
CHILDREN; Well behaved welcome
BAR FOOD; Snacks available
CREDIT CARDS; All major cards
VEGETARIAN; Several dishes
LICENSED; Yes
DISABLED ACCESS; Yes
ACCOMMODATION; Well equipped mobile homes

THE DOLBRODMAETH INN
Dinas Mawddwy, Machynlleth
Tel: 01650 531333.

This small, fully licensed hotel, situated on the banks of the River Dovey, is quite close to the picturesque village of DinasMawddwy and on the main holiday route, the A470, through Wales. All year round visitors can be sure of a warm welcome. Run by the owners, Jean and Graham Williams, the aim is to provide traditional hospitality with the benefits of modern comfort. There are 8 delightful, centrally heated, ensuite bedrooms including a family room and a suite of rooms on the ground floor which include self catering facilities - ideal for the disabled. Special arrangements can be made for dogs, which are welcome provided they are on leads.

The inn offers excellent international cuisine in a candlelit dining room. Meals and snacks are also served in the bar and restaurant overlooking the river. Diets can be catered for if notification is given. The Dolbrodmaeth Inn is as charming in the winter as summer. Roaring log fires spread warmth on cold days and throughout the year the views from the terrace are spectacular. Landscaped gardens slope to the river where a stretch of private fishing is reserved for hotel guests. The hotel grounds include a paddock and a nature walk. The food and wine are superb and who could wish for a more wonderful area, aptly called, 'Little Switzerland', ringed with beautiful mountain scenery. There is so much to do and see within easy reach. Once visited The Dolbrodmaeth Inn will never be forgotten. It was presented, deservedly, with the Green Guide to the Dyfi Valley Award, sponsored by Snowdonia National Park and presented by David Bellamy in recognition of the inn's environment-friendly practice over the 1994 season.

USEFUL INFORMATION

OPEN; All day.
CHILDREN; Welcome to stay and in restaurant.
CREDIT CARDS; All major cards
LICENSED; Yes
ACCOMMODATION; 8 ensuite rooms

RESTAURANT; Well presented food
BAR FOOD; Wide range
VEGETARIAN; Several dishes
DISABLED ACCESS: Excellent facilities
GARDEN; 4 acres with river

THE GOLDEN LION,
East Street, Newport
Pembrokeshire
Tel: 01239 820321
Fax: 01239 820423

You will find the fascinating Golden Lion on the A487 between Fishguard and Cardigan with the Preseli Mountains to the East and the sea to the West. It is an old 17th-century coaching inn full of character and run by two experienced and hospitable people, Glyn and Penny Rees for the last 25 years, who richly deserve their mention in the Egon Ronay Gride to Pubs. There are ten totally refurbished ensuite bedrooms with tea and coffee facilities, television and telephone, a friendly bar and a separate dining room as well as a beer garden. In fact it is a delightful place to visit whether it is to take a break, enjoy a drink or savour the excellence of the cooking which is done by Penny. The menu is not large but it includes many favourite dishes, all of which are cooked to order using fresh local produce where it is possible. At lunchtime you can enjoy simple pleasures like home-made soup or a fisherman's lunch with smoked mackerel, home-baked ham or shepherds pie for example. In the evening you can choose from a more extensive menu serving excellent grills, fresh fish and vegetarian dishes available both in the bar or in the restaurant. The prices are reasonable and it is good value for money.

USEFUL INFORMATION

OPEN; Weekdays until 11pm. Sun: 12-3pm & 7-10.30pm.
CHILDREN; Welcome.
CREDIT CARDS; Access/Visa :
LICENSED; Yes
ACCOMMODATION; 10 ensuite rooms.
DINING ROOM; Excellent home-cooked
BAR FOOD; Favourite dishes
VEGETARIAN; A choice
DISABLED ACCESS; Yes
GARDEN; Yes

THE LOWER NEW INN,
48 Newport Road,
Pontypool. Gwent NP4 5UT
Tel: 01495 762842

The original coaching steps and well-water pump are still at the front of The Lower New Inn which is constructed of local riverstone. It is a pub with a history. Used at one time as a courthouse in which 'Hanging' Judge Jeffries presided, it was discovered recently that there are cells below where prisoners were kept awaiting their fate. Oddly enough it has also been used as a church for the New Constitutionalists. Inside, the spacious pub is open plan with a restaurant at the rear converted from an old blacksmith's cottage. There are ample parking facilities and it is a hostelry much used by visitors as a stopping point before they set off to discover the many interesting places within close proximity. There are a number of attractive country walks along footpaths some of which pass Llandevaud Reservoir, renowned for its fishing and watersports. The towns of Cwmbran and Pontypool are only a short drive away. The constantly changing menu offers well cooked snacks and meals at extremely reasonable prices. During the week lunches are served in the bar but on Sundays the generous and excellent, traditional three course lunch is served in the restaurant. Food is only served at lunchtime.

USEFUL INFORMATION

OPEN; 11am-11pm daily.
CHILDREN; Welcome. Special menu. Lunchtimes only
CREDIT CARDS;:Access/Visa/Euro/Diners.
GARDEN; Small garden & play area
RESTAURANT;Traditional Sunday Lunch
BAR FOOD;Well cooked snacks & meals
VEGETARIAN; Several dishes
DISABLED ACCESS; Yes
ACCOMMODATION; None

EGERTON GREY COUNTRY HOUSE HOTEL,
Porthkerry, Nr Cardiff
South Glamorgan
Tel: 01446 711666

Ten miles from Cardiff and three miles from Barry, this is one of the most luxurious and beautifully run small hotels in Wales. The approach to this 19th century rectory is down a lane between thatched farm cottages. Once there, no other habitation or road is visible. It stands, graciously within seven acres of beautifully kept gardens, with views down to Porthkerry Park and the sea. There is a croquet lawn and an all-weather tennis court.

Inside there is an air of Edwardian elegance, with parquet floor, and panelling everywhere and a particularly fine carved Jacobean-style staircase. The cuban mahogany panelling in the intimate clerestoried restaurant adds to the pleasure of dining here by candlelight. Luncheon and dinner are both memorable experiences with delicious menus immaculately presented. Egerton Grey Country House is a wonderful place for a holiday break - a two or three day-break which includes breakfast and dinner is a rare treat. Many of the ten exceedingly comfortable bedrooms have superbly restored Edwardian bathrooms. The public rooms are a rich and harmonious blend of elegant furniture enhanced by porcelain and paintings. Owner, Anthony Pitkin is justly proud of this delightful hotel which also offers excellent facilities for conference and wedding receptions.

USEFUL INFORMATION

OPEN; All year
CHILDREN; Welcome
CREDIT CARD; Access/Visa/Amex/Diners
LICENSED; Yes
ACCOMMODATION; 10 ensuite rooms

RESTAURANT; Memorable food
BAR FOOD; Excellent value
VEGETARIAN; Several vegetarian dishes
DISABLED ACCESS; Restaurant access
GARDEN; Yes. Croquet. Tennis.

PORTMEIRION
Gwynedd LL48 6ET
Tel: 01766 770228
Fax: 01766 771331

One single word, Portmeirion, conjures up a magical place, somewhere that everyone should visit at least once in a lifetime. To spend a few days here
will refresh notonly the body but the soul as well. The Hotel Portmeirion is based on the early Victorian Villa near the shore. Opened in 1926 it played host to the famous. Writers such as George Bernard Shaw. H.G. Wells and Bertrand Russell were habitues. Noel Coward wrote Blithe Spirit here during a two weeks stay at Lower Fountain in 1941. During the 1960's Patrick McGoohan found in Portmeirion the perfect location for his television classis, 'The Prisoner'. You may stay either in the elegant and beautifully appointed main hotel building which houses bars, dining room and sitting rooms, or in the surrounding rooms, suites and cottages that make up the village. All the rooms have private bathrooms, colour television and direct dial telephones. The tariff reflects the time of the year and the standard of accommodation. Dogs are not accepted in any of the bedrooms. The Hotel is open all year except for three weeks at the end of January. The curvilinear dining room was added in the 1930s. Facing onto the Traeth Bach estuary, it seems, at high tide, almost to be afloat. Fresh local produce is used as the basis of a modern British cuisine, complemented by a distinguised wine list. Portmeirion is reached via a mile long private drive which winds through the woods and farmland of the peninsula. Surrounding the village on three sides are 70 acres of subtropical woodland gardens known as the 'Gwyllt'. These contain many century old rhododendrons, camellias and magnolias which flourish in the frost free climate .Miles of paths crisscross the woods, leading to rocky coves and sandy beaches all along the headland. The Hotel has an open air pool (heated May-September) and a hard surface tennis court. There is an arrangement for guests to play free of green fees at the local 18 hole Golf Club (3 miles away). Historic Castles, majestic Welsh mountains and to the West the Llyn Peninsula ring Portmeirion offering wonderful explorations. The kingdom of the ancestors of Portmeirion's founder,Sir Clough Williams- Ellis, is an ancient land of myths and legends, with its pwn unique literary and musical traditions, and where the Welsh language is widely spoken. Read more about Portmeirion under 'Places to Visit' in the back of this book.

USEFUL INFORMATION

OPEN; All year
CHILDREN; Welcome
CREDIT CARDS; All major cards
LICENSED; Yes
ACCOMMODATION; Ensuite rooms, Self catering

RESTAURANT; Superb food in the hotel
BAR FOOD; Available
VEGETARIAN ; Severl dishes
DISABLED ACCESS; Yes. Hotel & village

BARRATTS RESTAURANT
Tyn Rhyl,
167, Vale Road,
Rhyl, Clwyd
Tel: 01745 344138

Just out of Rhuddlan and just before you get into Rhyl you will come to Barratts Restaurant which also has two splendidly appointed rooms in which you can stay; something to be recommended if you really are going to do justice to some of the best food and wine in Wales.

Barratts is a wonderful period building built in the 16th century. It is full of atmosphere and no doubt was as welcoming to William Gladstone when he stayed here. His is not the only famous name to be seen in the Visitors Book. Wordsworth is there and so is Ruskin and a splendid Welsh lady, Angharad Lloyd, who was renowned as a hostess. David and Elvira Barratt are the proprietors, and it is David who is the inspired chef. He has a love and a sensitivity for food. The menu is not vast but includes some superb starters. Pearls of melon with fresh Figs and Mango, dressed with peach nuts, is just one of them. David also cooks a Honey glazed Duckling with Cognac and Apple sauce that is a masterpiece. Follow this with a delectable sweet from the trolley, a choice of cheese accompanied by one of the wines from the well chosen selection and you will have partaken of a gastronomic feast in a non-smoking restaurant.

USEFUL INFORMATION

OPEN; All year. Booking essential
CHILDREN; Yes, with parents
CREDIT CARDS; Eurocard/Visa/Master
LICENSED; Good selection of wines
ACCOMMODATION; 2 ensuite rooms
GARDEN; Front lawn & car park
RESTAURANT; Imaginative & delicious
BAR FOOD; Not applicable
VEGETARIAN; Always alternative dishes
DISABLED ACCESS; All on one level

HOLT LODGE,
Holt, Clwyd
Tel: 01978 661002.

Set in an attractive rural area Holt Lodge is owned and run by Andrew and Alex Smeaton who also own The Alyn at Rossett, six miles away. Both establishments are run with the same friendly and professional efficiency andeither is delightful to visit. Holt Lodge, unlike The Alyn, has 20 ensuite bedrooms which are furnished in keeping with the building. Each room has its own colour TV and that blessing, a beverage tray. The food is excellent and Holt Lodge is renowned for the daily carvery which offers a choice of freshly cooked meats and poultry with fresh vegetables. All the produce is acquired locally whenever possible. An ideal place to stay.

USEFUL INFORMATION

OPEN; All year every day.
CHILDREN; Welcome
CREDIT CARDS; Access/Visa/Switch.
LICENSED;; Yes
ACCOMMODATION; 20 ensuite rooms

FOOD:; Renowned especially for the daily carvery
BAR FOOD; Extensive menu
VEGETARIAN; Daily choice
GARDEN; Yes

THE ALYN,
Station Road,
Rossett, Nr Chester.
Tel: 01244 570368

This is a typical village pub but with the additional attraction of being on the riverside in the very pretty village of Rossett. It nestles in a quiet corner right next to the church, the old water mill and the bridge. On a summer's day one can wander out onto the terrace through the French windows and enjoy a drink, overlooking the river as it wends its bustling way downstream. The well maintained gardens illuminated at night, as is the enormous Weeping Willow which trails its branches in the river, are a delight. Indeed it is a thoroughly nice establishment and it is no wonder that it attracts not only local people but visitors from much further afield who enjoy its position and the excellent food on offer. Inside the riverside lounge is comfortable, attractively furnished, and in winter, the log fires send out a wonderful welcoming warmth which is echoed by the friendly landlords, Andrew and Alex Smeaton and their staff. Service and value for money are top priority at The Alyn. The menu is extensive - one of the most popular dishes is the famous steak and kidney pie. On cold days mulled wine is served. Children are welcome until 8pm. There is a special menu for them as well as a vast collection of toys and a wendy house at the bottom of the garden to keep them occupied. The Smeatons also own the welcoming Holt Lodge at Holt, six miles away. Run in the same friendly and professional manner and set in a beautiful countryside, it has 20 en-suite rooms and is renowned for its carvery.

USEFUL INFORMATION

OPEN; The Alyn; All day every day.
CHILDREN; Welcome, high chairs.
CREDIT CARDS; Access/Visa/Switch.
LICENSED; Yes
ACCOMODATION; No

BAR FOOD; Extensive. Home-cooked
VEGETARIAN; Yes
DISABLED ACCESS; Yes
GARDEN; Riverside garden

YE OLDE ANCHOR INN
2 Rhos Street,
Ruthin, Clwyd LL15 1DX
Tel: 01824 702813
Fax: 01824 703050

Ruthin is an ideal place from which to explore the many places of beauty and historical interest with easy reach. Snowdonia National Park is on the doorstep and the nearby Clwydian hills offer some delightful walks along Offas Dyke Path. The town itself is charming with historic streets, a half-timbered courthouse with its former gallows and Nantclwyd House, one of the finest medieval town houses in Wales.

There can be no better place to stay than the 18th century 'Ye Olde Anchor Inn' with its low ceilings and oak beams. Once it was a stopping place for drovers on their way from Holyhead to Shropshire now it welcomes 20th century travellers and offers them warmth and hospitality second to none. Rod England is the owner and the genuine welcome comes not only from him but from all his staff. You will find the whole inn is charming and full of character and the 14 guestrooms, each with a private shower or bathroom, have been tastefully decorated in co-ordinating colours. There is a suite of rooms suitable for families who are always welcome and so too are their pets, with prior notice. Every room has colour television with the added bonus of satellite and in-house videos. After a good nights sleep, guests start the day with a full English breakfast. The cosy bars are always good meeting places where traditional cask beer is on tap as well as a bar menu offering a varied selection, and there are always dishes suitable for vegetarians and children. 'Ye Olde Anchor Inn's' a la carte restaurant which has a fascinating 150 years old Dutch Stove, is open seven days a week. It is renowned in the area for its excellent cuisine and therefore it is always advisable to book. In 1994 it was awarded two rosettes by the AA for the standard of its cuisine. The extensive wine list offers something for everyone's taste and pocket.

USEFUL INFORMATION

OPEN; All year
CHILDREN; Very welcome
CREDIT CARDS; All major cards Not Amex/Diners
LICENSED; Full Licence
ACCOMMODATION; 14 ensuite rooms

RESTAURANT; A la carte.42 covers Renowned
BAR MEALS; Varied selection daily
VEGETARIAN; Several dishes daily
DISABLED ACCESS:Yes
GARDEN; No. Car Park, Yes

THE OLD MILL,
Llanddowror, St Clears
Dyfed
Tel: 01994 230836/230573

The Old Mill is a woollen mill which has been converted into a cafe and restaurant quite wonderfully. Set in ten acres of woodland it offers not only excellent food, but the opportunity to walk and relax in delightful surroundings. It is to be found on the A477 halfway between St Clears and Red Roses. The atmosphere in the restaurant takes one back in time. It has been lovingly and authentically restored to the period of the mill's best years long ago, and the furnishings complement this impression. It is in keeping with the village which is noted for the time at the close of the 18th century when Griffith Jones opened the first Bible College here, promoting literacy in Wales. The menu is not extensive but of the highest quality and delicious. In 1992 it was shortlisted for the Restaurant of the Year accolade as the best restaurant serving vegetarian meals. Indeed it is not only vegetarians who are well catered for but vegans as well. It is a wonderful experience dining in the restaurant with its wood burning stove and soft music adding to the ambience. The restaurant is only open in the evenings from 7pm for reservations but the cafe opens its doors every day from 7am-7pm.

USEFUL INFORMATION

OPEN; Cafe 7am-7pm every day. Restaurant; Evenings from 7pm Reservations only 7pm Reservations only.

CHILDREN; Welcome

CREDIT CARDS; All Major Credit Cards.

RESTAURANT; Award winning

VEGETARIAN; Yes & Vegans

DISABLED ACCESS; Yes + toilets

ACCOMMODATION; None

GARDEN; 10 acres woodland

ST NONS HOTEL
St Davids,
Pembrokeshire SA62 6RJ
Tel: 01437 720239 Fax: 01437 721839

St Non's Hotel which lies at the gateway to one of the most beautiful and peaceful coastal environments in Europe, the centreof Britain's only coastal National Park on the St Davids Peninsula, takes its name from the mother of St David, the Patron Saint of Wales. It is situated close to the Norman cathedral and fourteenth century Bishops Palace, whilst St Non's holy well and chapel (ancient monuments) are nearby on the coast. The original, listed part of the hotel was formerly known as Wellfield House and was sited near to a thirteenth century hospice later known as the 'Priory of Whytwel', which would have provided hospitality to pilgrims.

Today's guests at St Non's will see that the tradition of hospitality is upheld in the warm and friendly atmosphere that prevails throughout the hotel. It has a sense of somewhere in which can feel totally relaxed. It is both welcoming and informal - the latter is something that is only successful when a hotel is run superbly. There are twenty two centrally heated double, twin and family rooms with ensuite bathrooms. These mostly enjoy an attractive, westerly aspect and are available for single occupancy. Some are located on the ground floor for ease of access and all are provided with colour television, direct dial telephone and tea/coffee making facilities. There is ample private parking. The chefs provide a range of appetising dishes using fresh local ingredients which are excellent value. In the evening there is a choice of menus, including vegetarian dishes. Special diets can be catered for on request. Before or after a meal the cosy bar is both welcoming and well-stocked - ideal for enjoying a drink and discussing the day or planning for tomorrow.

USEFUL INFORMATION

OPEN; All year
CHILDREN; Welcome
CREDIT CARDS; All major cards
LICENSED; Full on Licence
ACCOMMODATION; 22 with ensuite bathrooms
PETS; By arrangement
GARDEN; Yes. Patio with tables

RESTAURANT; Wholesome food using fresh local ingredients
BAR FOOD; Well-cooked dishes
VEGETARIAN; Always a choice
DISABLED ACCESS; Yes. Ground floor rooms

RAMSEY HOUSE,
Lower Moor, St David's,
Pembrokeshire SA62 6RP
Tel: 01437 720321

Catering exclusively for adults, the non-smoking Ramsey House is very special. There would be few people who, once having savoured the unique informal, relaxed but totally professional standards, would not want to return speedily. One might be convinced already that the St David's Peninsula was the ideal place for a holiday but the icing on the cake must be the enjoyment to be found at Ramsey House. The owners, Mac and Sandra Thompson, do everything in their power to make your visit memorable. The en-suite rooms are furnished to a very high standard and the food is delicious. Ramsey House specialises in providing the best in Welsh food, combining quality local produce with quality cooking. In addition to its famous lamb and beef, Wales has a bountiful larder of fresh vegetables, superb seafoods and cheeses to rival the world's best. These ingredients are used to produce both traditional dishes and fresh imaginative ones. Ramsey House has a string of well deserved accolades including the Wales Tourist Board 3 Crown Highly Commended and Dragon Awards. RAC Highly Acclaimed, AA QQQQ Selected and Les Routiers Corps d'Elite Wine Award. and is a member of the 'Taste of Wales' Hospitality Scheme.

USEFUL INFORMATION

OPEN; All year including Christmas and New Year.
CHILDREN; No children
CREDIT CARDS; None taken
ACCOMMODATION; 7 En suite rooms
LICENSED; Yes. Non-smoking establishment

DINING ROOM; Traditional & imaginative
VEGETARIAN; Yes
DISABLED ACCESS; Ground floor bedrooms But not suitable for wheelchairs
GARDEN; Yes. Parking
PETS; Welcome

THE NEW INN
Bronllys Road,
Talgarth, Powys LD30HH
Tel: 01874 711581

The New Inn has recently been acquired by Peter and Sandra Lawson and in their hands it will undoubtedly go from strength to strength. They have all sorts of interesting plans for the inn including creating a Talgarth Ale Festival with other pubs and breweries in the area. Peter is a Real Ale enthusiast. The New Inn is a 17th-century building which was once two cottages and has enormous charm both inside and out. Oak beams and welcoming fires greet you as you enter its portals. It is believed to the the oldest inn in the area and what a wonderful area it is in the Brecon National Park. You will find it just 300 yards from the centre of Talgarth on the Bronllys to Brecon road.

Sandra aided by a local chef produces excellent food. Shespecialises in Steak and Fish but has found her Beef Stroganoff, Goulash and Indian Curries rapidly gaining renown. Everything is freshly cooked and as much local produce used as possible. There are two ensuite rooms and one family room for those wanting to stay - and who would not wish to do so when everything about the inn and the surrounding countryside pleases. Fishing, gliding, walking and golf are all within easy reach. There is no garden but a pleasant patio has tables and chairs to encourage one to drink and eat outside in warm weather.

USEFUL INFORMATION

OPEN; 7am-11.30pm
CHILDREN; Very welcome
CREDIT CARDS; None taken
LICENSED; Full Licence
ACCOMMODATION; 2 ensuit 1 Family
PETS; By arrangement
RESTAURANT; Home-cooked, Fish & Steak a speciality. European dishes & Curries
BAR FOOD; Varied and interesting
VEGETARIAN; Varied
DISABLED ACCESS; Easy access
GARDEN; No garden. Pretty patio

HOTEL MAES y NEUADD,
Talsarnau,
Nr. Harlech,
Gwynedd LL47 6YA

Guests from all over the world make a bee line for Hotel Maes y Neuadd which must be one of the finest in Wales. Everything about it is delightful, there are fascinating corners to be explored and enjoyed. Sheltered corners of the beautiful grounds and old trees provide welcome shade during the summer months. A pre-dinner drink on the terrace on warm summer nights allows you to enjoy the magnificent spectacle of the sun setting over the Lleyn Peninsular. You will find the house nestling into a wooded mountainside and situated amongst some of the most beautiful scenery in Britain, with spectacular views across the Snowdonia National Park. The oldest part of the house was built less than a century after Edward I's mightly castle at Harlech. 16th, 18th and 20th century additions to this gracious house, blend harmoniously. It is a much loved house and since 1981 has been in the personal care of the Horsfall and Slatter families who have sympathetically restored their home to provide the highest standards of comfort and luxury. Evenings draw guests to the oak-beamed bar with its ancient inglenook and recesses full of interesting curios. On cooler days a cheerful log fire burns. Dinner, in the gracious and elegant dining room is a truly memorable experience. Delicious dishes are created by talented chefs, using fresh produce for which Wales is renowned. The wines have been chosen with great care and offer choices from all over the world. There are sixteen bedrooms and suites, twelve in the main house and four in the adjoining Coach House. Many have fabulous views ofthe mountains or Tremadoc Bay and the distant Lleyn Peninsula. Each room is imaginatively designed and furnished with its own very individual style. There are a wealth of fascinating places to visit, magnificent walks, numerous drives and interesting pursuits to follow. Above all you will experience the especial Welshness of the area. Maes -y- Neuadd has joined forces with the world famous Ffestiniog Railway to create 'Steam and Cuisine' - an unique experience in Fine Dining. Imagine a gentle journey by narrow gauge steam train through some of the most spectacular scenery in the country and at the same time sipping champagne and enjoying a superb dinner. Wonderful for parties of 30-100 or weekly Dining Trains, Spring and Summer, on Wednesdays for individuals.

USEFUL INFORMATION

OPEN; All year
CHILDREN; Welcome
CREDIT CARDS; All major cards
LICENSED; Yes. Fine wines
PETS; By arrangement
ACCOMMODATION; 16 rooms & suites

DINING ROOM; Superb. Welsh produce
BAR MEALS; Not applicable
VEGETARIAN; By arrangement
DISABLED ACCESS; Limited
GARDEN; Delightful grounds

THE YSGETHIN INN,
Talybont, Nr Barmouth
Gwynedd
Tel: 01341 247578

This is an inn which has had many other names in its long history not as a hostelry but as a fulling mill, but this one cannot be changed whilst trees grow tall and the river runs. That alone makes one want to go and see it. It is a super place run by John and Stephanie Hewlett, experienced landlords who have built a great reputation for fine beers and excellent food. They employ mainly local staff, some of whom are Welsh speaking, which is a bonus for the regulars, and a joy for visitors who enjoy the lilt of the attractive Welsh tongue. The old fulling mill on the Afon Ysgethin has been working for centuries. It is only five years since it was turned into this delightful country pub. In the cosy atmosphere you cantaste real ale and real food too. There is a patio overlooking the river, and a children's adventure playground. By the patio is the old 'Pelton' Wheel which drove part of the machinery and there is history all around. Inside is the attractive Woolpackers Bar and family room, the main bar with an inglenook fireplace and bread oven as well as many other original features. In the winter the old range in the Inglenook bar is lit - not for the heat it gives but for the character, charm and atmosphere it creates. Nearby is the 'Anchorage' and Talybont Museum' with all sorts of agricultural and country life exhibits. There is a car park for patrons of the pub and museum.

USEFUL INFORMATION

OPEN: 11-3pm 6-11pm (7pm in winter)
CHILDREN; Welcome.
CREDIT CARDS;Access/Visa/Diners.
LICENSED; Yes
BAR FOOD; Delicious.
VEGETARIAN; Daily choice
DISABLED ACCESS; Yes
GARDEN; Yes

RHIW GOCH HOTEL,
Bronaber, Trawsfynydd
Gwynedd
Tel: 01766 540374/219

The Trawsfynydd Holiday Village and Ski Centre is an exciting place in its own right but the jewel in the crown is the 16th century Manor House, Rhiw Goch, which is now the Inn. Situated as it is between Dolgellau and Porthmadog and within the Snowdonia National Park, the scenery is spectacular and it is area which will delight any walker. The Rhiw Goch Hotel has served many masters in its time including the Officers Mess for the Royal Artillery. It has a very happy atmosphere everywhere. There are busy bars, an 80 cover restaurant with its own bar and dance floor, a family room, and a games room. The restaurant menu has a wide choice including daily specials. There are always five or more choices for vegetarians and in the bar, tasty snacks and sandwiches are readily available. Efficient, friendly service and high standards are the hallmark of the Rhiw Goch.

USEFUL INFORMATION

OPEN; 12-2pm & 7-11pm.
CHILDREN; Welcome
CREDIT CARDS; Most cards
LICENSED; Yes
ACCOMMODATION; Not in Inn but Log Cabins available ring 01766 540219

RESTAURANT; Excellent food. Good value
BAR FOOD; Extensive menu
VEGETARIAN; Daily dishes
DISABLED ACCESS; Yes
GARDEN; Yes
PETS; Not permitted

The Complex also offers award winning Dry Slope Skiing.

THE CASTLE COACHING INN,
Trecastle, Powys
Tel: 01874 636354

Just eleven miles along the A40 from Brecon is the village of Trecastle which is in the Brecon Beacons National Park. The Park is renowned for the grandeur of its mountains, waterfalls and gently meandering streams flowing through lush unspoilt valleys. An ideal place for walkng, riding or sightseeing. In the heart of Trecastle is the 17th-century Castle Coaching Inn, which takes its name from the Norman Motte and Bailey, the remains of which can be seen today. It is the most wonderfully atmospheric hotel, as indeed it should be in this land of the legendary King Arthur. A local lake Llyn-Y-Fach or 'Lady of the Lake tells a story of long ago. There are standing stones, stone circles and castles, all of which add to the romanticism of this enchanting place. To make the best of a stay here the hotel will arrange riding, shooting and Landrover trips as well as golfat the local course. There are ten ensuite bedrooms in the hotel, and all of them have colour TV and tea/coffee making facilities. The friendly bar is warm and comfortable with good solid benches, chairs and a welcoming fireplace. It is here that you can enjoy a good bar meal which will have been prepared with local produce. In the small restaurant, traditional fare is served which is both delicious and excellent value.

USEFUL INFORMATION

OPEN; All Year. 11am-3pm & 6-11pm
Lunch 12-2pm Dinner 6.30-9pm
CHILDREN; Welcome. Highchair & Cot + Baby alarm.
CREDIT CARDS; Access/Visa/Barclaycard
LICENSED; Yes
ACCOMMODATION:10 ensuite rooms, 3 star rating. Highly Commended.
RESTAURANT; Small, traditional fare
BAR FOOD; Traditional, wide range
VEGETARIAN; Selection
DISABLED ACCESS; Yes
PETS; Not permitted
GARDEN; Yes & patio with tables and chairs.

GOLFA HALL HOTEL
Llanfair Road,
Welshpool, Powys SY21 9AF
Tel: 01938 553399 Fax: 01938 554777

This fine country house hotel is just one and a half miles from Welshpool on the A458 Dolgellau road. It stands on a hillside overlooking a delightful wooded valley through which runs the famous narrow gauge Welshpool and Llanfair Steam Light Railway. Originally the Golfa Hall Hotel was a substantial farmhouse on the Powys Castle estate and was converted into an hotel approximately 10 yars ago. The hotel is run by Chef David Ostle and his Front of House partner, Sarah Pinson who describe themselves as a 'Tom and Jerry Double Act'! Such a description belittles the professional way in which the hotel is managed. It is somewhere to which you come as a stranger but leave as a friend. Golfa Hall gives one an immediate sense of welcome and well being; well behaved pets included. The 14 ensuite bedrooms are warm and comfortable, the food is superb in quality and supports a menu which is changed regularly, offering seasonal, fresh local produce. Light meals are available in the bar but definitely no chips! There is a friendly lounge bar and a non-smoking sitting room. The attractive restaurant is also a non-smoking area. Private parties of up to 20 can be held in the Drawingroom whilst the Conifer Suite accommodates 120 for seminars and functions of all kinds. There is plenty to see and do in the surrounding countryside and if you just wish to relax then the 8 acres of garden completewith tables and chairs for alfresco meals, could not be bettered.

USEFUL INFORMATION

OPEN; All year. Doors close 11pm approx
CHILDREN; Allowed, no special facilities
CREDIT CARDS;
Access/Visa/Master/Diners
LICENSED; Full. Good inexpensive wines
ACCOMMODATION; 14 ensuite rooms
PETS; Well behaved
GARDEN; 8 acres. Garden tables etc

RESTAURANT; Superb quality Fresh, seasonal,local produce
BAR FOOD; Light meals-no chips!
VEGETARIAN; Always 1 starter 1 main course
DISABLED; No steps but not very good facilities

PEPPERS RESTAURANT,
Puzzle Square,
Welshpool, Powys
Tel: 01938 555146

This is a purpose built, modern, attractive restaurant, in the front of which are tables and chairs making a pleasantly relaxing site after you have explored the centre of Welshpool. Puzzle Square is very central leading from a pretty walkway. Peppers is a favourite venue for local people who call in the morning for coffee and a home made-scone or appear at lunchtime to savour Peppers now famous, Cheese, Onion and Potato Pie. Powys Castle is only one and a half miles away, a fascinating place to explore. Welshpool also has the Montgomeryshire Canal wandering through its midst together with the very interesting Canal Museum. For those who enjoy the bustle of market days, Monday brings one to the town and people come from miles around to purchase the fresh produce, and to hunt for bargains. Llanfair Light Railway is within easy reach too. You can fish and play golf or if you feel in need of practice, Bulthy Driving Range will address the need. Wendy Waldron runs Peppers with her partner Judith Ward. These busy ladies are constantly cheerful and welcoming. The food is nourishing, tempting and very good value. Peppers caters for all kinds of appetites. Hot meals are available daily and never the same two daysrunning. Snacks, sandwiches, salads and delicious home-made cakes complete the range. Celebration Cakes are a speciality and made to order.

USEFUL INFORMATION

OPEN; Weekdays; 8-5pm Sun. 10-6pm.
CHILDREN; Welcome.
CREDIT CARDS;No credit cards.
LICENSED; Yes
ACCOMMODATION; No

RESTAURANT; Caters for all kinds Of appetites
VEGETARIANS; Always a choice
DISABLED ACCESS;Yes + toilets.
GARDEN; Yes. Patio with seating

The National Trust Restaurant,
ERDDIG
Wrexham, LL13 0YT
Tel: 01978 355314

Erddig is a very special place. Its appeal lies in the way in which this unique house tells the history of a bustling household community and reflects the lives of those who lived and worked here. Erddig's successive owners and their well documented relations with their staff give today's visitor a remarkable insight in the domestic arrangements of a historic country house and estate. The mellow brick facade of the late 17th and early 18th century makes a wonderful back-drop to the early 18th century garden with Victorian additions which has been restored by the National Trust. With its formal borders, canal and fruit trees it combines the decorative with the utilitarian and is one of the best surviving examples of the ordered and symmetrical Dutch and French fashions that took over British garden layout at the end of the 17th century. The lawn, enclosed by rows of pleached lime trees, is a particularly lovely setting for music on a summer evening and concerts are held here annually. The house and garden are surrounded by extensive woods and picturesque walks. The licensed restaurant at Erddig is sited in the former haybarn, just one of the carefully restored range of outbuildings at Erddig. The restaurant offers a wide choice of freshly baked and home-made dishes with a real emphasis on using fresh local produce in mouthwatering regional dishes. This year Pat Bodymore, the Catering Manager, is introducing Glamorgan Sausages onto the menu, a herby, meatless sausage made with Caerphilly cheese, Welsh leeks and fresh parsley. Also featuring on the menu are Welsh lamb shepherds pie, home made savoury flans and a carrot soup adapted from a late 18th century Erddig recipe among many others. The menu successfully combines a taste of Wales with a taste of history. Traditional cream teas for which the National Trust are famous are always available. Children of all ages arewelcome and an imaginative children's menu is available. There is a thriving Christmas lunch trade on Sundays in December. Bookings are essential. The restaurant can also cater for a wide range of special functions or celebrations on other days.

USEFUL INFORMATION

OPEN;   The restaurant is open from 1 April to 3rd November Wed-Sun 11am-5.15pm. 8 Nov-22Dec open Fri,Sat & Sun 11am-4pm

CREDIT CARDS;   Visa/Mastercard

DISABLED ACCESS; Access to gardens & toilets Restaurant is sited upstairs

ACCOMMODATION; Not applicable

RESTAURANT; Excellent, varied menu. Welsh flavours

CHILDREN; Welcome

LICENSED;   Restaurant

VEGETARIAN; Always available

GARDENS; Yes And canal terrace

LLWYN ONN HALL
Cefn Road,
Wrexham, Clwyd LL13 0NY
Tel: 01978 261225

This delightful, friendly and welcome Country House Hotel complete with two friendly ghosts, is everything one could wish for. It stands in its own substantial grounds about a mile south east of Wrexham and was built around 1700. Part of its charm is the total seclusion, quietness, peaceful gardens and extensive views, and yet one is by no means isolated.

LLwyn Onn Hall (pronounced Clewin Onn) is a family owned hotel where the concentration is on personal courteous service and a homely atmosphere - both of which are admirably achieved. Whilst over the years modern comforts have been added nothing has been done to detract from the charm and character of the house. The bedrooms have all been individually designed and have their own bathroom, shower and bath. Some of the smaller rooms have a shower alone. Every room has a colour TV, a telephone, a trouser press and a beverage tray. Continental breakfast is available in your room if required. Personal laundry can be arranged. Most of the rooms have views over Cheshire and Shropshire to the South or the Welsh mountains to the West. The menu is varied and interesting and offers a chance of trying something different. Indeed the chef will create dishes of your own choice upon request.

The elegant, beautifully appointed Jones Parry Room, named after the family who owned Llwyn Onn Estate for 400 years, is used for meetings or private dinner parties. The beautiful gardens provide an ideal setting for wedding photographs whilst indoors no bride could dream of a better reception.

USEFUL INFORMATION

OPEN; All year
CHILDREN; Yes - well behaved
No pets
CREDIT CARDS; All except Diners
LICENSED; Yes
ACCOMMODATION; 13 ensuite rooms

RESTAURANT; Fine, home-cooked food
BAR MEALS; Snacks available
VEGETARIAN; Yes & Vegan, prior notice
DISABLED ACCESS; To Bar & Restaurant
GARDEN; Beautiful gardens.

HOTELS, INNS, RESTAURANTS AND COUNTRY HOUSES

THE HEART OF ENGLAND

including Hereford and Worcester, Staffordshire, Shropshire, Warwickshire and the West Midlands

Includes

The Shoulder of Mutton	Barton-under-Needwood	p.129
Freshmans Restaurant	Belbroughton	p.130
The Longmynd Hotel	Church Stretton	p.131
The Plough	Claverley	p.132
Red Hart Inn	Flyford Flavell	p.133
Il Mago	Hanley	p.134
Hanmer Arms	Hanmer	p.135
The Cottage of Content	Carey, Nr Horwithy	p.136
Bulls Head Hotel	Inkberrow	p.137
Walter de Cantelupe Inn	Kempsey	p.138
The Swan Inn	Letton	p.139
The Two Boats	Long Itchington	p.140
Wheatland Fox Hotel	Much Wenlock	p.141
Restaurant Sebastian	Oswestry	p.142
The Loughpool Inn	Ross-on-Wye	p.143
The Sheaf & Sickle	Rugby	p.144
Granvilles	Stone	p.145
The Wheatsheaf	Stone	p.146
College Arms	Stratford-upon-Avon	p.147
The Red Lion	Thorncliffe	p.148
The Sutherland Hotel	Tibberton, Newport	p.149
The Roebuck	Uttoxeter	p.150
The Plough	Wall-under-Heywood	p.151
The Narrowboat	Whittington	p.152
The Old Rectory	Willersey	p.153

'Pulchra Terra Dei Donum' (This fair land is the Gift of God) is the county motto of Hereford and the more I see of this beautiful land, the truer I know that statement to be. Although Hereford is joined to Worcester for administrative purposes, the characters of the two counties have little in common. A perfect illustration of this is gained from the viewpoint atop the Herefordshire Beacon in the Malvern Hills. To the east lie the rich, fertile lowlands of Worcestershire, through which the Severn and Avon wander, whilst to the west, the undulating wooded scenery of Herefordshire extends to the lowering ridge of the **Black Mountains**, some forty miles away.

The M50 motorway is a western spur of the M5 and runs some five miles into Herefordshire before ending at **Ross-on-Wye**. Agriculture, light industry and tourism form the basis of the local economy and Ross (from the Welsh ros, meaning a spit of land) is ideally situated for exploring the glorious country of the Wye Valley. Its friendly and welcoming atmosphere owes much to the example set by the town's best loved inhabitant, John Kyrle (1637-1724). Trained as a lawyer he inherited a small fortune and never practiced, preferring to spend his time and money on good works and acts of great public generosity. He died, a bachelor, at the age of 89, having given all his money away but never incurred a debt. He is remembered as the 'Man of Ross' and among his many philanthropies were the provision of a town water supply, a causeway enabling the bridge to be used when flooding occurred, and a walled public garden known as Kyrle's Prospect. He built a summer house in the grounds of his home, now known as **Kyrle House**, and paid the poor and unemployed to find horse's teeth from animals killed in a nearby cavalry skirmish during the Civil War; these were set into mortar to create a mosaic in the shape of a swan. A much loved man.

The little town on its steep rock outcrop has been a favourite with visitors since the early Victorian era when, as now, the attractions of the surrounding countryside and the excellent salmon fishing brought people back year after year. Hotels, pubs and restaurants are plentiful. I was impressed by the enthusiasm and high standards to be found.

The Lost Street Museum is a charming and very well thought out museum in the form of an arcade of Edwardian shops containing all manner of period items including amusement machines, musical boxes, toys, costumes and gramophones. An unusual local industry is candle-making and **Ross-on-Wye Candlemakers** open their workshop to the public in old Gloucester Road. Two gardens are worth visiting. **Hill Court Gardens and Garden Centre** to the east of the town and **How Caple Court Gardens** to the north, are a gardener's delight.

At **Symonds Yat West**, the Jubilee Park offers a wide range of family entertainment including a maze, craft shops and a butterfly farm. **The Herefordshire Rural Heritage Museum**, set in an attractive rural location houses one of the country's largest collections of historic farm machinery and agricultural implements. About three miles downstream in the wooded Doward

Hills above the river is **King Arthurs Cave** where excavations have revealed that its occupancy by man dates back nearly 60,000 years! Five miles south of Ross and upstream from Symonds Yat are the romantic and massively impressive ruins of **Goodrich Castle**.

Goodrich is an entertaining though somewhat scattered little village and the 12th century castle is sited on a high, rocky spur overlooking a crossing of the river. Square in shape with a tower at each corner and surrounded by a moat hewn out of the red rock, Goodrich was besieged by Parliamentarians under the command of Colonel Birch, in 1646. Legend has it that Birch's niece, Alice, was inside the castle with her Royalist lover, and that they were both drowned in the Wye whilst trying to escape. Her shrieks of distress can still be heard on stormy nights when the river is in spate.

Heading north-east from Ross on the A449 and lying close to the eastern border of the county, is the attractive village of **Much Marcle**, blessed with a fine church of 13th-century origins, **St Bartholomews** and two historic houses. Just over four miles further along the A440 is the delightful ancient market town of **Ledbury**. Set by the old cross-roads to Tewkesbury, Hereford, Gloucester and Malvern, it has been inhabited since around 1500BC. The church of **St Michael and All Angels**, Herefordshire's premier parish church was built on an earlier Saxon foundation and has a Norman chancel and west door, and a magnificent medieval north chapel.

The wide main street, flanked by many half-timbered houses including the Elizabethan **Feathers Inn** was the scene of a desperate charge by Prince Rupert's cavalry during the Civil War, when a Parliamentarian force was routed. Bullets are still embedded in the church door and in the walls of **The Talbot** in New Street. Church Lane, cobbled and narrow offers, a delightful period view of St Michaels and opens out into a small close with handsome houses surrounding the church.

The south-eastern quarter of Herefordshire is the main hop-growing region and hopyards with their trellis work of poles, wires and strings can be seen throughout the area. At **Bishop Frome**, on the Ledbury to Bromyard road, **The Hop Pocket Hop Farm** is open to visitors interested in a form of cultivation that is regrettably in decline. Drying kilns, hop-picking machines and the hopyards are all open to inspection.

Further information on the history and practices of hop-growing can be found at the **Bromyard Heritage Centre** along with other displays relating to matters of local interest. **Bromyard** sits in a natural bowl, amongst rolling downland and was one of the most important towns in Herefordshire long before the Norman clerks started to compile the Domesday Book. It had a Saxon church in 840AD and the present church of **St Peter** was probably built on the same site about 1160. The town's wealth came principally from its market and local agriculture - later came an added bonus in the form of its geographical position halfway between Worcester and Hereford which led to its development as a coaching centre. Notable amongst the inns catering to the trade was **The Falcon** whose postboys wore a smart uniform of white hats, breeches and yellow jackets. Somehow I cannot believe they stayed smart for very long!

The River Teme wriggles through the three counties of Herefordshire, Worcestershire and Shropshire in the area around **Tenbury Wells**. A borough since 1248, Tenbury has remained an attractive small market town surrounded by hopyards and apple orchards.

Hope of wealth came in the 19th century with the discovery of saline springs - but the town lacked an entrepreneur of the quality of Doctor Wall at Malvern and the spa never became fashionable. The incongruous Pump Rooms survive known locally as the 'Chinese Temple' because of the syle of architecture.

Leominster (pronounced 'Lemster') a thriving market town, lies nine miles to the south-west and is Herefordshire's second largest town, set amongst a gentle landscape of fields, hills and meadows where river, stream and brook wander. The town's fortunes were based on the fine quality of the wool from the local breed of sheep, the Ryeland, an animal that thrives on the poorer grazing to be found on the neighbouring hills and the less fertile outcrops of sandy soil from which the name is derived. The demand for this wool was so great that at one time the fleece was known as 'Lempster Ore'.

Cider orchards along the road heading south to **Hereford** hint at one of the city's major industries. **Bulmer's** have been making cider in Hereford for well over a century and their premises in Plough Lane are open for tours and samplings. The contrast with modern automated production techniques with those of yesteryear are enormous, and a visit to **The Cider Museum and King Offa Distillery**, in Ryelands Street, is a real eye-opener.

Any town or city engaged in the convivial pursuit of brewing or distilling has a rather jolly atmosphere, and Hereford is no exception, although its early history would suggest otherwise. Never free of strife until the end of the Civil War in 1651, the city suffered numerous attacks and sieges over the preceding centuries, yet during that time, managed to become one of the most thriving medieval cities in England, a centre for both trade and scholarship.

Items relating to the turbulent past, as well as to more peaceful interests such as bee-keeping, can be seen in **The Hereford City Museum and Art Gallery** in Broad Street. The modern military presence in the city is restricted to the **Herefordshire Regimental Museum** at the TA Centre in Harold Street, and to the discreet gentlemen of the SAS, at Bradbury Lines. Hereford is rich in museums; apart from those already mentioned, there are the **Bulmer Railway Centre**, for steam enthusiasts, **The Churchill Gardens Museum**, displaying fine furniture, costumes and paintings of the late 18th and 19th centuries, **The St John Medieval Museum** containing armour and other relics relating to the order of St John, and **The Old House**, built in 1621 and beautifully furnished in period.

The medieval visitors to the city - scholars, men-at-arms, and traders - would have had their numbers swelled by large numbers of pilgrims, visiting **The Cathedral of St Mary the Virgin and St Ethelbert the King.** The cathedral was begun in the 7th century - in fact, the appointment of the first Bishop of Hereford dates back to that time. A large proportion of the Norman masonry work survives, particularly inside, but the siege and structural collapse in the 17th and 18th centuries led to extensive rebuilding and renovation. For all this, it is still a wonderfully handsome building, quite small compared to most cathedrals, and full of many unique treasures. Chief amongst these is the Mappi Mundi, a map of the world drawn around 1290 and of great importance because it shows us how the scholars of that time saw their world, both in spiritual, as well as geographical terms. The medieval draughtsmanship is superb with all manner of beasts, both fabulous and familiar. The cathedral also has a notable collection of manuscripts and early printed material in the Chained Library, including the 8th century Anglo-Saxon gospels still used when Hereford bishops are sworn in.

The choral traditions of the cathedral are long and the origins of the magnificent Three Choirs Festival can be traced back to an 18th-century chancellor, Thomas Bisse. To listen to soaring music in such surroundings is surely close to ' the rudiments of Paradise'.

The south-western region of Herefordshire and the Welsh Borders was known as **Archenfield** and stretched from the western back of the Wye to the long ridge of the Black Mountains, twenty miles away. It remained a Welsh enclave in England for around six centuries until well after the Conquest. Many of the laws and customs remained peculiarly Welsh until as recently as the present century. An attractive, yet sparsely populated region, with few large villages, but a wealth of churches, which point to the fact that this area had possibly the longest history of continuous Christianity in England.

Welsh Newton is still the scene of a yearly pilgrimage since the graveyard contains the last of Herefordshire's many saints. John Kemble, who was canonised as recently as 1970, was a Jesuit priest who administered to the many catholics in the area, including the wife and daughter of the man who arrested him for complicity in the Popish Plot. An innocent and greatly loved man, he was executed in the most barbaric manner at Hereford, in August 1679. He was eighty years old.

At **Kilpeck**, just off the A465 from Hereford, is the most famous of Archenfield churches, Saint Mary and St David. Saxon work remains in the north-east wall of the nave but the church is principally Norman and the local red sandstone from which it was built has survived the weathers of time remarkably well.

The real glory of the little church is its carvings; work of skilled masons who are sometimes referred to as the Herefordshire School, and who flourished during the 12th century. Behind the church can be found the remains, little more than a stump, of Kilbeck Castle, built around the same time that the carvers were indulging their strange fantasies with hammer and chisel. King John visited here a number of times, and it is recorded that a pretty widow, Joan de Kilpeck offered him a bribe of fifty marks and a palfrey (a small horse) if he would allow her to marry whom she pleased.

It was to the men of Archenfield that England looked in time of strife. From this area came the medieval equivalent of the machine-gun; the long bow, made from yew, and in the hands of a master, capable of piercing through the mailed thigh of a horseman and nailing him to the saddle at fifty paces or more. More importantly the next arrow would be on its way within seconds, whereas the cross-bowman would still be tensioning his weapon. Once the major disputes between English and Welsh were settled, it was the bowmen of Archenfield who led the armies in attack and held the rear in retreat.

Men-at-arms of higher rank, but of common experience, are remembered amongst the high, sheep grazing hills of **Garway**. These were the Knights Templar, Soldiers of Christian belief and noble birth who wore a red sign of the cross on simple white surcoats that covered their armour. Formed to protect pilgrims on the long and dangerous journeys to and from Jerusalem, they showed great bravery during the Crusades and later founded numerous religious houses throughout Europe. Garway was one of their estates and the church of **St Michael** is one of only six Templar foundations left in England. It seems strange to think of those grim monastic soldiers, used to the blazing sun and the desert battles with the Saracens, ending their days on these damp hillsides. The place is moving in its simplicity and well worth the meandering drive south.

The Golden Valley gets its name from a justifiable piece of linguistic confusion on the part of the Normans; they muddled the Welsh 'dwyr' meaning water with their own 'd'or' meaning gold - hence Golden Valley and the River Dore. Also **Abbey Dore**, a mile or so from **Ewyas Harold Castle** (pronounced Yewas) on the west side of the valley. This was a great Cistercian monastery until the Dissolution. The remains were carefully restored under the direction of the first Viscount Scudamore, and he and his craftsmen did a most excellent job. The present building possesses a simple grandeur and contains good glass, some interesting glazed tiles, and a knightly effigy of the grandson of the founder of the Abbey, Robert de Clifford.

Michaelchurch Escley sits tight under the lee of the Black Mountains, truly a dark and brooding mass, frequently blue or purple in tint. From these slopes the Celtic warriors of longago would rush in ambush, only to vanish into the woods and hills when ambush threatened. The trout laden waters of **Escley Brook** run parallel to those of the Monnow, into which it eventually merges, and the area is border country at its best - remote and beautiful.

The road running north alongside the Monnow passes through **Crasswall** with **Hay Bluff**, the source of the river rising high over the hamlet. The Order of the Grandmontines, an offshoot of the Cistercian order and named after their founding house in Limoges had their abbey here. The remote situation must have suited an order which emphasised strict discipline and reliance on alms and agricultural labour.

The road continues northward, climbing to around 1500 feet, before dropping down the steep, wooded slopes and into Wales at **Hay-on-Wye**. Hay changed hands several times in its turbulent early years, being burnt down five times, which may account for the fact that there are the remains of two castles in the small town. Hay is known worldwide for its bookshops. Second hand books in their millions line the shelves of the castle, the cinema, a garage, and shops that once catered for the more mundane demands of the local populace. Rare first editions and fine leather bindings lie in close proximity to heaps of dog-eared paperbacks and bundles of yellowing magazines. Sleepy little Hay woke up to the fact that it is now a tourist attraction in its own right - thanks to the wonderfully eccentric, but undoubtedly shrewd entrepreneur, Richard Booth, who started the whole idea.

Turning back from Hay towards Hereford, it is worth taking a detour to view the remains of Clifford Castle, whose ivy-clad ruins tower over a shallow bend in the Wye. It was built by Walter de Clifford in the early 1200's and first saw action not long after when it was captured, not by Celt or fellow Norman Marcher Lord, but by Henry III. This unfortunate episode was as a result of Henry's request that Walter's debts be paid off. Walter's reply was to make the King's Messenger 'eat the King's writ, waxe and all', so the incensed Henry promptly sacked the castle. The 'Fair Rosamund'; an earlier Clifford who was the mistress of Henry II, was probably born here. The King kept her hidden from the jealous Queen Eleanor, but eventually the Queen found Rosamund and forced her to drink poison. The Mortimers succeeded the Cliffords, so the old fortress was held by two of the greatest Marcher families.

Weobley (pronounced Wedbley) is where the first tough Hereford strain of cattle, dark red with white faces, bellies and hocks, were first bred on the Garnstone Estate. The village was evidently one of the more successful Norman settlements. Only the castle's earthworks remain today, but Weobley's prosperity is indicated by the wealth of half-timbered housing and the large parish church. Weobley is the place where the expression 'pot walloper' was first coined; the term referred to Shropshire tenants of the Marquess of Bath who had the right to vote in local elections - providing they had set up their cooking fires in the main street the previous night. Needless to say, during the corrupt political era of the 18th century, His Lordship took full advantage of this strange custom to ensure the successful return of his chosen candidates.

The half-timbered black and white theme is continued at **Eardisland** to the north of the A44. A picture postcard village by the banks of the Arrow, the enchanting Mill Stream Cottage was once the village school and was built in the 1700's at a cost of fifty pounds! Close by was the site of an ancient British settlement, now the site of Burton Court, a Georgian house of 14th-century origins which houses a fascinating collection of European and Oriental costumes and curios, together with natural history displays, ship models and a working model fairground.

Almost next door to Eardisland is the beautiful and unspoilt village of **Pembridge** with a wealth of 13th and 14th century buildings and none more beautiful than **The New Inn** which is a hostelry of warmth and atmosphere acquired over the centuries. Everything about it reeks of history. It was the Court House before it became an inn and even after that one room was used to administer the majesty of the law. It has two ghosts who refuse to leave!

It does seem extraordinary that in such an area, outstanding in its natural beauty, combining peace and solitude with the scenery of the hills, woods and rivers, should have been the scene of so much strife - yet reminders lie all around. Wigmore Castle has a connection with Brampton Bryan in that it was briefly owned by the Harleys before being dismantled by Parliamentarian troops, but it was first built by William Fitz-Osborn, Earl of Hereford, and then owned by the Mortimer family. The castle is impressively and strongly sited on a ridge in a most commanding position. It was to this great fortress that Prince Edward fled, before rallying his forcs against Simon de Montfort (he had been imprisoned at Hereford and escaped by the simple ruse of challenging his captors to race their horses. When the animals were exhausted, the cunning Prince produced a fresh beast that had been kept hidden by a sympathiser and disappeared in the proverbial cloud of dust.

Of this great family who held the castle, perhaps the most astute and savage of the Marcher Lords, little remains but a tablet in the nearby gatehouse, where once stood an Augustinian Abbey. 'In this Abbey lies the remains of the noble family of Mortimer who founded it in 1179 and ruled the Marches of Wales for 400 years.' Henry VIII took little notice, even though his mother was a Mortimer, and the tombs vanished with the Abbey. Their name is, however, commemorated a little further down the road where the A4110 intersects the B4362. This innocent looking junction in the valley of the River Lugg, was the scene in 1461 of 'an obstinate bloody and decisive battle'. Four thousand men died at what is now known as Mortimer's Cross; the first defeat to be inflicted on the Lancastrians by Edward, Duke of York - himself half a Mortimer, and later to become Edward IV. Before the fight began an extraordinary sight was seen in the sky - three suns appeared. We now know that this phenomenon is caused by the refraction of light through particles in the atmosphere, and is called a parhelion, but to the superstitious medieval warriors it appeared as an omen, a sign from God. The Yorkists took the three suns to represent the triumvirate of Edward, Duke of York, Richard, Duke of Gloucester and George, Duke of Clarence, and the ' sun in splendour' became a favourite heraldic badge with the House of York.

Turn to the east at Mortimer's Cross, and you will come to three large houses lying within a few miles of each other, the first of which acted as a rendezvous for the Yorkist forces. The Croft family have lived at Croft Castle since the time of Domesday, with the exception of 177 years - due to some unfortunate debts incurred by an 18th century Croft - and still live there, although the house and the estate is administered by the National Trust. In its present guise the castle is a massive but handsome house with turrets at each corner, and stands in beautiful parkland with an avenue of Spanish chestnut trees - said by some to have been grown from chestnuts carried in a galleon of the Spanish Armada. For all its troubled history, it is a wonderfully peaceful and attractive home. A strong feeling of continuity and service hangs in the air; as exemplified by the memorials in the little church to two more recent members of the family. Both the tenth and eleventh baronets, father and son, were killed while serving with the Herefordshire Regiment in the First and Second World Wars, nearly eight hundred years after their ancestor, Jasper de Croft, was knighted during the Crusades.

The other two houses stand almost side-by-side to the east of the Leominster to Ludlow road. The smallest is **Eye Manor**, a neat restoration house, built for a slave-trader and plantation owner from Barbados, with the exotic name of Sir Ferdinando Georges. Known as the 'King of the Black Market', he spent a good deal of his ill-gotten gains on the interior decoration, particularly the ornate and well-crafted plasterwork.

Berrington Hall has links with Moccas Court and Brampton Bryan, for the estate once belonged to the Cornewells, who sold it to the Harleys in 1775. Thomas Harley, a prosperous banker, employed Henry Holland, later responsible for the original Brighton Pavilion, to design the house, and Holland's father-in-law, Capability Brown, to lay out the grounds. They succeeded splendidly and Berrington is surely one of the most attractive and elegant Georgian houses in the country. Berrington Hall is now run by the National Trust but from 1901, it belonged to Lord Cawley. and there is a moving memorial in the Norman church at Eye to his three sons, all killed in the First World War.

It is tragic, that they, like their neighbours the Crofts and so many other thousands of Herefordshire's sons and daughters, could not have been laid to rest in the soil of their birth, the land that Henry James described as 'The copse-chequered slopes of rolling Hereford, white with the blossom of apples.'

HOTELS, INNS, RESTAURANTS AND COUNTRY HOUSES

WORCESTERSHIRE

This is an area of richness and contrast in terms of agricultural wealth, historical association and scenic beauty. The dark fertile soils of the Vale of Evesham produce the finest vegetables and fruits while farmers throughout the region happily indulge in the old-fashioned concept of mixed farming with seeming success. Orchards, arable fields and pasture lie happily grouped together while on the ancient western hills, contented sheep graze on both enclosed and common land. Man's presence on this rich, dark earth dates back to paleolithic times and its fertility was appreciated by Celt, Roman, Saxon and Norman as it is by the agricultural industrialists of today. Paradoxically, such pastoral splendour has also been the stage for savage blood-letting and the scene for king making and king-breaking. The power of the Barons was smashed at Evesham in 1265. **Tewkesbury** saw the Lancastrian claim defeated by the Yorkist Edward IV in 1471 and nearly two centuries later, Cromwell's greatest victory over the Royalists was at Worcester in 1651. Such viscious yet decisive battles, seem strangely at odds amongst such a gentle landscape where rivers meander through a countryside of quiet moderation and simple continuity; violence appears ill-suited to rolling hills and broad blossom strewn plains, lacking the bleak heathland or craggy peaks normally associated with such savageries.

The venerable Cathedral City of **Worcester** is capital to the region and reflects much of the contrasts to be found within the region as a whole with historical associations, architectural contrast and industrial, as opposed to agricultural wealth; yet even its industry has a bucolic air to it, for the black smoke and noisome forges of the industrial revolution have little place in the manufacture of gloves, Royal Worcester porcelain, or that secret blend of 'brown vinegar, walnut ketchup, anchovey essence, soy sauce, cayenne, and shallots' known world-wide as Worcestershire sauce.

I am extremely fond of the city for it has much of interest and has always been a welcoming and friendly face, but it has to be said that the twentieth century has not treated it kindly. William Cobbett (1763-1835) described Worcester as 'One of the cleanest and handsomest towns I ever saw, indeed I do not recollect to have seen any one equal to it'. Sadly his description no longer tallies; ring-roads, multi-story car parks, power stations and other civic developments have changed forever what was once 'the noblest Georgian townscape in the Midlands'. Nevertheless, there remains much that is good and visitors will find their time amply repaid.

The Cathedral of Christ and the Blessed Virgin Mary contains much of interest, particularly if you have a sharp eye. The craftsmen of old were noted not only for their skills but often for theirsense of humour, notably when it came to decoration: the 14th century choir stalls have a fine set of misericords (a rather grand name for a hinged support) and these represent a perfect riot of carver's fantasies - biblical characters, mythical beasts, scenes from both court and everyday life and even a wolf saying grace before devouring his victim! Memorials to the famous and the not-so-famous are scattered throughout but the real glory of the building, like so many of its kind, is in the construction and harmony of the interior which was skillfully overhauled in the last century by the famous Victorian architect, Sir George Gilbert Scott. Scott was responsible for many such restorations and was something of a workaholic, indeed he was so busy that he once telegraphed his London office from Manchester, with the perplexed request 'Why am I here?'

The Cathedral stands on a rise overlooking the River Severn and the Worcestershire County Cricket Ground, where traditionally, touring Test teams play their first county matches. Ornamental gardens cluster around the Watergate at the bottom of the rise where a ferry once ran when the city was walled and a tablet on the gate records the impressive heights gained by the river during floods.

It is a splendidly English backdrop, ideally suited to our summer game but in 1651 the area now dedicated to peaceful recreation would have seen the Royalist forces stumbling in retreat before Cromwell's invincible Model Army. The clash of steel and thunder of guns rang out where leather meets willow today. Relics, displays and mementoes of the Battle Worcester and other aspects of the Civil War are to be found in the Commandery, a fine 15th-century timber-framed building built on the site of an earlier hospital founded by St Wulfstan, and in the baroque 18th century Guildhall with its sumptious assembly rooms. The City Museum and Art Gallery attracts many people and apart from much of general local interest contains the Regimental Museum of the Worcestershire Regiment, who rejoiced in the stomach-turning nickname of the 'Vein-Openers'! Their heroism in battle earned them the approbation of Wellington who called them ;'the best regiment in his army', while the city's loyalty to the Crown was recognised by Charles II, who gave it the motto 'May the faithful city flourish'. Music is an important part of Worcester life and every third year it plays host to the world's oldest musical celebration, the Three Choirs Festival, which was started in 1717. The other cathedral cities involved are Hereford and Gloucester.

There is a great deal to see and do in Worcester not least Spetchley Park which is an early 19th century museum with a deer park and splendid formal gardens that are open to the public. Greyfriars, a splendid half-timbered building (Tudor with later addition) has been fully restored under the aegis of the National Trust and has a delightful walled garden. The five hundred year old Tudor House Museum is close by and has fascinating displays of social history while in Severn Street, the Dyson Perrins Museum contains examples of Royal Worcester porcelain dating back to 1751 and includes the dinner service made for the Prince and Princess of Wales.

The River Avon almost entirely encircles **Evesham**, a town which owes its beginnings to a vision of the Madonna seen by a local swine-herd called Eoves. Egwin, Bishop of Worcester, established a monastery on the site in 704 and became its first abbot. The Abbey rapidly became an important place of pilgrimage and a town grew round the site. The original shrine of Eoves'vision increased in importance with the canonisation of Egwin and then, 560 years after the Abbey's foundation came the battle which would lead to a third shrine within its precincts. The Barons, led by Simon de Montfort, fell out with Henry III over the interpretation of the Magna Carta and a short but bloody war resulted. The Barons held Henry captive after defeating him in battle but had failed to hold on to his son, who later became Edward I. The Battle of Evesham, which took place on the 4th August 1265, resulted in a crushing defeat for the Barons and was an astonishing feat of arms by the young prince who had left Worcester on the morning of August 2nd, marched to Kenilworth and captured it, then turned to the south to approach Evesham on the morning of the 4th - sixty miles in forty-eight hours, not forgetting the hand-to-hand combat on the way! De Montfort's body was dismembered but the trunk was buried before the High Altar of the Abbey where it soon became the shrine of a man the common people considered a folk-hero, and who is remembered today as the 'Father of Parliaments'. The Abbey grew evermore wealthy and two churches were built outside the monastic grounds to cater for the townsfolk and the pilgrims respectively, and these churches, dedicated to St Lawrence and to All Saints, still remain. The Abbey was pulled down during the Dissolution and the principal remains include the magnificent Perpendicular bell-tower, built by the last rightful abbot, Clement Lichfield who is also remembered in both churches.

The Almonry Museum chronicles much of Evesham's history and, although the town is a busy marketing and light industrial centre, its fascinating history is reflected in the ancient buildings and streets. It is also very much a town of, rather than by, the river since the Severn, has acted as a means of both defence and transport in times past and recreation today.
The Vale of Evesham was described by the American writer Henry James, as 'the dark, rich, hedgy flats of Worcestershire'. Since he wrote those words in 1875, the majority of the hedges have long gone in the pursuit of intensive cultivation of fruit and vegetables. All manner of varieties are grown in the fertile tilth including such exotics as asparagus and peppers, but it is the fruit that gives the area its greatest glory - albeit for only a short time. Generally around late March and early May, depending on the climate, the area becomes almost magical with blossom from cherries, apples, pears and plums. There are well marked Spring Blossom Trails that can be followed by car, bike or on foot and it is one of the most wonderful sights that the English countryside has to offer. It is nothing less than a total transformation and there are many who come back year after year to view the splendour. It is an interesting fact that although local farmers had appreciated the fertility of the vale's soil for centuries, it was left to a foreigner to reveal its true potential. Francesco Bernardi was a Genoese envoy in the 17th century who settled in the Vale after a dispute withhis country. He spent the enormous sum of thirty thousand pounds to begin, in effect, the local industry of market gardening.

Pershore is the second town of the Vale and was once the 'third town' of the county after Worcester and Droitwich. A handsome town with a predominance of seemingly Georgian architecture (many are facades built onto older buildings) it lies to the north of Bredon Hill amongst water meadows beside the Avon's meanderings. It too has an Abbey although considerably more survives than that of neighbouring Evesham. Pershore Abbey is still a magnificent building although much reduced in size, it has a splendid pinnacled tower supported on high Norman arches and a wonderful vaulted roof to the choir with much fine carving. The original religious settlement dates back as far as 689 but depradations from Danish pirates and disbelieving Saxons meant that little of import was established until the Benedictines founded a monastery dedicated to King Alfred's grand-daughter, St Eadburgh. Over the centuries the Abbey grew, surviving setbacks like the fire in 1288 which led to the rebuilding of the present tower, until the Dissolution of the Monasteries when the faithful citizens of Pershore bought the monastic part of the buildings for their own use at a cost of four hundred pounds. Pershore's prosperity, like Evesham, is strongly linked to the surrounding fertile land and to the River Avon which for many years enabled agricultural produce to be sent downstream to Bristol, including the famous Pershore Plums.

The Lower and Upper Avon Navigation Trusts have done tremendous work in restoring the numerous locks and weirs dating back to the 17th century that enable the river to be fully navigable. The advent of the railways meant that many of these riverine structures fell into disrepair and the work done by the Trusts has been extensive and of benefit to all. I recommend a boat trip to appreciate not only the beauty of this unique part of England but also to see and appreciate the work that has been and is being done.

To the south-west lies another small town of considerable appeal whose fortunes have also been linked to a river: **Upton upon Severn**. The Severn is stronger and more direct than the meandering Avon and for many years Upton possessed the only bridge across the river between Gloucester and Worcester and was such an important meeting place for river craft that what became known as the 'Bridge of Parliament' was held there. Obviously the bridge was of major tactical importance during the Civil War and the Royalists, based at Worcester, blew out two of the spans to prevent an outflanking movement - but in vain. Due to the negligence of a sentry, a small party of Roundheads crept across the plank that had been left across the gap and barricaded themselves in the church, resisting all efforts to displace them until relieved by their own cavalry which had crossed at an unguarded ford. Upton fell to the Parliamentarians and the church was partially destroyed. There is a romanitc sequel to this brief but savage skirmish; that evening Cromwell himself arrived to congratulate his men and saw, at an upstairs window, a beautiful girl in obvious distress. He asked her name and was told it was a Miss Morris whereupon he pardoned her brother whom he had just condemned to be shot. It is nice to know that Old Ironsides hadthe human touch.

Upton-upon-Severn is a charming little town where such a story seems eminently believable. The medieval church tower survives, crowned with a copper covered cupola and is now used as an heritage centre, whilst in the churchyard can be found the well known epitaph:

> *'Beneath this stone, in hope of Zion,*
> *Doth lie the landlord of the Lion,*
> *his son keeps on the business still,*
> *Resigned unto the heavenly will.*

Apt lines for a town that has a greater number of pubs per head of resident population than most - probably as a result of the old river traffic. Incidentally **The White Lion Hotel** is still thriving and is a delightful place to stay. All the pubs do a roaring trade during the many Summer events that take place here, such as The Steam Rally, The Water Festival, and The Jazz and Folk Festivals.

Worcestershire's greatest natural glories are to be found to the west of the Severn. **The Malverns** are perhaps the originators of that well-known phrase 'as old as the hills' for this ridge of pre-Cambrian rock is more than 500 million years old. The name means 'the bare hills' and they rise gently from fertile soils and woodlands to stand guardians against the prevailing winds. Although of no great height (the highest point is only 1394 feet) their appearance is impressive in contrast to the lowlands from which they spring, and the infinite permutations of light and shade sweeping over their bracken-strewn slopes and barren summits have inspired musicians, poets and artists over the centuries.

Walking the beautiful hills is one of the great pleasures of staying in The Malverns. The name is not only applied to the hills but to the struggle of six distinct settlements often referred to collectively as Malvern. These are **Little Malvern, Malvern Wells, Malvern Link, Great Malvern, North Malvern** and **West Malvern**.

Little Malvern is the smallest and southernmost of the Malverns nestling cosily in the lee of steeper slopes. The church of St Giles is all that remains of a larger priory church and was treated roughly by the Parliamentarians during th Civil War who removed the misericords and damaged some of the beautiful 15th century glass. They also left a sword behind in the graveyard which is now kept in a glass case. Next to the church is **Little Malvern Court** parts of which date back to the 12th century and which was the refectory of Prior's Hall of the original monastic foundation. Long a family home, it contains a priest-hole, a magnificent 14th century roof and a number of treasures including a travelling trunk and silk quilt belonging to Catherine of Aragon.

The shifting play of light and shadow on the ancient hills, sometimes dramatic, more often subtle and complex is nowhere better artistically represented than in the wonderful music ofSir Edward Elgar. It seems only right that this man of Worcestershire whose genius was acknowledged worldwide, but who remained a countryman at heart, should be buried, together with his wife and daughter, in the quiet peace of the Malverns at St Wulfstan's Roman Catholic Church.

The strict contemplative life of a monastic order would seem ideally suited to this region and Malvern Priory Church is the sole, but impressive remnant of a large priory which dates back to 1088. Unfortunately the monastic order was not always strict or contemplative for, in 1282, the prior was accused of adultery with twenty two women! Although the conventual buildings (the living quarters) were nearly all pulled down in the Dissolution, the church was retained by the payment of twenty pounds (in two instalments) - a wonderful bargain for a building which externally is a fine example of Perpendicular architecture with a light and airy interior which includes a six-bay Norman nave of the early 1100's. The 15th century stained glass is wonderfully complimented by some beautiful tiles of the same period, together with a fine set of misericords. Once again the humour of the old craftsmen has been given full sway, for example, there are three mice hanging a cat and a drunkard being beaten by his wife, to name but two. The Malvern Museum is housed in the other surviving part of the prior, the Abbey Gateway.

Great Malvern surrounds the church and is essentially 18th and early 19th century in character and is a product of the period's preoccupation with spa waters. There are distinct parallels with life today; our preoccupation with health, diet, fitness and beauty has led to the establishment of fashionable 'health farms' while the Georgian and Victorians had their spas and hydros.

Perhaps the only difference being the emphasis our ancestors placed on ailments affecting digestion - hardly surprising when one considers the amount they ate! Four meals a day, breakfast, lunch, dinner and supper were the norm, even for the lower middle classes and a menu from a local hotel, now defunct, offers the following delights:

Caviare
Soups: *Mulligatawny* or *Julienne*
Fish: *Brill* or *Stewed Eels*
Entrees: *Salmi of Wild Duck* or *Chicken Cream*
Roast: *Sirloin of Beef* or *Haunch of Mutton*
Sweets: *Orange Fritters, Benedictine Souffle* or *Ices*
Savouries: *Angel on Horseback* or *Cheese Straws*

All this was accompanied by copious quantities of the appropriate wines and liquers and eaten in tight restricting clothing; well-laced whalebone corsets being de riguer for the women and the vainer men. Consequently, anyone offering relief from such embarassing disorders as 'Constipation, Flatulence, Diarrhoea and Indigestion or similar ailments arising from Impure Blood or Disordered Stomach' was undoubtedly on to a winner.

The first entrepreneur to exploit the area's water was the founder of the Royal Worcester Porcelain Works, one Doctor John Wall. He had, however, one slight problem in extolling the curative properties of the liquid: it tasted pleasantly fresh and sparkling - quite the reverse of the generally foul-flavoured, mineral rich fluids experienced at other fashionable resorts. Doctor Wall was evidently made of sterner stuff and had a marketing ability that would have made him a target for all major executive recruitment agencies were he still alive today.

'Malvern Water, said Doctor Wall,
is famed for containing nothing at all.'

This was the essence of the campaign and it worked! His premise was quite simply, that since the water was so pure, the cure was effected faster ' as it could pass more rapidly through the vessels of the body.'

The town quickly became fashionable and hotels, pump rooms and lodging houses were built. The Victorians added a further refinement by introducing a form of 'water-cure' that was horrific by anyone's standards. This consisted of being wrapped tightly in cold wet sheets for hours on end, having hundreds of gallons of icy water dropped on you from a great height, cold baths, long walks, a strict diet and naturally nothing but water to drink. Recreation was strictly controlled with even reading being banned as 'too demanding'. It was a wonder that anyone survived; nevertheless, the resort attracted the likes of the Royal Family, Gladstone, Florence Nightingale, Macaulay, Carlyle, Wordsworth and Charles Darwin.

The waters have not been forgotten and are bottled and exported all over the world by Cadbury Schweppes, while the awful Victorian water treatments have been replaced by the delights of a 'water activity centre'. The Splash an indoor complex complete with water-slide, wave-making machine and 'beach'.

Above all Malvern are the hills, and to walk their eight mile length and savour the amazing views, is to see England at its very best. The Malvern Hills Conservators were set up by Parliament in 1884 to protect the common land from commercial exploitation and they have done their job wonderfully well. There are more than twenty six miles of footpaths, together with a number of discreet car-parks so that the hills can be enjoyed by all.

To the north, at the end of a lane in meadows bordering the Severn, lies the village of **Grimley**. Apart from some gravel pits and a number of farms, this would seem a quiet prosaic country community. However, in the churchyard lies Sir Samuel Baker (1821-93) an African explorer of renown, discoverer of Lake Nyanza and the Murchison Falls, big-game hunter and colonial administrator, While at neighbouring **Thorngrove** lived an even more exotic character, in the shape of Lucien Bonaparte. He was the younger brother of Napoleon and offended the Emperor by marrying the ex-wife of a planter. Napoleon offered Lucien the Kingdoms of Spain and Naples if he would renounce the woman, but Lucien refused and, in trying to escape to America, was captured by the British. He eventually settled with his wife in this remote corner of Worcestershire, where they happily whiled awaythe remaining war years by writing turgid epic poetry together.

At **Wichenford** the National Trust has restored a marvellous 17th century half-timbered Dovecote and the nearby **Wichenford Court** is said to play host to two female ghosts, both members of the Washbourne family. One stalks around holding a bloody dagger aloft (she was reputed to have murdered a French prince) and the other plays a harp whilst sitting in a silver boat drawn by white swans. Makes a change from grey ladies and headless horsemen!

The landscape of Worcestershire reveals many gems whether man-made or natural. The glorious blossom, the ancient buildings and the views from the hills - even in the most mundane little corner there is always something to interest and delight.

SHROPSHIRE

Shropshire is such a wonderful mixture of countryside, architecture, agriculture and industry. It has wonderful places to visit, history which is fascinating and at times awe inspiring, stately homes, gardens and all manner of other attractions. I cannot tell you as much about the county as I would wish but I hope it is enough to encourage you to come here.

The temptation when you come to South Shropshire, is to seek out immediately places like Ludlow, a place of historical romance and one of the most beautiful country towns in England. This is what I have always done in the past but this time I was invited to stay with friends in **Telford**, a new town that is light years ahead. My friends had moved there with reluctance when a new posting for the husband made it imperative. To their surprise they have found living in this new town a good experience. Some of their enthusiasm rubbed off on me and I, too, was agreeably surprised at the great effort that has been made to make it a 'green and pleasant land'. For example, over a million trees, plants and shrubs have been planted throughout the town. The park is a mixture of landscaped and natural scenery complete with a lake at the side of which is an amphitheatre and a sports arena. The town offers all sorts of facilities and seems to me to be full of young and enthusiastic people who enjoy what it has to offer.

One of the reasons that made my friends happy with Telford was the unique range of top class sporting facilities, with everything from golf and tennis to skiing provided in a range of superb modern sports centres. In addition to the National Sports Centre at nearby **Lilleshall**, Telford has six fully equipped sports and leisure centres of its own. The Telford Ice Rink is one of the finest in the Midlands, and it is the home of one of the country's top ice hockey teams.

Newport is only eight miles to the north-east of Telford and is as different as chalk from cheese. Here I found a pleasant, unspoilt market town, centred around the broad, elegant High Street, a street just asking to be explored. The town has a large and graceful church, **St Nicholas**, standing on an island site in the middle of the High Street. There is a font from the year of the Restoration, a coffin lid carved quite wonderfully 700 years ago, and a list of rectors going back to the Normans.

The most famous son of Newport was the wise and extraordinary man, Sir Oliver Lodge, who experimented in wireless and sent wireless telegrams long before Marconi. He interested himself in all sorts of things from the mysterious problems of telepathy to the conquering of fog.

Just 3 miles north of Junction 3 on the M54 is **Weston Park** on the A5 at **Weston-under-Lizard**. This classic 17th century statelyhouse is the historic home of the Earls of Bradford. The interior has been superbly restored and holds one of the country's finest collections of paintings, with originals by many of the great masters. There are fine tapestries from the famous 18th-century makers Gobelin and Aubusson, letters from Disraeli which provide a fascinating commentary on

Victorian history. It is quite wonderful. It is used all the year round for Conferences, Banquets, Product Launches, Wedding Receptions and for very special 'Dine and Stay' gourmet evenings which are open to the public. These are truly wonderful occasions and will long stay in your memory. If you are interested ring 01952 76207 and ask about dates.

From Weston Park it is only a short distance to **Boscobel House**, in which Charles Stuart sought refuge after his defeat at Worcester. As I drove along the quiet road I wondered if the King had wished he was just a simple Shropshire man, secure in his everyday life rather than a hunted royal. The Giffords of Chillington owned Boscobel and as staunch catholics they had honeycombed the house with hiding places for priests. If you see the house today many of them still exist. One will be pointed out to you as the King's hiding place, reached by a short flight of stairs leading to the cheese room.

William Penderel tenanted Boscobel and he was one of the six brothers who were loyal supporters of the Stuart cause. However it was not Boscobel which hid Charles Stuart but **Whiteladies**, where Humphrey Penderel lived. Here, he left all his retinue but Lord Richard Wilmot and became a countryman wearing a coarse shirt, darned stockings, a leather doublet with pewter buttons, a ragged coat and breeches, a battered old hat and rough boots. He darkened his face and his hands with soot and accompanied only by Richard, he crept out, avoiding troops that he knew to be in the neighbourhood. He was attempting to make his way over the Severn into Wales, stopping at Madeley, the home of Francis Woolf. The journey was fraught with danger and at one stage he and Richard were chased by a miller and a number of soldiers. The journey became so perilous that the only thing they could do was to return to Boscobel. The only way to do this was to swim across the river but Richard could not swim. Charles helped him over but by this time the King's feet were so blistered and torn and his boots so full of grit, that he felt he could not go on. It was Richard who kept him going and at last they reached the safety of Boscobel. Here Charles's feet were doctored, he was given a change of stockings and his boots were dried. Outside the house was a great oak and into this Charles climbed. He slept during the day but woke to the sound of Cromwell's men searching for him in the wood. There was a price of a thousand pounds on the king's head: something all the Penderels knew about but such was their loyalty that not one of them even thought for a moment about betraying him. They would have died in his cause if need be. For two or more days and nights Charles stayed at Boscobel, sleeping in the hole beneath the trapdoor in the cheese room until finally it was thought safe enough for them to set out on the long journey which would eventually end in France.

You must visit **Tong**. It is only a small village but the magnificent 14th-century church of **St Bartholomew** would not beout of place in a city. It is frequently referred to as 'the Cathedral of the West Midlands'. Just north of the village, off the A41, you can see a peculiar pyramid-shaped building set back a few hundred yards from the road. It is called the **Egyptian Aviary**, and it is a bizarre hen-house designed by a celebrated eccentric, George Durant in the early 19th century.

The whole of the **Ironbridge Gorge** is one big real life museum that tells you every chapter of the fascinating story, on the spot, where it happened. There is no place anywhere like it in the world. Make sure you allow yourself plenty of time to enjoy it.

The Severn flows through this deep gorge and the houses cling to the hillsides looking as though a puff of wind would blow them into the swirling river, but they have been there for hundreds of years and are as much a part of this incredible place as the Museums. The chief distinction is, of course, the bridge, believed to be the first iron bridge ever built. It was built by Abraham Darby of Coalbrookdale in 1777. It is 196ft long with one span of 100 feet and two smaller ones, the total weight of iron being 380tons. So much for the statistics, worth knowing but fading almost into insignificance alongside the many things to be seen. Over 250 years ago the Severn Gorge witnessed momentous events which culminated in the Industrial Revolution and it was the fortunate combination of coal, iron, water power and transport, all concentrated in this Shropshire Valley, which sparked off the series of events affecting all of us. Of the many places to visit perhaps **Rosehill House**, one of the elegant mansions where the Darby family lived in the 18th and 19th centuries, is probably my favourite. It is sheer pleasure to wander through the beautifully restored rooms with original period furniture. The house gives you an understanding of how a wealthy ironmaster would have lived.

In total contrast is **Carpenter's Row**, a terrace of workers' houses built by the company in the late 18th century. There is nothing grand about them. Four cottages have been restored and furnished to recreate a home from different periods between 1780 and 1930. Carpenters' Row is open to small groups by special appointment only. You will find many more places listed under 'Attractions' at the back of the book.

After the strenuous activity in Ironbridge it might be as well to take a look at **Broseley** across the Gorge. This was the great urban centre of the Coalbrookdale coalfield during the Industrial revolution. The ironmaster, John Wilkinson, built his furnace here, and in its heyday it was a rival to Coalbrookdale itself as a centre of the iron industry. John Wilkinson was the man who had the idea of building iron barges. He persevered in spite of being laughed at and he had the last laugh when, on one summer's day in 1787, the first iron barge was launched on the Severn. From this the idea of an iron ship was born and Broseley was its birthplace. John Wilkinson was so dedicated to the use of iron that he asked to be buried in an iron coffin!

Much Wenlock cries out to be visited; it is a lovely old market town full of history. Arthur Mee describes it as somewhere that' sleeps in the hills, dreaming of all that has been, stirring with the memory of warrior kings and the ancient strife of the Border valleys, and inspired by the natural spectacle of Wenlock Edge.

The steep wooded escarpment known as **Wenlock Edge**, runs for 16 miles and provides a series of spectacular viewpoints across to the Stretton Hills and the Long Mynd. It is essentially a geological phenomenon; the rock, Wenlock limestone, was formed more than 400 million years ago in a tropical sea. It developed as a barrier reef built up largely from the skeletons and shells of sea creatures.

Three miles north east of Much Wenlock, on the B4378 you will come to **Buildwas Abbey**. Standing in a beautiful situation on the banks of the River Severn quite close to Ironbridge Gorge, it is a worthwhile place to visit. It must be one of the country's finest ruined abbeys. Dating back over 800years to Norman times it is surprising that so much is still standing today. The imposing walls of the abbey church with 14 wonderful Norman arches remain. It was probably completed in 1200 with Norman and Early English architecture remaining virtually unaltered since the Dissolution in the 1530s.

When you are in Telford, Wellington, Ironbridge or Much Wenlock you should make the effort to reach the summit of **The Wrekin**. It is a curiosity and one of the most distinctive landmarks in the Shropshire Hills. The Wrekin is 1335 foot high, rising sharply from the flatness of the surrounding countryside. It is the site of the ancient Iron Age hill fort and it has been the focus of local legends and superstitions for hundreds of years. My favourite is that the hill was formed by a giant who had quarrelled with the people of Shrewsbury. The giant was determined to punish the townsfolk and set off with a huge spadeful of earth to bury the whole town. On the way he met a cobbler by the roadside carrying a sack of shoes to be mended. The cobbler thought the giant was up to no good so he persuaded him that Shrewsbury was too far to walk, showing him the whole bag of shoes he had worn out with walking the enormous distance from the town. The giant decided the cobbler was right: he ditched the spadeful of earth on the spot - and the Wrekin was formed.

Bridgnorth is two towns in one perched dramatically on a steep cliff above the River Severn. It is naturally beautiful and quite unlike anywhere else in England. This picturesque market town has High Town and Low town linked by the famous Cliff Railway, which climbs up a hair raising incline. The only other I know like it is the Cliff railway which joins Lynton and Lynmouth in Devon.

There is something reminiscent of old Italian towns as you climb the Stoneway steps cut sheer through the rocks, or wander about the maze of old half-timbered buildings and elegant 18th-century houses. One of these is the curious 17th century Town Hall. this timber framed building is built on an arched sandstone base partly across the roadway in the middle of the High Street. At the east end of the street is The North Gate, the only remaining one of five gates in the town's fortifications. There is a Museumover the arches.

Bridgnorth Castle is famous for its leaning tower which is 17 degrees out of straight. The leaning Tower of Pisa is only 5 degrees! It has survived safely for 850 years. The castle grounds are now a public park where you can admire a splendid view over the river and Low town. Take time out to discover this delightful town and its many interesting buildings which include the **Church of St Mary Magdalene, Bishop Percy's House** and the **Bridgnorth Costume and Childhood Museum**.

Ludlow beckoned and I happily answered the call. Here is a town that has few equals. Its river rings it like a moat and to walk about its castle and streets is quite thrilling. We are lucky to claim it as part of England because it is almost on the Welsh border. It became a fortress from which Wales's unruly and mutinous tribes were eventually knocked into submission. **The Church of St Laurence** soars upwards and vies with the castle for supremacy. It is an outstandingly beautiful Perpendicular church with an earlier foundation, twice restored in the 19th century. The church is open in summer from 9-5pm and in winter until 4pm.

The most exciting culinary event in Ludlow was the recent arrival of the celebrated international chef, Shaun Hill who opened a superb restaurant, **The Merchant House** - a must for any lover of good food.

There are some beautiful places to visit between Ludlow and Shrewsbury. One of my favourite haunts is **Stokesay Castle**. It stands just off the Ludlow-Shrewsbury road half a mile south of Craven Arms. There is a car park up the signposted lane and past the church, only a few yards from this romantic ruin.

The marvellous state of preservation does give a very clear idea of the conditions in which well-to-do medieval families lived. It is one of the earliest fortified manor houses in England with the oldest parts dating from the 12th century and the Great Hall from the 13th. It is an extraordinary structure with massive stone towers topped with a timber-framed house.

The A49 going towards Shrewsbury will take you to **Little Stretton** which must be one of the most beautiful villages in Shropshire complete with a little thatched church and its big neighbour, **Church Stretton** is somewhere else you should visit. Houses dot the valley and climb the slopes. To the west is the great moorland ridge of the Longmynd rising nearly 1700feet, with the beautiful Cardingmill Valley below and the prehistoric Portway running along the top. To the east are the rugged Caradoc Hills with Watling Street at the foot, and the banks and trenches of Caer Caradoc's stronghold 1500ft up.

The strange cross-shaped church goes back 850 years and in the old churchyard is a stone of 1814 to Ann Cook which says:

> 'On a Thursday she was born
> On a Thursday made a bride
> On a Thursday broke a leg
> And on a Thursday died.'

Thursday was not a lucky day for Ann Cook!

Bishops Castle to the west and surrounded by the beauty of the South Shropshire hills, was plundered by Royalists during the Civil War in 1645 but somehow missed out the inn, **The Boars Head Hotel**, in which Roundheads were slaking their thirst.

Here you are on the edge of the Clun Forest, a delightful place and if you have ever read A.E. Housman's 'A Shropshire Lad' you will know his description of the Cluns, he thought it a quiet area:

> *'Clunton and Clunbury*
> *Clungunford and Clun.*
> *Are the quietest places*
> *Under the sun.'*

And so to **Shrewsbury** where once again A.E. Housman says it all:

> *'High the vanes of Shrewsbury gleam*
> *Islanded in Severn stream;*
> *The bridges from the steepled crest*
> *Cross the water, east to west.'*

It is almost an island with its castle standing in a narrow strait and more than half-a dozen bridges crossing to and fro. It has old black and white houses, half-timbered of the Elizabethan era, fine brick buildings of the 17th century and wonderfully elegant Queen Anne and Georgian town houses, narrow streets and alleyways with strange names - Grope Lane, Shoplatch, Dogpole, Wyle Cop and Pride Hill. Everywhere oozes history and clamours for your attention.

There are people who may tell you that North Shropshire is dull. That is absolutely untrue; it may be flatter than the south but within it you will discover it has miles of gentle green countryside, reed fringed meres, the excitement of the Shropshire Union and Llangollen Canals, red sandstone hills, a wealth of small villages and five historic market towns, **Oswestry, Ellesmere, Whitchurch, Wem** and **Market Drayton.**

Oswestry is on the Shropshire side of the border with Wales and has very strong ties with the Principality. Apart from being a charming market town to explore it is equally splendid to wander the hilly, sparsely populated border country. This is a town that has much to offer ; you could well stay here for a month and still not have seen everything.

Market days are full of life with one of the busiest street markets in the county. Over 120 traders set up their stalls with every imaginable kind of product and produce. The Market days are all the year round on Wednesdays with an additional market on Saturdays in the summer. There is ample car parking near the town centre.

Canals are very important to the way of life in this part of Shropshire and provide so much more than just water transport. Following the canal or 'the cut' is a wonderful way of exploring North Shropshire whether you have a boat or not. The towpath is a splendid, traffic free footpath on the level for miles albeit in some places it is distinctly rough going and very muddy. You are rewarded though by the wildlife that abounds on the water, in the bankside vegetation, and along the hedges. You can learn so much from the canal which tells its own story of our industrial and architectural heritage.

At **Whittington** you will meet with the **Llangollen Canal**, which wends its way across the country right up into Cheshire where it joins the main Shropshire Union Canal close to **Nantwich**. Whittington is a very large village in the centre of which is Whittington Castle. All that you can see today of this important border castle is the magnificent gatehouse and the moat. It is a delightful place to visit, with a childrens play area, ducks to feed and a tearoom in which to relax. The village is reputed to have been the birthplace of Dick Whittington, the famous Lord Mayor of London and cat owner!

From here I went north a little until I came to **Chirk** where it is the only way to cruise from England into Wales. This is quite a place with a lot of history, right on the border of Shropshire and Clwyd; it has withstood the slings and arrows of outrageous fortune. **Chirk Castle** which belongs to the National Trust, is a place you must visit and you should make sure you get to **Llanrhaedr Falls**, another of the seven wonders of Wales. They are stunning.

The Shropshire Union Canal, a popular waterway for pleasure craft, has played a great part in the history of **Ellesmere**, and the **Old Wharf** with its warehouse and crane is a reminder of a prosperous period for the development of the town when it was a centre of plans for a link to the River Mersey (at what was to become Ellesmere Port). This was nearly 200 years ago when some of Britain's leading industrialists first met to discuss the project. Thomas Telford included. Circumstances caused them to build instead a most attractive canal from Llangollen's Horseshoe Falls to Hurleston junction near Nantwich.

Wem is a town that still manages to preserve more of the old market town atmosphere than most others. It is delightful and dates back before the Conquest in 1066. In fact it is the only town mentioned in the Domesday Book which can trace descendants from before and after the Conquest. The fire of 1677 destroyed many of the ancient houses and it suffered for its staunch support of the Protestant Cause in the Civil War, being the first town to declare for Parliament and hence became the prime target for the Royalists of Whitchurch and Shrewsbury who laid siege to it for a long period without success. The church dates from the 14th century and has an uncommon doorway of that period, and a Perpendicular style upper tower.

Whitchurch is the most ancient of the market towns dating from 60AD when it was founded as a garrison for the Roman legions marching between Chester and Wroxeter. Many Roman artefacts and buildings have been found in the town centre notably in 1967 and 1977, and Pepper Street, High Street and Bluegates occupy the same situation as the Roman streets.

Market in name and market by nature, ideally you should come to **Market Drayton** on a Wednesday and join in the bustling bargain hunting tradition that has been going on for over 750years. Since the Norman Conquest, this seemingly sleepy and isolated town has been the scene of revolt, riot, murder, adventure and trade; its links have extended worldwide. Clive of India was born here and he will never be forgotten. You will find much to enjoy including the celebrated product of local bakers' shops - Gingerbread Men, which come in a range of novelty shapes and packages, all faithful to recipes over 200 years old. A true taste of history.

You must find time to travel 6 miles down the A53 to **Hodnet** where the **Hodnet Hall Gardens** covering 60 acres, are unrivalled for their beauty and natural valley setting. The magnificent trees, lawns and lakes provide a background to an ever changing seasonal colour and interest. Between April and July the rhododendrons are fantastic. The gardens are famous nationally and have been the subject of several TV and radio programmes. This was a visit to remember among the very happy recollections I have of this county.

HEART OF ENGLAND

STAFFORDSHIRE

With limited time to spend in Staffordshire I decided to devote my time to a few places which interest me and in so doing hopefully stir in the reader a desire to see more of this most versatile and handsome county.

Thomas Telford's sixty-six mile canal was built to link the industrial city of Birmingham with the great port of Livrpool and was originally named the Birmingham and Liverpool Junction Canal. Looking at the peaceful waters running straight through the lovely countryside, it is difficult to see them as the 17th and 18th century equivalent of our motorways - yet that is what they were. Quiet tree-fringed stretches where the tranquillity is only disturbed by the quacking of the mallard and the puttering of an occasional leisure boat, were once bustling highways where entire generations of families lived their lives afloat. Goods of every concievable kind were carried by boat, together with passengers and even livestock, and a community such as **Gnosall**, situated beside both canal and major road, would have been important as a distribution centre. The popularity of the canals can be understood when one realises the appalling state of the majority of roads which were virtually impassable except by packhorse. Almost overnight the waterways enabled vast quantities of raw materials and finished goods to be moved quickly and economically - thus contributing enormously to the prosperity of the nation as a whole.

It is easy to forget the logistics involved in such a venture, as our own century place an enormous reliance on powerful and sophisticated machinery to construct the roads and motorways - today's equivalent of the canal systems. Labour in enormous numbers had to be accommodated, fed and paid during the building of such projects; to drive the great waterways through the heart of our country relied chiefly upon the speed and expertise of men aided with little more than picks, shovels and wheelbarrows.Theproblems were not over once the canal was built, for there was the continuous problem of maintenance - reinforcing banks, clearing weed, surfacing towpaths, breaking ice in winter and all the more skilled work involving locks, their gates and associated machinery. Failure in any of these departments could lead to blockage of the canal, or worse still, to loss of water, leaving boats and their cargoes stranded for days, even weeks. Gangs of men were allocated a length of canal to maintain, and many spent their lives working to keep the waterway running. Close to the aqueduct carrying the 'Shroppy' across the attractive countryside at **Shebdon**, is **The Wharf Inn**, once headquarters for a maintenance gang of 'lengthmen'. These gangs were noted for the prodigious amounts of food and drink they could consume - the Wharf obviously did a good job in these departments and carries on the tradition by catering to today's visitor with the same cheerful generosity.

Shebdon is close to the Shropshire border, a mile or so to the north of the A519 which runs through **Eccleshall**. The beauty of the surrounding undulating and wooded countryside, together with the architecture and charm of this small town make it one of the most attractive communities in Staffordshire. Pronounced 'Eccle-shawl', it has a long history dating back to a Roman settlement and over the centuries became an important strategic, ecclesiastic and market centre. Soldiers, bishops and traders have all gone but their legacy remains in the buildings they left behind. **Eccleshall Castle** was the principal residence of the Bishops of Lichfield for 600 years. Bishop Muschamp was granted a licence to fortify his house in 1200 and this led to the construction of the castle. Interesting to note that bureaucracy ruled even then, and one wonders whether there is still a department deep in the bowels of Whitehall dealing with requests of this nature. **The Church of the Holy Trinity** has been described as one of the finest 13th-century churches in the country. Restored in 1868, it is a tall, light and lofty building of considerable grace and contains the tombs of five of the Bishops of Lichfield.

Stone is a thriving and good-looking town. Two local stories account for the name; some say it comes from a cairn of stones that marked the graves of two Christian Mercian princes murdered by their pagan father, while others maintain it derives from a mineral-rich local stream that petrifies plant life. Whatever the truth, the area has been inhabited for a long time - as shown by the number of fine stone axe-heads found locally. A market town which did well out of the Canal era (the River Trent and the Trent and Mersey Canal run parallel south of the town), Stone produced two notable figures; Admiral John Jervis, later Earl St Vincent (1735-1823) and the water colourist Peter de Wint (1748-1849). The neat 18th-century Gothic Church of St Michael, with its galleries and box pews contains a memorial to the Admiral who lies with other members of his family in a small palladian-style Mausoleum.

South down the A34 is the county town of **Stafford**, the city constructed on the site of a hermitage built by St Pertelin some 1200 years ago. Commercial development has left the town surprisingly untouched - apart from the jutting intrusion of afew tower blocks. Stafford still wears the bucolic air of a country town, even though it has been an important manufacturing centre for centuries; manufacturing internal combustion engines and electrical equipment since the beginning of the present century. Nevertheless its ancient heritage is on proud display for all to admire. Here you have **Stafford Castle** built in 1070, an impressive example of an early Norman fortress. The central building in Stafford is the late Georgian Shire Hall, a most handsome building that fits the part well, while not too far away is a positive triumph of the timber house builders art, **The High House**. Built in 1595 for a wool mnerchant, John Dorrington, it is the largest timber-framed town house in the country. Nor must one forget **Chetwynd House**, a handsome Georgian building that is now the Post Office. Here the ebullient playwright, theatre-manager and MP for Stafford, Richard Brinsley Sheridan, would stay on visits to his constituency.

Due west of Stafford, on the very tip of Cannock Chase, is **Shugborough Estate**, ancestral home of the camera-wielding Earl of Lichfield. A beautiful mansion, dating back to 1693, and set within a magnificent 900 acre estate. Shugborough contains fine collections of 18th-century ceramics, silver, paintings and French furniture. **The Staffordshire County Museum** is housed in the old servants quarters and there are splendid recreations of life behind the 'green baize door'.

Shugborough Park Farm is a working agricultural museum where rare breeds are kept, horse drawn machinery used and an old mill grinds corn.

Whether you arrive by canal or car, **Cannock Chase** remains the greatest attraction of the region. As its name implies it was once a Royal hunting ground, but Richard I, in need of funds, sold it to the Bishops of Lichfield. In those times it was a much larger area, extending from the River Penk in the west to the Trent in the east, with Stafford to the north and including Wolverhampton and Walsall to the south. Now it is around 26 square miles of forest and heath land that have been declared an 'area of outstanding natural beauty'. Medieval industrial activities meant the loss of much of the native oakwoods while the southern part was given over to coalpits, but these activities have long ceased and the deer and wildlife have returned to their natural habitat. The highest point is at **Castle Ring** with wonderful views over the countryside and the site of an Iron Age hill fort, dating from around 500BC.

Close to the eastern side of Cannock Chase lies the ancient city of **Lichfield** with its unique **Cathedral of St Mary and St Chad**, a magnificent red sandstone structure with three spires, known as 'the Ladies of the Vale'. The Cathedral is considered the Mother-church of the Midlands and is the third building on the site since it was consecrated in 700AD by St Chad. The present structure is a magnificent example of Early-English and Decorated work, a triumph of medieval craftmanship. The surrounds of the cathedral are equally beautiful with attractive houses of the 14th and 15th centuries surrounding the green lawns of **Vicar's Close**.

Uttoxeter is the mecca for Midlands horse racing fans. This cheerful little market town (every Wednesday since 1309) hasthree different ways of pronouncing its name - 'Uxeter', 'Utcheter' or 'U-tox-eter' - and its name has been spelt in seventy-seven different ways since it was first recorded in the Domesday Book as Wotochesede. The town evidently suffers no neuroses and goes about its quiet business, waking up for market days and race meetings.

There is a tendency to think of the Peak District as belong exclusively to Derbyshire, but natural physical features have a distressing habit of ignoring man-made boundaries, and there is more than a little truth in the local boast that 'the best parts of Derbyshire are in Staffordshire'. This is fascinating countryside, almost cosy in scale one minute and then possessed of a wild grandeur, the next. North-east of Oakmoor, through the hills and dales, lies one of the most beautiful valleys in the region, The Manifold Valley. The village of **Ilam**, standing at the southern end, makes a good starting point for exploring the area, and the old mansion Ilam Hall, is now a Youth hostel. The valley is relatively flat at this point but becomes increasingly deep and narrow as one journeys northwards. The River Manifold has a disconcerting habit of disappearing underground and at Ilam Hall it re-emerges from its subterranean journey from Darfur Crags.

Obviously this beautiful area has long been a favourite with those who love what is described in the glossy-brochure trade as 'the great outdoors' even if writers of such hyperbole rarely get nearer to the fresh air than kicking the cat out last thing at night! Over three hundred years ago, two learned gentlemen, close friends and 'Brothers of the Angle' rambled the length and breadth of the glorious river valleys in pursuit of the shy brook trout. Izaak Walton and Charles Cotton could discuss the classical poetry of Homer or the merits of a fishing lure with equal facility and enthusiasm, and had a particular fondness for the river that runs down the border between Staffordshire and Derbyshire, the Dove. Cotton, who was to contribute a chapter on the art of fly-fishing in Walton's 'Compleat Angler' was a poet and author in his own right who lived at **Beresford Hall** near **Alstonfield**. The Hall was pulled down in the 1800's but the fishing lodge by the river still survives, and the village church still contains the Cotton family pew.

Longnor is a tiny market town in the farthermost corner of north-eastern Staffordshire on the same road the intrepid Greyhound rattled its way across the rutted potholes over the moors. The road may have improved, but Longnor is little altered; good looking 18th-century facades and a square with a small Market Hall dated 1873. Stone lined streets and alleyways with determined little houses of the same material give a sense of dogged continuity.

Wandering westwards one comes across the highest village in England, set close by the high road from Leek to Buxton. The oddly named **Flash** claims the title at 1,158 feet above sea level. A Nepalese would doubtless fall off his mountain laughing, but it is a respectable height for our 'sceptr'd isle' and probably just as cold in winter as the Himalayas.

'The Metropolis of the Moorland' was how one writer described **Leek**, though Doctor Johnson was not so charitable ' An old church but a poor town'. nowadays it is a neat mill town standing in magnificent countryside. Like so many of its kind Leek has a cheerful and generous nature and welcomes visitors; particularly on Wednesdays when the old cobbled market square is thronged with stalls and the air filled with cheerful banter. There are a surprisingly large number of antique shops and many of the mills have their own shops.

The great canal-builder, Brindley, started his working life as a mill-wright and the Brindley Mill in Mill Street, tells the story of his life and graphically demonstrates the many facets of this one, important craft. One of his later works was the Caldon Canal which runs with the River Chernet in the valley alongside the hillside of Cheddleton. Cheddleton Flint Mill ground up flints from Kent and Sussex for use in the pottery industry, and the waterwheels and grinding equipment are on display, together with other items associated with the trade, including a restored canal barge. The canal's successor, the railway, is also commemorated at the Cheddleton Railway Centre, with displays, mementoes, engines and other paraphernalia set in and around the attractive Victorian station.

The two different forms of transport were obviously of major importance to the development of the industries of the north-western sector of the county, Newcastle-under-Lyme and Stoke-on-Trent lie side by side, geographically close yet separate in terms of history and character.

Coming from the east, the first is **Stoke-on-Trent**, a combination of the six communities of Tunstall, Burslem, Hanley, Longton, Stoke and Fenton - known the world over as The Potteries. The companies based here, both large and small, have a world-wide market for their products and their heritage dates back many centuries. Wherever fine china-ware is used and appreciated, such as Spode, Copeland, Minton, Coalport, Royal Doulton and Wedgwood are revered and respected.

The Potteries have the flavour of a rural area; a feeling of continuity and a sense of tradition. The same family names crop up time and time again and, even in these difficult times, there is a pride in the past and has made enormous efforts to clean up the detritus of yesteryear and make Stoke an attractive place in which to work and live. Trentham Gardens cover 800 acres of parklands, gardens and lakes with numerous sporting facilities. Festival Park, is an amazing 23 acre complex which includes a sub-tropical aquatic playground with flumes, water slides and rapids.

The architecture is predominantly Victorian red-brick since the city was in a constant state of development, but there are exceptions; the Minton family brought over French artists to decorate their wares and built them ornate Italianate villas - their sense of geography being obviously inferior to their business acumen.

Newcastle-under-Lyme is the oldest of the two cities, dating backto its incorporation as a borough in 1180, at a time when the neighbouring Potteries were hamlets or villages. Although Stoke-on-Trent and Newcastle have grown into each other, they still retain their separate identities; the delicate craft of the Potteries being complemented by the ruder skills of the iron workers and colliers of their older neighbour. Modern Newcastle is an attractive town with much good architecture and is host to Keele University. Markets and a Fair date from medieval times.

Staffordshire is a little-known county of remarkable contrast, interest and beauty that will repay the curious a thousandfold.

WARWICKSHIRE

'This other Eden, demi-paradise, This fortress built by Nature for herself....'

These lines from Richard II conjure up images of a rural idyll and doubtless the beautiful countryside around Stratford-upon-Avon did much to inspire Warwickshire's most famous son. More than two centuries later, Shakespeare's affection for his native county was to be echoed in the words of the eminent novelist, Henry James, who described Warwickshire as 'the core and centre of the English world; mid-most England, unmitigated England... the genius of pastoral Britain'. James was an American and his words have done much to encourage his fellow countryman and women to visit this quintessentially English region Although the twentieth century has left its mark with evidence of industrialisation, the construction of motorways and some of the less appealing manifestations of the intensive tourist industry, there is still much of gentle grace and beauty beloved by both men; turn off the coach-laden main roads and one can enjoy pastoral scenery little changed since the Bard's day or, turning away from a modern shopping precinct, one can delight in architectural gems that would have been equally familiar to the great playwright and his contemporaries.

If Warwickshire can be described as the Heartland of England then the Avon must be its principal artery in that its waters have provided the means of irrigation, transport and power. **Stratford-upon-Avon** is without doubt the central tourist attraction of the county - perhaps of the entire country. Shakespeare may be synonymous with Stratford, but the town was of importance long before his birth (reputedly on St George's Day, 23rd April 1564) and had its beginnings as a Roman camp, and a Saxon monastic settlement. The name Stratford simply means 'a ford where the street crosses the river' and a market was first recorded in 1196. King John granted the right to hold a three-day fair in 1214 and in 1553 the town was incorporated as a borough and, regardless of Shakespeareama, Stratford is still an attractive and prosperous market town. The central part of the town which contains its chief attractions is arranged along the north bank of the Avon with three streets running parallel to the river and three at right angles, the names being unchanged since before Shakespeare's time. The predominant style of architecture is Tudor/Jacobean half-timbering, much of it genuine but with more than the occasional false facade; nevertheless the overall effect is pleasing and the town is an attraction in its own right.

Holy Trinity Church, lying beside the banks of the Avon, is an excellent place to start exploring the town, for it is a dignified and graceful building that reflects both the early importance and history of the town as well as being the last resting place of England's greatest dramatist. The proportions and spaciousness are almost cathedral-like and the church was granted collegiate status by Henry V in the year of Agincourt (1415) and remained as an important theological centre until the Reformation in the 16th century. Throughout the building there are numerous memorials to many local worthies and associations and the former Lady Chapel is almost entirely given over to the Cloptons who contributed much to the growth and development of Warwickshire and to Stratford-upon-Avon in particular. They, like many of their medieval neighbours, made their fortune from the wool-trade and Sir Hugh Clopton is doubly remembered for having built the multi-arched bridge upstream from Holy Trinity and for being a Lord Mayor of London in 1492.

William Shakespeare died at the age of fifty-two on St George's Day, April 23rd 1616 and is buried, along with his wife Anne and other members of his family, in the chancel, and every year, on the anniversary of his death, the whole area around the tomb is covered with floral tributes from all over the world. We sometimes forget how great a man he was and just how much his works are appreciated throughout the world; he would not be forgotten even if he had been buried in an unmarked grave and perhaps this is best summed up by the epitaph written by his friend and contemporary, Ben Jonson:

> '*Thou art a monument without a tomb,*
> *And art alive still, while thy book doth live,*
> *And we have wits to read, and praise to give.*'

At the age of eighteen Shakespeare married Anne Hathaway and it is believed he earned his living at this time as a schoolmaster although a year or so later after his marriage he left for London. However he was to return to Stratford at regular intervals and, with the prospering of his fortunes, he purchased **New Place** in 1597 and twelve years later settled there permanently with his family. That the house no longer exists is ascribed to the fact that a later owner, the Reverend Francis Gaskell, irritated by the rating assessments and constant pestering by Shakesperean enthusiasts was moved to pull down the entire house! That there is nothing new about the pressures that can be caused by tourism is evidenced by the fact that the demolition took place in 1759. The foundations have been preserved together with a beautifully re-created Elizabethan garden. The entrance is by way of **Nash's House**, once the home of Thomas Nash, who married Shakespeare's grand-daughter, and now containing what is effectively the town museum.

Quite rightly, Stratford-upon-Avon is home to the **Royal Shakespeare Theatre**. Originally known as the Memorial Theatre, it was designed by Miss Elizabeth Scott, a niece of the great Victorian architect Sir Gilbert Scott, and was opened by Edward, Prince of Wales in 1932. Considered controversial and innovativewhen first built, it stands massively beside the river and is a wonderful place to spend an evening being entertained by one of the greatest companies in the world. In the **Bancroft Gardens**, adjacent to the theatre is the impressive Shakespeare Monument, cast from sixty-five tons of bronze which shows the dramatist seated on a plinth surrounded by four of his principal characters (Hamlet, Lady Macbeth, Falstaff and Prince Hal.) Also in close proximity to the theatre are the **Other Place**, a small intimate theatre which presents a wide range of drama, and the **Black Swan Inn**, a favourite theatrical haunt that is better known as the Dirty Duck.

On the whole the town copes well with its immense number of visitors and has developed an infrastructure that operates extremely efficiently but it should be appreciated that Stratford-upon-Avon is perhaps the country's premier tourist attraction. A little planning will pay dividends in enabling you to enjoy your visit and the **Tourist Information Centre** at **Bridgefoot**, Stratford-upon-Avon (Tel: 01789293127) can provide considerable help and advice including details of guided tours.

Kenilworth will always haunt me because of the extraordinary and impressive sight of tall windows rising beside a massive fireplace in the ruins of the 14th-century Great Hall of Kenilworth Castle. Looking at it my imagination runs riot and I see the arrival of Queen Elizabeth I and her entourage to attend a lavish banquet in her honour. The whole castle would have been alive and busy. No doubt Her Majesty and her followers would have to be housed and their individual staffs cared for. On one occasion she stayed fifteen days. Quite wonderful. You will see the red-sandstone castle keep standing four-square on a grassy slope, aloof from the bustling market town below, serene in its own world. Though its towers are crumbling and its windows as blank as sightless eyes, it still retains the imposing strength and grandeur that made it one of England's chief strongholds in Norman times.

Approach it on foot across the causeway that leads from the car park on the south side and you will see that much of the castle's outer wall still stands. Beyond it is the Norman Keep standing dignified and alone, separated from the ravages of war, time and weather from the buildings added to it in later centuries. Only the walls remain of th great banqueting hall built by John of Gaunt in the 14th century and little more of the buildings added by Robert Dudley, Earl of Leicester in the 16th century.

The castle has not been lived in since the Restoration and the best preserved parts are Dudley's gatehouse, which was designed to impress distinguished visitors and still impresses with its tall corner towers and battlemented parapets. Then there are the stables built of dressed stone with a timbered upper storey. The Roundheads held the castle during the Civil War and destroyed the keep's north wall after the war.

Shipston-on-Stour dating from Saxon times has the flavour of other days about it. The streets are lined wih houses and inns of the Georgian period built when the woollen industry made Shipston a more prosperous place than now. It is charming withweathered roofs of Cotswold tiles, quaint little dormers and handsome doorways with old brass knockers. I came here to visit the **George Hotel** which dates back to the 15th century and a fireplace in the Front lobby dates to 1508. Queen Victoria stayed here before she became Queen and in more recent times it has been the haunt of famous racing people, actors and writers including George Bernard Shaw.

The Grand Union Canal and the River Avon make their way through **Royal Leamington Spa**, whose tree-lined avenues, riverside walks and wealth of handsomely proportioned architecture are laid out in a grid pattern. Named after the River Leam, a tributary of the Avon, Leamington (or Leamington Priors as it was then known.) was little more than a hamlet until the beginning of the 19th century when the fame of curative powers of the local spring-water became more widely known. Speculators and developers created the town we see today at the most astonishing speed; some idea of the rapid development that took place may be gained from the fact that in 1801 there were 315 inhabitants and yet by 1841 there were 13,000! As the town rapidly expanded, the rich and fashionable flocked in to see and be seen, to promenade, to take the waters and indulge in entertainments. One writer declared the town to be the 'King of Spas' and Queen Victoria, shortly after coming to the throne in 1837, granted the prefix 'Royal'. The locals must have been somewhat bemused since the original use for the salty waters was for seasoning meat and curing rabid dogs! Although the town has expanded further since the 19th century, much of the architectural interest has been retained around the centre and the original source of prosperity, the spring water, can still be sampled at the **Royal Pump Room and Baths**. This elegant building designed in the classical style with a colonnade, was first opened in 1814; the waters are described as being a mild aperient (a polite word for laxative), and 'particularly recommended in cases of gout, chronic and muscular rheumatism, lumbago, sciatica, inactivity of the liver and the digestive system, anaemia, chlorisis and certain skin disorders'.

The town is blessed with many parks and gardens, perhaps the best known being **The Jephson Gardens** whose entrance lodge faces the Pump Room. Originally planned as an arboretum, these spacious gardens contain mature specimens of many unusual trees together with magnificent floral displays, a lake and two fountains modelled on those at Hampton Court. The gardens were named after Dr Henry Jephson who did much to promote the curative effects of the waters as well as much Charitable work.

Warwickshire is a wonderful county - enjoy it.

HEART OF ENGLAND

WEST MIDLANDS

It seems only fitting that the West Midlands, like so many of its products, should be of modern invention, being an amalgamation of the most heavily industrialised areas of Staffordshire, Warwickshire and Worcestershire. Created in 1974, the region covers an area of 347 square miles and incorporates the cities of Coventry and Birminghams with a population in the millions.

It is an area preoccupied with production, effectively createdby the Industrial Revolution and vastly expanded by the insatiable demands of Empire. It has been touched by the dread hands of War and Recession, yet continues to thrive, producing goods and providing services that are in demand all over the world. Thousands of its acres have disappeared under industrial and suburban sprawl and it is soil scarred and riven by roads, motorways, canals, mines and railways, yet there is still much of beauty and a great deal of value. It can be both depressing and inspiring but if the poet's vision of the 'Heart of England' referred to the rural charm and historical assets of neighbouring Warwickshire then the West Midlands is where the pulse can be felt.

Droitwich in the south west of the region, was probably a Roman centre for the salt and mineral trade which was well developed by the time of the Domesday Book. The town lies on the western side of the M5 and the production of salt continued until quite recently. It was in the 1830's that John Corbett, the Droitwich Salt-King rose to prominence by modernising and developing the salt-mines and workings, particularly around **Stoke Prior** where he achieved the astonishing feat of turning the annual output of salt from 26,000 tons to 200,000 tons. Very much a man of his period, he had started life as the son of a bargee and at the peak of success controlled a vast empire. He built himself an ornate home, now an delightful hotel, the **Chateau Impney**. He was an enlightened employer providing his workers with gardens, schools, a dispensary and cottages.

The many rivers, streams and canals that vein the entire Midland region mean that angling is one of the most popular local past-times and **Redditch** has been providing fish hooks for generations, as well as many other items of fishing tackle. The hooks are a natural adjunct to the town's chief industry and claim to fame, that of being the headquarters of the needle-making industry, indeed **The National Needle Museum** is situated here.

Between **Bromsgrove** and **Kidderminster** lies the pretty village of **Chaddesley Corbett** with its fine timbered houses and church dedicated to St Cassian, a schoolmaster who was condemned to death by his own pupils! The building is a good example of 14th-century architecture on an earlier base and has a handsome 12th-century carved font. Nearby are **Chaddesley Woods** with nature trail and reserve and **Harvington Hall**, a late medieval moated manor house which has a number of ingenious priestholes.

Weaving and carpet-making built up the wealth of **Kidderminster** and the industry continues to this day. I do not know whether this trade is particularly renowned for its friendly spirit but certainly the town's good natured atmosphere is as tangible today as it was over two hundred years ago when one John Brecknall established a charity to provide every child or unmarried person living in Church Street with a plum cake every Midsummer's Eve.

Stourport-on-Severn is unusual in that it is almost entirely a product of the Industrial Revolution, and an attractive one at that. The canal systems of the Midlands were the fore-runners of the Victorian's railway networks and our own motorways, opening up the country's industrial centres to national andinternational trade and Stourport was created as a 'new town' around the point where the Staffordshire-Worcestershire canal ran into the River Severn. Neat rows of cottages were built tidily around the central basin, which is almost an inland port, and the town still has a pleasant late-Georgian feel to it, although it has grown considerably since the days when the hard-working and often hard-driving bargees would gather to exchange cargoes, swap horses and gossip.

A couple of miles to the north-west lies **Bewdley** which also contains many fine Georgian houses but also architecture of earlier periods. It also rose to prosperity because of water-born traffic but that of the pre-canal era utilising the natural facilities of the River Severn in the 15th and 16th centuries. It was also a centre for weaving, manufacturing saltpeter, brass, horn goods, and cap-making (apparently this trade was so important that at one time the citizens of Bewdley were compelled to wear caps on pain of a fine). The image of grime, poverty and pollution in the Midlands may be out-moded now but it has a basis in truth and particularly applied to that area known as the Black Country, banded by **Wolverhampton** to the north and **Stourbridge** to the south and so-called because of the region's numerous open-cast coal mines and smoke-belching factories. Thomas Carlyle, visiting in 1824 described it as; '...a frightful scene...a dense cloud of pestilential smoke hangs over it forever.. and at night the whole region burns like a volcano spitting fire from a thousand tubes of brick. But oh the wretched thousands of mortals who grind out their destiny there!' Paradoxically, from this vision of hell on earth came skills and objects of beauty that were to be admired and coveted the world over and a tough, warm hearted people proud of their heritage. The mining has gone, along with the old style furnaces but many of the skills, trades and industries survive albeit in a cleaner more efficient, and pleasant surroundings. Stourbridge was, and still is, a great centre for the glass-making industry. Familiar names such as Royal Brierley, Stuart and Thomas Webb still produce glassware of the finest quality. To see how glass is made and the incredible standards and varieties that are available, go and visit the **Broadfield House Glass Museum** in **Kingswinford**. The factories themselves welcome visitors and I particularly enjoyed the Stuart Crystal factory with its amazing glass cone; a brick structure like an elongated beehive which housed the furnaces and the glass-makers.

As with so much of the region, canals played a large part in the growth of industry and the **Stourbridge Branch Canal and Wharf** is worth visiting to see the old restored Bonded warehouses and canal company offices and also to take a trip on one of the boats.

Industrial, political and social history all combine at **Dudley** in the heart of the Black Country, together with varied architecture and attractions. The ruined castle, standing on a wooden rise above the busy industrial town, dates back to the 11th century although the basic structure that we can see today is principally 14th century. **Dudley Castle** has had a checkered history and was first destroyed in 1175 when the then owner madethe tactical error of backing Prince Henry in the revolt against his father, Henry II. A century later, rebuilding began but proceeded slowly; one of the reasons being the unpopularity of the bullying and dishonest John de Somery, whose forcible taxations and reluctance to settle debts led to a natural disinclination on the part of the locals to help with construction. The Dudley family took over during the reign of Henry VIII, but John Dudley followed in the footsteps of his predecessor by backing Lady Jane Grey for the throne and paid the supreme penalty. The family fortunes, like those of the castle, must have declined somewhat for in 1585 a report was submitted that the castle was unfit for Mary, Queen of Scots to visit - and she was a prisoner at the time! The massive ruins still stand and are well worth a visit especially as they are now part of the well known **Dudley Zoo**.

You should make the effort to visit the **Black Country Museum** at Tipton Road. An open-air site, it is essentially a reconstruction of a 19th century Black Country village complete with canal, mine, houses and factories where all the skills and crafts are demonstrated. Its authenticity can be judged from the fact that special permission had to be sought to contravene the regulations of the Clean Air Act so that cottages could burn coal!

Working museums are always fascinating with their emphasis on ancient skills and crafts and to the north-east of the Black Country can be found at the **Walsall Leather Centre Museum**. Leather working developed alongside the specialist metal trades in stirrups, bits, buckles and spurs with hides being provided by the sheep and cattle of Shropshire anbd Warwickshire and bark for tanning coming from the surrounding oak forests. Saddlery and tack manufacture are still local trades to this day, surviving amongst the more high-tec industries of the 20th century. **Walsall** is proud of its past and possesses a charter dating from the early 13th century and yet has always taken a progressive and enlightened approach to its own affairs, having been one of the first towns in the country to have its own police force, library and cottage hospital.

As I drove south to **Birmingham** I reflected on the facilities offered by **The National Exhibition Centre, The International Convention Centre and The National Indoor Arena**. These impressive and still expanding buildings are equipped to the highest standards and play host to a multitude of events as diverse as opera, international athletics and Cruft's Dog Show as well as numerous conferences and trade shows which attract several million people a year representing some 95 countries! Nevertheless these massive centres are not alone and it is typical of Birmingham's ability to react to market demand that numerous other conference venues are available from five-star hotels to stately homes, together with an impressive infrastructure that covers everything necessary, such as accommodation, travel, leisure facilities and marketing. Perhaps more than any other skill, it is this ability in the market place that has brought Birmingham from being a 'vill of ten adults and value at £1' in 1086 to to-day's priceless 65,000 acre metropolis of one million inhabitants.

The city is constantly changing and intensely alive so it is difficult to know where to start in order to give you some idea of this vibrant place. Perhaps the best place is the **Birmingham Museum of Science and Industry** in Newhall Street which amongst many other fascinating exhibits features the world's oldest working steam engine. For an insight into an early example of mass-production allied to social concern (plus a thoroughly enjoyable time) visit **Cadbury World** at **Bournville** - a must for every chocoholic! Old skills still relevant today can be seen in the **Jewellery Quarter** in Hockley whilst the network of canals provide a unique opportunity to explore the many waterways that wander through the city - Brum has more miles of canals than Venice!

The rural area lying between Birmingham and Coventry is well worth exploring containing a number of villages and small towns of interest such as **Knowle**, with its timbered buildings, Guildhall and church with beautifully carved chancel screen. **Temple Balsall** is a unique and historic hamlet which owes its origins to the Knights Templars, a religious order of knights who fought in the Crusades. They are remembered in the lovely 13th-century church which reflects much of the pageantry of those long-past times and in the village's name whilst charity and kindness of a later period is marked by the almshouses that were founded in 1670 by Lady Katherine Leveson. **Hampton-in-Arden**, a mile or so to the north, slopes down to the River Blythe, where there is a fine pack horse bridge built for salt-traders. The village has connections with Shakespeare, being the setting for 'As You Like It' and with the Peel family; Sir Robert Peel (1788-18750) founded the Metropolitan Police Force and was twice prime minister.

The region's second city is **Coventry** and although smaller than Birmingham is much older, originating in the 7th century. It was the centre of the old cloth-weaving industry from the 14th to the 17th century, was the fourth city in England in importance and from its iron-worker's skills developed the engineeering expertise which led it to become the centre of the British motor industry. The city's proud past was very nearly wiped out on November 14th 1940, when German bombers destroyed 40 acres of the city centre, killing or wounding 1500 inhabitants. The fire-gutted ruins of St Michael's Cathedral remains as a moving memorial and a charred cross made from the remains of two oak beams was set up in the ruined church with the words 'Father Forgive' inscribed on the wall behind. Immediately adjacent is the new cathedral designed by Sir Basil Spence and consecrated in 1962. It contains works by Graham Sutherland, John Piper, Jacob Epstein and many others and the whole is a moving testimony to the faith and optimism of the people of Coventry.

Re-building of the city centre began shortly after the war and the occasion was marked by the erection of a statue to one of Coventry's earliest notable citizens, Lady Godiva, who is best remembered for having ridden naked through the streets in order to persuade her husband, Leofric, to reduce the heavy taxes that he had imposed upon the townsfolk. History records that Leofric relented but I doubt that today's Inland Revenue would take much notice!

Although the city centre is now a bustling modern development some notable remnants of the city's medieval past escaped the Blitz and are well worth a visit. **The Guildhall** contains some splendid glass, wonderful carvings, the Arras tapestry and a minstrel's gallery with a display of medieval armour. Mary, Queen of Scots was once incarcerated in its tower. **Bond's Hospital** and **Ford's Hospital** are both 16th-century almshouses and are still used as such while **Spon Street** is a re-constructed medieval cul-de-sac with ancient houses enjoying a new lease of life as shops and galleries. The 14th-century **Whitefriar's Gate** is a renovated Carmelite friary housing a number of exhibitions including a charming **Toy Museum**. The immediate past has not been forgotten and in Hales Street can be found the **Museum of British Road Transport**, which includes the Land Speed record holder, Thrust II, while at nearby **Baginton** there is the **Midlands Air Museum**.

One of our greatest novelists who made much use of this area of the Midlands in her books was Marian Evans (1819-80), better known under her pen-name of George Eliot. She was born north of Coventry at **Nuneaton** where her father was steward at nearby **Arbury Hall**, a fine example of Gothick Revival built onto an earlier Elizabethan house and with a porch and stables that were designed by Sir Christopher Wren. There are fine landscaped gardens and the stables are now home to **the Pinkerton Collection of Cycles and Motorcycles.**

Tamworth, once capital of the ancient Saxon Kingdom of Mercia is a pleasant town with some attractive architecture but surrounded by modern development; nevertheless the town is well worth visiting, particularly for its splendid castle. The predecessors of **Tamworth Castle** were destroyed by the Danes in 874 and 943AD but the present structure has stood firm since Norman times and, apart from the odd ghost, has an almost homely feel about it! A Jacobean manor house was built within the circular keep and occupation has been continuous until recent times. There is now a museum in the castle and the attractive grounds are open to the public and include a garden for the blind and disabled.

Tamworth is like so much of the region with modern development and ancient heritage happily co-existing; forward-looking yet concerned with the older values of a caring and friendly society. The West Midlands is continually evolving to meet the challenges of tomorrow whilst acknowledging the traditions and achievments of the past.

HOTELS, INNS, RESTAURANTS AND COUNTRY HOUSES

THE SHOULDER OF MUTTON
16 Main Street,
Barton under Needwood
Tel: 01283 712568   Fax: 01283 716349

Barton-under-Needwood is a charming village in the heart of the Staffordshire countryside, just off the A38 and near to the canal. In its midst is The Shoulder of Mutton, a much loved village inn, used regularly by place in which strangers are rapidly made to feel at home. The building is old, dating back to the 17th century and it is full of character. Oak beams, old pictures and memorabilia decorate the walls. It is comfortable and unpretentious; somewhere to relax, enjoy a pint of real ale or select a glass of wine from th list, have some good conversation and tuck into a delicious meal that will delight your taste buds and do no harm to your bank balance. This is a pub to visit all the year round, but in summer the children occupy themselves safely in the new Smugglers Cove play area, whilst you relish a glass of chilled white wine. The menu has many familiar dishes and you can eat here seven days a week either at lunchtimes or in the evenings (except Sunday evenings). The chef changes the menu monthly and there are always two or three dishes on the daily special board. All the dishes are served with fresh vegetables and prepared to order. Vegetarian dishes are included in the menu, there is also a children's menu.

USEFUL INFORMATION

OPEN; Mon-Thurs 11-3pm & 5.30-11pm. Fri/Sat;11-11pm. Sun:12-3pm&7-10.30pm.
CHILDREN; Welcome. Skittle alley.
CREDIT CARDS;No credit card
ACCESS;Yes
GARDEN; Garden with tables,
FOOD; Excellent, familiar home-Cooked dishes
VEGETARIAN; Catered for
DISABLED
LICENSED;Yes
ACCOMMODATION; chair/benches.

FRESHMANS RESTAURANT,
Church Hill, Belbroughton DY9 0DT
Tel: 01562 730467

Freshmans

Adjacent to Belbroughton Church, Freshmans has a unique quality achieved through the talents of Annette Wheatley and her daughter Rebecca Bodsworth. They have an undoubted flair which has turned this once, village workhouse and coaching inn, into one of the most charming restaurants in the county. One can never forget, nor would wish to do so, the age of thebuilding with its sturdy oak beams. Everywhere glistens with the patina of age and the sparkling crystal hardware. An abundance of fresh flowers decorate the intimate split-level dining rooms and it is here that you will discover why Freshmans has such a high reputation. Both mother and daughter are inspired cooks and the delightful style of cooking is based on the use of the freshest market ingredients, frequently resulting in imaginative and unusual flavours. Immense attention to detail adds the finishing touches to dishes which may be the simplest of fresh lobster salads, or fresh supreme oysters, simply flash fried in a subtle garlic butter, placed inside its shell with a topping of Mozzarella cheese and herb breadcrumbs and grilled. There are exciting sauces and interesting vegetables and puddings that will destroy any idea of dieting! There are often daily specialities, particularly fish, on offer as well. The wine is excellent with a good, honest French house wine from £10. Other wines are also sensibly priced. A wonderful place to be and somewhere in which weddings and special occasions are a speciality for up to 80 covers if needs be.

USEFUL INFORMATION

OPEN; Lunch: Tuesday-Friday; Dinner Tuesday to Saturday. Booking essential.
CHILDREN; Welcome.
CREDIT CARDS; All major credit cards.
RESTAURANT; Delightful. Wonderful Food. Daily specialities
VEGETARIAN; Several dishes
DISABLED ACCESS; Yes
LICENSED; Yes

THE LONGMYND HOTEL
Church Stretton SY6 6AG
Tel:01694 722244 Fax: 01694 722718

The South Shropshire Hills are renowned as ideal walking country and Church Stretton is a popular centre for exploring well known local features such as Carding Mill Valley, Wenlock Edge and the Stretton Hills. Many other places of outstanding interest such as Ludlow, Shrewsbury, Ironbridge and Clun are within easy reach by car. This makes all the more reason for staying at The Longmynd Hotel in Church Stretton. It is set in 10 acres of private woodland, high in the lovely breathtaking South Shropshire Hills and overlooks the old market town as well as commanding panoramic views across the Welsh Border landscape. This 3 star hotel is family run and the resident proprietors together with their excellent and experienced staff ensure high standards of service - something that is frequently missing in group owned establishments. The hotel has Honeymoon and Luxury Suites and 50 bedrooms all with private bathroom,central heating, video and satellite TV, direct-dial telephone as well as tea and coffee making facilities. There is a passenger lift to all floors. Also available for a family holiday or mini-break are 1 and 2 bedroom luxury, self-catering Cottages in the hotel grounds, offering accommodation for up to 6 persons. All guests have membership of the Leisure Club. The food is outstanding. There are two charming restaurants and snacks are available at the bar. The Longmynd also provides the ideal venue for a wide variety of functions from Wedding receptions to a Conference Centre for up to 100 delegates with an office and secretarial capacity if required. There is parking for over 100 cars.

USEFUL INFORMATION

OPEN; Every day, all day.
CHILDREN;Welcome
CREDIT CARDS; All major cards
LICENSED;Yes
ACCOMMODATION:50 ensuite rooms
Leisure & Conference facilities

RESTAURANT;Charming restaurants
BAR FOOD;Snacks available
VEGETARIAN; Daily choice
DISABLED ACCESS;Yes
GARDEN;10 acres of woodlands
PETS;Yes. £2per night per dog

THE PLOUGH AT CLAVERLEY
Aston Lane,
Claverley,
Nr Wolverhampton.
Tel: 01746 710365

Sometimes it is hard to realise that the busy industrial Wolverhampton is only a little way from the delightful village of Claverley, surrounded by beautiful Shropshire countryside and home to a host of charming half-timbered cottages as well as the excellent Plough Inn. It is a marvellous centre for those who enjoy walking. The River Severn flows its majestic way through picturesque Bridgnorth just 4 miles away. The Plough was constructed in the 18th century largely from reclaimed ships timbers. It has an open fire with a heavy copper canopy and many brasses which catch the reflection of the roaring fire whichever way you turn. Someone here at sometime must have had a keen interest in foreign travel for there is one of the biggest collections of foreign currency that you will see in the county. The Plough is a happy pub owned and run by David and Irene O'Gorman. Their pleasant personalities are echoed by the friendliness of the attentive staff. The large lounge bar has cosy alcoves where you can enjoy the various tempting dishes on the menu, perhaps with a glass of Traditional Ale, wine, or if you prefer freshly made coffee. Adjoining this is a Children's room. The ever changing menu has many favourite dishes on it including a super Beef and Guinness Pie. There are tender steaks, fresh fish and a good selection of the popular daily 'specials'including Vegetarian options. The home-made sweets are certain to tempt those with a sweet tooth.

USEFUL INFORMATION

OPEN; 12-3pm & 7-11pm
Sun:12-3pm & 7-10.30pmlunches & party
CHILDREN; Children's room
CREDIT CARDS; Access/Visa
VEGETARIAN;At least 2 original dishes
LICENSED; Full Licence
ACCOMMODATION;Not applicable

RESTAURANT; Open for Sunday
bookings at other times
BAR FOOD; Imaginative, freshly Prepared.
DISABLED ACCESS; Easy access
GARDEN; Large garden with swings & seats. Larger parties (25-40) catered for by special arrangement in the Barn Restaurant.

THE RED HART INN,
Kington, Flyford Flavell
Worcestershire
Tel: 01386 792221.

Situated in the village of Kington, the inn is wonderfully situated for anyone wanting to enjoy the countryside roundabout and is in easy reach of the Cotswolds, the Vale of Evesham and the Malvern Hills. You will find it on the A422, halfway between Worcester and Stratford-upon-Avon. The pub is over 400 years old and much of the original black and white building remains, together with a tasteful extension built in, which is in total harmony with its ancient counterpart. Over the years it has become known as 'The Sportsmans Pub' because of its great cricketing connections. Regular 'Sportsmans' lunches are held here and you are very likely to find a well known sporting personality or two in the bar who have just popped in to visit 'Drinkers', the landlord, David Drinkwater, who played for the World International Wanderers. It is a fascinating place and you will get as much pleasure in looking at all the bits and pieces of cricketing memorabilia and a substantial number of fishing rods, as you will in partaking of the excellent food and drink. The A La Carte restaurant seats 50 and there is a comfortable lounge area with a bar where 40-45 people can be seated. The new banquetingsuite is used for all sorts of purposes including the Sunday Carvery Lunch, wedding receptions etc. From Easter to September breakfast and a super afternoon tea are available. It is one of the happiest pubs to be found.

USEFUL INFORMATION

OPEN; 11-2.30pm & 6-11pm Longer Easter to September. Easter-Sept Breakfast & Teas
CHILDREN; Welcome
CREDIT CARDS; Access/Visa.
LICENSED; Yes
ACCOMMODATION; No. Banqueting facilities

RESTAURANT; A la Carte & Sunday Carvery
BAR FOOD; Wide range
VEGETARIAN; Daily choice
DISABLED ACCESS; Yes + toilet
GARDEN; Large garden with wooden Tables and chairs

IL MAGO

28 Cobridge Road,
Hanley, Stoke-on-Trent
Tel: 01782 274644.

Il Mago is an imaginative delightful restaurant in the heart of the Potteries just out of Hanley town centre. It is easily accessible from the M6 and is situated on the A53 road from Newcastle to Leek opposite the Festival Park. Formerly a pub, Il Mago was transformed into this exciting restaurant by its present owners some ten years ago. It has a wonderful, traditional Continental ambience which beguiles you into relaxation in readiness for a superb meal. An aperitif in the Reception Bar whilst you study the menu gives you time to soak up the atmosphere. The choice is difficult because it is all so tempting. Only fresh produce is used. There is a large selection of fresh fish, prime meats and an extensive selection of fresh, hand-made pastas which are made on the premises by their own chefs. Vegetarian Dishes are also available. The choice is yours.

USEFUL INFORMATION

OPEN; Mon-Sat: Lunch 12-2pm Dinner from 7pm.
CHILDREN; Children welcome.
CREDIT CARDS; Visa/Access/Master/Amex.
LICENSED; Yes

RESTAURANT; Traditional Continental
VEGETARIAN; Several dishes
DISABLED ACCESS; Level access Step to toilet
ACCOMMODATION; None

THE HANMER ARMS
Hanmer, Nr. Whitchurch,
Shropshire SY13 3DE
Tel: 01948 830532 Fax: 01948 830740

Lovely, typically English village which geographically is in Wales. It is peaceful and friendly with The Hanmer Arms central to the village and set in the shadow of St Chads Church. Always thought of as a village inn but has 26 traditionally designed ensuite apartments, most of which have been converted from the original farm buildings, and are situated around a cobbled courtyard. Welcoming village bar, excellent Restaurant with views to the west of the Berwyn Mountain Range, and to the north to the Cheshire Plains. The Bar also provides for the service of Morning Coffee, Lunch, Afternoon Tea and Light Snacks.

USEFUL INFORMATION

OPEN; All day, every day.
CHILDREN; Welcome
CREDIT CARDS; Access/Visa /Amex.
LICENSED; Yes
ACCOMMODATION; 26 Ensuite rooms
Price Band: B-C

RESTAURANT; Super food
BAR FOOD; Wide range
EGETARIAN; Daily selection
DISABLED ACCESS; Yes 2 bedrooms for Disabled

THE COTTAGE OF CONTENT
Carey,
Nr. Horwithy,
Herefordshire
Tel: 01432 840242

With a name like The Cottage of Content who could resist trying to find it? You would not be disappointed. It is in the heart of the country between Ross-on-Wye and Hereford, very near the M50 and conveniently situated for anyone wanting a meal, a drink or accommodation, before or after exploring some of the finest country and interesting tourist attractions in the vicinity. It is reached down a winding lane, which opens slightly to reveal the beauty of this lovely old pub. Surrounded by beautiful gardens and an attractive patio, it is wonderful to drink outside on a summer's day. Inside it is full of 'olde worlde' character with oak beams and an open fire, which throws out a welcoming warmth in the cold winter months. In the years that the Cottage of Content has been a pub it has given thousands of people refreshment and great pleasure. It is doubtful if anyone ever left here discontented. The traditions of the past are continued today, with a landlord and his staff working so well together, that the pub exudes friendliness.

The food is renowned and is the creation of an imaginative chef who does not adhere to any particular theme but produces dishes from around the world, some exotic, some simple. The Cottage of Content has always been famous for its home-made pies and these do feature regularly - there would be an outcry if they did not! A large Blackboard announces the 'Daily Special's which change constantly,and are delicious and sensibly priced.

USEFUL INFORMATION

OPEN; Mon-Sat 12-2.30pm & 7-11.30pm
CHILDREN; Permitted
CREDIT CARDS;; Visa/Access
LICENSED; Full Licence
ACCOMMODATION; 4 ensuite rooms
GARDEN; Lovely garden, patio, tables.

RESTAURANT; Not applicable
BAR FOOD; Innovative & international
Home-made pies a speciality
VEGETARIAN; 2-3 dishes daily
DISABLED ACCESS; Yes

THE BULL INN,
The Village Green,
Inkberrow, Worcestershire
Tel: 01386 792233/793090.

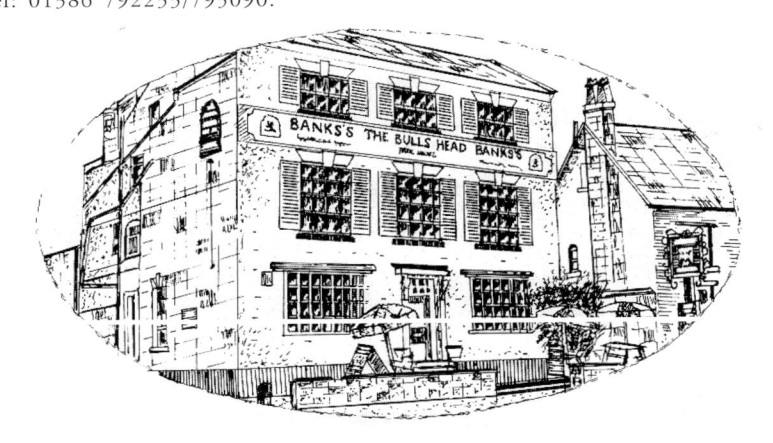

Situated in the very heart of Worcestershire countryside, Inkberrow is very well known by the many 'Archers' listeners as being the basis for the village of Ambridge. In its main street opposite the village green is an old pub, The Bulls Head Inn which offers everything a traditional should. Real log fires glow in the Inglenook fireplaces, original 14th-flagstone floors gleam with the patina of age and there are a wealth of exposed beams. The cosy, well furnished bars open their arms in welcome, and the well appointed table areas tempt you to sample some of the items on the extensive Bar Food and Restaurant Menus. This is a family run business with Sarah and Garry Cant at the helm assisted by their friendly staff. If you stay here you will find the bedrooms all have en-suite facilities, colour TV and tea/coffee making equipment. You will come down in the morning after an excellent night's sleep to a classic English breakfast which is included in the tariff. The Bulls Head Inn is only 15 minutes from Stratford-Upon-Avon and Worcester, within minutes of Ragley Hall and Coughton Court and many other places of interest. It is ideally placed for a day at the races. The menu at The Bulls Head Inn is both exciting and traditional with much of the produce being sourced locally from the Vale of Evesham as well as local cheesemakers, game dealers and established butchers. The food personally cooked and supervised by the owners, is the best you will taste anywhere. Children are most welcome and the traditionally served Sunday Lunch allows you to remain at your table and be truly pampered. Why stay at home to eat?

USEFUL INFORMATION

OPEN; All day April-September.
11-3pm & 5-11pm Sept-April
CHILDREN; Welcome
CREDIT CARDS; Access/Visa/Master/ Euro
LICENSED; Yes
ACCOMMODATION; Ensuite rooms

RESTAURANT; Home-cooked
BAR FOOD; Wide range
VEGETARIAN; Several dishes
DISABLED ACCESS; Yes
GARDEN; Fenced garded
Tree house etc

WALTER DE CANTELUPE INN,
Main Road,
Kempsey, Worcester
Tel: 01905 820572

Just by the village Post Office and set back from the busy A38, one of the most used holiday and tourist routes in the country, the Walter de Cantelupe brings not only a colourful name but a wonderful array of various hues in the hanging baskets and window boxes that adorn the outside of the building. The history of the village is fascinating going back to 1237-1266 when Walter de Cantelupe was Bishop of Worcester and chose to live in Kempsey. It was he who helped Simon de Montfort, Earl of Leicester to cross the River Severn at Kempsey. He discovered that the ford was unguarded and under cover of darknedd he led de Montfort and his 5,000 troops across the river. The following morning, August 3rd 1265, the Bishop said Mass in the church for the troops before they left for Evesham expecting to be joined by reinforcements. This was not to be, Royalist Troops led by Prince Edward defeated them. Simon de Montfort was killed and his men massacred. Bishop Cantelupe fled but was captured, excommunicated and deprived of office. The interior of the pub is delightfully furnished with antiques some of which come from India. The bar is one large area and from it French windows lead to a paved hidden garden, which is wonderful on a balmy summer's night. The inn is a joy to visit and the food lives up to the high standards set by Martin Lloyd-Morris, the proprietor. Everything is fresh, home-made and good to eat.

USEFUL INFORMATION

OPEN ;Easter-Mid-October 10am-11pm.
October-April 10am-3pm & 5.30pm-11pm.
CHILDREN;Welcome.
CREDIT CARDS;Access/Visa
LICENSED;Yes
ACCOMMODATION;No
RESTAURANT;No
BAR FOOD;High standard
VEGETARIAN:Yes
DISABLED ACCESS:Easy access
GARDEN:Hidden Garden

THE SWAN INN,
Letton,
Hereford
Tel:01544 327304.

Ten miles out of Hereford, cottages. The main rooms are heated by open log fires or wood burning stoves, which add to the warmth of the hospitality that is outstanding. The owners, Mike and Julia Boardman and her mother, Joyce Chapman, universally known as 'Mother' have that indefinable touch which makes people feel at home. There are two comfortable bedrooms, one en-suite and the other with exclusive use of a bathroom and each with tea/coffee making facilities - please note the milk is always fresh, so much nicer than the plastic abominations. There are also facilities for Camping and Caravans main route between Hereford and Brecon, you will find Letton, a charming spot with the 17th-century Swan Inn in a short row of picturesque black including hard standing electric hook-ups. Simple, reasonably priced food is available throughout opening hours. The menu is varied and changes daily - usually depending on the whim of Mike who does all the cooking. You may find yourself choosing an exotic Indian dish or the simpler delight of a delicious rabbit pie made with shortcrust pastry that melts in the mouth. Home-made soups are a meal in themselves or you may settle just for a pot of tea. Games for children and a Caravan Club CL for 5 caravans are also available.

USEFUL INFORMATION

OPEN;Mon/Tues: 11-3pm & 6-11pm Wed/Sat:11-11pm. Sun: 12-3pm & 7-10.30pm.
CHILDREN;Welcome
CREDIT CARDS;No credit cards
LICENSED;Yes
ACCOMMODATION;Caravans & Camping

RESTAURANT;Not applicable
BAR FOOD;Simple or exotic
VEGETARIAN;Daily choice
DISABLED ACCESS:One low step
GARDEN:Yes.Fishing in area

THE TWO BOATS
Southam Road,
Long Itchington, Nr Rugby.
Tel: 01926 812640

Canals have a great deal of fascination for most people and to find a pub where you can sit outside in the summertime watching all the waterway activity is most people's idea of heaven. The Two Boats, a Free House, is just such a pub. Owned by Alex Mckerlie and Richard Wormell, two very professional men, this is one of the nicest pubs in Warwickshire. Their friendly dispositions and the warmth of their welcome has ensured that people who visit are keen to return. The pub is on split levels with a comfortable lounge and a nice public bar. The Forge Bar which was opened in 1992, has enhanced the pub and given it more room. It is needed because of the increasing number of people using the canal from Stratford to Rugby who tie up alongside the pub, and for all those who have discovered how delightful the pub is. There is ample car parking. The menu has many interesting dishes on offer as well as the tried and tested favourites.

You can choose from a simple basket meal, fish, succulent steaks, an enormous mixed grill or two dishes in Crockpots; Lasagne Verdi and Chicken Curry. Fresh Batches and Steakwich's are made to order and there is a daily selection of specials. Vegetarians will enjoy the excellent Broccoli and Mushroom Mornay or the Courgette and Mushroom Lasagne.

USEFUL INFORMATION

OPEN; 11-11pm.
CHILDREN; Welcome
CREDIT CARDS; No credit cards.
LICENSED; Yes
ACCOMMODATION; None
RESTAURANT; Not applicable
BAR FOOD; Interesting & varied
VEGETARIAN; Several dishes
DISABLED ACCESS; Yes
GARDEN: yes + Children's area

THE WHEATLAND FOX
High Street,
Much Wenlock,
Shropshire TF13 6AD
Tel: 01952 727292

The Wheatland Fox Hotel is a Grade II listed building, the main structure with its half-timbering was built originally in 1669, and at a later date the Georgian frontage was added. It is a charming small hotel offering friendly service under the personal direction of the owners Peter and Caroline Reeve, retaining standards required by business people and travellers alike.

Conveniently situated in the main street of the medieval town of Much Wenlock, the hotel with its own private car park, offers peace, comfort and tranquillity and is English Tourist Board Three Crown Commended and AA**

Accommodation provides for a maximum of ten guests in five comfortable bedrooms. All the attractively styled rooms have their own bathrooms, colour television, radio and alarm, tea and coffee making facilities, direct dial telephones and central heating to ensure comfort all year round. The public rooms furnished with antiques and paintings throughout, plus the exposed beams, open fires and tasteful decorations contribute to the restful atmosphere and natural character of the hotel. The friendly bar offers a good selection of beers, wines and spirits in comfortable surroundings. The delightful Dining Room serves a variety of interesting dishes using top quality local produce, which receives consistent praise from regular diners. The wines are carefully selected to offer a good choice to suit everyone's taste.

USEFUL INFORMATION

OPEN; 12-3pm & 7-11pm All day for residents
CHILDREN; By arrangement, Childrens menu
CREDIT CARDS; Visa/Amex/Access
LICENSED; Full. Well chosen wine list
ACCOMMODATION; 5 ensuite rooms
RESTAURANT; Traditional. Home-cooked
BAR FOOD; Specials daily
VEGETARIAN; 3-4 dishes daily
DISABLED ACCESS; No
GARDEN; Patio. BBQ

RESTAURANT SEBASTIAN,
45 Willow Street,
Oswestry SY111AQ
Tel: 01691 655444

A delightful 1640 merchants Jacobean Town House in which Sebastian and Michelle Fisher have established a restaurant 'par excellence'. Welcomed personally by Michelle you will be offered food prepared to order and exclusively from fresh produce. Even the variety of breads and petit fours are all home made. Sea food and shell fish are amongst the most popular items. Sebastian goes to great lengths to select and often collect his fresh fish each day. The wines are superb specialising in lesser known wine areas of France which produce particularly fine wines at affordable prices. Wines can be purchased 'off licence' at competitive prices. Dine unhurriedly by romantic candlelight, pop in for an alfresco lunch - served on a nice day on the vine covered terrace. Stay overnight and enjoy a memorable breakfast in this little bit of 'France' in the town centre of Oswestry.

USEFUL INFORMATION

OPEN;;Tues-Sat 11-2pm & 6.30-10.30pm last orders. All year Except Christmas Day
CHILDREN; Welcome
CREDIT CARDS;All major cards
LICENSED; Yes
ACCOMMODATION; Stay overnight
RESTAURANT;Everything home-cooked. Fish a speciality
BAR FOOD;Alfresco lunches
VEGETARIAN;Daily choice
DISABLED ACCESS:Yes
GARDEN;Vine covered terrace

THE LOUGH POOL INN,
Sellack,
Ross-on-Wye,
Herefordshire

If one wanted to conjure up in ones mind the perfect pub in a wonderful setting, that is what you would find at the Lough Pool Inn at Sellack, just 4 miles from Ross and 8 miles from Hereford, close to the River Wye and the Wye Valley. The location is a secluded one, next to the pool from which the pub takes its name. The gardens are delightful, complete with an old cider press, and equipped with tables and chairs for dining outside, when the weather permits.

The pub is a 16th century black and white timbered building which is as delightful inside as out. The unspoilt timbers, the nooks and crannies, the flagstone floors and large open fireplaces just enhance the warm and welcoming atmosphere. Malcolm and Janet Hall are the owners and in the short time they have been here they have become firm favourites locally. One of the pleasures for visitors is listening to the contented chatter of regulars at the bar who are not averse to discussing anything from sport to politics, religion and the European Community with a little local gossip thrown in for good measure. The food is home-cooked, imaginative and sensibly priced. The menu has something to offer everyone from the young to the elderly and includes several vegetarian dishes.

USEFUL INFORMATION

OPEN; Daily 11.30-3pm & 6.30-11pm
Sun: 7-10.30pm
CHILDREN; Yes. Not under 14 in bar
CREDIT CARDS; Visa/Access/Master/Switch
LICENSED; Full Licence
ACCOMMODATION; Not applicable

RESTAURANT; Good, home-cooked fare
BAR FOOD; Wide range. Value for money.
VEGETARIAN; Always a choice
DISABLED ACCESS; Easy access
GARDEN; Yes, with tables/benches for 30/40 people

THE SHEAF AND SICKLE
Coventry Road,
Long Lawford,
Rugby, Warwickshire
Tel: 01788 544622

What better way to enjoy a pint than doing so whilst watching a cricket match from the gardens of a pub! This you can do at The Sheaf and Sickle on the edge of Long Lawford village, believed to be the only such named pub in the country. The pub is blessed with a cricket pitch at the rear, and three or four matches are played there every week in the season.

Talking to the contented regulars, who have been coming here for years, they will tell you that not only does The Sheaf and Sickle have the bonus of cricket but it has also a remarkable couple as mine hosts. Shan and Steve Jones, they tell me, are specialists in a friendly atmosphere, good beer, good food, and good fun. You certainly get this impression from the moment you enter the pub. Somehow everyone makes you feel 'special'. The pub is included in the CAMRA Good Beer Guide and has a good reputation for traditional beers. It is regularly awarded certificates by local CAMRA drinkers. There is a large bar with a darts area, a cosy cottage style lounge, which is home to Shan Jones' ever increasing collection of pottery ducks, and the new, comfortable, pretty restaurant to the rear of the pub which opened in 1993 and already has an excellent reputation.

The traditional home-cooked dishes on the menu, and the Daily Specials are super with the emphasis on quality, variety and value for money. Vegetarian dishes are always available and so are children's portions.

USEFUL INFORMATION

OPEN; Mon-Fri: 12-2.30 & 6.00-11pm
Sat: 12-11pm. Sun: 12-3 & 7-10.30pm
CHILDREN; Made welcome
CREDIT CARDS; All major cards
LICENSED; Full Licence
ACCOMMODATION; Not applicable
RESTAURANT; Cottage style, 44 seater
BAR FOOD; Home-cooked. Quality and value
VEGETARIAN; 3 dishes always & Specials
DISABLED ACCESS; Yes
GARDEN; 2 Beer Gardens. Play area

GRANVILLES

Restaurant and Wine Bar,
Granville Square,
Stone, Staffordshire
Tel: 01785 816658.

Every year since an existing small cafe was turned into the exciting Restaurant and Wine Bar that it is now well over a decade later, the standard has increased and every year sees some improvement. The latest is a new Gallery and Bar upstairs overlooking the Bistro, with live music downstairs. This is a friendly, fun place to be and offers excellent English and French food with a wide range of attractively priced wines. It is a favourite haunt of the famous and is renowned for its live music, mostly jazz from internationally famous actors, including George Melly, Aker Bilk, Humphrey Lyttleton and less known but accomplished local groups. Everything about Granville's is charming including the garden which was just an overgrown jungle. Hard work and green fingers have produced what is now a wonderful walled oasis.

USEFUL INFORMATION

OPEN; Rest; Tues-Sat 7-10pm Wine Bar: Mon-Sat 12-2pm & 7-10pm
CHILDREN; Welcome
CREDIT CARDS; Access/Visa/Amex.
LICENSED; Great wines
ACCOMODATION; Nor applicable
RESTAURANT; Exciting food
BAR FOOD; High standard
VEGETARIAN; Catered for
DISABLED ACCESS; Shallow step
GARDEN; Wonderful walled oasis

THE WHEATSHEAF

Kibbleston Road,
Oulton, Stone,
Staffordshire
Tel: 01785 812767

Oulton is one of the many pretty villages in the Manifold Valley. Close to the busy little town of Stone, it is also near the Wedgwood Visitor Centre, The Potteries, Cannock Chase and Barlaston Downs. This is one good reason for coming here and the second is The Wheatsheaf, a charming hostelry built in the Victorian era.

In the competent, friendly hands of landlords Barry and Jean Holland, it is run to a very high standard. They are assisted by talented chef and a very good Restaurant Manager who between them make lunching and dining at The Wheatsheaf a pleasureable experience. An inspired Vegetarian Menu, a real Sunday Lunch (for which it is advisable to book) and excellent Bar snacks are additional reasons for coming to what is one of the nicest pubs in Staffordshire.

The Restaurant is an ideal setting for wedding receptions or private parties and you will find that immaculate attention to detail by the Hollands ensures that special occasions are just that.

USEFUL INFORMATION

OPEN; 11.30-2.30pm & 6.30-11pm
CHILDREN; Welcome
CREDIT CARDS; Access/Visa
LICENSED; Full On
ACCOMMODATION; No

RESTAURANT; International a la carte
Closed on Mondays & Sunday evening
BAR FOOD; Wide range
VEGETARIAN; Inspired menu
DISABLED ACCESS; Limited

THE COLLEGE ARMS,
Lower Quinton,
Stratford-upon-Avon
Tel: 01789 720342

Lower Quinton is a delightful village between Cheltenham and Stratford-upon-Avon, on the very edge of the Cotswolds. Chipping Camden is closeby and Warwick too, so it is a wonderful place to use as a base for exploring this magical countryside. The place to stay is The College Arms, where in an establishment that reeks of history, you get comfortable accommodation, great food and hospitality as well. The inn was owned originally by Henry VIII who gave it to one of his wives as a gift. Sometime later it was purchased by Magdalen College, Oxford and remained under its ownership for 400 years. Because of this connection The College Arms is the only public house in England permitted legally to display the College Coat of Arms. Accommodation is limited and booking is advisable. There is a dining area just off the lounge and an attractive bar with inglenook fireplaces; but it is the restaurant on the first floor which will delight the architectural buffs. The College Arms has a darts team, pool team and quiz nights during the winter when barbecues are not possible. Lynn and Tony Smith, the proprietors, are a popular couple who have an excellent relationship with their regulars and visitors. Most of the food, which is varied and traditional, is home-cooked. Whether it is a snack or a full restaurant meal, the quality is outstanding. Specialities are Gammon and eggs, Game in season. Sunday lunch is very popular and it is advisable to book in advance.

USEFUL INFORMATION

OPEN; Mon-Fri: 12-2.30pm & 7-11pm
Sat & Sun: 12-3pm & 7-11pm.
CHILDREN; Children welcome to stay or eat.
CREDIT CARDS; Access/Visa.
LICENSED; Yes
ACCOMMODATION; Limited ensuite

RESTAURANT; Varied & traditional
BAR FOOD; Outstanding quality
VEGETARIAN; Catered for
DISABLED ACCESS; Yes
GARDEN; No. Outside seating
On enclosed terrace

THE RED LION INN
Thorncliffe, Nr Leek,
Staffordshire
Tel: 01538 300325

Take the A53 Buxton road and turn right on to the Thorncliffe road about a half a mile out of Leek and your reward will be the excellent Red Lion Inn which has served the locals in the village since 1787. Much has been done to it since those days but never to the detriment of the old world atmosphere. Ron and Sheila Mitchell have owned the pub since 1984 and it is they who are responsible for the good food. The warm friendly atmosphere pervades the whole pub and makes it a happy place to visit. The Red Lion has comfortable bars and a separate restaurant. It is also able to provide Conference facilities plus now being a great centre for weddings. It is licensed for marriages and for any couple contemplating a wedding complete with a reception in one venue, The Red Lion would be ideal. It is a welcome stopping place for coach parties - the coach driver is always given a courtesy meal. There is a large car park. In the garden children are safe and able to play with special equipment. Fishing and hang-gliding are two of the sports on offer and frequently the Mitchells will cater for Outings and Mystery Tours. The food is traditional, home-cooked and wherever possible fresh local produce is used. Juicy steaks are cooked to perfection and there is a delicious range of fish. The Red Lion is Vegetarian recommended so there are always at least eight dishes from which to choose. Children have their own menu and for those merely wanting a quick snack, the sandwiches are fresh, beautifully garnished and with a wide variety of fillings. Sunday lunch is very popular and very good value for money, as indeed, is everything.

USEFUL INFORMATION

OPEN; Mon-Fri 7-11pm.
Sat: 12-3pm & 6-11pm
Sun: 12-3pm & 7-10.30pm.
CHILDREN; Welcome to eat.
CREDIT CARDS; Access/Visa/Switch
LICENSED; Yes
ACCOMMODATION; 1dbl ensuite 1dbl shared bath
1 twin shared bath. Licenced for Civil Weddings

RESTAURANT; High standard
BAR FOOD; Varied & home-cooked
VEGETARIAN; Several dishes
DISABLED ACCESS;
PETS; Not permitted
GARDEN; Yes. Safe for children

THE SUTHERLAND HOTEL
Tibberton,
Newport,
Shropshire

Tel: 01952 550533

Tibberton was once part of the land belonging to the Duke of Sutherland hence the name of the village pub, The Sutherland Arms. What a pretty rural village this is and yet it is no distance from the shopping centres of Telford and Shrewsbury, Weston Park or Hodnet Hall and Gardens, the Ironbridge Museum, The Wrekin, the 'House that Jack Built' at Cherrington and a host of other places. This makes the village and especially The Sutherland a good place to visit before or after exploring some of these interesting places.

Jonathan Morris and his wife Sheila who run The Sutherland are an unusual pair. For years Jonathan was the lock-keeper on the Shropshire Union Canal and at one time with Sheila, he ran the horse drawn trip boat Iona, at Norbury Junction. Their joint experiences make them very good with people and you can see this in the friendly, lively and happy atmosphere of the Sutherland. Every year the Morris's endeavour to make the pub that much better and recently they have started serving meals in the evenings and have made a better entrance for wheelchairs. Sheila cooks delectable dishes every day as well as producing a good cold table. There are always sandwiches, freshly cut, a Vegetarian selection and Burgers and Bangers for the children. You can play darts, dominoes and pool and the playing fields nearby allow enough room for everyone to let off steam. This is a true pub and one you will want to return to.

USEFUL INFORMATION

OPEN; 12-2.30pm & 6-11pm.
Sat+12-4pm & 7-11pm
Sun: 12-3pm & 7-10.30pm
CHILDREN; Welcome
CREDIT CARDS; None taken
LICENSED; Full on and off Licence
ACCOMMODATION; Not applicable

RESTAURANT; Excellent pub grub
BAR FOOD; Good value pub fare
VEGETARIAN; 4-5 dishes daily
DISABLED ACCESS; Garden only
GARDEN; Award winning with tables and benches

THE ROEBUCK
Dovebank, Uttoxeter,
Staffordshire
Tel: 01889 565563

Half a mile from Uttoxeter's pretty racecourse and just 5 minutes walk from the Town Centre, you will find The Roebuck Inn. It is so conveniently sited on the main route for Alton Towers, Tutbury Castle, the Potteries and many other places. The age of the pub is uncertain. Certainly it goes back to the beginning of the 1600s and probably earlier. It is constructed of brick-quarry tile, has wonderful oak beams, inglenooks and a fine open log fire place. David Lankester and John Smith, the Proprietors and their wives have developed the Roebuck into one of the most popular pubs in the area. With 2 comfortable double bedrooms available, it is an ideal place in which to stay either on business or as a base from which to explore the area as well as the Peak District National Park. There is excellent fishing, game and coarse, locally and shooting facilities in the immediate area. The large beer garden is very pleasant on a summer's day. Freshly cooked specialities and country fare are the backbone of the food served at The Roebuck. All meals are cooked to order so please be a little patient. One of the house specialities is 'Chicken Roebuck Style' - a large boneless breast of chicken, stuffed with ham, cheese and herbs, and gently cooked with white wine, garlic, mushrooms and fresh cream. Absolutely delicious and comes to the table with an assortment of fresh vegetables.

USEFUL INFORMATION

OPEN;11-11pm
CHILDREN;Welcome in Anteroom And garden
CREDIT CARDS;None taken
LICENSED;Yes
ACCOMODATION;2 letting rooms

RESTAURANT;Not applicable
BAR FOOD;Excellent. Cooked to order
VEGETARIAN;Daily choice
DISABLED ACCESS;Yes
GARDEN;Beer Garden

THE PLOUGH INN
Wall under Heywood,
Church Stretton,
Tel: 01694 771221

Wall under Heywood is situated in the beautiful Ape Dale and is easily reached from Church Stretton 4 miles away. Much Wenlock is 6 miles distant and Shrewsbury 15 miles. There are several interesting places to visit nearby such as Wenlock Abbey, once a monastery and the Wenlock Edge walking trail which gives hours of delight to lovers of the countryside. Fishing is a popular pastime too. One of the most visited places is Acton Scott Working Farm Museum, and another the old Roman village of Rushbury. In the midst of Wall under Heywood is The Plough, which is not only the village pub but also a good restaurant, renowned locally for the standard of its home cooking and the traditional Sunday lunch. The latter is so well attended that it is essential to book. The Dining Room which is separate from the bars, is somewhere in which smoking is banned. This attracts many people to The Plough although it is the overall friendliness and hospitality of the proprietors, Lloyd and AnnNutting, which makes the pub just that extra bit special. The garden is an attractive spot in summer with its lawned areas and colourful flower beds. All the year it is interesting however because of the display Aviaries. Whether you have a full meal or just a bar snack, you will find the food tempting and excellent value for money.

USEFUL INFORMATION

OPEN; 12-2.30pm & 7-11pm.
CHILDREN; Welcome to eat
CREDIT CARDS; Access/Visa.
LICENSED; Yes
ACCOMMODATION; None
GARDEN; Yes & Aviaries

DINING ROOM; Renowned home-cooking Traditional Sunday Lunch
BAR FOOD; Wide range
VEGETARIAN DISHES; Good choice
DISABLED ACCESS; Easy access

THE NARROWBOAT
Ellesmere Road,
Whittington,
Nr. Oswestry
Tel: 01691 661051.

For almost two hundred years only a cottage and an orchard marked Bridge No 5 on the Llangollen Canal, the official address of which is Ellesmere Road, Whittington. Fifteen years ago the enterprising and multi-talented Hill family changed all that. Colin built what he calls the largest 'Narrowboat' of them all, which is now the pub of that name. It is a delightful place just outside Welsh Frankton, surrounded by farmland and next to a boatyard also owned by the Hills. Here 24 narrowboats tie up ready for hiring and it buzzes with activity. The extension to the old cottage is long and narrow to fit into the space between the road and the canal. It is certainly different and the very genuine welcome you get from Colin and his wife Elaine and son Martin makes visiting the pub a truly memorable experience. They will tell you that the motto of The Narrowboat is 'Eat, Drink and be Nautical.'

The Hills work tremendously hard. On a Sunday morning you will see Elaine cleaning the pub, Martin restocking the shelves and Colin organising the kitchen in which he will personally cook the succulent roast beef and Yorkshire Pudding which has become traditional. All the food is delicious and the prices are quite ridiculously inexpensive. Book for Sunday lunch to avoid disappointment.

USEFUL INFORMATION

OPEN; Mon-Sat; 11-3pm & 7-11pm. Sun: 12noon-10.30pm.
CHILDREN; Welcome
CREDIT CARDS; None taken
LICENSED; Yes
ACCOMMODATION; None
RESTAURANT; Not applicable
BAR FOOD; High standard
VEGETARIAN; Yes
DISABLED ACCESS; Yes
GARDEN; Beer Garden

THE OLD RECTORY

Church Street,
Willersey, Nr Broadway,
Worcestershire WR12 7PN
Tel: 01386 853729
Fax: 01386 858061

Built of mellow Cotswold stone the 17th century Old Rectory at Willersey is quietly tucked away at the end of a lane, sitting opposite the 11th Century church with a backdrop of the picturesque Cotswold Hills. The Old Rectory welcomes visitors from all over the world who delight in the friendly glow the house offers. Within the solid walls of this gracious old building six bedrooms have every comfort to offer, and are tastefully furnished and decorated to a high standard. A further two bedrooms are now available in the old Coach House, one of these is a romantic fourposter room with ensuite bath and shower. Overlooking the beautifully maintained and colourful walled garden, many honeymooners have enjoyed the privacy of this room.

An excellent breakfast is served in the elegant Georgian dining-room. In winter a blazing log fire will greet you morning and evening. The very friendly owners, Chris and Liz Beauvoisin, do not serve dinners, as the surrounding area has a great number of restaurants to choose from, including the excellent Bell Inn just 300 yards down the lane.

The Old Rectory garden is blessed with a 300 year old Mulberry tree at one end, which at the end of each summer is heavily laden with fruit. A family of woodpeckers live in the garden and are often seen in the tree. Behind the house a local colourful character who for many years was one of the Queen Mother's jockeys, now rears sheep and welcomes Old Rectory guests to visit and watch the lambs being born. The Old Rectory is very well placed for visiting the many places of interest in the area, and you are assured that you will always be given a warm welcome by Chris and Liz.

USEFUL INFORMATION

OPEN;All year except at Christmas
CHILDREN;Welcome over 8 years old
CREDIT CARDS;Access/Visa/Euro/Master
LICENSED;No, but do bring your own
ACCOMMODATION;6 ensuite/2 with Private shower

RESTAURANT;Not applicable
BAR FOOD;Not applicable
VEGETARIAN;Yes, by arrangement
DISABLED ACCESS;Ramp available
GARDEN;Large and colourful Enclosed car park at the side

HOTELS, INNS, RESTAURANTS AND COUNTRY HOUSES

LEICESTERSHIRE, NOTTINGHAMSHIRE, DERBYSHIRE & NORTHAMPTON

Includes

The George	Alstonfield	p.171
Renaissance	Bakewell	p.172
Pack Horse Inn	Bakewell	p.173
Montagu Arms	Barnwell	p.174
Greyhound Inn	Burton-on-the-Wolds	p.175
Falcon Inn	Castle Ashby	p.176
Monkton Arms	Glaston	p.177
Skillet Restaurant	Hayfield, Stockport	p.178
Weavers Wine Bar	Leicester	p.179
Three Swans Hotel	Market Harborough	p.180
New Ferry Restaurant	Newark	p.181
Quorn Grange	Quorn	p.182
Woolpack Hotel	Thrapston	p.183
The Pickwick Restaurant	Towcester	p.184
The Old Friar	Twywell	p.185
The Fox Inn	Wilbarston	p.186

It is difficult to enthuse about **Leicester Cathedral** as I have done about so many others. Although St Martin's has a medieval plan, what one sees is almost entirely Victorian. Its finest attribute is the soaring spire between the nave and the chancel, designed by Raphael Brandon in 1867, rising to 220feet; it manages to dig itself out and away from the ever encroaching buildings of the 20th century which cramp its style. Whilst St Martin's in the main dates from 1867 it did not become a cathedral until 1927. The spire of the cathedral was once the most prominent of Leicester's landmarks but it has now become hemmed in by so many modern blocks that the church has become quite difficult to find. You will find it close to the Clock Tower, in the very centre of the city.

Visitors are encouraged to tour the building and what impressed me most was the fine roof, the decent Victorian glass throughout the church and the stone and wood carvings. The North Chapel contains many memorials to the old Leicester family of Herrick with the earliest dating to 1589, with many tomb slabs erected around the walls. The father of the poet Robert Herrick was born in Leicester and the mother of Dean Swift, who was a Herrick, is also buried here. In the floor of the chancel is a slab inscribed:

RICHARD III
King of England
killed at Bosworth Field
in this county
22nd August 1485
Buried in the church of the Grey Friars
in this parish

What it does not tell you is that Richard's body was brought back to Leicester via Bow Bridge - where there is a plaque - after the Battle of Bosworth. He was buried in Greyfriars Friary but his bones were later thrown into the River Soar from the bridge. The plaque recalls the spot near where ' lie the remains of Richard III, last of the Plantagenets, 1485.

It is not just for the cathedral that you should visit Leicester. people have lived and worked here since before the Roman Conquest. The Romans established Ratae Corieltauvorum as a flourishing regional capital and remains of its public baths are still visible today at Jewry Wall. The Romans recognised its position as worthy because of its many trade routes. Today it still has an enviable central location within two and a half hours drive of many of Britain's largest centres of population. Leicester is Britain's first Environment City and it shows in its surroundings and green spaces - those used to more built up cities will be impressed by the parks and gardens, green wedges,foot and cycle paths and wildlife sanctuaries in the city centre itself.

LEICESTERSHIRE, NOTTINGHAMSHIRE, DERBYSHIRE & NORTHAMPTON

Leicester has some fourteen museums and a host of other places to see so I am going to to ask you to look in the Visitors Attractions in the back of this book which will give you details of them. I always think of the North West of Leicestershire as being 'Ivanhoe' country. Sir Walter Scott brought it to life for me in his stirring book set in this region of natural beauty. The historic town of **Ashby de la Zouch** whose unusual name comes from the Breton la Zouch family who acquired Ashby Manor in 1160, is a charming place which, in the 19th century, was quite a fashionable spa town. It is a place of mellow half-timbered buildings, impressive churches, delightful green parks and the ruins of an old castle which underlines its historic past.

Anyone with an interest in industrial archaeology should make a point of visiting **Moira**, where what is probably the best preserved Blast Furnace in Europe is now open to the public. From Ashby you will have the ideal opportunity to visit **Staunton Harold** of which Nikolaus Pensner wrote in his famous 'Buildings of England' series, 'For position, Staunton Harold, the house and chapel are unsurpassed in the country - certainly as far as Englishness is concerned.'

The splendid Georgian stable block behind the Hall is busier now than it has been for a hundred years. The decline of the horse and of the family fortunes, meant that it was largely redundant by the time of the First World War, and its condition deteriorated steadily until the estate was sold in 1954. The roof repaired, a new use proved hard to find until a potter, Geoff Herbert, took over several rooms for a craft pottery in 1977. This led to other rooms being let for craft workshops and exhibition gallery, gift shop and tea room. Sharing in the popularity of the whole Staunton Harold area, the public facilities at the craft centre now cater for over one hundred thousand visitors per year.

Coalville, as its name suggests, is an industrial town originally centred round coal mining. I mention it because it is pleasantly situated on the fringe of **Charnwood Forest** and within walking distance of **Bardon Hill**, the highest point in Leicester.

Castle Donington is another nice small town. The Norman castle built to command the River Trent crossing was demolished by King John to punish the owner for supporting Magna Carta. It was rebuilt in 1278 and no less than four of its subsequent owners were executed. Chaucer wrote 'The Fair Maid of Kent' whilst he was visiting Richard II's mother at the castle. The 13th-14th century church has a spire that reaches for the heavens, the timber-framed houses are delightful and the shops will tempt you to spend money.

At **Donington Park**, where the vast Hall of 1793 was built in the 'Strawberry Hill' Gothic style, is the famous motor racing circuit, racing car collection and a new exhibition centre. TheDonington Collection is the result of one man's love for a sport that has thrilled him since the mid 30's when, as a spectator at the Donington Grand Prix, he witnessed the giant German cars powering themselves to victory. For Tom Wheatcroft, founder of this incredible collection, the love affair had begun.

Today the Collection numbers somewhere in the region of 150 racing cars plus the Speedway Hall of Fame and numerous other vehicles of interest. You can understand why so many past and present racing drivers come here quite regularly.

Between Ashby and Castle Donington is **Breedon-on-the-Hill** from which nothing blocks quite the most stunning and panoramic views in Leicestershire. Its Norman and 13th-century church stands with The Bulwarks, remains of an Iron Age Fort, on one side and to the east a limestone quarry drops precipitously down creating an unbelievably beautiful setting.

Kegworth is a small country town situated on a rocky bank above the meeting of the River Soar and the Grand Union Canal, crossed by Kegworth bridge. It is full of buildings of interest including 18th and 19th century cottages and workshops used for framework knitting and hosiery industries. There is a 1698 house with a fine hipped roof and the church of St Andrews which lives up to its reputation as the 'almost faultless' late Decorated church, mainly 14th century with some stained glass and a splendid Royal Arms dated 1684.

Market Bosworth found fame nearly five centuries ago when the Wars of the Roses ended on the stricken Field of Bosworth two miles away. It has slumbered ever since, almost as if it was happy to step back into obscurity. It attracts visitors of course and quite rightly so. **The Bosworth Battlefield Visitor Centre and Country Park** is signposted from the town off the A5, A444, A447 and B585. This site of the Battle of Bosworth between Richard III and the future Henry VII has fascinated every generation. In the Visitor Centre you will find a comprehensive interpretation of the Battle including exhibitions, models, film theatre, book and gift shops. From time to time there are special medieval event days. Almost on the border of Warwickshire and just off the M1 is **Lutterworth** one of the loveliest places in Leicestershire, even today, where the High Street climbs steeply from the bridge across the shallow River Swift and leads the way to its famous church, with a tower stretching upwards as if to reach the heavens.

Market Harborough is an old market town and a pleasant place in which to wander. It is deep into hunting country - in this case, the Fernie Hunt. The town was the creation of Henry II. Here in the three days of 1645 the balance between King and Commonwealth swung. It was the eve of the battle of Naseby and the streets and square were filled with royalist soldiers. At the end of the three days the church of St Dionysius was filled with royalist prisoners. The first part of this dramatic turn of events took place when Charles I, sleeping at nearby **Lubenham** was roused at two in the morning with the news that Fairfax had marched fromNorthampton to Naseby. He came riding down the street in the darkness to meet his Generals at a Council of War. He allowed the rashness of the Cavalier, Prince Rupert, to prevail and the Royalist Army marched from its entrenched positions to give battle to the New Model Army. At midday the fight began and by nightfall the king was a fugitive, his army destroyed and his throne lost. While he fled to Leicester the church was packed with wounded soldiers, and Oliver Cromwell sat down to write to the Speaker of the House of Parliament in which he described the destruction of the King's Army.

Market Harborough was to see Charles I twice more. The first time he would not have been recognised in his disguise as he passed through on his way to join the Scots. The second time the townsmen stood in silence as he passed through, a prisoner, on his way south.

Finally in Leicestershire I want to take you to **Melton Mowbray**. Since the Bronze Age horsemen have been riding along its trackways. The Romans lived here and then vanished and the Saxons made sure we knew about their occupation by the burial ground they left behind. Then the Norman Mowbrays set their seal on the place. Today it is still famous but now it is for pies, Stilton cheese, Melton Hunt cake and hunting. You will want to stay in and around Melton for a while both to savour the town itself with its quaint customs, attractive buildings and a parish church that Leicestershire men acclaim as the most beautiful in England.

Melton country is the home of the Quorn Hunt and much of the activity of the area is centred on the town. Until late in the 18th century, huntsmen wore green but a surplus of red cloth used for 'redcoat' soldiers after the American War of Independence brought about a change. A tailor named Pink produced hunting coats of this material, which more easily distinguished the hunt principals. Thus hunting 'pink' came into vogue.

We know the expression 'Painting the Town Red' to mean having a good time. in 1837 in Melton Mowbray it meant precisely what it says. The town was full of fox hunting people among them the eccentric Marquis of Waterford who with some of his friends decided after a day's hunting to so some unsolicited redecorating on parts of the town's buildings, including one of the town's toll gates and even the unfortunate toll keeper, by painting them bright red! So when anyone out for a night's enjoyment refers to 'painting the town red' this is where that boisterous activity originated.

What we know as 'Stilton' Cheese has been made for over 300 years in the farmhouses of the Vale of Belvoir. There are several legends about its origin. One says that a Mrs Orton, housekeeper at Little Dalby Hall in the time of Queen Anne, is reputed to have 'perfected' it. Another says that Mrs Paulet, a farmer's wife at Wymondham, is said to have supplied cheese to her brother-in-law at the Bluebell Inn at Stilton on the Great North Road for the delectation of travellers. Today, the Cheeses are renowned all over the world. Whether you take it as an after dinner delicacy with a glass of port or a main snack with crispfresh bread and butter and a cool glass of ale, the enjoyment of Stilton is a gourmet's delight.

As for Melton Mowbray Pork Pies - who could want for anything finer. Succulent pork in a crisp crust mildly spiced with a lining of pork gell is always acceptable. The oldest remaining pork pie bakers, Dickinson and Morris are to be found in Nottingham Street and by prior arrangement you can see the traditional pie being hand raised around a wooden mould and baked without any means of support. This method ensures thorough cooking and the crusts, resembling cups without handles are filled while still warm.

A delicacy you may not have heard of is Melton Hunt Cake. It is a rich mix of currants, raisins, selected nuts with a mild seasoning for added 'warmth' on a cold day and a touch of spirit for extra dash.

Wherever you go in Leicestershire you will find warm-hearted people. Leicester has become a renaissance city with so much to offer. Yes, I was disappointed in the cathedral compared to the might of **Canterbury** and the beauty of **Wells** but it is still a joy to see and the regeneration of the city makes it a place that should come high on any visitor's itinerary.

Rutland, the smallest of all counties, is a gem but in reality and officially it does not exist in its own right but merely as an appendage to Leicestershire, although, as I write, there is a move to restore its independence. Meanwhile anyone who lives here will tell you without equivocation that they live in Rutland and not in Leicestershire. It would take 300 Rutlands to make up England and 40 to cover Yorkshire but that does not phase this little brother of the Shires.

The earliest mention of Rutland as a county was seven centuries ago, in the days of King John. The north part of the county is a fertile plateau of grassland; it has the Leicestershire Wolds to the west and the Lincolnshire lowands to the east, the River Welland separates it from Northants on the south. It perhaps lacks some of the grandest English scenery but from its high places there are some wonderful views. It has gentle wooded hills, fertile valleys and serene villages with thatched cottages. Industry takes very much a back seat. Its unique qualities are summed up in its motto 'multum in parvo' - much in little.

I started my journey in **Uppingham**, a small town which is home to one of England's finest schools, known throughout the world. The great school with its splendid halls and courtyards appears to stand sentinel over the quiet town with its attractive bow fronted shops, peaceful streets and sombre ironstone houses.

From April to September you can visit **The Bede House** at **Lyddington** just a couple of miles to the south of Uppingham. It was built by Bishop Russell as an episcopal residence late in th 15th century and has not changed much since. The home of bishops for over a century it was refashioned by Thomas Cecil, the son of Elizabeth I's Lord Burleigh. He converted it into analmshouse for a warden, 12 men and two women, adding to it, for the comfort of pensioners, the stone-roofed verandah running along the north side. The old house is domestic Gothic at its best.

I would like you to take a look at **Glaston**, a neat little place which has a good pub, **The Monkton Arms** and a very unusual church with its central towers described as being ' crowned with a Peter Pan of spires that seem never to have grown up high enough to give the church dignity'. A perfect description.

Just up the road is **Wing** which has one of the oddest survivals of any English village. The ancient turf maze is forty feet across and still preserved, a wonderful example of the mazes that once were commonplace in England. Here the maze is made up of little turf banks about a foot high, winding round and round. If you ever wondered for what purpose mazes were built, tradition has it that they were devised by the Church as a means of penance, the wrongdoer was put in and left to find his own way out! The old church still watches over this one but modern man is too smart not to find his way out.

Tinwell is a small village complete with a green and an excellent hostelry, **The Crown**. Just a few yards from the A6121 between Stamford and Ketton, it is very close to the magnificent **Burghley House**, home of the Cecil family. It is no surprise therefore to know that the pub is actually owned by the Burghley estate.

The village church has a massive tower and a saddleback roof, the only one in Rutland. The nave arcade and the chancel arch are 13th century, the chancel and the clerestory 15th century. In the chancel lies Elizabeth Cecil, sister of Lord Burleigh, Elizabeth I's counsellor and founder of the house of Cecil.

There are many places I want to revisit in England and one of them is definitely Burghley House. It is one of the finest examples of late Elizabethan design in England. Entering it is like walking into an Aladdin's cave, full with every imaginable treasure. There is one of the finest private collections of Italian Art, unique examples of Chinese and Japanese porcelain and superb items of 18th century furniture.

The remodelling work of the 17th century meant that examples of the work of the principal artists and craftsmen are to be found here; amongst others Antonio Verrio, Grinling Gibbons and Louis Laguerre made major contributions to the beautiful interiors.

If the interior beauty was not sufficient, you have the additional thrill of walking in a 300 acre Deer Park landscaped by the inimitable Capability Brown under the direction of the 9th Earl. Capability Brown created a lake and delightful avenues of mature trees. The park is open all the year round and the house from Good Friday to October 1st every day from 11am-5pm.

From Tingwell you are only moments away from the man made masterpiece, **Rutland Water**. Spanning 3,100 acres, it is the largest man-made lake in Western Europe. Built in the 1970's to satisfy the rising demand for water from the developing towns of Northampton, Peterborough, Corby, Milton Keynes, Daventry and Wellingborough, the reservoir's storage capacity of 124,000million litres provides not only water for domestic and industrial consumption but also gives recreational facilities and enormous pleasure to everyone who visits it.

What do you look at first? I am not sure so I will just try and tell you some of the pleasureable things you can see and do. For example visit **The Barnsdale Drought Garden** which is completely innovative. Created by Anglian Water its purpose is to demonstrate the wide variety of attractive plants and shrubs which can be grown successfully in the British climate and which require no extra watering.

From the car park at **Whitwell** you can board the Rutland Belle giving yourselves a chance to cruise around the reservoir taking in the views that are usually only enjoyed by fishermen and sailors. A regular service runs each day during the season except Mondays, but including Bank Holidays. The trip takes about 45 minutes.

Rutland is noted for its fine churches covering th whole range of architectural styles. One of these you will find at the medieval village of **Empingham**, and for me it is the most beautiful. Set amongst fine trees with the river Gwash running drowsily by, its 14th century tower has a spire ornamented with arcading that rises gracefully towards the sky. Inside peeps of old wall paintings and old glass strengthen the impression of past glory. Empingham also has one of the most unusual and magnificent of dovecotes. Built of stone, it is circular and has over 700 nests.

You may wonder how the village of **Edith Weston** got its name. Edward the Confessor was responmsible, for he gave his Queen Edith this western part of Rutland. What a lovely village it is, lapping the edge of Rutland Water, with its thatched cottages and stately trees. The tower and spire of St Mary the Virgin are well over 500 years old and well justify the rhyme inscribed in the church below:

> '*Crown of all the neighbouring lands,*
> *High and lifted up it stands.*'

My journey around Rutland Water finished at the capital of this small county, **Oakham**. It is the very heart of Rutland and quite lovely. The wide streets have delightful houses and flower filled gardens. Glimpses of green hills and wooded lanes can be seen even from the ancient cobbled market square. All that is good has been preserved including th ancient stocks and buttercross. It is all quaint and it would not evoke much surprise if one saw a prisoner in the five hole stocks.

Oakham is famous for its magnificent church, its old school and what is left of its castle. If you look upwards you will see high above All Saints, Cock Peter, a weather vane which must be the oldest in England. It is said to have shown the way of the wind to men who went to the Battle of Agincourt.

Oakham Castle is part of a late 12th-century manor house of which the timber buildings and most of the fortifications perished longago. What we see today is an aisled hall with curious carvings on its doors. It is beautiful and is enhanced by a unique collection of horseshoes dating from the 11th century when William I's farrier lived here. Through many centuries it has been the custom to take a horseshoe from every peer passing through the town, and on the walls is one said to be given by Elizabeth I.

You should take a look at the 14th-century merchant's dwelling known as Flore's House. It has an early 14th-century doorway between two faces, and a stone washing bowl with a head carved from foliage. It may once have been the home of a group of priests in the 13th century but it was certainly the home of Roger Flore, who put the top on the church spire. Titus Oates was born in Oakham in 1649 and in Jeffrey Hudson's Cottage an interesting thatched building on the Melton Road, was born a little man of that name in 1619. Nine years later he gained fame by hopping out of a pie in the presence of Charles I. He was only eighteen inches high!

One of the pleasures of writing a guide book is that your attention is constantly drawn to places and areas that are entirely new to you; even though the names have been familiar since childhood. As far as I am concerned the County of Nottingham is a prime example of this and I think the reason has as much to do with the shire's legendary hero, Robin Hood, as with its geographical position close to the Heart of England. Bounded to the West by the country's first motorway, the M1, and with its predecessor, the A1, running up through from the East, there is a natural tendency to take this fascinating county for granted as we travel north or south; we feel we know the area because of the exploits of the 'Merrie Men' on page and screen, and we are reluctant to stop because we are on the way to somewhere else. We could not be more wrong.

Nottinghamshire is a delight, redolent in history, landscape and culture, yet intensely alive; taking advantage of its very centrality to attract business and visitors from all over the world. The land is fairly flat with the highest country being in the western region - perhaps the only off putting fact about the county is that its name is derived from the Saxon for 'the followers of Snot'!

Nottingham has everything from its restored and converted castle to theatre and concert hall, museums, pubs and hotels. Trent Bridge caters for cricket fans at county and Test level, whilst soccer enthusiasts can choose between the oldest football league club in the world, Notts County, or Nottingham Forest. Particularly impressive is the National Watersports Centre at Holme Pierrepoint, a 250 acre country park complete with 2,000 metre Olympic rowing course and white water slalom canoeing course - all this just four miles from the city centre.

Newstead Abbey, the ancestral home of one of England's greatest poets, Lord Byron, strictly speaking was a priory and never an abbey. It is an appropriately romantic house with a dramatic past set in extensive parklands. It owes its origins to the guilt that Henry II felt over the murder of Beckett, for it was on this spot that he founded a monastery in memory of the dead Archbishop. After the Dissolution the estate was bought by one, Sir John Byron of Colwick, who turned the priory into a home for himself and his descendants. Two and a half centuries later, one of these descendants, the lame and impoverished Lord George Gordon Byron, first set eyes on Newstead and later recorded his impressions.

> 'Through thy battlements, Newstead, the hollow winds whistle
> Though the hall of my fathers are gone to decay
> In thy once smiling garden the hemlock and thistle,
> Have choked up the rose which late bloomed in the way.'

The reason for this somewhat gloomy description was that his great uncle, whom Byron succeeded, had let the place fall into disrepair after having been ostracised by society, as a result of killing his cousin in a duel, and was convicted of manslaughter. The poet was greatly attached to Newstead, but, deeply in debt, was forced to sell. The buyer, an old friend, spent over a quarter of a million pounds on remodelling the house into its present style incorporating the ruins of the priory. It is a site worthy of a romantic such as Byron, and the surrounding parkland with its lakes and waterfalls and gardens provide the appropriate backdrop. Thanks to another two great benefactors the house and land were presented to the City of Nottingham, whilst a third bequeathed a unique collection of Byronic relics.

Newark, is almost a guide book cliche - an ancient market town with a strong sense of its own importance in the history of our country. Situated where the ancient Fosse Way crossed the Great North Road and by the banks of the River Trent, where the wool was once shipped to Calais via the Lincolnshire port of Boston, it was an important geo-political centre from earliest times and it was considered the Key to the North in the turbulent days of the first King of All England. The town's buildings reflect its importance in historical terms, particularly around the large cobbled market square with an enchanting blend of architecture, predominantly medieval and Georgian inlet with narrow streets and alleys.

The tall and well proportioned spire of the parish church of St Mary Magdalene rises to well over 200ft from behind the square and the building is mainly 14th century, although there has been a church here since Saxon times. The beauty and elegance of the construction is counterbalanced by a strong human element in its decoration; for both internally and externally, the church bears witness to the skills of the carver in both stone and wood with inumerable gargoyles, figures, scenes and shields to be found wherever one looks. However, to my mind, the town's greatest glory is to be found in the forbidding and noble ruins of Newark Castle, which stands guard over the entrance to the old town from the north. It is a wonderfully impressive structure and I think best viewed from one of the cruise boats that sail past its ancient walls.

LEICESTERSHIRE, NOTTINGHAMSHIRE, DERBYSHIRE & NORTHAMPTON

Before leaving Nottinghamshire I went, once again, to what has been described as 'England's least known Cathedral', thebeautiful Mother Church of Nottinghamshire, Southwell Minster. If you admired the carvings in St Mary Magdalene, Newark, then you will be staggered by the work to be found in the 12th century Minster with its octagonal chapter-house and twin spires.

Southwell itself is an attractive small town and was once described by the late Sir John Betjeman as 'unspoilt', a description that is true today. The heavily beamed Saracens Head Hotel, an old coaching inn, was where Charles I spent his last night of freedom whilst **Burgage Manor** was the residence of Lord Byron prior to his taking up residence at Newstead Abbey, and it was friends in the town who first encouraged him to publish his poems.

I have always had an affinity with Derbyshire and this time I concentrated on **Eyam** as an example of one of the villages of the peak. Each has its own charm and history and none more so that Eyam, known as the 'Queen of the Peak'. Here the old stone houses line the long, wide, old world street looking up to Eyam Edge towering 400ft above the village and reaching down to the gorge of **Middleton Dale** with its own delightful Cucklet Delf and Eyam Dale shut in by rocky heights. It looks at peace with itself but that is on the surface for no one living here has ever forgotten the terrible days of the plague.

It was in September 1665 that a box of tailor's cloth and some old clothes came from London to the cottage by the church, and with it a time that turned the village into a place of death, for it brought the plague that had raged in London for months. First the journeyman died within four days, five more by the end of the month and in October more than twenty. It continued its terrible path for the whole year only abating in winter. The warmer weather set it off again and by March 56 had perished.

All through this the villagers had been courageous and stoical people, who in the face of death, resigned themselves to their fate. Names that will live on forever are those of William Mompesson, the rector, his wife Catherine, and Thomas Stanley who had been ejected from the church for nonconformity, but had remained among his people. They set about isolating the village for the sake of other villages. They arranged for food to be brought from outside and left at certain places on the boundaries, the money left for payment being placed in vinegar to act as a disinfectant. One of these places became known as Mompesson's Well and is covered with a block of stone, half a mile north of the village.

Deaths became so frequent that the passing bell ceased to be tolled. The graveyard could no longer take the dead. Graves were dug in gardens and fields often by the families of those who had died. One woman watched helplessly whilst her husband and six children died within eight days. Their graves can still be seen, a pathetic circle of six headstones and a tomb.

Eventually the rector closed the church and took his ever decreasing flock to Cucklet Delf where Mompesson, whose wife Catherine was dead by this time, found comfort for himself and his followers in preaching from a picturesque rock with naturalarches. By October the plague had run its course. Out of 350 villagers, 259 had died as well as 58 children. Mompesson and Thomas Stanley saw it through until the bitter end. Mompesson left the village afterwards and eventually became a Prebendary of York. Thomas Stanley, who remained at Eyam until he died, was not given such recognition. In fact had it not been for the Earl of Devonshire he would still have been turned out of the village for nonconformity.

It is a horrendous but moving story in its courage and bravery. Eyam people are strong and welcoming, as can be witnessed when you visit the great church of St Lawrence. Be sure to see the 17th century wall paintings of emblems of the 12 tribes of Israel, the magnificent 8th-century cross, carved with bold vine scrolls and angels, and the 18th-century sundial.

In Water Lane is **The Miners Arms**, a 17th-century inn with a great story to tell. It was usd in lead mining times as the meeting place of the Great Barncote Court, which upheld the ancient and unique lead mining laws. The lead miners depended entirely on this Court to settle any disputes. Ghosts frequent The Miners and they could well be disgruntled lead miners who found the Court's decisions had gone against them. The pub is fun, the food excellent and there is attractive and comfortable accommodation.
For me Eyam is the epitome of what Derbyshire is all about.

They call Northamptonshire the Rose of the Shires. It is a true description, for this small county tucked away is quietly beautiful with its petals opening more and more gloriously as you penetrate into it. I knew nothing of it until I stayed in **Northampton** for a few days attending a seminar which gave me just enough free time to explore a little. The little whetted my desire to know more and the research for this book has given me the opportunity.

Northampton itself is the busiest place in the county, famous for its boots and shoes since King John bought a pair of shoes here for ninepence in the early 13th century but there is so much more. It is a thriving market town and a wonderfully covenient plac to use as a base for seeking out the beauty of the county.

If you want to find peace amidst the bustle of Northampton you will discover that it has no less than 1500 acres of parks and gardens. The largest, Abington Park, has boating, tennis, bowls, pitch and putt and something you rarely see or hear today, Band Concerts. **The Central Museum and Art Gallery** in Guildhall Road not surprisingly has a strong collection of boots and shoes, the largest in the world. Until you see it you would not believe how many different designs have been used, some look even more uncomfortable than the dreadful winkle pickers of the sixties and the platform shoes of the seventies. It also covers the history of Northampton from the Stone Age, and has decorative and fine arts on show. Another interesting museum is **The Leathercraft Museum** in Bridge Street which contains leatherwork from Ancient Egypt, Roman Britain, the early Middle Ages, gloves, Spanish leather, saddlery and the work of leathersellers. It is anamazing collection and very well displayed.

The Norman church of **St Peter** in Marefair is beautiful with no structural separation between nave and chancel and when you consider that much of medieval Northampton was destroyed by fire in 1675 it is good that the rare round Norman church of **Holy Sepulchre** survived. It was built by a returning crusader in 1100.

One of the most famous stately homes in all England is **Althorp**. The home of the Spencer family since 1508 it is known throughout the world now as the birthplace of the Princess of Wales. It lies only a few miles to the west of Northampton off the A428. Althorp has been altered over the centuries but in one sense it has changed little, the site is the same and the basic structure is Elizabethan.

To wander through it is to relive history. Everywhere you go there is something of great beauty or interest to attract you. The setting of the house, between formal gardens and in the middle of the park, is essentially a picture of Northamptonshire at its very best. It is a house that has been loved throughout its life and that shows in its dignity.

Another masterpiece of English architecture is **Castle Ashby** which lies on the outskirts of the village of the same name and a mere seven miles from Northampton. The building was started in 1574 by Henry, 1st Lord Compton. The original plan of the building was in the shape of an 'E' in honour of Queen Elizabeth I, and about sixty years later the courtyard was enclosed by a screen designed by Inigo Jones. The most interesting feature of Castle Ashby is the lettering around the house and terraces. The inscriptions when translated read 'the Lord guard your coming in' and 'The Lord guard your going out'. The Compton family are still there today so I think the prayer has been answered don't you?

Turner's Musical Merry Go-Round to be found near the village of **Wootton** off the A508 has the most unusual collection of mechanical musical istruments. The collection must be unique. If you enjoy gardens you will be well advised to visit **Holdenby**, six miles north west of Northampton off the A50. It is a tiny place but it contains one of the jewels of Northamptonshire. **Holdenby House** was the home of Queen Elizabeth's Chancellor, Sir Christopher Hatton who became her favourite Lord Chancellor. Hatton Garden, home of the diamond dealers in London was named after him. It was at Holdenby that he wrote impassioned and intimate letters to the Queen in which he said:

'To serve you is heaven but to lack you is hell's torment. Would to God I were with you for one hour. My wits are overwrought with thoughts, I find myself amazed. Bear with me, my dear sweet lady. Passion overcometh me. I can write no more. Love me for I love you.'

The original house is no longer there but its successor is a building of great beauty and dignity with fine transformed windows, seven picturesque dormers in the roof and some arresting chimney stacks. The grounds are of particular interest, with one of the finest Elizabethan gardens in England. As you wander around the fragrance of the silver borders assails your nostrils. It is quite lovely.

Coton Manor Garden off the A50, 10 miles north east of Northampton, owned by Commander and Mrs Pasley-Tyler, is another gem. It forms the framework for a charming 17th century stone manor house. You can wander round the gardens to your hearts content watching th activity of the water gardens, admiring the herbaceous borders, revelling in the glorious colours and scent of the roses. It is beautifully kept and home to a collection of waterfowl, cranes and flamingoes. Sample the home made tea after your visit and forget all about the need to diet!

Racing on the pretty course at **Towcester** is a very pleasant outing but even if there is no racing it is still a delightful place to visit and historically the oldest town in the county. Britons, Romans, Saxons and Normans have all had their share in building it. It has tremendous atmosphere and generally an air of tranquillity. Market days are apt to change this and so do Race days, of course, and I am not only referring to horses. Silverstone Motor Racing Circuit is only four miles away.

Stoke Bruerne is just to the east of Towcester. It is a pretty place in its own right with its thatched cottages climbing the hill, but most people come here to see the canal winding slowly by until its waters are raised by seven locks and vanish into a tunnel. **The Stoke Bruerne Canal Museum** will keep you interested for hours and give you a deep insight into 200 years of history and tradition on the canals and waterways. It has interesting shops from which you can buy many things including mementoes of your visit. One of the pleasantest features is the narrow boat trip you can take which will bring home to you all that you have seen in the museum.

Rockingham Forest was annexed by William Rufus for his personal hunting grounds and much of it is still there for us to enjoy. On a hill overlooking the thatched and slated village of **Rockingham** is the magnificent castle which dates from Elizabethan times. William the Conqueror gave orders for the keep to be built and King John used it as his hunting lodge. The castle was host to Charles Dickens on many occasions and it was to the then owners, the Watsons, that he dedicated David Copperfield.

Fotheringay is not far away, a village with solid limestone cottages and an 18th-century bridge over the River Nene on the edge of Rockingham Forest. It has an imposing church St Marys and All Saints, which has a cathedral air about it. Its setting is lovely too as it stands overlooking watermeadows fringing the river. See it from a distance with the sun flooding it with warmth and light and you may think it dreamlike and liable to float away before you reach it. Not so, it is firmly rooted as it has been since before Agincourt.

Most visitors come here to see the remains of the 14th-century castle where Mary Queen of Scots was executed in 1587. All that remains of this sad place is a mound on which grow wild Scotch thistles said to have been planted by the tragic Queen. There is a sad melancholy about the place that never disappears no matter how beautiful the day. Henry VIII gave it to the unhappy Catherine of Aragon, the bloodstained Richard III was born here and Mary Stuart lost her head in the banqueting hall. Thiscastle of such awesome memories was pulled down in 1627 and two hundred years after this they found a gold ring with a lover's knot entwined round the initials of Mary and Darnley.

Between **Grafton Underwood** and the village of **Geddington** is another wonderful stately home, **Boughton House**, the Northamptonshire home of the Duke of Buccleuch. Lets talk about Geddington first, because it is here that the best of all the Eleanor Crosses still stands in memory of the night in 1290 when King Edward lay uneasily in bed in his hunting lodge whilst his beloved Queen Eleanor lay in her coffin within the walls of the palace that once was here. There were nine crosses in all but only three remain, this one and the others at **Hardingstone** and **Waltham.** Geddington is a delightful place.

The beauty of Boughton lies in the wonderful light from the 366 windows - one for every day of the year and an extra one for leap year. It has been described as a vision of Louis XIV's Versailles transported to England. You will find it full of lovely things including some 17th-18th century tapestries, French and English furniture and the masterpieces of Murillo, El Greco and many others. It should be remembered that Boughton House is an integral part of a thriving and progressive rural estate of some 11,000 acres. The 350 acres Park has broad avenues of 200 year old trees with river and lake walks, nature trails and an Adventure Woodland Play Area.

Where the A6 joins the A6116 is the little village of **Islip** separated from its bigger neighbour, **Thrapston** by the fine old bridge that spans the River Nene with many arches. Both places are like magnets for our American visitors. At Islip it is the elegant medieval church they come to see with its great east window. It is as fine inside as out and high on the south wall of the sanctuary is a monument to Mary Washington, whose husband was John Washington of Thrapston, uncle of Laurence Washington who sailed to America in 1657, bcoming the great-grandfather of the President.

The Americans themselves have contributed to the glory of this church. They presented it with a fine modern brass to take the place of the lost brass of one John Nicoll who died in 1657. The Americans are also responsible for the oak chancel screen and the reredos in remembrance of their predescessors, including Matthias Nicoll, who, born about 1630, was a Plymouth preacher's son and went to America with the Duke of York. Matthew Nicoll drew up the first code of English laws for the Governor, which he signed with his own name. His commonsense approach has been regarded as very important to the Americans.

Higham Ferrers is still sufficiently small to encourage you to abandon your car and wander through its streets. Just off Market Square you will be amply rewarded by the sight of the church of the Blessed Virgin Mary in the centre of a group of ecclesiastical buildings of medieval origin. The beautiful spire looks across the valley of the Nene to another lovely church in the village of **Irthlingborough**. Here the Nene is crossed by an impressive 14th-century bridge. St Peters Church fills you with a sense of 'God's in his heaven and all's right with the world.' It seems untouched by time.

In the west of the county **Daventry** will always be thought of for its association with radio communications but it goes back to the Prehistoric Age when it was a fortified camp and the stronghold for men of the Stone Age. It lies on Borough Hill and is part of the ride which forms the Water Divide of the Midlands. From its highest point the line of the ancient Watling Street may be followed. When the day is clear you can see into seven counties.

It is in **Oundle** in the north of the county that I leave you. This is a treasure of the county with its fine houses, ancient pubs and St Peters Church with its glorious Decorated tower and spire. The church is both simple and sumptuous and somewhere which will keep you delighted in mind and eye.

If all this were not enough Oundle has one of the country's oldest and most famous public schools. The streets are wide and the gentle waters of the River Nene embrace it on three sides. Oundle illustrates all that is best and beautiful about this lovely county.

THE GEORGE
Alstonfield,
Nr. Ashbourne,
Derbyshire
Tel: 01335 310205

Situated in lovely countryside six miles north of Ashbourne off the A515 is the little village of Alstonfield. Nothing disturbs its peace too much, apart from the visitors who come to enjoy the many wonderful walks and the scenery in what has become known as Isaak Walton country. In the midst of the village at its focal point is The George, which has been caring for travellers and local people for over 250 years. It is a simple, happy and comfortable pub in which Richard and Sue Grandjean have been mine hosts for almost thirty years. There is little the Grandjeans do not know about the area and they are happy to share their knowledge with their customers. There are all year round camping facilities attached to the pub which attracts many families. They take themselves off during the day to explore and return in the evening to enjoy the hospitality and the fun in the bar. Chatsworth House and Haddon Hall are within striking distance and so are Alton Towers and Tittersworth Reservoir. For those who like golf, Buxton Golf Club welcomes visitors. Whatever you choose to eat at The George will be home-cooked using fresh produce. The Order for all meals is taken at the Kitchen Door, which makes it homely and friendly. Brown Bread is used for the fresh, well-filled sandwiches, a selection of home-made puddings is listed on the Kitchen Door every day. It is a delightful place and good value.

USEFUL INFORMATION

OPEN;11-2.30pm & 6-11pm
CHILDREN;Welcome
CREDIT CARDS; No credit cards
LICENSED; Yes
ACCOMMODATION;Camping facilities
RESTAURANT;Not applicable
BAR FOOD;Home-cooked, wide range
VEGETARIAN;Varied dishes
DISABLED ACCESS;Easy access
GARDEN:Village green & garden

RENAISSANCE,
Bath Street, Bakewell
Derbyshire
Tel: 01629 812687

This charming and quietly sophisticated restaurant in the heart of Bakewell is half-timbered in Tudor style and in summer is pleasingly festooned with hanging baskets and window boxes, ablaze with colour. It is painted externally in black and white and is quite eyecatching. At the rear is a beautiful perfumed garden. The French windows from the restaurant and the next door eaterie are opened onto this on sunny days. The pace in the restaurant is leisurely and the food memorable. There is a fixed price menu a la carte for four courses at 15.95 and a lunchtime menu in the Eaterie Room from 5.50. The wine list is well chosen and offers a wide range of wines from around the world at sensible prices. Special gourmet evenings occur regularly and special evening catering is available on request. A truly delightful place to be, Renaissance should not be missed. The Restaurant and the Eaterie Room open Tuesday lunchtime until Sunday lunchtime. Well behaved children welcome. All major credit cards. Easy access for the disabled. Vegetarian dishes cooked to order.

USEFUL INFORMATIOM

OPEN; Tuesday lunchtime until Sunday lunchtime
CHILDREN; Well behaved welcome
CREDIT CARDS; All major cards
LICENSED; Fine wine list
RESTAURANT; Memorable food
VEGETARIAN; cooked to order
DISABLED ACCESS: Easy access
GARDEN; Beautiful, perfumed
ACCOMMODATION; Not applicable

THE PACK HORSE INN
Little Longstone,
Nr. Bakewell, Derbyshire
Tel: 01629 640471

Three miles from the busy market town of Bakewell is a hamlet that has to be one of the most beautiful and unspoilt in Derbyshire. It is Little Longstone and the focal point is the small country inn, The Pack Horse, where Lynn and Mark Lythgoe welcome all their customers in the tradition of the pub which has been continuous for 200 years. The building is a lot older than that dating back to the 16th century when it was simply a labourer's cottage. What would the labourer make of it now? He would find a place that is not marred by the passage of time and is full of character and charm, with beamed ceilings and open fires providing a warm and friendly atmosphere but with far more comfort than he would have found in his time.

Both Lynn and Mark were born and raised locally and it is this background that has helped them to locate and form an excellent working relationship with some of the best butchers, grocers, fishmongers, bakers and vintners for miles around. Their efforts have ensured that the food and wines you enjoy are of the highest quality. You can eat either in the small and intimate dining room or in the bars. Wherever you are you will find the furnishings are totally in keeping with the buildings and encourage you to relax and enjoy The Pack Horse. Wisely the menu is not vast but includes interesting and beautifully cooked dishes. It is a delight to be here.

USEFUL INFORMATION

OPEN; 11-3pm & 5-11pm
CHILDREN; Welcome
CREDIT CARDS; None taken
LICENSED; Yes
GARDEN : With goats & rabbits

DINING ROOM; Excellent fare, local produce
BAR FOOD; Interesting and good value
VEGETARIAN; Several dishes
DISABLED ACCESS; Difficult

THE MONTAGU ARMS,
Barnwell, Northants,
Tel: 01832 273726

Barnwell was until recently the home of the Duke and Duchess Gloucester and what better setting could a pub have! The Montagu Arms is situated opposite the stream. The A605 is close as is the new £14 link road. Edward Montagu was chief justice to the court of the King's Bench during the reign of Henry VIII, and he purchased the manor from the Abbot of Ramsey at the time of the Dissolution of the churches about 1540. The Montagu Arms was built specifically for the workmen to live in during the erecting of the Manor house. It is one of the oldest inns in Northamptonshire and very much unchanged apart from a section that has been added in recent years to provide a new lounge, dining area and accommodation suites. This has been constructed so graciously that it merely adds charm and certainly does not detract from the overall look of the Inn. There are 5 twin en-suite rooms and a reasonable sized conference or meeting suite which can be used also for parties. The food is excellent, well presented, freshly cooked and at sensible prices. Specials dominate the blackboard everyday offering a tasty choice. Children are extra welcome and enjoy the large crazy golf area and the wide assortment of recreation aids on the lawns. Barbecues are a regular feature in the summer months. The Montagu has a successful darts team as well as its own football eleven. Two fairly high profile ghosts have been encountered by staff and customers. It all adds to the tremendous atmosphere which the licensee, Bill Wilson does much to foster.

USEFUL INFORMATION

OPEN; Summer: 11-3pm & 6-11pm. Winter: 11.30-2.30pm & 7-11pm. Sunday: 12-3pm & 7-10.30pm
CHILDREN; Very welcome.
CREDIT CARDS; None taken
LICENSED; Yes
ACCOMMODATION; 5 twin en-suite rooms.

RESTAURANT; Freshly cooked, sensible prices
BAR FOOD; Wide range
VEGETARIAN; 3 dishes daily
DISABLED ACCESS; Yes
GARDEN; Very large recreational garden.

THE GREYHOUND INN,
25 Melton Road,
Burton on the Wolds
Leicestershire
Tel: 01509 880860

One of the most attractive pubs in the area, it is a white three-storey buildings with a verandah and adjoining coach house. In addition to snug bars, comfortable seating and open fires there is a large dining area which has French windows opening onto a paved patio and lawn - ideal for private parties and wedding receptions. The bill of fare is available seven days a week and has the emphasis on fresh food. All the bread, meat and vegetables come from local suppliers. There are home-made soups and pate, daily 'Specials' and a varied full bar menu complemented by a comprehensive wine list. Philip and Ann Ashley, the proprietors, have developed their own vegetarian menu consisting of six home-made dishes. This is an inn that deserves its many accolades including Les Routier recommended.

USEFUL INFORMATION

OPEN; Mon-Fri 12-2.30pm & 5.30-11pm Sat & Sun: 12-3pm & 7-11pm.
RESTAURANT; Emphasis on fresh food
BAR FOOD; Traditional, home-cooked
CHILDREN; Well behaved welome
VEGETARIAN; Always a good choice
CREDIT CARDS; All major cards
DISABLED ACCESS; Yes
LICENSED; Yes
GARDEN; Beer Garden & Patio
ACCOMMODATION; Not applicable

THE FALCON HOTEL,
Castle Ashby,
Northampton NN7 1LF
Tel: 01604 696200 Fax:01604 696673

Just six miles south east of Northampton, this traditional 16th Century B Watsons have an eye for beauty which is apparent throughout the hotel. The overall atmosphere is cosy, warm and comfortable and enhanced in the winter with a blazing log fire. In summer the pretty restaurant which seats 60 and the pavilion marquee overlook a luscious green lawn, surrounded by willow and walnut trees. The restaurant teems with life - lunch and dinner - seven days a week. With good reason for the food is undoubtedly the highlight. All 16 bedrooms have private bathrooms. Friendly faces greet you on arrival; French, Spanish and German is spoken. Fresh flowers abound. Special weekend breaks are available; private parties, weddings or small conferences can all be catered for. Nothing is too much trouble.The hotel is a member of the Best Western Consortium and a Relais du Silence.

USEFUL INFORMATION

OPEN; All year.Bar 12-3pm & 6.30-11pm
CHILDREB; Welcome.
CREDIT CARDS;Visa/Access/ Master/Amex/ JCB.
LICENSED; Yes
ACCOMMODATION; 16 ensuite rooms
RESTAURANT; Superb food
BAR FOOD; Wide range
VEGETARIAN; Daily choice
DISABLED ACCESS; Yes
GARDEN; Yes

THE MONCKTON ARMS,
Main Road,
Glaston, Leicestershire
Tel: 01572 822326

This charming 16th/17th-century inn is on the main A47, 2 miles from Uppingham and on the chief holiday route from Leicester to the East Coast. Since Spencer Dainton took over with his excellent chef, Mark Goode early in July 1995 there has been extensive refurbishment and decoration. They have been extremely careful not to destroy the olde world charm of the Monckton Arms Hotel and have succeeded in making it a delightful place to stop. It is one of those quiet restful places with no loud music to disturb the peace. There are 11 well furnished en-suite bedrooms, some twin, some double and a family room, but all have TV and tea/coffee making facilities. Other facilities include laundry and ironing services, trouser press etc. In the mornings you can either tuck into a splendid traditional English Breakfast complete with local bacon, sausage, tomatoes, mushrooms and fresh eggs or a lighter Continental one. It is a great start to the day after a restful night. In the restaurant you can choose from a wide variety of well presented dishes either from the A La Carte menu or from the Table d'Hote. In particular you may want to try the very good honey roasted duck served with Cherry apples in a Plum sauce. Whatever you decide upon you will have a very good meal and be agreeably surprised at the reasonable prices. In the Bar there is an extensive range of good home-cooked Bar Meals including particularly good Ploughmans, and on Sundays the traditional Roast lunch is available with a choice of meat or poultry. There are Conference facilities for 50 people. Special weekend break prices £49.95 per two people per night, Dinner, bed and breakfast (Min 2 night stay)

USEFUL INFORMATION

OPEN; Every day 11am-11pm. Sun: 12-10.30pm
RESTAURANT; A la Carte or Table d'hote
CHILDREN; Welcome
BAR FOOD; Excellent value
CREDIT CARDS; Amex/Access/Visa/Switch.
VEGETARIAN; Several dishes
LICENSED; Yes
DISABLED ACCESS; Limited
ACCOMMODATION; 11 ensuite rooms
GARDEN; Beer garden. BBQ
PETS; Welcome -special rooms for guests with pets

THE SKILLET RESTAURANT
Steeple End Field,
Hayfield, Stockport
Cheshire
Tel: 01663 743119

Two 17th century stone cottages were extended in the 19th century to provide a small eating house serving the station. Today this has become The Skillet Restaurant catering for discerning palates for many miles around the small Derbyshire village of Hayfield, which lies between Glossop and New Mills and no distance from Chapel-en-le-Frith. It is surrounded by superb moorland which provides wonderful vistas for walkers. Kidder Scout looks down benevolently on the village. Paul Hughes and Colin Bolton, using their considerable talents and experience have transformed The Skillet. There is one main dining room catering for 40 covers, and one large, separate bar area which seats 30 comfortably. The surroundings and the food once savoured will not be forgotten. Theme evenings are tremendously popular. You may find yourself part of an old English evening with a Minstrel in attendance or embraced by the liveliness of an Italian extravaganza. A traditional lunch is served on Sundays. Neither the good selection of wines nor the excellent food are at anything but affordable prices.

USEFUL INFORMATION

OPEN; Tues-Sat 7-10pm. Sun 12-3pm.
CHILDREN; Welcome. No facilities
CREDIT CARDS; Access/Visa
LICENSED; Yes. Affordable wines
ACCOMMODATION; Not applicable
RESTAURANT; Memorable food
BAR FOOD; Not applicable
VEGETARIAN; 4 dishes daily
DISABLED ACCESS; Level entrance
GARDEN; Small garden. Car park

WEAVERS
54 King Street,
Leicester,
Tel: 01509 412167

Weavers recalls 19th century Leicester and in its pleasant surroundings it provides a Wine Bar which is very much of this century but has that almost intangible relaxed air that was so much part of the bygone centuries in bars and coffee houses catering for those with good taste. Seven original terraced weavers cottages have been tastefully renovated, their courtyard bedecked with an impressive Victorian conservatory. All of which give the impression of a 'street scene' whilst retaining the intimate charm of 'one up and two up down' living and working environment of the era. The original York stone paving set against the rustic pitched pine bar and wrought ironwork lends itself to an ambience of times gone by. In addition to wines from the well stocked cellar, food is also available all day, ranging from morning croissants, afternoon tea, to wholesome traditional dishes as well as hot and cold snacks. There are traditional cask beers, lagers popular bottled beers, interesting wines and hot drinks. Weavers is under the ownership and managment of the able Jeremy Lord who owns Quorn Grange in Wood Lane, one of the finest, small hotels in the county.

USEFUL INFORMATION

OPEN; 11am-11pm with a 12 o'clock supper license.
CREDIT CARDS; Yes
LICENSED; Yes
CHILDREN; Welcome
RESTAURANT; Available all day
BAR FOOD; Hot and cold snacks
VEGETARIAN; Several dishes
DISABLED ACCESS; Yes

THE THREE SWANS HOTEL
High Street,
Market Harborough
Leicestershire LE16 7NJ
Tel:01858 466644 Fax: 01858 433101

The Three Swans never fails to delight its guests with its warm welcome, efficient service and an ambience that combines olde world charm with the ultimate comfort and style of the 20th century. Just to remind you of its historic past, on June 13th 1645, the day before the Battle of Naseby, King Charles I took refreshment at the Three Swans Hotel and nearly 300 years later the Prince of Wales was brought to the hotel following a hunting accident. Today the hotel has been thoughtfully extended and refurbished. It combines the hospitality befitting its 16th Century origins with every modern comfort and amenity. There are 36 individually decorated en-suite bedrooms. All have direct dial telephone, remote control colour TV, tea/coffee making facilities, trouser press and hair dryer. Three rooms have antique four poster beds. Swans Restaurant is renowned throughout the Midlands for its aw Whilst the Swan's Nest Conservatory offers a less formal environment to take refreshment and during the summer months you can enjoy a drink al fresco, in the courtyard. ard winning cuisine. The hotel has held an AA Rosette for good food and wine for the past six years. The lounge bar and cosy 'Fothergills Bar' attract many of the local characters, so there's always a good atmosphere and plenty of company. The relaxing cocktail bar complements the ambience of the restaurant. Wonderful for weddings and licensed for Civil Marriages, it is also a popular place for seminars and conferences which provide the perfect environment for productive meetings.

USEFUL INFORMATION

OPEN; All year
CHILDREN; Welcome
CREDIT CARDS; Access/Visa/Amex/Diners/Switch
GARDEN; Courtyard .
PETS; Not welcome
ACCOMMODATION; 36 ensuite rooms. Old School House Conference Centre with 11 rooms & excellent facilities

RESTAURANT; Renowned for its food
BAR FOOD; Wide range daily
VEGETARIAN; Several dishes daily
DISABLED ACCESS; Yes. 2 Bedrooms. Bars & cloakroom

THE NEW FERRY RESTAURANT,
Riverside,
Farndon, Newark
Nottinghamsire
Tel: 01636 76578

This is a restaurant in which the owners, Pam and Jose Gomes fiercely maintain the old fashioned elegance now lost in so many restaurants. This does not mean that it is not relaxed. The silver-service staff are beautifully trained by Jose, and he personally flambe's some dishes at his trolley. No table is ever double booked, so you can linger over your meal for as long as you wish. You will find The New Ferry in the pretty village of Farndon, just off the Fosseway (A46) and one and a half miles out of the historic town of Newark. Mentioned in the Domesday Book, the village church and the Ferry crossing attract a lot of visitors. The old towpath from Newark ends just outside the restaurant. To continue on to Nottingham you have to cross the River Trent on the ferry. The old winching gear used to take the horse across in the days of the horsedrawn barges, is still to be seen next to the slipway. The restaurant has a large car park on the riverside, with moorings for customers' boats. Jose comes from Madeira and this is apparent in the interior with lots of woodwork, wicker furniture, marbletopped bar with masses of different liquers decorating the shelves. He is a Fellow of the Academy of Wine which is reflected in the splendid and reasonably priced wine list. The A La Carte menu, available at lunchtimes and in the evenings, usually has dishes from Portugal. At lunchtime there is also a Snacks menu and a Dish of the Day. Sunday is the day for the traditional English Roast Beef and Yorkshire Pudding. It is a delightful place.

USEFUL INFORMATION

OPEN; Tues-Sun: 12-2.30pm, 7pm until late.
CHILDREN;Children welcome.
CREDIT CARDS;Access/Visa.Amex/ Diners.
GARDEN;Al Fresco garden overlooking the river.

RESTAURANT Wonderful, varied menu
BAR FOOD; Lunchtime snack menu
VEGETARIAN ; Several dishes
DISABLED ACCESS; Yes. Wide doors

QUORN GRANGE
Wood Lane, Quorn
Leicestershire LE12 8DB
Tel: 01509 412167
Fax: 01509 415621

This elegant, mellow and ivy clad country house is the epitome of what a good hotel should be. It is under the personal supervision of the welcoming owner, Jeremy Lord who masterminds the apparently faultess running of the establishment. Without doubt his skills have communicated themselves to his staff who have the same dedication and offer a friendly, efficient service to guests. There are 19 ensuite bedrooms, each furnished with cheerful fabrics, tasteful decor, good beds and bathrooms. They all overlook the immaculately kept gardens and the gentle Leicestershire countryside. The dining room, with its pretty drapes and soft colour scheme, has become synonymous in the area with good food. It is as popular with local people as it is with those who come to stay. The menu is a mixture of traditional and dishes which come from the inspirational hands of the chef and his team. An ideal venue for a wedding reception or private function, the hotel also has gained acclaim for the excellence of its Conference facilities for 25-30 people. Every back up facility is available for the businessman. Places of interest to visit from here abound. Bradgate Park and The Beacon, both of Leicestershire. Nottingham Castle; Belvoir Castle and many more. With adequate notice Horse Riding, Swimming, Golf, Squash, Angling and Clay Pigeon Shooting can be arranged.

USEFUL INFORMATION

OPEN; All year.
CHILDREN; Welcome
CREDIT CARDS; None taken
LICENSED; Yes
ACCOMMODATION; 19 ensuite rooms Conference facilities
RESTAURANT; Inspired menu
DISABLED ACCESS; Yes
VEGETARIAN; Daily choice
GARDEN; Yes
PETS; By arrangement

THE WOOLPACK HOTEL
6, Kettering Rd,
Islip, Nr. Thrapston
Northamptonshire
Tel: 01832 732578

This is a truly delightful hotel overlooking the River Nene. The sort of place that having visited for the first time you would take your leave knowing that a return visit would not be too far off. It is easy to find on the A14 just ten miles from Kettering. Recently the hotel has been completely refurbished, and whilst doing it, all sorts of unexpected things were uncovered including the attractive stonewalls and inviting inglenook fireplaces. All the bedrooms are furnished to a high standard with modern and antique furniture, and have either views of the River Nene or across the fields to Islip Church. As one would expect all the rooms are en-suite and equipped with Television, Radio and a beverage tray. There are special breaks throughout the year at excellent prices. Children under 12 stay free if sharing a room with their parents. Open to non-residents, the food is superb, the comfortable bars offer a wide range of bar meals and at weekends in the summer there are delicious cream teas from 3-5pm.

USEFUL INFORMATION

OPEN; 11.30-2.30pm 6.30-11pm.
CHILDREN; Welcome
CREDIT CARDS; Yes
LICENSED; Yes
ACCOMMODATION; 13 ensuite rooms
RESTAURANT; Superb menu
BAR FOOD; Wide range
VEGETARIAN; Daily choice
DISABLED ACCESS; Limited
GARDEN; Yes. Cream Teas in summer

THE PICKWICK RESTAURANT,
201 Watling St,
Towcester, Northamptonshire
Tel: 01327 350692.

The name Watling Street immediately conjures up an historical atmosphere and when, just ten minutes from Towcester National Hunt Racecourse and 4 miles from Silverstone, you come across the delightful Pickwick Restaurant, which dates from 1600, you have found a treasure of the past. This establishment which looks quite small from the outside, is quite misleading. There are three separate downstairs dining rooms, and upstairs private facilities for wedding receptions and celebration parties for 12-60 people. As one would expect in a building of this age there is a wealth of old oak beams and it is rumoured that it is haunted by a friendly ghost. The Pickwick has been in the same ownership since 1949 and under the same management since 1968 with a fully trained staff, many of whom have been there ten years or more. It is a happy place in which to work and eat. In the 1800s it was used as a bakery and a post office, with the Mail Coaches stopping outside to drop the mail into the cellar through a hatchway. It was the Ward family, from whom the present owners purchased the property, who first made the now celebrated Towcester Cheesecake which is still served in the restaurant and sold today in the Pickwick Shop, 2 doors below. The Pickwick serves food all day, every day, except Sundays and some Bank Holidays. There is a wide range of tempting snacks always available, except Saturday evenings, and a very comprehensive A la Carte menu, all of which is home-cooked. The prices are extremely reasonable and the portions generous. A good place to visit.

USEFUL INFORMATION

OPEN; Mon-Thurs 9-9pm Fri/Sat 9-10pm. Closed Sundays.
CHILDREN; Children welcome.
CREDIT CARDS; All major cards
LICENSED; Yes
RESTAURANT; Excellent food all day
BAR FOOD; Snacks always available
VEGETARIAN; Several dishes
DISABLED ACCESS; No
GARDEN; Pretty garden for use in summer.

THE OLD FRIAR,
Twywell, Nr. Kettering.
Northamptonshire
Tel:01832 732625

This is one of those delightful old pubs that are so much a part of rural Northamptonshire. It is just 7 miles from Kettering and only 2 miles from Thrapston which makes it ideal for people who live in either place to use for lunch or dinner or even just a quiet drink. The Old Friar is a 16th-century building to which extensions have been tastefully added. The delightful restaurant which seats 65 is in the original building complete with beams, and in keeping with the name there are carvings of Friars everywhere adorning fireplaces and carved into the woodwork. In winter the open fires add a warmth to the friendly, welcoming atmosphere that has been created over the centuries and added to by the Crisps, the present owners, who have been here themselves for well over a quarter of a century. There are several interesting places to visit in the vicinity one of them being Broughton House, the home of the Duke of Buccleuch. A house full of history and fascinating because it has a window for every day of the year. Yvonne Crisp is an excellent cook and the full A La Carte menu offers some deliciousdishes. The main feature however is a first class carvery. In addition there is a wide range of Bar food.

USEFUL INFORMATION

OPEN; 11-2.30pm & 6-11pm.
CHILDREN; Welcome
CREDIT CARDS;Access/Visa
LICENSED; Yes
ACCOMMODATION; None

RESTAURANT; Excellent carvery. Full A la carte
BAR FOOD; Wide range
VEGETARIAN;Large choice
GARDEN; Yes

THE FOX INN,
Church Street,
Wilbarston, Market Harborough
Leicestershire
Tel: 01536 771270.

There are parts of this interesting pub, which has always been a hostelry, that date back to the 14th century. Do not expect to find a ghost because there is definitely not one! Quite surprising really because it is such a welcoming place that it would make an excellent haunting home for any up market ghost. The Fox Inn is owned by the McHarg family, two brothers, Bert and John, and their wives Sheila and Barbara. It is a very happy place to visit and best described as a traditional style village inn situated in the heart of Wilbarston. It is a very pleasant part of the Welland Valley in the Rockingham Forest area. An ideal place to stop for a drink, a meal or to stay in one of the bedrooms which have been built in a converted outbuilding. The are 4 bedrooms, 2 double, 1 twin-bedded and one family room. All of them are extremely comfortable and ensuite with colour TV and tea/coffee making facilities. There is a pleasant lounge bar, public bar, games room and a dining room. The McHargs are extremely hospitable and insist on very high standards of service. Once you have stayed here you will want to return. The menu, whether it is for Bar Food or in the Dining Room, is based on simple, well cooked and presented traditional dishes. The prices are extremely reasonable and the quality undoubted. There are never less than four interesting vegetarian dishes.

USEFUL INFORMATION

OPEN; Bar: 12-2.30pm & 6.30-11pm
Restaurant: Tues-Sat 6.30-9.45pm + Sunday Lunch
Bar Food: Mon-Sat 12-2pm & 6.30-9.45pm.
CHILDREN; Welcome to stay and in dining room.
CREDIT CARDS; Visa/Mastercard
LICENSED; Yes
ACCOMMODATION; 4 ensuite rooms

RESTAURANT; Well presented. Traditional
BAR FOOD; Extremely reasonable. Wide Choice
VEGETARIAN; 4 + daily
DISABLED ACCESS; No
GARDEN; Patio with tables & chairs Boules pitch.

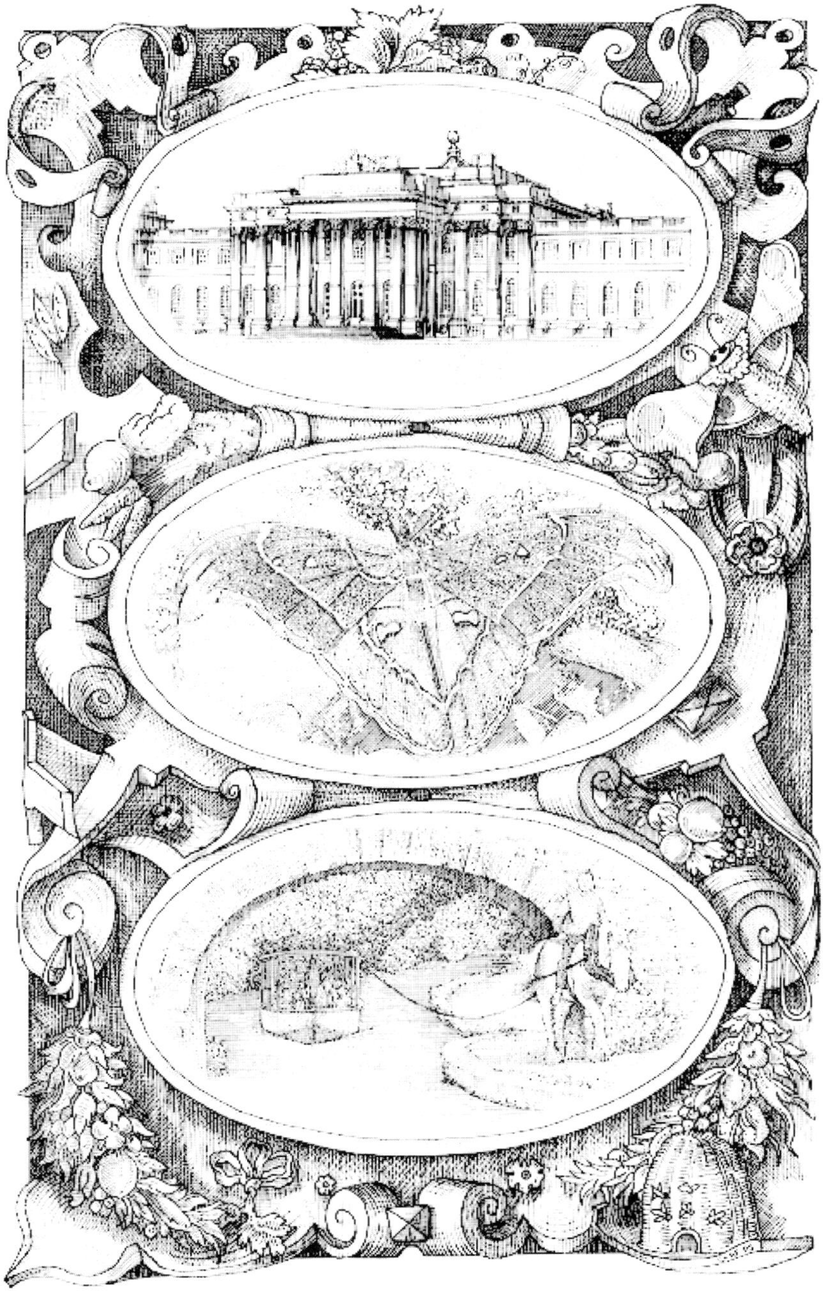

GLOUCESTERSHIRE, OXFORDSHIRE & THE COTSWOLDS

Includes

Abingdon Lodge Hotel	Abingdon	p.200
The Crown of Crucis	Ampney Crucis	p.201
The Crown Hotel	Blockley	p.202
Lansdowne Villa	Bourton-on-the-Water	p.203
The Old New Inn	Bourton-on-the-Water	p.204
Buckingham Lodge Hotel	Buckingham	p.205
Elm House Hotel	Burford	p.206
Bull at Charlbury	Charlbury	p.207
White Hart Royal Hotel	Moreton-in-Marsh	p.208
Stow Lodge Hotel	Stow-in-the-Wold	p.209
Witney Lodge Hotel	Witney	p.210

The City of Gloucester makes a wonderful springboard for the chapter which will take me to some of my most favourite places in the whole country. They say that 42 Kings have visited the city, to say nothing of Queens, Princes, Princesses and other Royal personages. The Saxon Kings had their own royal palace here, giving the name to the district of Kingsholm. Gloucester owes much to one Saxon 'royal' Aethelflaeda, daughter of Alfred the Great, who undertook the restoration of the city after its period of decline.

Gloucester sits in an enviable position and is able to claim it is part of the West Country as well as being in the Heart of England. Whichever it chooses to be it is bustling and prosperous. A wonderful base from which to explore so many places. Close to the Cotswolds, no distance from the Severn Vale, and a short drive to the Royal Forest of Dean. Wherever you are in the city you cannot miss the Cathedral. Whatever one's opinion of the less than sympathetically developed City of Gloucester nothing can detract from the magnificent grandeur of the body nor the glorious symmetry of the Cathedral tower. Inside it has so much beauty that one is left almost bereft of speech and it takes a while to re-adjust to the hurly burly of the twentieth century when you leave it hallowed portals.

The great round columns of the nave lead us to the choir where the beauty is so wondrous it is almost miraculous. There are soaring columns, a great lierne vault and the largest stained glass window in England which somehow has survived six centuries, and is still full of superb 14th century glass. There are flying arches and angelic musicians forming the bosses in the vault above the high altar. There are no adequate words to describe the beauty. It is for you to see and make up your own mind.

Gloucester Cathedral is a favourite of mine and in amongst its stunning beauty there are some very simple and moving things to see as well. For example, only a few steps away from the tomb of Edward II, perhaps the finest of all royal effigies, is a very different piece of stonemasonry - a tiny cross, obviously fashioned by a loving, but amateur hand. This is the cross of Colonel Carne VC, carved with a nail in the Chinese prison camps by the brave and valourous Commanding Officer of the Glorious Gloucesters, who preferred to go into captivity with his men rather than escape to freedom after the heroic battle at Solm-ri on the Imjin River during the Korean War in April 1951.

With a love of things ecclesiastical it would be a pity not to take a look at Gloucester's fine churches. There is an old saying which is supposed to relate to the amazing number of churches in Gloucestershire. 'As sure as God's in Gloucestershire'; something that certainly applies to the number and variety in this county capital. At the north-west corner of the Cathedral precincts, is the Green of **St Mary's Square** which has a massive memorial to the martyred Bishop Hooper and it also has a pleasant church, St Mary de Lode, which just might be the site of one of the earliestplaces of Christian worship in Britain. Just a stroll from the cathedral is the ruined priory church of **St Oswalds** which is Gloucester's oldest building. English Heritage have the care of **Blackfriars**, the most perfectly preserved example of a Dominican Friary in Britain. **Greyfriars** is a fine example of an early 16th century Franciscan Friary, ruined after the Dissolution. It forms a most dramatic backdrop to the delicate beauty of **St Mary de Crypt** church and the modern architecture of **Eastergate Market**.

Llanthony Priory has undergone a massive programme of restoration after years of neglect. Probably the most intriguing of all Tourist Information Centres in the country is housed in **St Michaels Tower**, all that is left of a medieval church. No less than seven Mayors of Gloucester are buried in **St John's** in Northgate Street, founded by the Saxon King Athelstan in about AD931 and later rebuilt by the Normans. The pulpit is all that remains of the 'three-decker' from which both George Whitfield and John Wesley are known to have preached.

Gloucester is a multi-racial city and many new churches have been welcomed into it. The buildings have certainly added a new, handsome and spectacular dimension to the architecture of the city. None of these is more remarkable than than the Mosque Jamal.

One of my favourites is the delightful tiny **Mariner's Church** which is incorporated into the redevelopment of Gloucester Docks. It is a Victorian foundation, provided for the spiritual well-being of the sailors and dock workers, who perhaps felt uncomfortable in the town churches. Gloucestershire poet and composer, Ivor Gurney, was choirmaster here for a while.

You could travel all over Britain and Europe today and see nothing quite like **Gloucester Docks**. They represent a resource of national importance and one of England's most exciting new tourist attractions. Charles Dickens description of the port in days gone by explains succinctly, what it was like.

> *'You will see, suddenly appearing, as if it is in a dream, long ranges of warehouses, with cranes attached, endless intricacies of dock, miles of tramroad, a wilderness of timber in stacks, and huge, three masted ships wedged into little canals, floating with no apparent means of propulsion and without a sail to bless themselves with'.*

That was Gloucester Docks at the height of their wealth and prestige. Now where dockers and mariners once toiled and strived, tourists can sit or stroll at leisure. Where grain, salt and timbers were stored, there are bars, restaurants, an antique centre and three museums. Dickens 'long range warehouses' have been restored to their former glory and this is only one part of the miracle that has occurred. A decade or so ago public opinion was so strong that the acres of dereliction which existed were nearly demolished with the objective of starting something new from scratch. Fortunately there was an acceptable alternative made possible by British Waterways Board and Gloucester City Council, and so now we are able to see the most complete example of Victorian Dockland in existence anywhere in the world. The Docks are a mecca for film and TV companies who have used the Dock as a period setting on many occasions including the memorable 'Onedin Line'. One could spend at least a day exploring Gloucester Docks taking in everything from the exciting **National Waterways Museum, The Regiments of Gloucestershire Museum, The Robert Opie Collection Museum of Advertising and Packaging** or 'Merchants Quay' a new green steel and grass pavilion on the edge of the main dock basin which forms the heart of dockland shopping. Here you can hire a ball gown, buy a postcard enjoy a cup of freshly ground coffee with a doughnut, have a pizza or relax with a pint looking across the water from **Doctor Foster's Public House and Restaurant.**

Cheltenham now a town of flowers, which has many times won awards in the Britain in Bloom Competitions, three hundred years ago was just an ordinary village and not the elegant place we know today. The story of how it became a Spa is undoubtedly far fetched but nonetheless an enjoyable thought! A resident watched a flock of pigeons who appeared particularly healthy. Daily they came to drink from the same spring. Samples of the water were taken and it was found that it had health giving minerals. This brought people flocking to the town to gain the same benefits as the pigeons and so the spa was born. You may not believe the tale, but Cheltonians do - they have seen fit to include a pigeon on the town's crest! By the end of 1783 the first Pump Room was established and it attracted such distinguished visitors as George III and the Duke of Wellington. There is no question that the waters were beneficial and still are.

Today you can take the waters at the **Town Hall** as well as the Pittville Pump Room which has to be the most notable of all Regency buildings. The whole town has an air of elegance withits fine crescents and distinguised mansions. The Regency Promenade, laid out in 1818, must be one of the most gracious thoroughfares in Britain. It was built as a carriage drive leading from the High Street up to the Spa, now the site of the impressive **Queens Hotel.**

People come to Cheltenham for many reasons but probably more than any other for the horse racing at the Cheltenham course, one of the prettiest in the country. As every meeting comes around so the town fills up, every hotel is full for miles around and the whole place seems to become preoccupied with the sport of kings. It creates a wonderful atmosphere.

Who could not love **Tewkesbury**. Situated where the Avon meets the Severn, it is the northern gate to the Cotswolds. It grew up around the Abbey, first founded in the 8th century, one of England's most magnificent Norman churches which was saved from sacking at the time of the Dissolution when the townspeople decided to buy it. It cost them the vast sum of £453. Everything about it is so beautiful. Each time I visit it I find something new to revel in, but perhaps the superb Quire windows - seven of them, all of which have 14th century stained glass, and the dazzling splendour of the Beauchamp Chapel, are my favourites.

We have King Canute in 1016 to thank for the glorious 27,000 acres which today make up the Forest of Dean. He decreed this should be a royal hunting ground. It is a world of its own with beauty spots, picnic areas, walks, trails, camping sites and a myriad of other activities. It is magical, mysterious, tranquil and yet it is still a source of industry in coal mining and timber.

Beneath the tree clad hills, Britain's free miners continue to dig for coal. Quarrying for stone is still active and the last of the stone-cutting factories can be found at **Cannop**.

To understand more of the past, a visit to **Clearwell Caves** near **Coleford** will help and fascinate at the same time. Eight caverns are open to the public in addition to which there are excellent geographical and mining displays which bring home, with clarity, the dangerous and courageous lives our miners have always led. You will be taken on a guided tour into the Bat Chamber, which is the home of the hibernating Greater and Lesser Horseshoe Bats in the winter. Since the cessation of mining calcite has grown everywhere, and it provides a beautiful backdrop. As you progress through Old Churn, 100ft below the surface, you are at the deepest point open to the public. It brings home the labour involved in bringing ore to ground level. It horrifies me to think that small boys not much older than my eleven year old grandson were expected to manhandle the loads which could well weigh 70lbs a time.

Nearby is a charming place, **Puzzle Wood**, which was created out of some open cast iron workings which were left to gather moss. In the 19th century it was landscaped creating a puzzle path with steps, seats and bridges. You can take picnics here in the very pretty garden.

Is the Forest more beautifully clad in spring or autumn? I do not know, either is wonderful. The spring has the joyous arrival of the soft green unfurling leaves when the ground is carpeted with bluebells, but autumn is a delight to the eye when the Larch turns to russet gold. Wildlife abounds with deer and badgers leading a protected life. Forest sheep thrive and munch their way through the pasture. At **Nagshead** near **Parkend** you will see birds of all kinds in the reserve. Peregrines dominate the scene coming from their breeding ground in **Symonds Yat Rock** in Herefordshire.

The Forest is encompassed by three rivers, the mighty Severn, the Wye and the little Leadon. The Severn Valley has everything. It is fertile and full of orchards. Drive along and you will be invited to stop time after time to select fresh fruit, vegetables and flowers from wayside stalls. The Severn Bore is known by most and if you want to see it at its most spectacular then **Newnham** will provide you with a grandstand view. For those who have not met this natural phenomenon before, it is caused by the river flowing seawards and meeting the incoming tide from the Bristol Channel. In the late spring or autumn it reaches its greatest height causing a wave sometimes as high as 10 feet. Lesser bores happen throughout the year and give an endless challenge to surfers and canoeists.

Cinderford and **Coleford** are the two main towns in the forest, aptly called because of their connection with coal. I found Cinderford interesting more because of its people than its architecture. Coleford may not be so pretty but it is surrounded by picturesque villages which are a pleasure to explore. Choose either **Newland** or **Broadwell** and you will have chosen well! Newland has **The Ostrich Inn** which dates back to the 13th century when it was a hospice for the workers building 'The Cathedral of the Forest'.

The Dean Heritage Centre at Camp Mill, **Soudley**, near Cinderfordon the B4227, will provide you with a wealth of information and understanding about the Royal Forest. If you are more interested in visiting places you may enjoy **Littledean Hall**, which is 2 miles east of Cinderford. The family owned house is renowned for its claim to ghostly hauntings. The site was originally used by the Romans and the remains of a Roman temple were found there in 1984 and identified as Springhead Temple. It is now the largest restored ground plan of such a temple in Britain. Legends abound about Littledean Hall. Most of them seem to stem from 1664 onwards. Tragic events in the dining room led to poltergeists being active. A servant is said to haunt the landing outside his bedroom. Two members of the family fell in love with the same woman and ended up shooting each other at the dining table. They have not yet found rest! Phantom blood stains appear alongside the fireplace where two officers of the King died in the Civil War. Finally in amongst this motley collection of ghosts, is a monk who came to give Holy Communion to the family in the days when Catholocism was illegal. No one has slept in the Blue Room with its four-poster bed since the 1950's because sleep is disturbed by the sound of footsteps and the clashing of swords!

St Briavels Castle southwest of Coleford is interesting. What is left are the remains of a 12th century castle adjacent to a Norman church. It stands high above the Wye valley amid glorious scenery. The church is a beautiful example of Norman and Early English architecture. It is open 10am to dusk daily. There is an amusing custom which takes place in the village after evensong on Whit Sunday. Bread and cheese is thrown by a local forester towards the people and it is considered a good omen for the year ahead if you catch a piece. It is a 700 year old custom which used to take place in the church.

A bird's eye view of The Cotswolds is all that I am able to give you in the permitted space in this book. At worst it will whet your appetite to know more and at best it will instil in you a little of the sheer joy the area has given me over many years.

The Cotswold Hills extend from near Bath in Avon across to North Oxfordshire and part of Northamptonshire. At first their wooded slopes descend steeply to the Severn Vale. Later however they shake off the trees as they roll towards the Midland plain. Near Cheltenham and again above Broadway, they reach heights of over 1000ft. Drystone walls, towns and villages built of mellow stopne or that silvery-grey limestone which shimmers in the light, characterise the Cotswolds. The wool industry, once the wealth of this area has gone into decline but sheep continue to roam the hills, and cloth is still woven around **Stroud**.

For the ardent walker there are almost one hundred miles of footpath which will take you through ever changing scenery, sometimes climbing steeply or descending abruptly, following the escarpment for much of the time. It will never fail to delight you as you walk along beside burbling streams, over rickety bridges, through woods and in and out of 'kissing gates'. You will sometimes find yourself on a golf course and the next moment wandering through fields of corn. There are long barrows, hill forts and picturesque Cotswold villages. The route will take you from Kelston Round Hill, near Bath through Tormarton and theSodburys, Nibley Knoll and Stinchcombe Hill. The route continues to Freocester Beacon, Painswick Hill Fort, Cooper's Hill and Birdlip by the Devil's Chimney high up on Leckhampton to the highest point in the Cotswolds at Cleeve Cloud and then down to Winchcombe, the ancient capital of Mercia. Not far on is Hailes and then another climb to Beckbury Camp. Down again to Stanway and Stanton and on to Broadway and so to Chipping Camden. Much too long a trail for most of us but you can join it anywhere along the way.

It would be sacrilegious to miss out **Sudeley Castle** which is close to Winchcombe, just off the A46. It is rich in history and contains some fine art treasures. The grounds are beautiful and include an Elizabethan garden, and there are regular Falconry displays. You will need to allow some considerable time here if you are to get the best out of it.

Nestling peacefully in its sheltered wooded valley, the village of **Temple Guiting** is one of the Cotswold's best kept secrets. Its close neighbour **Guiting Power** is a village of simple, uncontrived beauty; its typically Cotswold cottages with gables and stone-tiled roofs converge upon the sloping mound of the village green in a perfect grouping. Further down the river **Windrush** village sits on a steep slope overlooking its river namesake. A small triangular green is surrounded by attractive cottages and one of the most fascinating village churches; the beaked and bearded head carvings around the Norman South porch are grotesque and still stand out despite the passing of eight centuries.

Upper and Lower Slaughter close to Stow-in-the-Wold, I find to be beautiful and breathtaking but almost too perfect. Both have excellent, expensive, superbly run hotels and many lovely houses.

Hailes Abbey is a beautiful medieval abbey lying in ruins but with a romanticism about it that makes it a must for visitors. Then there is **Stanway House**, a golden Jacobean manor, just to the north east of Hailes, which demands your presence. The house has only changed hands once in the last 1300 years or thereabouts. And so to **Snowshill**, just west of the tiny hilltop village of **Bourton-on-the Hill** with a church that has a fine Norman South Arcade. **Snowshill Manor** is a charming Tudor house with a 17th-century facade. It has an incredible mixture of displays inside. Anything from weavers and spinners tools to Japanese armour and musical instruments. The owner filled up the house so much with his collections that he had to move to an adjoining cottage. His name was Charles Wade and his coat of arms bears the motto 'Nequid Pereat' - 'Let Nothing Perish'!

South of Bourton is **Sezincote**, famous for its house and garden. The house was remodelled by a wealthy 18th-century Nabob, Sir Charles Cockerell. He loved all things oriental and had his house constructed in Indian style with oriental gardens.

So impressed was the Prince Regent when he came to stay in 1807 that he decided to use a similar design for his own Brighton Pavilion.

Broadway, unfortunately for those who love it, has become almost too popular. It is so attractive that it brings people from all over the world to savour its loveliness only to find that theover crowding disguises its true beauty. See it early in the morning or just as evening is drawing on and you will see the real Broadway. There can be very few people who have not heard of **The Lygon Arms**, one of the country's leading inns. A place of charm, character and furnished quite beautifully with genuine country furniture. It goes without saying that the food and hospitality are superb.

One of the great Cotswold wool towns in the Middle Ages was **Chipping Camden**. Here you will see a flawless 'wool church', St James, beloved of Sir John Betjeman. It represents the wealth of the time and piety thrown in for good measure. It has a splendidly decorated West Tower, tall nave arcades with light that floods from the clerestory and window over the chancel arch. **The Woolstaplers Hall**, which was a 14th-century merchant's house, now holds a wonderful collection of things pertinent to the history of the town. Traditions dating back to 1612 are still celebrated annually in the town, in the form of Scuttlebrook Wake and Robert Dover's Cotswold Olimpick Games, whose disciplines include the ancient and honourable sport of shin-kicking!

Gardens always attract me and right in the High Street is the **Ernest Wilson Memorial Garden** which opens daily. It is in memory of Ernest Wilson who was dedicated to the study of Chinese and Japanese botanical specimens. Two other gardens are quite nearby. **Hidcote Manor Gardens** lying 3 miles to the northeast, were created early this century by a noted horticulturist, Major Lawrence Johnstone. He strove successfully to build a series of formal gardens separated by walls or hedges of different species. If you are here in July you may be lucky enough to catch a performance of a Shakespeare play which takes place in the grounds. **Riftsgate Court** is right by Hidcote and is full of unusual plants and shrubs as well as a wonderful display of hydrangeas.

Blockley comes under the heading of villages you should not miss. It is probably the most unspoilt of all the Cotswold villages. It suffered like so many others, from the decline of the woollen industry but it was saved by the continued production from its eight silk mills.Many of the houses on **Blockley Brook** at the southern end of the village were once mills. It has a collection of genuinely ancient inns which will provide you with food and particularly good Real Ale.

Another small town of much character is **Moreton-in-the-Marsh**. It is right on the Fosseway and has a High Street full of splendid 18th and 19th-century buildings, among them the former manor house in which Charles I sheltered during the Civil War. Although not one of the principal markets during the heyday of the Cotswold wool trade. Moreton now claims the largest open-air street market in the Cotswolds. Every Tuesday, thousands of visitors arrive by coach, car and train, to browse around the 200+ stalls.

Surrounded by pretty villages like **Bledington** with its Kings Head Inn and **Upper Oddington** with The Horse and Groom, **Stow-on-the-Wold** stands high on a hill beside the Roman Fosse Way. It was a centre for wool in medieval times and today is a picturesque town which will give you a great deal of pleasure. The big square, complete with its old stocks, seems to encompass the whole life of the town. The busy shops, with a preponderance of antique shops, a wealth of pubs, eating houses and hotels all make for the hustle and bustle of a well kept, well loved place. I love the different shapes and sizes of the buildings which dominate the square.

Another village just off the Fosse Way is the incomparable **Bourton-on-the-Water**. It is infinitely photographable and because of this, like Broadway, it does suffer from a surfeit of visitors. There are several places to visit, amongst them **The Model Railway Exhibition** which will endear itself to young and old with its 400sq ft of model railway layouts. At the **New Inn** in the High Street is **The Model Village** which has been in situ for over fifty years and is a model of the village built in Cotswold stone.

Two more places beginning with the letter B are Cotswold favourites of mine. **Burford** which is actually in Oxfordshire,is somewhere that rekindles happy memories whenever I go there. Many years ago I used to stay in **The Bay Tree** in Sheep Street when I was attending the Cheltenham Spring Meeting. It was a wonderful time and from what I can see the hotel has simply grown in stature over the years, adding modern comforts to rooms of all shapes and sizes in this very old, atmospheric building.The steep main street leads down to the River Windrush from the Wolds. There is only one way to see Burford and that is on foot. **Bibury** is the second B. In the 17th century it was a famous horse racing centre and home of England's oldest racing club. Take a look at Arlington Row with its picturesque cottages. **Arlington Mill** is built on a Domesday site. It is a 17th-century corn mill, which, with the adjoining cottages, has become a museum with 17 exhibit rooms. Looking for somewhere to stay then the 17th century **Swan Inn** is delightful. Once a coaching inn, it is full of character, lies by the river and has fishing rights.

Northleach is very special because of its church mainly which dominates the small town. Built in the 15th century when the woollen industry was at its height, it is magnificent. The south porch has original statues under canopied niches, great crooked pinnacles and a stair turret crowned with a delightful spirelet. It is open daily from 9am-dusk.

To the south of the A40 from Northleach to Burford, The Cotswolds are split by fertile river valleys along which villages havegrown. The wolds of this southern section are not as well populated as the north. The difference between the populated valley and empty wold is marked. The first valley was cut by the River Leach that flows by Northleach, and in its upper reaches the leak drains bleak wold. It is not as pretty as the Coln nor does it have the character of the Windrush but it is beautiful and gives its name to **Lechlade**, the town that separates the Cotswolds from the Thames Valley. It is a nice small town well known to Thames cruisers for it is the highest point of navigation on the river. There are some fine Georgian buildings and a church whose roof boss above the nave shows two carved wrestlers. It has the look of Lincoln cathedral but nowhere near as grand.

Fairford is somewhere I always try to see for two reasons. The first is the superb Perpendicular church of St Mary the Virgin built at the end of the 15th century by John Tame, a wool stapler and cloth merchant, except for the base of the tower which was built by the Earls of Warwick.

Everything about it is wonderful but the greatest glory is the 28 windows of opulently coloured glass, contemporary with the church, which may be the work of Barnard Fower, Henry VII's master glass painter. It is ablaze with colour, a sublime sight, unparelleled in any of England's parish churches. In the Market place there are fine 17th and 18th century houses including the well loved and well established **Bull Hotel** which sits in a corner by the church. This is the meeting place for people from miles around and it is fun just to listen to the general chatter at the bar whilst enjoying a good, home-cooked meal. An ideal base for anyone wanting to enjoy the atmosphere of an old inn and be well situated for exploring both the Cotswolds and Oxfordshire.

Cirencester is a strange place. It does not seem to value its tremendous history. I know I love the graceful Georgian buildings in which the town is rich. The church is dazzling and will give you hours of pleasure. Then there is **The Corinium Museum** in Park Street which contains one of the largest collections of Roman artefacts in the country. If you would rather be out of doors, at the top of Cecily Hill is the entrance to **Cirencester Park**, a wonderful expanse of greenery which is owned by Earl Bathurst. Cars and cycles are not permitted but you can walk or ride to your hearts content, in woodland and parkland laid out in the 18th century by the 1st Earl Bathurst helped by a friend, the poet, Alexander Pope.

South of Cirencester is **Tetbury** dating from 681, one of the most popular Cotswold towns. Inspite of being famous as the home of the Prince of Wales at Highgrove House, the town has remained comparatively unspoilt. Both the fine parish church and the Market House of 1655 have been well restored. The town still accommodates a busy general and antiques market every Wednesday and Tetbury is world famous for its antique shops. A walk down the old Chipping Steps leads to Gumstool Hill, site of the ever popular Woolsack races, dating from the 16th century, in which teams of men and women race up and down the 1-in-4 hill carrying 65lb woolsacks on their backs!

Westonbirt House and Gardens, roughly three miles south of Tetbury is an excellent place to visit. The Arboretum contains one of the world's finest collection of temperate trees and shrubs. It is a place of startling contrasts. In the spring the magnificent rhododendrons bloom and in autumn the fantastic colour of the leaves is stunning.

I have visited **Chavenage House** twice and enjoyed it each time. It is on the B4014 just northwest of Tetbury. It is an Elizabethan manor house thought to be haunted by Charles I and has Cromwellian associations. It has a great air about it which is intangible but charming.

Oxfordshire's contribution to the Cotswolds is not to be ignored. When I was travelling about the Cotswolds garnering information for this book and drinking in the autumnal beauty of the area I felt that every road led to **Chipping Norton**! Here is a busy town with a sloping main street that appears to be tiered. It has a great deal of character and much to recommend it.

Banbury is no longer part of the Cotswolds but very much part of the life of the county. The town is best known for its cakes and its cross of nursery rhyme fame. It disappoints many because here you have a town that dates from Saxon times but few pre-17th century buildings survive. The people of Banbury throughout the ages have always wanted something up to date and in their quest destroyed much of their history. In the 17th century they petitioned Parliament to pull down their great castle so that the stone could be used to repair damage caused to the town by two Civil war sieges. In the 18th century they blew up the church rather than restore it. The original Banbury Cross was destroyed too, in an upsurge of Puritanism 300 years ago. The present cross dates only from 1859. The 'fine lady' of the rhyme is believed to have been a member of the Fiennes family, who still live nearby at Broughton Castle. The ride to the cross was probably a May Morning ceremony.

Down the A4260 from Banbury you will come first to **Deddington** and if you take a left turn there onto the B4031 you will happen upon **Clifton**. Not specially remarkable as a hamlet but it is a must because here I found **The Duke of Cumberland's Head**. This exciting hostelry has all that is required of an inn which has been in situ for three hundred years, and much more. Walk through the main entrance and the smell of logs burning in the big fireplace plus the air of well being that pervades the atmosphere, and you will recognise that you have found somewhere that will remain in your memory as one of the good things of life.

Just off the Oxford to Swindon road I started an immediate love affair with **Fallowfields Hotel at Kingston Bagpuize**. This is the family home of Anthony Lloyd and his wife. It is a magical house with high ceilinged rooms downstairs and wonderfully spacious bedrooms with vast beds and beautifully drapes and furniture upstairs. It is a house that is loved and everyone who stays there seems to acquire the mantle of well-being it gives out.

Wantage is a quiet town with cobbled streets and 17th and 18th-
century houses. It lies at the foot of the Berkshire Downs in the Vale of the White Horse. King Alfred the Great was born herein 849 and his statue stands in the market place. Parts of the church of St Peter and St Paul date back to the 13th century. It has a 15th century hammerbeam roof, some fine wood carvings and the tombs of the members of the Fitzwarren family, into which Dick Whittington married.

I have deliberately left **Oxford** until last. So much has been written about it by generations of people. Matthew Arnold's city of 'dreaming spires' bewitches all who come here. It maybe that much of the outskirts is industrialised but it is of no importance. Oxford remains a University town, par excellence, its street dominated by the stone built walls and quadrangles of its ancient colleges and in term-time by flocks of black-gowned undergraduates on foot or on bicycles. The Broad, where that famous Oxford institution, Blackwell's Bookshop, is to be found, the High, Cornmarket and the narrow lanes leading off them are the centre of University life and where most of the old colleges, public houses, good restaurants and shops are to be found. In Spring and Summer the University Parks and the Rivers Cherwell and Isis, as the Thames is known here, come into their own. On May Morning at 5am the Cherwell is packed with punts at Magdalen Bridge to hear the Choristers of Magdalen sing a Latin hymn to salute May Day from Magdalen Tower. Something, which once heard will never be forgotten.

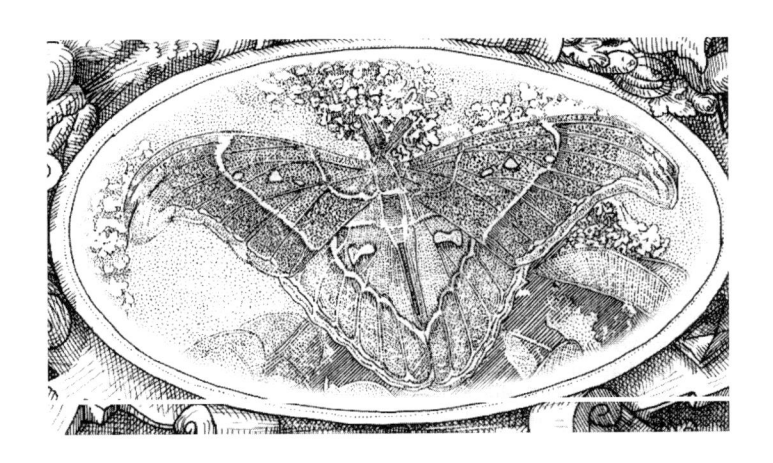

ABINGDON LODGE HOTEL,
Marcham Road Abingdon OX14 1TZ
Tel: 01235 553456 Fax: 01235 554117

The Four Pillars Group of Hotels are all ideally situated for both business and pleasure. Each has its own charm and personality and emphasises the pre-eminence of customer care. What is so nice about the Abingdon Lodge is that it is purpose built. All the sixty three bedrooms have been decorated to provide a relaxed and comfortable atmosphere and each has its own private bathroom and television with satellite stations. The light, airy and tastefully decorated restaurants serve imaginative and beautifully presented food using fresh produce whenever possible. The excellent conference facilities have been designed to meet the needs of today's conference organiser and can cater for two to 130 delegates. Those are the factual details of this nice hotel but it has much more to offer. Firstly the well-trained, dedicated staff make sure you are well cared for and secondly the hotel is geared for special occasions. Murder Mystery Breaks, Dinner Dance Weekends, School's out - a chance to treat the family to a half term mid-week break. A New year Winter Warmer with dancing will take away the empty feeling after the Festive Season and then there are fun packed Country and Western Rock and Roll weekends when it is time to dig out the gingham shirts and stetsons and Jump and Jive or Doce Do the weekend away. Easily reached from the M4 the Abingdon Lodge offers first class accommodation, great comfort and all at realistic prices.

USEFUL INFORMATION

OPEN; All year.
RESTAURANT; Imaginative, well-presented
CHILDREN; Welcome
VEGETARIAN; Several dishes
CREDIT CARDS; All major cards
DISABLED ACCESS; Yes
ACCOMMODATION; 63 ensuite rooms
LICENSED; Yes

Sister hotel of the Witney Lodge Hotel, Witney, Buckingham Lodge Hotel, Buckingham Ring Road and The Osterley Hotel, Isleworth, Middlesex

For further details call Freephone 0800 374692

THE CROWN OF CRUCIS,
Ampney Crucis, Cirencester
Tel: 01285 851806 Fax: 01285 851735

This is a former coaching inn dating back to the 16th century, built in the traditional Cotswold style and gracing the pretty village of Ampney Crucis. The village is delightfully quiet but it is only three miles from Cirencester, the gateway to the Cotswolds with all its attractions and only 20 minutes from Swindon and the motorways. What makes The Crown of Crucis so worth while is the very special atmosphere, which not only embraces those who stay a while, but also those who just call in for a drink in the warm and friendly bar or to enjoy lunch or dinner in the charming dining room. With mainly English cooking the full a la carte restaurant is open every day and is highly popular. The bar also has its own menu for lunchtime and evening meals seven days a week. The Dish of the Day is always a favourite both for its variety and value. All 25 twin/double bedrooms have private bathrooms, colour TV, video and tea/coffee making facilities and have AA 3 Star and English Tourist Board 4 Crown ratings. Every bedroom, furnished to complement the traditional Cotswold building, surrounds a delightful courtyard and most overlook the pretty Ampney Brook and village cricket ground. A super place to spend a holiday or a weekend break and equally desirable for those on business. The Cotswold Room, catering for up to 100 people is ideal for all private parties and wedding receptions. A large banqueting menu is offered. The Crucis Room is also popular for smaller parties. Full Conference facilities with audio/visual equipment are available and can accommodate up to 70 theatre style and 30 boardroom style.

USEFUL INFORMATION

OPEN: All year except Christmas Day
CHILDREN; Welcome
CREDIT CARDS; All major cards
LICENSED; Yes
ACCOMMODATION; 25 Ensuite rooms

RESTAURANT; Mainly English
A la Carte
Own menu 7 days a week
VEGETARIAN; Yes
DISABLED ACCESS; Yes

THE CROWN INN & HOTEL
High Street,
Blockley,
Moreton in Marsh
Gloucestershire GL56 9EX
Tel: 01386 700245
Fax: 01386 700247

The Crown Inn and Hotel built of mellow Cotswold stone, festooned with gently climbing creepers and with a wealth of colour from its hanging baskets and flower filled tubs, is everything one could imagine, and wish for, in an inn in this glorious part of the Cotswolds. It stands in the High Street in what is regarded as one of the most unspoilt and attractive villages in the Cotswolds. Everyone who comes here is encompassed by the sense of peace and tranquillity which is enhanced for those who stay at The Crown or even pop in for a drink and a meal. The Champion family have just celebrated their 10th anniversary as proprietors of this splendid establishment. It is run to a very high standard for the benefit of guests and still retains a relaxed and friendly ambience which makes it so popular with local people as well as visitors. The lounge bar has comfortable leather seating and is the perfect place to spend a pleasant hour or so chatting to friends. The split-level hotel bar offers a beamed ceiling, a choice of real ales and frequently some local 'characters to give it added flavour! The delightfully appointed Coach House Restaurant offers the very best in English and French cuisine - all freshly prepared to order while the Grill Room specialises in fish and grills. The well stocked cellar provides an excellent choice of wines from around the world. Mellow stone walls and old beams take pride of place in many of the beautiful bedrooms. There are several charming suites available - some even featuring four poster beds. Careful design has discreetly incorporated modern appointments such as en-suite bathrooms, colour TV, radio, hair dryer, and tea and coffee making facilities. Conveniently close to all major motorway routes and 5 miles from the rail link at Moreton in Marsh with direct connections to London etc, Blockley is easily accessible from anywhere in the UK. Surrounded by famous towns and beautiful villages The Crown Inn is ideal for holidays, for conferences, special breaks or wedding receptions.

USEFUL INFORMATION

OPEN; All year
CHILDREN; Over 10 years
CREDIT CARDS; All major cards
LICENSED; Full. Well-stocked cellar
ACCOMMODATION; En suite & suites with fourposters
GARDEN; No -Patio

RESTAURANT; English & French cuisine
Grill Room: Fish & Grills
BAR FOOD; Wide range
VEGETARIAN; Always a choice
DISABLED ACCESS; Yes. No special facilities
PETS; By arrangement

LANSDOWNE VILLA,
Lansdowne, Bourton-on-the-Water
Tel: 01451 820673

Bourton-on-the-Water is described as 'A year-round experience'. A very fair description of somewhere that is as good in the depth of winter as it is in the height of the summer. It is made even better if you stay in Lansdowne Villa, a large stone Victorian house set at the quiet end of this beautiful village - everyone's idea of the perfect place in the Cotswolds. Tony and Marie-Baker are the resident proprietors who have both had immense experience in the hotel and catering trade in both the Seychelle islands and other parts of the Cotswolds. Their ability to make their guests feel relaxed and at ease is apparent as soon as you enter the house. Each of the twelve bedrooms have en-suite bathrooms, colour TV, radio alarms, and tea/coffee making facilities. For your comfort there is also a TV Lounge. Breakfast, a memorable meal, is served in the pretty dining room where, if you wish, you can also enjoy a 3 course table d'hote meal between 6-7pm. Lansdowne Villa is licensed for residents and their friends. The Guest House has its own car park. If you are thinking of taking a winter break Lansdowne Villa is ideal and there are frequently special offers.

USEFUL INFORMATION

OPEN; All the Year
CHILDREN; Welcome
CREDIT CARDS; All major cards
LICENSED; Residential
ACCOMODATION; 12 ensuite rooms - Winter breaks

DINING ROOM; Memorable Breakfast
3 course a la carte evening meal
VEGETARIAN; Catered for
DISABLED ACCESS; No special facilities

THE OLD NEW INN,
Bourton-on-the-Water GL54 2AF
Tel: 01451 820467   Fax: 01451 810236.

This traditional country inn is not one to be missed. The Inn originally came into being as an amalgamation of two cottages and a barn in 1714. It was a lodging for those people on their way via Burford to Oxford across Westcote Heath. The Heath at that time, was renowned for footpads and robbers - who came from the Oxfordshire side of the hill from the Wychwood Forest - and was not safe to cross except in broad daylight. After the railway arrived, the Inn became a stop over for Commercial Travellers, who would hire horses and traps to visit the local villages with their samples. For the last sixty years The Old New Inn has been in the loving and capable hands of the Morris family. It has log fires andthree bars where guests can enjoy a drink and a chat. In the heart of the Cotswolds, close to the River Windrush, Bourton-on-the Water is an ideal centre for a country holiday and you will not do better than to stay in the Old New Inn. The welcome is there for you immediately on arrival. The prettily furnished bedrooms are mainly ensuite and all have TV and Tea/Coffee making facilities. The Hotel has two lounges reserved for residents and a separate TV Lounge. The large and delightful garden is for the use of residents. You will have a sumptuous full English Breakfast. If you want to lunch here the food is excellent with light meals and bar snacks available. Packed lunches can be provided when required. In the evening a comprehensive table d'hote menu is served accompanied with wines from around the world. You cannot fail to visit the world famous Model Village at the rear of the Inn. It is a 1/9th replica in local stone of the actual village. The village was measured by Win and Bo Morris, then built by six local men and opened on Coronation Day in 1937.

USEFUL INFORMATION

OPEN; Every day except Christmas Day
CHILDREN; Welcome
CREDIT CARDS; All major cards
LICENSED; Yes
ACCOMMODATION; Pretty, mainly ensuite 3 Crown ETB Commended
RESTAURANT; Delicious food
BAR FOOD; Wide range
VEGETARIAN; Catered for
DISABLED ACCESS; No
GARDEN; See Model Village

BUCKINGHAM LODGE HOTEL,
Buckingham Ring Road,
Buckinghamshire
MK18 1RY
Tel: 01280 822622 Fax: 01280 823074

This hotel in the Four Pillars Group which includes The Witney Lodge, Witney, The Abingdon Lodge, Abingdon and The Osterley Hotel, Isleworth, Middlesex, Buckingham Lodge is delightful. The interesting architecture provides a sophisticated but informal atmosphere, and the personal service extends to guests a warm welcome and an enjoyable stay. Each hotel is this small, privately own group sets a very high standard both in the furnishings and the food but also in the choice of hand-picked staff in every department, training them well to provide a professional but at the same time personal and friendly service. You are a person when you stay in any of these hotels not just a room number! The seventy bedrooms are all ensuite with all modern facilities including satellite television. The Leisure Club, open to all residents has been designed so that a quiet swim or a full workout can both be enjoyed to the full. The excellent conference facilities have been designed to cater for every need. With air conditioning, from 2 to 150 delegates can be assured of the utmost comfort. This is a hotel, like its sister hotels, which provides the very best in theme weekend and mid-week breaks. The emphasis is on fun, relaxation and enjoyment, and covers just about something for everyone from a first class Christmas package to a Murder Mystery Weekend, a DancingWeekend to a School's Out programme for families at half term. Well run and conceived, these special breaks are sensibly priced and excellent value for money.

USEFUL INFORMATION

OPEN; All year
CHILDREN; Welcome
CREDIT CARDS; All major cards
LICENSED; Yes
ACCOMMODATION; 70 ensuite

RESTAURANT; Good food
BAR FOOD; Extensive menu
VEGETARIAN; Severl dishes
DISABLED ACCESS; Yes

You will find the Buckingham Lodge Hotel on the A421 off the M40 Bicester junction. For further details call Head - Office freephone 0800 374692.

ELM HOUSE HOTEL
Meadow Lane, Fulbrook,
Burford OX18 4BW
Tel: 01993 823611

Nestling on the valleyside of the River Windrush and less than a mile from the picturesque and historic wool town of Burford, is Fulbrook a peaceful village which has, at its heart, Elm House. This fine example of a Victorian Manor style house built circa 1897 and using the famous honey coloured Cotswold stone is totally welcoming. The attractive partially walled garden complete with babbling brook and croquet lawn provides the perfect setting. Inside deep mullion windows and Minster stone fireplaces, the elegant original oak staircase which leads to the seven individually styled Guest rooms, and the comfort everywhere are very appealing. To add to this you are personally greeted by your hosts on arrival and escorted to your room after which you are invited to take tea in the Drawing Room or on the terrace if the weather is kind. Every bedroom is regularly provided with fresh flowers and has its own bathroom, colour television, trouser press, main service telephone and provision for early morning refreshment. Original decorative Brass and Iron beds adorn most of the Double or Twin bedded rooms, whilst a Victorian Louis XIV style Upholstered King-size Double bed stands majestically in the hotel's most favoured Guest Room. The Dining Room is charming and here you will enjoy both breakfast and a splendid dinner of fine home-food. The wines have been carefully chosen and complement a meal beautifully. Adjacent to the Dining Room is the Drawing Room a super place to have a pre-dinner drink or coffee and liqueurs afterwards, where in season, you will find a cheerful log fire greets you. Elm House relishes a celebration, so should your visit revolve around, or coincide with a special day or event, just let the hotel know when you are reserving your room and be assured of an extra special welcome.

USEFUL INFORMATION

OPEN; All year except Christmas Day
DINING ROOM; Fine, home-cooked fare
CHILDREN; Welcome over 12 years
VEGETARIAN; On request
CREDIT CARDS; Access/Visa/Master
DISABLED ACCESS; No
LICENSED; Yes
GARDEN; Yes
ACCOMMODATION; 4 doubles, 2 twin, 1 double or twin
Strict code of practice concerning accommodation of young adults above the age of 12. Smoking is not permitted in Guest rooms, Dining Room or rooms visibly marked 'No Smoking'.

THE BULL AT CHARLBURY
Sheep Street,
Charlbury,
Oxfordshire OX7 3RR
Tel: 01608 810689

Charlbury lives in a quiet world of its own yet it is situated three miles west of the A44/ A3400, the main Oxford-Stratford road. The town has its own mainline railway station, with London Paddington one hour away. It is here that the Flynns have created a superb venue in a 16th century coaching inn. This has been done by people who have a great understanding and feeling for old buildings and know exactly what it is that customers want. Everywhere is attractively furnished in a manner that compliments the rough stone walls, the old flag stone floors shine with age and the air is redolent of that tantalising smell that comes from a log fire. The whole place has a sense of well-being. The Flynns are charming, hospitable people who enjoy talking to their clientele. Local people use the bar almost as a club. They meet to enjoy a drink and possibly to be regaled with an interesting nibble or two.

The food is outstanding and at sensible prices. The menu, which varies daily has a number of exciting and innovative dishes as well as tried and tested old favourites. Everything is cooked on the premises and as much local produce is used as possible. The wine list is as well chosen as the food with bottles and half bottles from around the world. Upstairs there are several ensuite rooms which are gradually been refurbished and brought up to the excellent standard the Flynns demand. It would be very difficult to find fault with anything in this delightful establishment which has blossomed under the present ownership.

USEFUL INFORMATION

OPEN; Bar. 12-2pm & 7-9pm
Rest: 7-9pm. Sunday lunch 12-2pm
CHILDREN; Welcome if well behaved
CREDIT CARDS; All major cards
LICENSED; Yes. Fine wines
GARDEN; No. Patio. Car park
ACCOMMODATION; 5 ensuite rooms

RESTAURANT; Home-cooked, innovative Fresh produce
BAR FOOD; Wide range interesting food
VEGETARIAN; Yes. Options daily
DISABLED ACCESS; Front entrance Not accommodation

WHITE HART ROYAL HOTEL,
High Street, Moreton-in-Marsh.
Tel: 01608 650731
Fax: 01608 650880

The atmosphere, redolent of history and emitting a sense of contented permanence, is what strikes me every time I enter the fascinating cobbled entrance hall. The inn was originally a 17th century manor house, and found favour with Charles I as a peaceful refuge in the summer of 1644 during the Civil War. Today The White Hart Royal Hotel enjoys pride of place in the centre of Moreton, overlooking the historic Fosse Way, the Roman Road that runs from Seaton to Lincoln. You would have to be without soul not to be enchanted by beauty everywhere from the original stone walls to the mellow beamwork. The hotel's majestic bar called 'The Cavalier' houses a massive fireplace, radiating the warmth of welcome to be found here. The restaurant offers an exciting a la carte menu plus a daily menu. Children are well looked after with their own menu, or they may choose from the main menu at a reduced price. Every bedroom is ensuite, centrally heated and with remote control colour television, telephone, razor sockets and a hostess tray. Baby listening services and cots available. Perfect for a family holiday at any time of the year. The honeymoon suite features a fourposter bed, with private sitting room. The hotel has excellent conference facilities, with ample parking and good road communications. It is within easy reach of Oxford, and a British Rail link direct to London, Stratford on Avon, London and Birmingham. Robert M. Steen, the Resident Managing Director has created a staff in his own image and in so doing has ensured that every guest receives personal, friendly and first class service.

USEFUL INFORMATION

OPEN; All year.
CHILDREN; Welcome. Own menu
CREDIT CARDS; All major cards
LICENSED; Yes
ACCOMMODATION; En suite rooms, Conference facilities.
RESTAURANT; Exciting menu
VEGETARIAN; Yes + low fat dishes
DISABLED ACCESS; Yes
GARDEN; Courtyard and Garden.

STOW LODGE HOTEL
The Square,
Stow-on-the-Wold GL54 1AB
Tel: 01451 830485

This is an oasis of tranquillty standing back within its own grounds. Away from the bustle of the busy market square of Stow-on-the-Wold, one of the most fascinating of the Cotswold towns. The hotel is everything a traditional English hotel should be. It is furnished with great taste and a great regard for comfort. Relaxed and friendly, the efficient Staff make sure of your enjoyment and pleasure, headed by Val and David Hartley who with their two sons, Chris and Steve, together with Chris's wife Amanda and Steve's girl friend, Nicky, make up the management team. It took some years for the Hartleys to acquire the high recognition that they have today and it is something they guard jealously. Every bedroom is attractively and individually furnished and each has its own bathroom as well as Colour TV, direct dial telephone, radio and a hostess tray. The welcoming Lounge with its open fire and genuine priest hole, has an old-world charm. In the Dining Room you will find a first class menu created by Steve Hartley and Head Chef Robert Dryburgh who has been at the hotel for over 20 years; they mix the traditional English favourites with innovative dishes. Local produce is used whenever possible and the end result is delicious food. If you are a wine buff or eager to learn about and enjoy good wines, Chris Hartley is fast becoming a connoisseur and has compiled a fascinating and quite unusual wine list yet managed to keep the price within the realms of commonsense. The pretty garden makes an ideal spot in which to lunch on a summer's day choosing from a selection of excellent bar meals. Stow Lodge is a gem and a very happy hotel in which nothing is too much trouble.

USEFUL INFORMATION

OPEN; All year. Closed for Christmas, open for New Year and closed January 3rd for 4 weeks.
CHILDREN; Welcome over 5 years.
CREDIT CARDS; Diners Club/Amex/Euro.
LICENSED; Unusual wine list
ACCOMMODATION; All en suite

RESTAURANT; Traditional & Innovative
BAR FOOD; Good selection
VEGETARIANS; Daily choice
DISABLED ACCESS; Yes. Ground Floor bedrooms; not for wheelchairs
GARDEN; Pretty, eat out in summer

WITNEY LODGE HOTEL,
Ducklington Lane,
Witney, Oxon OX87TJ
Tel: 01993 779777   Fax: 01993 703467

This is another hotel in the Four Pillars Group of Hotels which is a shining example of the high standard set by this small privately owned group. Others in the group include The Osterley Hotel, Isleworth - ideal for anyone wanting to spend a few days in London - Buckingham Lodge Hotel on the Buckingham Ring Road and the Abingdon Lodge Hotel, Abingdon. Witney Lodge is easily reached either from the M40 and then the A40 or from the M4 which you leave at Newbury taking the Didcot/Abingdon road. Built in the Cotswold style The Witney Lodge is well in keeping with its locality. It has that air of contentment about it that is only achieved when a hotel is run for the good of the guests - sadly not always the case. It is much used by local people as well as visitors who all find the Buttercross Restaurant serves delicious home-cooking which is of special note. All the seventy-four bedrooms are beautifully furnished to the highest standard with private bathrooms and all modern comforts including satellite television. With everyone in mind, the facilities have been designed to cater for every need, including children. The indoor swimming pool is a prime example. Designed for the conference market The Witney Lodge has excellent facilities meeting almost every requirement. It caters for up to 150 people in air-conditioned comfort. Like its sister hotels The Witney Lodge has tempting weekend breaks which include Christmas - a very special time -, Murder Mystery Weekends, Country and Western, Dancing Weekends, School's Out -a means of taking the children away for a mid-week break at half term. Every break is extremely good value.

USEFUL INFORMATION

OPEN; All year.
CHILDREN; Welcome
CREDIT CARDS; All major cards
LICENSED; Yes
ACCOMODATION; 74 ensuite

RESTAURANT; Interesting menu
BAR FOOD; High standard
VEGETARIAN; Daily choice
DISABLED ACCESS; Yes
GARDEN; Yes

For further details call Head Office Freephone 0800 374692

HOTELS, INNS, RESTAURANTS AND COUNTRY HOUSES

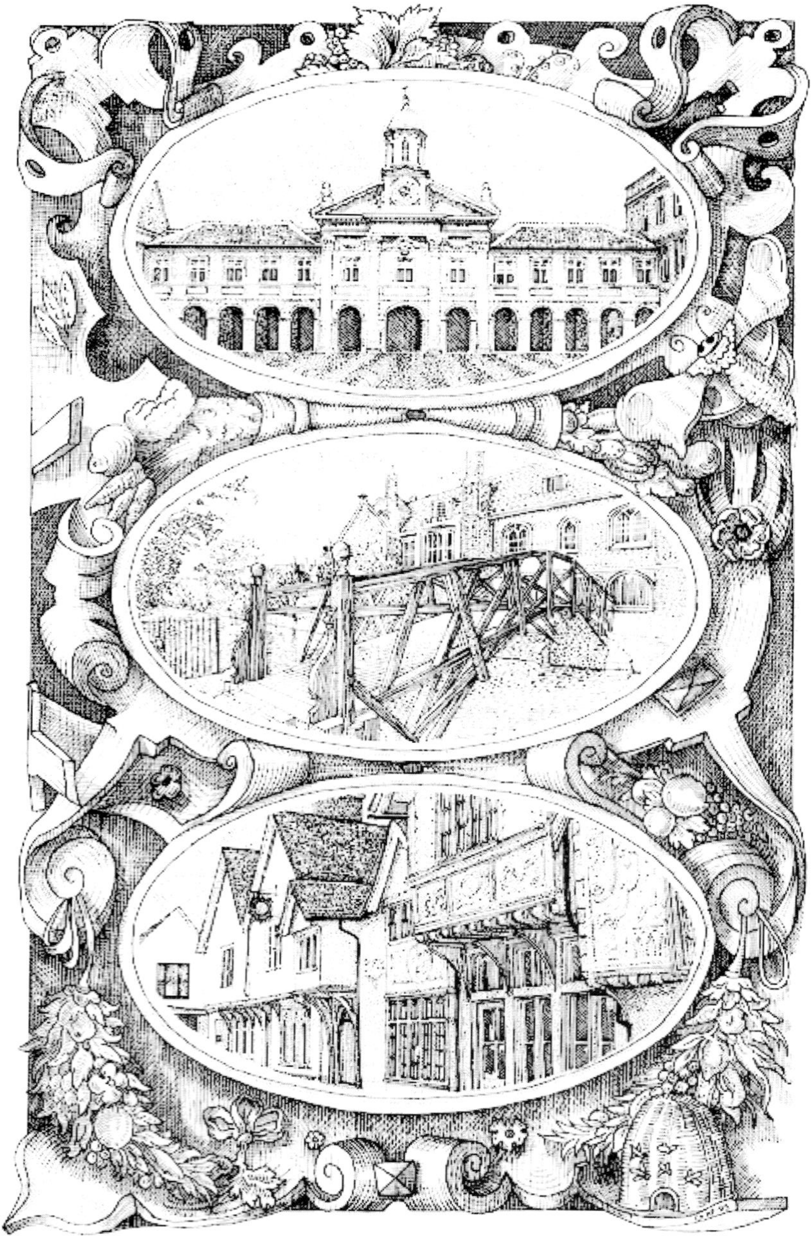

BEDFORDSHIRE, BERKSHIRE, BUCKINGHAMSHIRE AND HERTFORDSHIRE

Includes

Grove Farm	Leighton Buzzard	p.219
The Ibex Inn	Newbury	p.220
The Lord Lyon	Newbury	p.221
The Copthorne Hotel	Slough	p.222
The Christopher Hotel	Eton, Windsor	p.223

The whole of the Royal County of Berkshire is really overshadowed by the majesty of Windsor Castle and its surroundings. This enormous fortress which dominates Windsor, is the largest inhabited castle in the world. It has been one of the principal residences of the sovereigns of England since the days of William the Conqueror, who built it. When you come to examine it closely you will see that almost every monarch since William's time has taken a hand in the rebuilding. For our present Sovereign Lady, Queen Elizabeth II, the rebuilding has been forced upon her by the devastating fire of 1992 which destroyed much of value, although the works of art, furniture and books were saved by a human chain passing these priceless masterpieces gently down the line, hand to hand - hands that included the Queen, the Duke of York and many local peple.

The damage has now been restored and the castle is as magnificent and awe inspiring as ever. Three wards, or enclosures, make up Windsor Castle. The Round Tower in the Middle Ward was built by Henry II to replace the wooden Norman fortress; George IV added its upper half in 1828-32. The Lower Ward contains St Georges Chapel and the Upper Ward has the State Apartments.

Within the Castle, parts of which are open to the public, you must not miss the 15th and 16th century St Georges Chapel. It boasts some of the finest fan vaulting in the world, the helms and banners of knights, the tombs of Henry VII and Charles I and a memorial to Prince Albert. The State Apartments also must not be missed. These magnificently furnished rooms on the precipitous north flank of the castle are still used on official occasions. On a quite different scale is the world's most famous Doll's House designed by Sir Edward Lutyens in the 1920's for Queen Mary.

Everywhere in Windsor there are Royal connections. Indeed the town grew up because of the presence of the castle. In St Albans Street, the Royal Mews has the elegant Scottish State Coach of 1830 in pride of place. Next door Burford House, built in the 1670's for Nell Gwynn, is used to display gifts presented to the Royal Family. Colourful uniforms of the Blues and Royals are on view at the Household Cavalry Museum in Combermere Barracks. Exhibits cover the history of the Regiments of Household Cavalry - bodyguards and escorts of the sovereign - from their beginnings in Charles II's reign through to the age of armoured and motorised transport. Then there is the Royalty and Empire Exhibition, mounted by Madame Tussaud's of London in the restored Eton and Windsor Central Station; a stunning recreation of Jubilee year in 1897.

Windsor in its own right is delightful, with a good theatre, attractive shops and a beautiful parish church built in 1820 on the site of an earlier church. The building was supervised by Jeffry Wyatt who later, as Sir Jeffry Wyatville, designed the Castle's Waterloo Chamber for George IV.

BEDFORDSHIRE, BERKSHIRE, BUCKINGHAMSHIRE AND HERTFORDSHIRE

Windsor Great Park off the A332, south of Windsor, is the remnant of a much vaster royal hunting forest. It is marvellous for walking and has some superb views which include the vista up the famous Long Walk - a 3 mile avenue leading from the statue of George III on horeseback, known as the Copper Horse, to the walls of the Castle. The park at its south-east corner, stretches into Surrey where two beautiful gardens - Savill Garden and Valley Gardens - spill to the shores of Virginia Water.

Eton is always inextricably mixed with Windsor but it is a little town with its own character and style. It has always had a fascination for people specially because of the world famous school, Eton College. It is an excellent place in which to stay because it is so convenient for London, and central for anyone who wants to explore the beautiful countryside surrounding the River Thames. There are some wonderful drives along the River Thames to small towns and villages, **Maidenhead and Taplow**, amongst many. I always enjoy visiting **Cookham** the home of the artist Sir Stanley Spencer (1891-1959). He loved his birthplace with an intensity that shows in his paintings. Cookham High Street, the parish church, the River Thames, the meadows, are all recognisable in his works. It is fitting that Cookham should be the home of the **Stanley Spencer Gallery**. It stands in the centre of Cookham in the former Wesleyan Chapel to which he was taken as a child by his mother. Pride of place is held by the immense, unfinished Christ preaching at Cookham Regatta. There are also some touching reminders of this talented man; his spectacles, easel, palettes, sunshade and folding chair, and even a baby's push chair that he used to carry his equipment when he was off on a painting expedition.

Newbury is a busy, prosperous town which drew me because of its **Newbury District Museum** in the Wharf off Newbury Market Place. It is situated in the town's beautiful **Jacobean Cloth Hall** and extends into a picturesque 18th-century Granary. Its purpose is to tell of the history of Berkshire where, in centuries past, the **Berkshire Downs** were great sheep hills and Newbury was a thriving cloth town. There are all sorts of things to see connected with the history of local weaving. You can learn about the **Kennet and Avon canal** which runs closeby. You can admire the old town stocks and there is an audiovisual show dramatising events of the Civil War at Newbury.

Bedfordshire is a green and peaceful county where water meadows flank the River Great Ouse and the rolling downs climb towards the mighty Chilterns. John Bunyan was born in the village of **Elstow** in 1628. Later he was imprisoned for his religious views in the county town of **Bedford**. Both places have much to remind us of this great man. **Elstow Moot Hall** is a beautiful timber and brick building built about 1500. Its purpose to house the goods for the famous May Fair at Elstow. it was also used as a court house and it has been suggested that Bunyan might have had Elstow Fair in mind when he described the worldly 'Vanity Fair' in the Pilgrim's Progress. The Hall belonged to the nuns of Elstow Abbey and after the abbey was dissolved at the Reformation, the Moot Hall continued as a court house. For centuries it was neglected until in 1951 it was restored. The upper floor has been opened up to display the superb medieval roof, with massive beamsand graceful uprights.

Two miles south west of **Dunstable**, the rolling hills of **Dunstable Downs** form the northern end of the Chilterns chalk escarpment and from them there are wide views over the Vale of Aylesbury and beyond. Thousands of years ago they were a highway for prehistoric man, who trudged along the Icknield Way (now the B489) at their foot. In a 300 acre area the ground has been left untreated by chemical weedkillers or fertilisers and the result is stunning. Rare plant species flourish, including fairy flax and chalk milkwort. Little muntjac deer browse among the scrub, and whinchats and grasshopper warblers dart over the hillside.

At Whipsnade Heath there is a reminder of the First World War. Here is the Tree Cathedral, in a sun dappled grove, laid out to a plan of nave, transepts and chapels. It was planted in the 1930's by Edmund Kell Blyth in memory of his fallen friends. Quite moving and very beautiful.

Nearby on top of the downs, more than 2000 animals roam over 500 acres of **Whipsnade Park Zoo**, in conditions as nearly as wild as climate and safety will permit.

Magnificent views over Dunstable Downs are just one of the many reasons that bring regular visitors to **Grove Farm, Leighton Buzzard**. This extensively modernised 1890 farmhouse is very much the family home of Tony and Elizabeth Milhofer, and their three grown up sons. Everyone who stays here feels immediately welcome as friends of the family. It is wonderfully situated for anyone wanting to explore London, Windsor, Oxford or Cambridge; they are all within an hour's journey. Equally Heathrow will take you less than 60 minutes to reach.

If you are a narrow gauge railway enthusiast you will want to visit **Leighton Buzzard Narrow Gauge Railway**. An average speed of five and a half miles an hour might not seem much by today's standards but it is quite enough for the locomotives of the Leighton Buzzard Railway which was built to carry sand from the quarries north of the town to the main London and North western railway. Due to be scrapped at the end of the 1960's, it was saved by a band of enthusiasts who have acquired steam and diesel engines from as far away as India and the Cameroons, constructed rolling stock, and built an engine shed for maintenance.

This is a county full of wonderful stately homes including **Woburn Abbey**, the showplace home of the Dukes of Bedford and **Luton Hoo** standing in 1200 acres of a park laid out by Capability Brown. The plain exterior hides a glittering treasure house.

Arthur Mee described **Buckinghamshire** as 'The Country of the Chiltern Hills'. It is a county that has inspired many. It sheltered John Milton, encouraged Alexander Pope and enthralled William Cowper. Edward the Confessor gave one of its villages to the Church and another was given by Henry VIII to Catherine of Aragon before he tossed her aside for Anne Boleyn. Shelley was here and Gray wrote his famous Elegy. Buckinghamshire gave us three great Prime Ministers, the two Grenvilles and the fascinating Disraeli, who spent his boyhood at the home of his famous father at **Bradenham** and lived and died at **Hughenden**.

BEDFORDSHIRE, BERKSHIRE, BUCKINGHAMSHIRE AND HERTFORDSHIRE

I lived for a while in **Penn** close to **Beaconsfield**. Here lived the ancestors of some of the descendants of the great Quaker, William Penn, who stamped a continent with his ideals. The 14th century church was given as a wedding present by Henry the Eighth to Sybil Penn who had been Elizabeth's governess. From the tower of the church you can see a dozen counties and look down at the peaceful churchyard where some of the earliest Penns are buried and where too lies David Blakely, murdered by Ruth Ellis, the last woman to hang in Britain. The church is full of interest including a great medieval treasure which came to light during the restoraton of the church in 1938. A number of oak panels covered with broken plaster were removed from the wall above the chancel arch, and were being carted away as rubbish when a workman detected paint beneath the plaster. He halted the work and an expert was called in. The boards were cleaned, and a superb medieval painting of the Last Judgment was revealed.

It is the Stuarts who gave Buckinghamshire its immortal place in history. John Hampden was born here. He had started the Civil War by refusing to pay the Ship Money demanded by the king. A much honoured man. When he died he was brought from Chalgrove Field with arms reversed, drums muffled and heads uncovered.

Everywhere you go you will find entrancing villages and small towns like **Iver** and **Denham**, the market town of **Aylesbury** with its fine square and old inns, winding ways and narrow passages, **Amersham** with black and white fronts to its houses and an old street with watermills at both ends, a splendid Market Hall and good inns. **Beaconsfield** appeals with its wide main street. **Waddesdon** has fine views over the rolling country of the Vale of Aylesbury, charming houses, old and new. Splendid names like Weston Turville, Chalfont St Giles, Water Stratford, and Lillingstone Dayrell add to the voyage of discovery in this pretty county.

Buckinghamshire is a popular county for commuters today. London is within easy reach both by road and rail and Heathrow is not far removed. But it is for its beauty and friendliness that I will always remember this corner of England which for a while some forty years ago was my home.

Hertfordshire for me is principally **St Albans** with its fine cathedral in which thousands of years of worship have continued on the site of St Alban's martyrdom. Many centuries ago Alban was the first Christian martyr in this country and his shrine has always attracted pilgrims in search of spiritual and physical healing. It is a beautiful place which emanates strength. You feel as if the Almighty is reaching out for you and endeavouring to pour into your soul the fortitude shown by St Alban, and at the same time give you hope for the present and peace eternal. The history of the cathedral is well documented and you will do no better than to purchase the beautifully presented, colourful Pitkin Guide to St Albans Cathedral which will cost you about £2 and be a constant reminder of your visit.

Almost surrounded by motorways, St Albans is easy to reach andhaving done so you drive into quieter realms and begin to realise that here you are going to discover, in this one place, which offers the unusual combination of the dignity of a Cathedral City and the intimacy of a rural market town, the full span of British history. For a moment or two the sense of history is overwhelming. St Albans is full of museums, beautifully laid out and providing easily digested information.

A totally different atmosphere you will find at **The Mosquito Aircraft Museum** in Salisbury Hall, **London Colney**. The historic site of moated Salisbury Hall, mentioned in the Domesday Book, was chosen by the de Havilland Aircraft Company in 1939 to develop in secret the wooden, high speed, unarmed bomber the Mosquito; with 41 variants of the type of the most versatile aircraft of the war. This began the museum's long association with Salisbury Hall making it the oldest Aircraft Museum in the country. Visitors to the museum soon discover that it can offer more than a collection of static aircraft. Close inspection of the exhibits provides a unique hands-on experience. Members are always on hand to assist the visitor and demonstrate the working displays. With a varied programme of regular events that include flying displays, vintage car and motor cycle rallies and model exhibitions, there is always something to appeal to all ages.

From the air to the ground, **The Royal National Rose Society** at Chiswell Green, St Albans on the outskirts of the town, invites you to enjoy the world famous 'Gardens of the Rose' at the Society's showground where there is a collection of some 30,000 roses of all types. The 12 acres of gardens are a marvellous spectacle for the casual visitor and fascinating to the rose enthusiast. The gardens are being continuously developed - in particular by associating roses with a great many other plants - to create greater interest for visitors and to stimulate ideas leading to more adventurous gardening.

The British Rose Festival is a spectacular national event held every year in July. It includes a magnificent display of roses organised by the Society and the British Rose Growers Association on an excitingly new and different theme each year. The competition is for the leading national amateur rose exhibitors and floral artists. All the best of British roses can be seen at this unique show.

GROVE FARM

Grove, Leighton Buzzard,
Bedfordshire LU7 0QU
Tel: 01525 372225
Fax: 01525 374900

Magnificent views over Dunstable Downs are just one of the many reasons that bring regular visitors to Grove Farm. This extensively modernised 1890 farmhouse is very much the family home of Tony and Elizabeth Milhofer and their three grown up sons, and everyone who stays here feels immediately welcome as friends of the family. The house is beautifully furnished with antiques, and has all sorts of interesting features. The three well apointed bedrooms each has its own bathroom, the elegant,comfortable drawing room just asks to be used for those who simply want to relax, and for the energetic,the heated indoor forty-foot swimming pool invites use. No longer a working farm, Grove nonetheless has the benefit of windows that look outover the ha'ha's to the thirty acres of paddocks, where thoroughbred horses graze contentedly.

Elizabeth is a proficient and imaginative cook who conjures up wonderful meals in which she uses as much as possible the organic vegetables they grow themselves. Dinner is a delight; restful, frequently conversationally thought provoking and always entertaining. After a peaceful nights rest you will come down to an excellent breakfast which caters not only for those who like a full English breakfast but also for those who are either watching their weight, vegetarians or restricted by dietary needs.

Grove Farm from the south is found by leaving the M1 at junction 9 towards Dunstable on the A5. Turn left at Dunstable on B489 until Invinghoe, then turn right twice on B488 for 5 miles towards Leighton Buzzard. Watch for lane on right signed Grove Church. The farm entrance is first on the right. From the North leave A5 on A505 towards Aylesbury and after about 5 miles turn left at roundabout on B466 and sign for Grove on left after half a mile. Entrance then first on right. Grove Farm is wonderfully situated for anyone wanting to explore London, Windsor, Oxford or Cambridge; they are all within an hour's journey. Equally Heathrow will take you less than 60 minutes to reach. Children are very welcome but pets are not permitted. A non-smoking house. Grove Farm is a member of the Wolsey Lodge consortium.

USEFUL INFORMATION

OPEN; All year
CHILDREN; Welcome
CREDIT CARDS; Access/Visa
LICENSED; No
GARDEN; Two & half acres
A Non-Smoking house

RESTAURANT; Delicious, imaginative food Using home grown organic produce
BAR FOOD: Not applicable
VEGETARIAN: On request
DISABLED ACCESS; No
PETS; Not permitted

THE IBEX INN
Chaddleworth, Nr Newbury
Berkshire RG16 0ER
Tel/Fax: 01488 638311

Chaddleworth is a sleepy hamlet in the heart of the Berkshire Downs with superb uninterrupted views wherever you look. It is approximately 8-10 miles from Junction 13/14 of the M4. The focal point of Chaddleworth is The Ibex with its three busy bars. Here you will find the racing fraternity whether it be stablelads, grooms, jockeys, trainers or owners. The landlords of the pub, John and Sylvia Froome own race horses themselves. Several well known yards are closeby. As you may imagine much of the conversation is devoted to this sport of kings but no one coming in for the first time need feel out of it. They are a friendly, outgoing crowd, full of fun and there is always the chance you may pick up a tip or two!

The Ibex is a typical country pub, built of mellow brick, long and low and furnished in a relaxed, comfortable manner. On the walls both in the bars and restaurant you will find paintings, the work of John Froome, a talented artist. This is very much a family run pub with Gaye, the Froome's daughter helping behind the bar at weekends and son Justin also lending a hand wherever he is required. Sylvia is an excellent cook and with Jackie Mills who has been cooking at The Ibex for many years they make a formidable team. The results of their efforts are eagerly awaited both in the restaurant and the bars. The menu is based on good, home-cooked English food using local produce wherever possible. Ibex Pies have become renowned in the area; the pastry melts in your mouth and the various fillings are always tender and tasty. There is a good selection of inexpensive wines as well as the well kept ales.

In the summer the large, safe garden with direct access to the bar and tables for eating, is very popular. The Ibex is a happy establishment and one not to be missed.

USEFUL INFORMATION

OPEN; 11am-11pm Mon-Sat
RESTAURANT; Good home-cooked, English
CHILDREN; Welcome
BAR FOOD; Wide range. Renowned Ibex Pies
CREDIT CARDS; Visa/Switch/Master
VEGETARIAN; 4-5 dishes daily
LICENSED; Full & Supper Licence
DISABLED ACCESS; No
ACCOMMODATION; Not applicable
GARDEN; Large. Safe. Direct access to Bar. Tables for eating. Car Park.

THE LORD LYON
Stockcross, Newbury,
Berkshire RG16 8LL
Tel: 01488 608366

Stockcross is a small village just three miles from Newbury with easy access to the M4 motorway. It stands amidst the lovely Berkshire countryside with a host of woods and some beautiful walks. Newbury Racecourse is no distance away and being close to Lambourne Downs The Lord Lyon has a strong connection with the racing fraternity. In fact the pub was named after the racehorse which was the first horse to win the Triple Crown in 1866 - for those not in the know the races included the 2000 Guineas at Newmarket, the Derby at Epsom and the St Leger at Doncaster; quite an achievment. Inside the Lord Lyon you will find photos of horses and jockeys everywhere and naturally the conversation at the bar is frequently equestrian orientated.

The Lord Lyon is a traditional village pub with pool and darts teams and on a Wednesday evening live music is enjoyed by everyone. Brian and Sheila Priestley, the landlords, have only been here a short while but they have been readily accepted locally. They enjoy the countryside and are happy to share their discoveries with their customers. The beer is well kept, especially the Arkell cask ales for which the pub is renowned, and on the menu you will find a large selection of tasty meals and bar snacks at sensible prices. These are available at lunch and in the evening every day of the week. You can stay here if you wish. There are two comfortable bedrooms and a guarantee of a substantial breakfast to set you up for the day. Newbury is always good to visit with a market in the Square on Thursdays and Saturdays and a good museum. The Kennet and Avon Canal runs through the town as it does through Hungerford, another nearby town of interest.

USEFUL INFORMATION

OPEN;11-3pm & 6-11pm
CHILDREN;Allowed in to eat
CREDIT CARDS;Visa/Master/Euro
LICENSED; Full On
ACCOMMODATION;2 letting rooms
RESTAURANT;Not applicable
BAR FOOD;Hot & cold meals. Snacks etc
VEGETARIAN;3-4 dishes daily
DISABLED ACCESS;Yes
GARDEN;Yes. Patio. Large Car Park

THE COPTHORNE HOTEL
Cippenham Lane,
Slough, Berkshire SL1 2YE
Tel: 01753 516222 Fax: 01753 516237

This striking four star hotel in Royal Berkshire just minutes from Windsor and the M4, stands out even amongst the excellent chain of Copthorne Hotels in this country and in Europe. The reason? The personal attention of the General Manager, Simon Read and his staff who manage to make this 219 bedroom hotel as friendly and welcoming as a much smaller establishment and at the same time are able to offer you a range of facilities that is second to none. That it is so readily accessible is a virtue. London Heathrow is only 15 minutes away, the InterCity Railway Station 5 minutes and the M4 Motorway at Junction 6 only 2 minutes.

The beautifully appointed bedrooms comprise Classic, Connoisseur Floors and suites; rooms for disabled guests and non-smokers. All with ensuite bathrooms, tea and coffee tray, mini-bar, colour TV with movie and cable channel including 'Sky Sports' direct dial telephone, radio, trouserpress and hairdryer. There is 24 hour room service, comprehensive Business facilities, a Connoisseur Lounge, Same-day laundry and dry cleaning, a Concierge, Baby-sitting, Car rental and Theatre reservations. Within the hotel is 'Waves' a Club which offers swimming pool, sauna, Turkish bath and spa baths, gym and solaria. And finally a Snooker table.

The Restaurants and Bars offer you an excellent choice. In Reflections you can dine from an extensive, beautifully presented A La Carte menu whilst The Veranda Brasserie with a more informal atmosphere has a range of imaginative dishes. Dukes Bar is spacious and relaxing; ideal for meeting friends before a meal. Within easy reach of the hotel you can visit Windsor Castle, Thorpe Ascot, Ascot and Windsor racecourses, Eton or perhaps take a river boat trip on the Thames.

USEFUL INFORMATION

OPEN; All year. 24 hours

CHILDREN; Welcome. Baby-sitting
CREDIT CARDS; All major cards
LICENSED; Full on
ACCOMMODATION; 219 ensuite rooms
Including suites, non-smoking & disabled

RESTAURANT; Reflections-A La Carte
The Veranda Brasserie - informal, both
Have imaginative, varied menus.
BAR FOOD; Full range of sandwiches etc
VEGETARIAN; Many choices
DISABLED ACCESS; Yes + rooms
GARDEN; Not applicable

CHRISTOPHER HOTEL
110 High Street,
Eton, Windsor,
Berkshire SL4 6AN
Tel: 01753 852359

Eton has always had a fascination for people not only because of the world famous school, Eton College, whose pupils are to be seen about the town, but because it lives its own life almost protected by the more wordly and much grander Windsor. Its streets are narrow and full of interesting shops in which antiques predominate. It is an elegant, restrained town, with the River Thames running through it, but one so worthwhile exploring and a truly delightful town in which to stay. The Christopher Hotel stands in the High Street, as it has done for centuries when it was a coaching inn. In those days it offered succour and hospitality to visitors and today it does just the same for the 20th century traveller who can appreciate all the many modern comforts that are available. Recently the hotel has been refurbished with loving and thoughtful care which has ensured that none of its olde world charm has been lost.

Every bedroom is ensuite and has telephone, satellite colour TV, tea/coffee making facilities, trouser press, welcome tray and baby listening service. Free accommodation is available for under 16's sharing parents room with meals charged as taken. Children in own room over 16 charged 75% of the parents rate. In the bar you will find congenial company and the attractive restaurant with its soft lighting, pretty drapes, sparkling glass and shining silver, offers a menu that is mouthwatering and covers a whole range of tastes from English traditional to the more adventurous French and worldwide dishes. The wine list is equally exciting with a good selection from many countries including the New World. There is car parking for 23 cars - invaluable in this area.

In Windsor, apart from the glories of the Norman Castle, there is a delightful racecourse with several meetings a year and a very good theatre which attracts some first class productions.

USEFUL INFORMATION

OPEN;All year
CHILDREN; Welcome.Baby listening
CREDIT CARDS;All major cards
LICENSED;Full On. Fine wine list
ACCOMMODATION;8sgl 4twin 18dbl

RESTAURANT;Imaginative menu, freshly Cooked
BAR FOOD;Bar snacks available
VEGETARIAN;Several dishes daily
DISABLED ACCESS;Yes
GARDEN;No Car Park

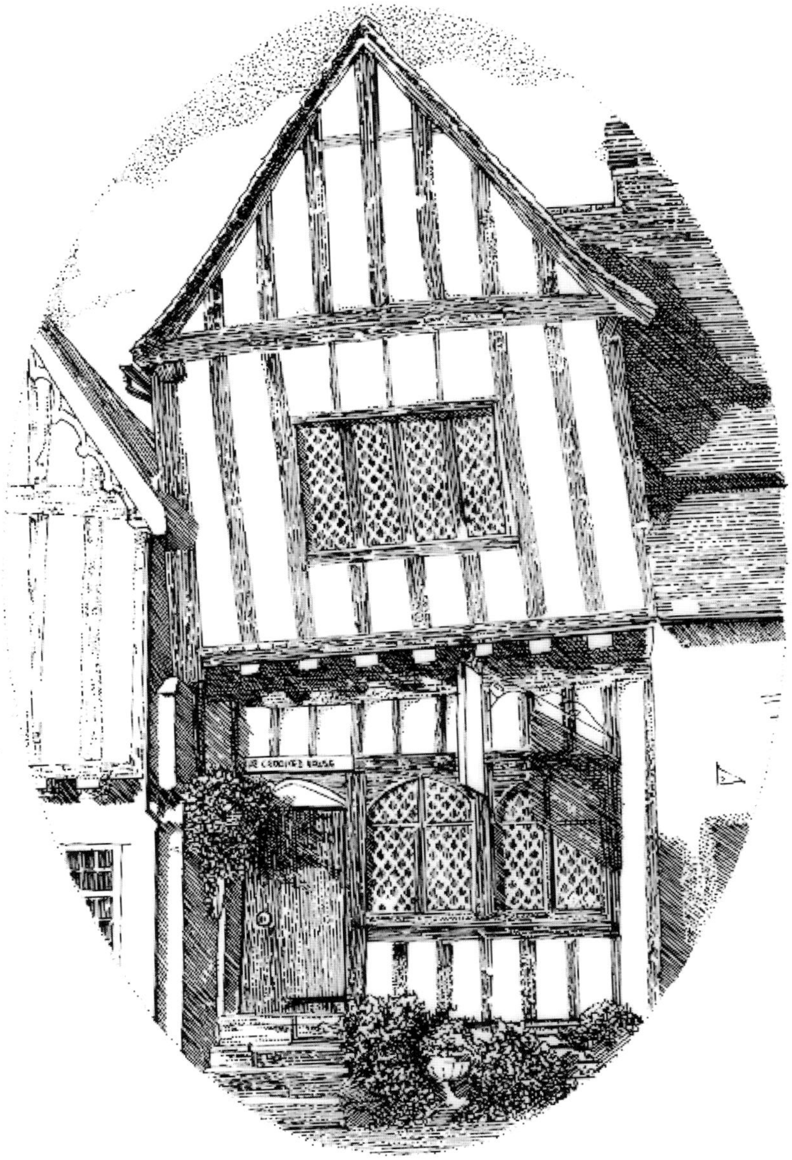

EAST ANGLIA

Includes

Suffolk

Outney Meadow Caravan Park	Bungay	p.252
Brook Hotel	Felixstowe	p.253
Suffolk Grange Hotel	Ipswich	p.254
Martello Coffee House	Lowestoft	p.255
Darsham Old Hall	Saxmundham	p.256
Cedars Hotel & Restaurant	Stowmarket	p.257
The Captains Table	Woodbridge	p.258

Norfolk

The Malt House	Palgrave, Diss	p.259
The Limes Hotel	Fakenham	p.260
Wensum Lodge	Fakenham	p.261
Caldecott Hall Golf & Leisure	Gt. Yarmouth	p.262
Brasteds	Norwich	p.263
Cubitt Cottage	Sloley, Norwich	p.264
Dormy House Hotel	West Runton	p.265

Lincolnshire

The Kings Arms	Boston	p.266
The Red Lion Inn	Boston	p.267
The Brackenborough Arms Hotel	Brackenborough	p.268
Ye Old Dun Cow	Cowbit	p.269
The Marmion Arms	Haltham	p.270
The Poachers	Kirton Holme	p.271
White Hart Hotel	Spilsby	p.272

East Anglia is so full of charm from its county town's like Norwich to its country villages, its busy coastal resorts and the timeless beauty of the Norfolk Broads, that it is impossible to include everything. Explore it for yourself and use my input as a basis for a memorable tour.

NORFOLK

Norwich gets its European air from the fact that it is almost as quick to get to Amsterdam as it is to London. In the past this has certainly been a facet of its trading habits. Whatever the reason this is one of the most exciting cities in the country. It is full of history but that has never prevented the City fathers from seeing into the future and continuing to do so today. It is a city with two sides to its face. The first in this day and age has to be its commercial face which shines with success, the second and the one in which I am primarily concerned is its past and its leisure.

The very special atmosphere of the city might first of all be savoured in the market place where stalls are covered by brightly coloured 'tilts' - awnings to those of us who do not know the local terminology. It is a bustling place and it is with some difficulty that you will pass down the narrow lanes between the stalls. One of the landmarks of the city is **St Peter's Mancroft Church** in the marketplace which is dramatically floodlit at night, as are many of the city's wonderful buildings. There is no other word for it but stunning. The building which dominates the market place is City Hall. It is a most popular place with the people of Norwich but Pevsner described it as 'likely to go down in history as the foremost English public building between the wars. For me it is the Guildhall which delights the eye with its striking pattern of stone and flint. It was begun in 1407 and constructed by forced labour.

Norwich is somewhere you should explore on foot. For example at the Back of Inns is the Royal Arcade which has a tesselated pavement, laid by imported Italian workmen and over the delightful Victoria/Edwardian shops, the walls and glass roof can only be described as Art Nouveau. In Theatre Street is the Assembly House set back behind wrought iron gates and well manicured lawns. It is the venue for thousands of people every year who flock here to enjoy concerts, exhibitions and meetings.

Norwich has more pre-Reformation churches than London, York and Bristol put together. One of them is St Stephens in Theatre Street. It was the last of a great series of Norwich churches to be built. It is eye catching. The tower is superbly decorative in contrasting flint and stone in roundels, diamonds and window outlines. The 16 clerestory windows have some notable glass and the sun shining through them throws immense light on the glorious hammerbeam roof. Chapelfields once was the place where archery was practised in Elizabeth I's reign. This was not for fun but was enforced; a sort of conscription. Bacon's House in Colegate on the corner with St George Street is one building that has been tenderly restored. It was the 16th century residence of a prosperous worsted merchant who was Lord Mayor of the city. It is a fine timber framed house.

Regency houses line Quayside and will lead you to Fye Bridge built in medieval style. The bridge stands at the beginning of Magdalene Street which was rescued from decay by the Civic Trust in the 1950's. The houses flow with colour and every now and then one will surprise you with its charming medieval courtyard. Using Fye Bridge and Wensum Street as your guide, the first turning to the right is Elm Hill, surely the showpiece of the city. It has everything. narrow winding streets are covered in cobblestones, the quaint houses partly dating from the 15th century, are painted almost all the colours of the rainbow. There is the 16th-century half-timbered Pettus house, the 17th-century Flint House and the 15th-century church of St Simon and St Jude, now a centre for the Norwich Boy Scouts. As in almost every part of central Norwich there are more alleys to explore. Wrights Court just up from the church, was rescued from decay and takes its name from Wright and Son who, in the last century, had a factory on Elm Hill employing something like fifteen hundred hand-loom weavers. Within its courtyard, on the first floor facing the street, is a long weaver's window which was the only way, at that time that Wrights would have been able to give maximum light to their workroom. In spite of Elm Hill looking almost like a film setting, it is a busy place full of shops carrying on trade that harmonise with the surroundings, yet create business in their own right.

A visit to the Castle and the cathedral are musts. The battlements of the castle provide a vantage point to look down on many of the sights and streets you have already seen. It really does dominate the city and all the streets go round it. Built by Roger Bigod in the 12th century its purpose was to block the way to the city. Its peaceful role today is that of a museum which has the reputation of being the finest provincial museum in the kingdom.

Unlike many cities, the cathedral does not dominate the skyline. It is quite low lying and surrounded by buildings which make its spire one of the tallest in the country, hiding its beauty for privileged eyes. What a wonderous place it is. Before you enter you will find yourself embraced by the arms of Cathedral Close. Its effect is immediately to make you feel withdrawn from the modern world. You can choose to enter this enchanted world through Bishop's Gate in Palace Street, the Erpingham Gate or St Ethelbert's Gate in Tombland. Any of them reveal the stunning beauty of Upper Close or Lower Close as well as Green Yard and Almery Green. The grander houses are in Upper Close with delightful cottages in Hook's Walk. At every corner there is another vista on which to feast your eyes. Lovingly tended gardens are an offering to the Lord, and when the sun shimmers on the mullioned windows you know you are in a magical land.

The Cathedral was begun in 1096 by Bishop Herbert de Losigna on the orders of the Pope, as a penance for the sin of simony. The penance could not have been performed better. I have my ownspecial favourite spots in the cathedral, one of which is going in through the south transept door, passing through the transept and then turning left into the nave south aisle until I reach the end of the nave. From here I have a view of the full length of the building which takes my breath away every time.

It is almost a relief to leave so much beauty and if your departure happens to be at eventide when The Close is at its best, I suggest you walk slowly through to Pull's Ferry from which you can turn back and see the cathedral from the river, remembering its glory.

You could spend a long time in Norwich and never see all its treasures. This makes it all the more reason to come back.

Now for all the places I have visited on this tour of Norfolk.

Banham on the B113 from Forcett St Mary is a lovely village, just 5 miles northwest of Diss and has a wealth of historic houses. It surrounds a rectangular green. The beautiful 13th-century church has a churchyard from which, at the eastern end, you can see the Priory, a fine Georgian house with Dutch gables and, beyond is the timber-framed Guildhall with a jettied upper floor. If you wonder where the brick came from to build all these fine houses, there used to be kilns at Hunts Corner, half a mile to the west of the village. They supplied much of South Norfolk with brick and tile.

Billingford just west of Diss, has a handsome five storeyed windmill. It has been lovingly tended by the Norfolk Windmills Trust and is open to the public at weekends in summer. The village is dominated by a fine lofty church, with some remains of the 13th and 15th centuries. The tower is octagonal and embattled. Two fine arcades with clustered pillars divide the nave and aisles and over them are the quatrefold windows of the clerestory. The bench ends are carved with 15th-century tracery and old poppyheads, but it is the lectern which is most interesting. Some 450 years old, it is vast with four lions at the foot. It is said to have come from the same foundry as its mighty counterpart in Peterborough Cathedral. Of little importance today is that the village was once the home of Sir Simon Burley, a favourite of Richard II who despatched him to Bohemia to bring Anne to England to be his Queen. His fame and fortune did not serve him well; he died not in peaceful Billingford but by losing his head on Tower Hill.

Blickling, one mile north of Aylsham, has Blickling Hall owned by the National Trust, undoubtedly Norfolk's most wonderful Jacobean house. You approach it along a drive between clipped hedges of yew and rows of limes, and then over an ornamental bridge astride the dry moat. At the end of the drive the Tudor splendour of the house bewitches you with its gables, turrets and oriel windows.

In the great park of some 600 acres, a lake glistens in the sunlight and every now and again you come across a little statue at one point, a summer house, which is a copy of a Greek temple, at another. The fountains which toss their floating streams of water in the air, come from Oxnead. What appears to be a pyramid is the tomb of the second Earl of Buckinghamshire and his family. He was our Ambassador to Russia and sufficiently respected by the Court of the Tsars to be presented by Catherine the Great, with a tapestry of Peter the Great at the Battle of Poltawa.

This is now in the house with portraits by Gainsborough and Zucchero amongst others. The massive library has a remarkable plaster ceiling with rows of symbolical figures representing learning and the Five Senses in the centre. There is a priceless collection of manuscripts including a copy of the Maintz Bible - the first one printed - a Miles Coverdale Bible and two books printed by Caxton.

Brancaster Staithe, just three miles from Burnham is renowned for its salt marshes and is said to be the least polluted in Europe. It certainly produces the finest quality mussels and other seafood delicacies which you can enjoy at many of the areas restaurants and inns.

HOTELS, INNS, RESTAURANTS AND COUNTRY HOUSES

Bressingham just outside Diss, off the A1066 has an interesting steam museum in which there are hundreds of steam driven things plus Victorian fairground gallopers. A visit here will enthrall both young and old.

Buckenden is a little village which once had a ferry. Those days have gone but there are still some delightful cottages and a village green whilst nearby there is a steam museum for your entertainment.

Burnham Market. When you see the signposts for Burnham just off the A149 Sheringham to Hunstanton coast road, you might be confused because in all there are seven pretty villages in this group. Three of them, Westgate, Sutton and Ulph have joined together and become the small town of Burnham Market. All the villages seem to be in sight of the sea and you reach them through a network of high hedged narrow lanes. The village green is surrounded by pretty 18th century buildings with red-tiled roofs.

Burnham Overy has a fine group of 18th-century mill buildings, **Burnham Norton** is an unspoilt hamlet and **Burnham Deepdale's** church contains one of the finest fonts in East Anglia..

Beaulugh lies one mile off the B1354 south of Coltishall. Worth making th effort if only to stand on the high bank in the churchyard of St Peters. There is nothing below but the River Bure and you get an extraordinary sense of tranquillity as though you had left the world outside momentarily.

Burgh-next-Aylsham. On the Blickling road is **Aylsham Old Hall** surrounded by Dutch-gabled farm buildings. It is a perfect example of a late 17th-century house. **Millgate** will take you to the River Bure and give you a chance to look in wonder at the 18th-century mill.

Colkirk is almost into Fakenham and is a pretty village standing on high ground. It gets on with its own life quietly, enjoying the luxury of being surrounded by beautiful countryside.

Coltishall is a village you must find time for. It is at the head of navigation on the River Bure and a favourite place for boating people. It has pleasant, mellow brick Georgian houses with many of the gardens running down to the river bank. Roman urns have been unearthed and Roman tiles frame two of the Saxon windows in the hilltop church. There is still Saxon masonry in the walls although most of the church is of the 13th and 14th centuries.

Cromer is a fishing village that was developed into a seaside resort by the coming of the railways at the end of the 19th century and has been bustling ever since. It has great charm especially round the centre which highlights the old flint buildings of the fishing village it once was. Here stands the church of St Peter and St Paul, at 160 feet the tallest of any parish in Norfolk. The sea has always been important to Cromer and even today crab boats work daily except in the stormiest conditions. With the sea so much a part of the life of the community it is not surprising that the town's little lifeboat has one of the most decorated histories of any in Britain. There is a lifeboat museum in The Gangway which will tell you much of the bravery of these men.

Dickleburgh. This friendly village is steeped in history. It is only three miles from Diss and has an Otter Trust nearby as well as Wild Life Parks, and is also within easy reach of the coast.

Edington two miles to the north of North Walsham has All Saints Church which keeps watch as it stands on a little hill alone in a field. It has a delightful thatched nave and is worth the trek. Wellies might not be a bad idea though. A little 14th century church, still lit by oil lamps at **Crostwight** also called All Saints stands bravely facing the elements in another field. One that looks on the sea in splendid isolation is the Saxon church of St Margarets at **Witton**.

Fakenham has all you might expect of a market town. Go there on Thursday and you will find it transformed into an open market full of bustling shoppers and friendly chatter. It is a splendid centre for antique auctions too. There is a racecourse with regular meetings and on the outskirts of the town is the village of **Thursford** which is the home of **The Thursford Collection**. I was there a few years ago when this exciting place was playing host to Songs of Praise. It was magical.

Forncett St Mary to the east of Attleborough is a tiny village which is the home of the **Forncett Industrial Steam Museum**. It houses an amazing collection of large stationary steam engines, including one of the pumping engines which started its life as the force that went behind the opening of Tower Bridge.

Fritton is a straggling village scattered around a vast marshy common. Its glory is the church of St Catherine reached up a grassy track. It is a thatched building with a little round tower. Nearby is **Fritton Lake Country Park** part of the **Somerleyton Estate**, which offers hours of interest and activity to the visitor. The lake is two and a quarter miles long and probably one of the most beautiful expanses of water in EastAnglia. A house filled with love is how I would describe **Somerleyton Hall**, family home of Lord and Lady Somerleyton and their five children. It is a perfect example of a house built to show off the wealth of new Victorian aristocracy. Sir Morton Peto made a vast fortune from the railways, and promptly spent a large part of it taking what was a comparatively small 17th-century manor at Somerleyton and creating around it an extravagant concoction of red brick and white stone. Inside he made it nothing less than lavish. He went too far and subsequently went bankrupt, selling his beloved house to Sir Francis Crossley, whose great grandson is the present Lord Somerleyton.

Gorleston-by-Sea just four miles from Gt Yarmouth is as different as chalk from cheese. It has two faces, one side of it is the dockland of the River Yare but then you come to the beach and the whole scene changes. This quiet, slightly old fashioned place has a special fascination. The great church stands on a bank and it was quite likely that Felix, Bishop of Dunwich built a small wooden church on the site in the

7th century. The fine flint tower stands 90ft high and if you want to climb to the top you will need a lot of puff; there are 127 steps. The marine drive which goes along for about two miles is wonderful and not an amusement arcade in sight.

Great Ryburgh nestles in the verdant Wensum valley approximately 3 miles south east of Fakenham in North Norfolk. This is a delightful corner of rural England, teeming with wild life - there are over 20 nature reserves and bird sanctuaries in the county.

Great Snoring is a small rural village just 2 miles north east of Fakenham from the A148 King's Lynn-Cromer Road. It is quiet and peaceful and has **The Old Rectory**, a secluded haven that dates back to the 1500s and promises the discerning traveller old fashioned charm with a homely warmth and friendliness.

Great Yarmouth is one of the busiest places, sometimes a bit too garish but nonetheless a town that delights many visitors year in year out. It is long and narrow, hemmed in by the River Yare. Once its economy relied entirely on the herring fisheries but when the Victorians discovered its sandy beaches and started coming for holidays, the town changed its thinking away from the fish quays and concentrated on this new way of making a living. There is a happy balance between the two fine 18th-century buildings on the South Quay. The seafront is totally different and has become engulfed in all the 20th century holiday attractions.

Happisburgh is a coastal village not far from North Walsham. It is full of charm and a favourite haunt of Sir Arthur Conan Doyle who was a regular visitor to the village.

Herringfleet just a mile to the west of Somerleyton Hall, has an odd little round-towered church with an east window filled with foreign glass. A south window however makes up for it with two figures of the 14th-century. One curious thing about the church is that its priest is never instituted.

Hevingham three miles south of Aylsham is beautifully wooded through the generosity of Robert Marsham, a member of a local family, who was a keen naturalist and squire of the next door village, **Stratton Strawless**. This was in the late 18th century and many of the trees he planted then still line the A140. Hevingham has benefited too from H.P. Marsham, who in 1881, gave St Botulph's Church a number of stained glass panels. These were originally made in Germany for a monastery but were looted at the end of the 18th-century by French soldiers who sold them into willing English hands.

Horning is one of the best loved Broadland boating centres. It is a charming place with one long street containing a happy mixture of inns, shops, cottages and boatyards. Many of the buildings have reed thatch and most of them are built with brick that has mellowed with age. The pretty half-timbered houses have moorings and thatched boathouses alongside. The river winds in and out until it nears the old church, which hides its face behind trees but still manages to catch glimpses of the shining water and the gaily coloured sails of the boats.

Ingworth has the little church of St Lawrence of which only the stump of the tower remains and that is thatched. Inside the church is simple but it is the views down the Mill House and water meadows which make it so pleasing. A humped back bridge over the river at **Oxnead** lets you see the old mill on the right and there is yet another clapboard mill by the Bure as you reach Burgh-Next-Aylsham.

King's Lynn you will either love or hate and you will learn to refer to it as 'Lynn'. There is so much that is beautiful here and so much that has been spoilt in careless development because of the new for new industry, which became obvious immediately after World War II. Saturday Market is probably the best place to start a tour of Lynn, St Margaret's Church here reflects the wealth resulting in the medieval port's export trade in wool and cloth. Lynn's most famous building is The Guildhall. It is fabulous, with its handsome facade of chequered flint and stone. Built in 1421, it was originally the hall of the Trinity Guild, a wealthy merchant guild, existing before King John gave the town its charter. Since it was first built it has had extensions built on either side at different times but you would be hard put to differentiate which is which. Inside the 15th-century Hall leads to the Georgian Assembly Rooms and the Card Room. If you are outside at night when the light shines through the massive windows, illuminating Saturday Market, you will think you are in fairyland.

Langley is one of Norfolk's prettiest villages. It has a fine 18th-century mansion, **Langley Park,** which architecturally pinches its design from Holkham Hall. It is a school now and not open to the public but you can catch glimpses of the park with its spring carpet of snowdrops and daffodils. On the edge of the park is the church whose 13th century doorway leads into a 14th century church with a 15th-century tower. It is very long and a bit barnlike with no arch between the nave and the chancel. The nave is filled with high-backed horsebox pews, from one of which rises a three decker pulpit. The font is 600 years old.

Litcham has hooded doorways which remind one of days long gone by. One house by the bridge that crosses the little river Yar was once a house of rest for pilgrims. The church is mainly 15th-century with a font that has a traceried shield.

Loddon is everything one would wish for in a busy little market town. It has houses. Shops and inns that are mainly 17th and 18th century. The buildings lining the square are mainly Georgian with the exception of the flamboyant Gothic school built in 1857. The impressive church which lies to the east suffered at the hands of careless restorers but it does have some good paintings.

Lound you might possibly ignore because it has nothing about it except for the duckpond. What is different is the rather severe church with its round tower. The inside has been restored by the 20th century genius, Sir Ninian Comper.

Mundesley has one of the nicest sandy beaches on the Norfolk coast. It is a unspoilt, a place for families and for those who just enjoy a walk across an uncrowded beach watching for the 'lowies' at low tide. This is the odd name locals use for the small rock pools.

Neatishead in the Broadland triangle of Wroxham, Stalham and Potter Heigham is an attractive village with Georgian houses, standing at the head of a wooded creek which runs westward from Barton Broad.

North Elmham. Like all villages and small towns in this part of Norfolk you are surrounded by lovely countryside but in fact very close to Norwich. It has a long village street lined with high brick and flint walls which sadly hide some of the fine houses from public view. There is a splendid parish church of St Mary the Virgin with an imposing Perpendicular tower attached to a church of Norman origin.

North Walsham's quaint Market Cross, built by the Bishop of Norwich in 1550 is still the focal point of this prosperous market town which caters for Mundesley, Bacton, Happisburgh and the northern part of The Broads. It has a handsome cross with three tiers of bell-like roofs each lessening in size. The Paston Grammar School taught Horatio Nelson for three years before he went to sea.

Northwold near Thetford is situated in the centre of East Anglia and is very central for the Norfolk and Suffolk coasts, four National Trust properties and the historic cities of Norwich, Cambridge, Bury St Edmunds and King's Lynn. There are wonderful forest walks and superb activity for birdwatchers.

Oulton Broad is one of the finest inland yachting lakes in the country. The road crosses the lock connecting the eastern end of Oulton Broad with Lake Lothing and so to the sea. At the other end there is a dyke that links the River Waveney and the Broadland water system.

Overstrand next to Trimingham is where Lutyens designed two quite lovely houses, The Pleasaunce and The Hall. The Pleasaunce originally had gardens laid out by Gertrude Jekyll but these have been considerably modified.

Reedham is an interesting small place. Once it was a North Sea port and a battlefield for Romans, Danes and Saxons. The River Yare runs beside its streets. It is an area of marshes in which grow reeds which gave it its name. The big church of St John the Baptist suffered badly from fire in 1981 but it produced something unexpected when the plaster was stripped from the walls after the fire. There was a Saxon nave wall constructed from alternate courses of herringbone and horizontal tiles.

Sale pronounced Saul, has the marvellous church of St Peter and St Paul which rises high above the land. The foundations were laid in the 15th-century and it was built to last, as it has done and been saved the fate of restoration by the sometimes over zealous Victorians. The noble families included the Boleyns, and there are many brasses to the family but none to the sad Anne, Henry VIII's second Queen. It has been said though that she is secretly buried here and not in the Tower of London.

Sandringham, 'Dear old Sandringham, the place that I love better than anywhere in the world' wrote King George VI about this most private and beloved Royal home.

Only Edward VIII hated it and spent just one night there. The present house was built in 1869-71, it has a front 150 yards long and stands in an estate of 20,000 acres taking in several villages. The grounds at Sandringham are open to the public from April to September, when the family are not in residence. Do make time to visit the museum in the grounds which is full of royal possessions. You can see Royal Vintage Motor cars and a wonderful collection of photographs. Edward VII might have been a leader of society but he never neglected his attendance at the 16th-century church at the corner of the park where the family still worship today. Here too are reminders of the Royal family with memorial brasses and two little headstones over graves in the churchyard are of little princes. One of the brasses to the Duke of Clarence, Edward VII's oldest son, says 'To my darling Eddy, from his mother, Queen Alexandra.'

Sheringham on the North Coast is designated an area of outstanding natural beauty. This small, attractive town has one of the finest seaside golf links to be found anywhere.

Stody close to Melton Constable, is a village that came into being entirely as a railway town in 1881. The village is very pretty with a church standing quietly above a stream. Nearby lies Stody Lodge built by the first Lord Rothermere which has a very pretty water garden with glorious azaleas and a superb display of rhododendrons.

Surlingham's church has a round Norman tower which was given its octagonal belfry when the rest of the church was made new in the 14th century. A short distance away is one of the loveliest places on the Yare riverside, Bramerton Woods End. Here the trees dip down to the water and the wide and grassy banks invite you to get out of your car and stay for a while.

Swaffham is an elegant small town with some lovely buildings situated around a triangular market place. One of them is the Assembly Room, built in 1897. The Butter Cross which is not a cross at all, immediately demands attention. It is a circular pavilion built by Lord Oxford in 1738 and at its apex sits a life size figure of Ceres. East of the Market Place is the church of St Peter and St Paul in which the north aisle was built by a wealthy man, John Chapman, known as the Pedlar of Swaffham. Legend has it that he discovered two pots of gold in his garden.

Wells-Next-The-Sea has a name that enchants. It manages to combine a working port with tourism successfully. Wandering the narrow yards (lanes to us) is a delight. Staithe Street with its Edwardian and Victorian shop fronts is a place to browse.

West Runton is the home of the Norfolk Shire Horse Centre and County Collection. A visit is a must to recapture times past when these beautiful, majestic animals worked the countryside.

Wolverton railway station is now a museum filled with royal memorabilia but once it played hosts to Kings, Tsars and other Royals from many countries when they were on their way to Sandringham.

Worstead is a village you might like to seek out to the south of North Walsham. In medieval times this was a busy place renowned for its worsted cloth. Today it is quietly prosperous and has a square flanked by Georgian and Queen Anne houses.

Worthing is a tiny hamlet lying a mile to the south east of North Elmham in the Wensum valley. It has a delightful mill pond and a tiny Saxon church with a round tower. It looks almost abandoned, standing as it does alone by the river. I am assured however that it is well used.

Wroxham which considers itself to be the unofficial capital of the Broads, is linked with Hoveton by a hump back bridge over the River Bure. The banks of the river are alive with boatyards and the waterway is so busy that traffic lights would not come amiss. The marina is the place to go if you would like to take a boat trip by paddleboat or motor launch through the adjacent broads.

I think it is a wonderful way of taking in this amazing area. It has everything, the colourful activity of the boats and then the peace of the less used areas where wildlife abounds and you get the chance to see the enormous amount of work carried out by the Broads Authority, which was set up in 1978 to stop the degeneration of broadland. It has to walk a very tight rope when you consider that it must please so many people. You have got a cross-section of nature lovers, sailors, holidaymakers, farmers, water authorities and one must never forget the most important of all, the people who actually live here.

SUFFOLK

Going back to happy stomping grounds can produce feelings of dismay because what was once treasured has disappeared to be replaced by foreign objects or simply erased to make way for anew road. My return to Suffolk in the 1990's has given me nothing but pleasure. Of course things have changed, but in most cases it has been for the good. I start my journey in Ipswich, a city close to where I once lived. It is England's oldest heritage town and as Suffolk's county town it is a major commercial and shopping centre.

Ipswich offers a choice of many things to see and do. For a start there are no less than 12 medieval churches. The lovliest of these is St Margaret's. Flanking the north side of St Margaret's Plain. It is almost as beautiful as Norwich's St Peter's Mancroft, with a spectacular 15th century roof, painted in the time of William III. Five of these churches are floodlit at night and most are open in daylight hours. Each of them has something to offer and will provide you with much interest.

The Tudor **Christchurch Mansion**, which was built in 1548 is furnished as a country house and contains the finest collection of Constable and Gainsborough paintings outside London. **The Worsley Art Gallery** is another must on a visitor's list remembering that Cardinal Wolsey was one of Ipswich's most famous sons. My favourite building is **The Ancient House** in the Butterwalk. Once a hiding place of Charles II, it is the finest example of pargetting in the country and is now used as a bookshop.

One must not forget that Ipswich is still a busy port but much of the marine activity on the waterfront today is for leisure with yachts large and small berthing there.

Whichever way you decide to drive deeper into Suffolk from Ipswich, it will be a delightful experience.

Aldeburgh has always been a gentle backwater and only came to prominence with the advent of the composer Benjamin Britten who, together with his friend Peter Pears, the opera singer, lived here for many years. **The Moot Hall** is one of Aldeburgh's treasures. It is a herringbone brickwork building of the 15th century and is still used at the Town Hall.

Battisford just outside Stowmarket is a place you might pass by without realising it was the home of Sir Thomas Gresham, the found of the Royal Exchange in London. An immensely rich and powerful man he became King's Agent to Henry VIII and retained the position with hardly a break through the reigns of Edward and Mary, and in the early years of Elizabeth I. Four centuries before his birth the village had famous builders in the Knight;s Hospitallers who raised one of their hospitals here.

Beccles is a little town that is very much a part of the life of The Broads but one that could easily put you off because so much has been eaten up by Industrial estates, especially on the eastern perimeter. The church of St Michaels dominates the town. Narrow lanes or what are known locally as scores run from the river bank to the foot of the tower. Severely damaged by fire in the 17th century it was lovingly restored and refurnished by the Victorians.

When you stand before the altar of St Michaels church you can tell yourself that it is here that one of the most thrilling chapters of English history began. In 1749 the curate of Beccles was married to Catherine Suckling; he was Edmund Nelson. Their son, of course, was Horatio Nelson.

Bentley on the other side of Alton Water from Holbrook has a Victorianized medieval church set in a churchyard which seems almost oppressed by conifers. I always believed it was in this churchyard that I would find this splendid epitaph - but I was wrong; it is in Suffolk somewhere.

> 'Here lies the body of Margaret Chowder,
> Who died through drinking fizzy powder.
> Oh may her spirit in heaven be blessed.
> Why should she have waited until it effervesced.'

Delightful isn't it?

Bildeston, halfway between Sudbury and Needham Market, is another charming spot. It has houses of rich cream plasterwork and dark oak half-timbering of the kind especially concentrated in the late medieval clothing towns. The church of St Mary Magdalene stands on a hill half a mile from the village. It is 15th century and well worth climbing the hill to see its splendid portal. Ironically its Perpendicular tower collapsed on Ascension Day in 1975 and has never been restored.

Bramford close to Ipswich is a village of picturesque houses and a beautiful church, St Mary the Virgin. It has a handsome 14th-
century tower with an 18th-century lead spire. Look closely and you will see panelled stone parapets and carved figures, including a monkey wearing a monk's cowl and hurling stones. The extraordinary presence of boulders round about it are thought to indicate a pagan sacred site.

Brandeston not far from Kettleburgh is where, in the 17th-
century, they hung their octogenarian vicar for witchcraft. Also in the village is the cottage of Margaret Catchpole, whose misdeeds caused her to be transported to Australia.

Bury St Edmunds is one of the most delightful and splendid of Suffolk towns. It is full of treasures and has managed to remain almost untouched by large scale modern developments. Almost 1,000 of its buildings have preservation orders on them. Wander into Churchgate Street and you will see the impressive group of buildings erected by Abbot Anselm. The massive Norman Gate was begun in 1121 as a belfry. It was Abbot Anselm who gave Bury its two great churches. St Marys in Crown Street and the 12th-century St James's which in 1914 became the cathedral of the diocese of St Edmundsbury and Ipswich. The broad square oddly named as Angel Hill, has fine Georgian and Regency buildings. Charles Dickens gave two of his celebrated public readings in the Athanaeum in the square and also made the nearby Angel hotel forever famous by using it as the setting for one of Mr Pickwick's adventures. There is also the beautiful Theatre Royal and Abbeygate, surely one of the loveliest shopping streets in the country.

Buxhall, just 3 miles south west of Stowmarket was the birthplace in 1512 of Sir William Coppinger. He, like Dick Whittington, became Lord Mayor of London. Half his estate he left to the poor and half to his relations, whose hospitality was such that it produced a local saying 'To live like a Coppinger'. It was one of those relatives, Walter Coppinger to whom Henry VIII gave permission to wear his hat in the royal presence and the document giving this permission and signed Henry R, is in the possession of the lofty church, which is well over 600 years old.

Cavendish to the west of Long Melford is a name that takes us back to one of the most ancient struggles between Government and workers: Wat Tylers rebellion. St John Cavendish, Chief Justice to the King's Bench lived here. His son helped to kill Wat Tyler and the news of this angered the mob so greatly that they ransacked Sir John's house, dragged him away and beheaded him after a mock trial. The old home of the Cavendish family is here by the beautiful well manicured green. St Marys Church has a tower built in the 13th century with a stair turret in one corner. The tower's ringing chamber is furnished as a living room with window seats in the casement window, and a fireplace whose chimney strikes one as being more than slightly eccentric, perched as it is on the impressive tower.

Clare named after the long line of the Earls of Clare from William the Conqueror. Gilbert the 7th earl, was one of the most powerful men in the land during King John's reign and his son founded the famous Priory of Clare. The town is beautiful with handsome houses, several of which are pargetted - intricately patterned plasterwork.

Dunwich just fell into the sea and was no more! How did it happen? It really started in the 12th century when, instead of riches from its trading success, silt came from the Suffolk shore and clogged the harbour which gave the storms and high tides the opportunity to batter the sea walls. Year after year the sea relentlessly swallowed up parts of the town. In the 13th-century 400 houses, shops and churches disappeared and in the 14th century, the churches of St Martin and St Nicholas crumbled. By 1677 the sea had reached the market place and by the 18th century the Town Hall and St Patrick's church were no more. By then at low tide, ghostly buildings could be seen above the shingle. Nothing survives now except for the ruins of a friary, founded on the spot where St Felix landed in the 7th century bringing Christianity back to East Anglia.

East Bergholt was the birthplace of John Constable in 1776 who wrote ' I even love every stile and stump and lane in the village'. He painted innumerable pictures of the village of which 21 are now in the Victoria and Albert Museum in London.

Felixstowe gained popularity as a south facing Edwardian seaside resort, round a wide shingle bay with totally safe bathing. It lost its Pier at the end of World War II but it is still a favourite place for Ipswich people to come at weekends. Much of the activity in the newer part of Felixstowe is connected with the docks and the port handles well over a million containers annually. A little way up the coast is Felixstowe Ferry whichcrosses from one side of the River Deben to the other.

Framlington is a little town of great charm and dignity. Its streets are very narrow and graced by many fine buildings. The hilltop castle keeps a watchful eye on all that goes on in the town but it cannot find much of which to disapprove.

Kedington was the home of Lord Barnadiston, one of Cromwell's generals and inside the medieval church you will find stone figures of seventeen members of the Barnadiston family. If you ever wondered how the Roundheads got their name, you will find the answer in the Barnadiston family. The story is that Charles Stuart's Queen was looking out a window when she noticed a short-haired youth, Samuel Barnadiston, among a rebellious crowd in the street and commented' Look at that handsome roundhead below'. The name stuck although Samuel took no part in the Civil War, biding his time until he was able to welcome Charles back to the throne, and so well was his welcome received, he was knighted.

Kersey is designated as the prettiest village in Suffolk. It is just two miles north west of Hadleigh and set in something like a natural letter V, with the church looking down from one hill and lovely timbered houses with glorious gardens creeping up the other. It is several centuries since the clack of looms could be heard weaving the now famous Kersey cloth, but as you look at the weaver's cottages, you can almost conjure up the sound and the smell of the cloth. The ruins of a 13th-century Augustinian priory crown the slope opposite the fine church of St Mary.

Lavenham is somewhere that must be visited. Jane Taylor who wrote the nursery rhyme'Twinkle, twinkle little star' lived here. Quaint streets will lead you into enchanting medieval prospects, including those of the Guildhall, the Old Wool Hall, Tudor Shop and Woolstaplers in Prentice Street, a house that is 14th century at the back and 16th century at the front. Set at the end of this miraculously intact timber-framed Tudor wool town is the incomparable church of St Peter and St Paul, built by rich clothiers to celebrate the end of the War of the Roses in 1485.

Leiston pronounced Lacet'n, on the B1122, stands on farmland near the beautiful stretch of coast. It has the most extensive monastic remains in Suffolk and one of the most interesting museums. **The Long Shop** tells the history of the Garrett family, who in the 18th century started a forge to manufacture ploughs, threshers and cast iron work, then went on to build steam powered units for factories, mills and farms. No longer operational it is an exciting place to visit.

Long Melford approached from the south might disappoint you, but be patient and you will come to a mile long High Street lined with timber-framed Georgian houses which delight the eye. As the High Street narrows again to cross the Chad Brook, it reaches a wide green, bounded by the walls of Melford Hall, one of the best moated houses left from Tudor days, on one side and the beautiful church of the Holy Trinity on the other. Long Melford is unfairly blessed with two beautiful houses. The second, Kentwell Hall lies to the north. This is a mellow, red-brick Tudor manor house which stands at the end of a mile long drive, guarded by limetrees. It is moated and work was begun on it in the mid 16th century. the church is best of all and one of the great spectacles of England. It stands across the green with the Tudor almshouse in front of it. Its tower was burnt down but rebuilt at the end of the 19th century. The rest of it has not changed in 550 years. It is 260ft long and must have at least one hundred windows. You can see its great walls and proud tower for miles.

Moulton to the east of Newmarket has one of the loveliest packhorse bridges in Suffolk, sitting astride the River Kennet.

Newmarket is where horse racing started 2,000 years ago when Boadecia set up camp at **Exning**, 2 miles down the road. The Jockey Club controls the regulations of racing from their headquarters at Newmarket. If you come here for the racing you will find that in the summer it takes place across the Heath where the crowds are free to mingle with the horses whilst they wait to be led into the paddock. Racing on the Rowley Mile which takes place in Spring and Autumn is different. The Newmarket Classics are run here.

Orford always conjures up visions of the past. It was once a seaport but the greed of the giant gravel bank, Orford Ness, has gobbled up the entrance. It was on this exposed but secret shingle spit that scientists made their first experiments in radar in 1935. Orford has remains of a great 12th-century royal castle, and if you climb the hummocky ramparts to the top of the formidable polyganal keep, you get a wonderful view over lush countryside and the coast.

Otley is a quiet village north of Ipswich and just five miles west of Woodbridge. A rural retreat, it is totally restful and relaxing to visit.

Pin Mill. Take the B1456 out of Ipswich and you are following the river down to the sea at Shotley opposite Harwich. This is a wonderful area for anyone who loves birds and marine life.

Saxmundham is an unsophisticated small town dating back to Norman times and before that to the Danish Conquest. The church has suffered too much restoration but it is still of interest, particularly the south chancel aisle which has nine panels of Flemish glass in a nice Victorian setting.

Saxtead is a little village close to Framlingham which has **The Saxtead Green Windmill**. This gem is preserved in beautiful order. It is an 18th-century post mill with a three storey roundhouse. There are four patent sails, two pairs of stone and a fantail.

Snape is the home of the Aldeburgh festival. Set right on the banks of the River Alde, it is the trustee of a wonderful collection of 19th-century buildings which includes the Snape Maltings Concert Hall.

Southwold with Blythburgh and Walberswick, cradle the River Blyth in their beautiful arms. The tower of Holy Trinity Church soars out of the reed beds. The devil is supposed to have caused thespire to topple in 1577 and to have left his signature in scorch marks on the north floor. The beach is famous for its coloured pebbles and the old Edwardian pastel painted beach huts. You will not find fast food shops, arcades or souvenir shops. There is a small lighthouse, a collection of fine Georgian houses and contrastingly simple fishermen's cottages. St Edmunds Church rises proud and tall, a monument to light and airiness. 'Southwold Jack' stands by the tower at the rear of the church. It is he who strikes the bidding bell to mark the beginning of a service. He has been doing this since the War of the Roses.

Stoke-by-Nayland has a church standing on a hillside among the trees which Constable put into his famous Rainbow picture. Its 120ft high tower is a proud Suffolk landmark and certainly one of the grandest.

Stowmarket does not have the architectural beauty of some other Suffolk towns although it is a lively market town under which many a relic of Roman and Saxon England can be found. It has a fine medieval church with a timbered 16th-century vicarage where the poet Milton used to visit his tutor.

Sudbury has never lacked the courage to change over the centuries but has managed to save much of its heritage for the president residents. It was the centre of the wool-weaving industry and later of silk production which gave it wealth. There are many fine buildings in this town. The house in which Gainsborough was born in 1717 stands in the street named after him at the bottom of the market hill. It is now a museum used to display his painting and those of his contemporaries. Wander further along the street until it becomes Sour Street. Here there are some delightful if slightly ornate, timber-framed houses. There is Salters Hall, a merchants house, and the old Moot Hall. Both date back to the 15th century and have oriel windows and some splendid carvings. St Gregorys Church has stood much as we see it now, since the 15th century but has relics of an earlier age. The treasure of the church is the ancient cover of its modern font, one of only three covers of its kind. Apart from beauty, what is exceptional is that the lower pushes up ingeniously telescopwise.

Westleton, a prize winning village has a wonderful thatched church whose dignity remains unimpaired even though the low steeple is the result of the village fathers trying to build something grander on the base of the ancient tower which could not take the weight and collapsed in 1770.

Woodbridge does not have one ugly building to my mind. Once a busy commercial port it is now a haven for those who love to sail. St Marys Church is a must for you to visit. The 15th-century tower and north porch are magnificently decorated. The font is of a type only found in Suffolk and Norfolk, depicting the Seven Sacraments.

Yoxford is known as 'The Garden of Suffolk'. This once coaching town is a pretty place with some charming old houses set in landscaped parks, through which flows the River Yox. It is a centre of arts and crafts galleries and good antique shops. TheChurch of St Peter is medieval with a 14th-century tower and lead spire guarded by gargoyles.

CAMBRIDGE

The most obvious place to begin a journey through Cambridgeshire is of course in the historic city of **Cambridge**. Steeped in tradition it is a place that needs time to discover. It is a place the traveller will return to again and again each time discovering new treasures that abound in this ancient seat of learning.

I listened to Jeffrey Archer once talking about Cambridge, a city he loves, and one in which he almost lives at Granchester, made famous by Rupert Brooke, only two miles away. He gave some good advice to people wanting to visit the city. 'Do not allow the academics and students to make you feel you have no right to be there. Cambridge is as much your city as theirs.' Good advice, for this famous seat of learning can be a bit intimidating.

There are all sorts of things you need to know about Cambridge. For example during the year there is constant activity and one thing is for certain one visit will not suffice. No matter when you come it is lovely and very special but if you remember that accommodation is difficult during major events such as May Week, Degree Days and the Festival, that may influence your decision. If you have thoughts of going to Evensong in Kings College Chapel, for example, the service only takes place during the University terms. Lastly during the University examination period, May to mid-June, many of the colleges are closed to the public.

So when are you going to visit Cambridge? Will it to be to tour the Colleges? A wonderful experience. Strangers frequently ask 'Where is the University?' Once an easy question to answer but today far more complex. The oldest buildings which now accommodate the administration form the complex called Old School's opposite Great St Marys Church. This really is the heart of the University but its lecture halls, laboratories and libraries are spread through central Cambridge and west of the river as far as Madingley. You will see undergraduates darting about from one college to another in pursuit of their studies and of their social lives. The only way to make the most of the joys of this magical city is on foot and the way I was shown many years ago, is probably the best way. Over a period of days I was taken on various walks which took in the central area of Cambridge, including th oldest College and University buildings.

There are many brilliant museums and perhaps I should mention that the beautiful green areas in front of the Colleges are known as 'Courts' whereas at Oxford they are called 'Quads'. You are welcome to visit these grounds and wander about at will but please remember that they are private establishments, and that their members live and work in them all year round. Many visitors take this opportunity and because of this there are occasional restrictions, especially during examination times. At most other times you can walk through the courts to visit the chapels, andin a few cases, the Halls and Libraries. Picnicking is not permitted nor may you bring prams, pushchairs or dogs.

I have to admit that most people come to Cambridge to take a look at the University but a spin off from this is the excellence of the shops. The big stores are represented but the specialist shops are the really interesting ones and usually housed in old buildings.

From Monday to Saturday you can walk around the bustling market which hides the unusual in the centre and keeps the outer stalls for fruit, flowers and vegetables. Keep looking and around the area you will find Flea Markets and in the summer All Saints Gardens provides a setting for displays of art and craft as well as artists selling their own paintings.

I went just a little way west on the A45 to **Stow-cum-Quy** and **Anglesey Abbey**, a place of great beauty bequeathed to the National Trust in 1966 by Lord Fairhaven whose nephew the third Lord Fairhaven now lives there.

Its history has been chequered with several owners since the 16th century one of whom was a carter from Cambridge by the name of Hobson and from whom we have derived the expression 'Hobson's Choice'. Of the original Augustinian priory only the chapter house and the vaulted monks' parlour survive. It is a wondrous place to visit and the gardens are nothing short of superb.

In spring cowslips cover the meadows and the sweet scent of some 4,000 white and blue hyacinths pervades the air. Next come the daffodils and their golden glory is replaced by dahlias and brilliantly coloured herbaceous borders. The autumn reminds us that winter is coming but throws out a warmth of its own with the varied array of trees and shrubs in every shade of bronze and red.

Then taking the A45 out of Cambridge again going west, I made for **Caxton**. The village is on the A1198, 11 miles north of Royston and 10 miles south of Huntingdon. Here lies Church Farm, a member of the Wolsey Lodge Consortium, set in three acres of beautiful grounds, a spacious and elegant, listed farmhouse. From here Heritage Leisure courses are run which enable the participants to enhance their knowledge of our heritage.

A little further north from here is **Waterbeach**, a pleasant village with the River Cam flowing nearby. The church is 500 years old and well worth a visit.

If you went further west and then drove northwards up the A1, the Great North Road, you would come to the historic village of **Buckden**. In 1533 King Henry VIII imprisoned his wife, Catherine of Aragon in Buckden Towers following the annulment of their marriage, allowing him to marry Anne Boleyn.

8 miles south west of Cambridge on the A603 is **Wimpole Hall**, the largest country house in Cambridgeshire with a landscape of rare historical worth. Not to be missed.

Sawston lies to the south of Cambridge. This small town has a bustling High Street and abounds with delightful eating places in which to refuel and stoke up energy ready for a visit to the mighty **Imperial War Museum** at **Duxford** two miles away.

This is much more than a museum. It is a different and fascinating outing for the whole family. It is fun, full of surprises and educational as well. There is the finest collection of military and civil aircraft in the country together with an incredible variety of tanks, vehicles, guns - even a lifeboat and midget submarines. The collection dates from the First World War right up to the Falklands conflict and the Gulf War.

Melbourn was an important place in the Middle Ages. It still has moated houses and a medieval church as well as many attractive cottages and is an ideal place to stop and relax in after visiting the museum. Here one can sit and watch the world go by in pastoral surroundings.

Another delightful village within 2 miles of the Duxford Museum and also only 4 miles from the historic **Audley Hall**, is **Hinxton**. It sits just one mile inside the Cambridgeshire border, 6 miles from Saffron Walden. It has no shops, just one street and its biggest disturbance is the River Cam flowing nearby. The tiny spire of the old church rises from a dome set in the battlement of a 650 year old tower. The story of the church is older than that. It begins in 1080 and from that time comes the font and a doorway blocked up in the nave. The church is mainly 14th and 15th century. The chancel has old benches and there are old beams in the roof. A wonderful inspiring house of God.

Wisbech is situated in an area renowned for bulb growing and fruit cultivation, and fruit canning is an important local industry. The town stands on the River Nene, 12 miles from the sea - though at one time before changes in river patterns altered its relationship to the Wash, it was only 4 miles away. From the North and South Brinks, an impressive array of Georgian houses, several with Dutch characteristics, looks across the quays and the river; the most noticeable is Peckover House, belonging to the National Trust and built in the 1720's, displaying some fine rococo plasterwork. The church of St Peter and St Paul is mainly Norman and Perpendicular with a fine 16th century tower. **The Wisbech and Fenland Museum** splendidly illustrates Fenland life.

The small village of **Welney** on the edge of Norfolk, is a quiet tranquil place which is known for its fishing of the rivers ' Delph' and 'Bedford'. In addition the well known Pisces fishing lakes are also very popular with birdwatchers, largely because of the Wildfowl and Wetlands centre which has its headquartersin Pintail House, Hundred Foot Bank, Welney. It is one of eight national centres encouraging visitors to develop close personal contact with a total of 7000 wetland birds of 200 different types; some species owing their very existence to the Trust. At Welney you can get close to nature along a carefully planned walk, with 21 camouflaged observation hides and a visitor building that provides warm, comfortable shelter from the harshest elements. **Ely** will be somewhere you will not want to leave out. Charming in its own right it is enhanced by the glory of its beautiful cathedral, which can be seen for miles around.

Now for **Huntingdon**, a county within the county of Cambridgeshire and famous at present as the home and constituency of Prime Minister, John Major. There are many picturesque villages to visit which are a shining example of rural life. Inns with a story to tell abound, waiting to welcome the weary, thirsty and hungry traveller.

Enjoy Huntingdon which is rich in history and has attractive countryside. It is a land of wide skies and church spires, pretty riverside villages, historic market towns and tranquil waters.

HOTELS, INNS, RESTAURANTS AND COUNTRY HOUSES

LINCOLNSHIRE

My first stop and my first love in Lincolnshire is the wonderful town of Stamford. It took me quite a while to get to know this fascinating county. Until I did I had always thought of it as nothing else but fens and tulips with the occasional sausage and pork pie thrown in for good measure. It is no such thing and it burst forth upon me with a matchless and unique beauty of its own. I suppose today I should refer to it as the County of Lincolnshire and South Humberside which is its official title.

You find yourself suddenly across the border from Norfolk or Rutland into an area of Fenland which closely resembles a chequerboard with a skyline that is nothing short of phenomenal. It has a richness and a tranquillity, a sense of going backwards in time and a disbelief when you see the comparatively small amount of traffic on the roads.

This time I was determined to spend more time in and around **Stamford**. What an elegant town it is, probably the finest in the county, standing at its southern gateway, where Lincolnshire, Northamptonshire and Rutland meet and where the bustling River Welland makes a last dash down from hilly country to enter the Fenland plan. It was one of the five towns, Lincoln, Stamford, Leicester, Derby and Nottingham from which the Danes ruled Lincolnshire and the Midlands. For nearly a thousand years it has been a market town. Its beautiful buildings range mostly from medieval times to the Georgian era, and despite the centuries that separate them, the harmony is superb. No intrusion from either the 19th century, the age of the Industrial Revolution, or of our own 20th century have been allowed to spoil Stamford. It is full of surprises and charms which the centuries have bestowed. There are stone-slated roofs, steep gables, little bow windows, Tudor windows, Queen Anne houses, and Georgian mansions. Even inside these delightful houses, beautiful fireplaces, magnificent staircases and panelling still survive.

You will have much to explore when you stay here including perhaps a visit to **The Steam Brewery Museum** in All Saints Street, where you can watch the brewing process from start to finish. In All Saints Place is a church of that name, one of the five medieval churches in the town. I visited three of them and found All Saints the most beautiful, with an exterior distinguished by the 13th-century blank arcading and its fine Perpendicular steeple. It is a church that makes a statement about the wealth of the rich merchants who endowed the church and to whom there are splendid brasses.

A little to the east of Stamford along the A16 is **Market Deeping** where the market is still a busy place and the rest of its name (with the other Deepings) reminds us that once its deep meadows were flooded every year by the River Welland from time immemorial. There are records that will tell you that the land was so fertile, gardens of great beauty were made out of its pits and bogs. The lands are still fertile, the floodings gone and the little town is a thriving place. The Old Market Place is where the A15 and A16 converge as well as several minor roads.

The history of the Deepings is fascinating and centres around the great Wake family to whom Hereward the Wake belonged; he who resisted the Conqueror and Hugh Wake, who looked after the affairs of the Forest of Kesteven for Henry III. Over a period of three hundred years the family grew in power and gained great possessions scattered all over England and into Scotland. Joan, the Fair Maid of Kent, was the heiress of the Wake family and daughter of Edmund Woodstock, Earl of Kent. Joan owned the Deepings, among her 26 manors, most of them in Lincolnshire. She married her cousin, the Black Prince, as her second husband, and one of their two sons became Richard II.

In addition to Market Deeping there is **Deeping Gate**, and **Deeping St James** which today are really suburbs of Market Deeping. Deeping St James stretches alongside the Welland, a place of wide streets and many lovely old houses, stone-walled and stone-roofed with a particularly beautiful rectory beside the 15th-century church.

It would be a pity not to take a look at **Woodhall Spa** which you will find on the B1292 off the A153 between **Sleaford** and **Horncastle**. No longer operative as a spa town, the unique spa town atmosphere is still very much in evidence. It has excellent accommodation including the **Eagle Lodge Hotel** in The Broadway. Purpose built in 1891 it reigned supreme when Woodhall Spa was as well known to high society as it is now to the golfing fraternity of the world.

By **The Golf Hotel** situated next door to the famous Woodhall Spa Championship Golf Course, there is a little **Cottage Museum** which will tell you how the town started and became a spa. You will then understand the enterprising John Parkinson, who set out with three aims in the early 19th century; 1. Build a town. 2. Plant a forest. 3. Sink a coalmine. The town sadly was not built in Woodhall but a street of fine town houses lies in the nearby village of **New Bolingbroke**. The forest was planted near Woodhall. As for the coalmine, John Parkinson chose a spot in Woodhall. When the shaft reached a depth of 540 feet, there was an inrush of clear, salty water. So the Spa began. The Museum is open daily from Easter to October.

Throughout the year the woodlands in and around Woodhall Spa provide a cavalcade of colour. There are picturesque walks. The Viking Way, a long distance footpath from the Humber to Rutland Water, goes through the village.

Going further towards the east coast, I made for **South Thoresby** at the foot of the Lincolnshire Wolds. You will find it one mile off the A16 and nine miles south of Louth. Ideal place for anyone to stay who wants to take a look at the coast. An invitation to a race meeting at **Market Rasen** took me up the A16 to Louth and then on the A631 to the bustling town. Here is a delightful course, just east of the town and is acknowledged as one of the finest small tracks in the country. The recently built stand in the course enclosure is excellent, and for those who want to bring the children, there is a picnic area and a children's playground. The course sees seventeen days of National Hunt racing annually with a mix of exciting steeplechase and hurdle races. Particularly popular are the four evening meetings during May, June and August. A telephone call on 01673 843434 will give you the dates of the fixtures.

Market Rasen is a pleasant and prosperous small market town. The setting is lovely with woodlands all around, and the high Wolds sheltering it on the east. From the Wolds, at Bully Hill, the dancing little River Rase flows contentedly into the town. There is nothing spectacular about its architecture, the big church by the square has been considerably rebuilt but the richly moulded Norman doorway within the porch is superb.

OUTNEY MEADOW CARAVAN PARK
Bungay, Norfolk NR35 1HG
Tel: 01986 892338

This family run Camping Park is in the Waveney Valley Countryside within easy walking distance to the Historic Market Town of Bungay. Ideally situated, between the river Waveney and the Golf Course at Bungay, on the Norfolk/Suffolk border. Fishing is available on the park and there are Rowing boats and Canoes for hire. For walkers, 'The Bigod Way' is close by. It passes through areas of outstanding natural beauty and offers a variety of wildlife, rare plants and sites of historical interest. Dogs are welcome on the Park but must be on a lead and excercised on the signed dog walk.

The Camping area is grass with some trees for shade and shelter. Electricity 'hook ups' are available to certain pitches. The Amenity toilet and shower block has hot showers, shaver points and a hairdryer and the Laundry as a Coin Op. washing machine spindrier and tumble dryer. You can discover the Historic Town of Bungay which has two fine old churches, a 17th century Butter Cross and the remains of Bigod's Castle. Restaurants, cafes, and pubs providing traditional ales and food are closeby. Bungay has an indoor heated swimming pool, tennis courts, golf course and a cinema. It is a wonderful area to explore. You may make a Reservation by telephone as deposits are not required.

USEFUL INFORMATION

OPEN; All year
CHILDREN; Welcome
CREDIT CARDS;; Not applicable
RESTAURANT; Not on site but nearby
DISABLED ACCESS; Yes
PETS; Welcome but must be on a lead

THE BROOK HOTEL
Orwell Road,
Felixstowe,
Suffolk IP11 7PF
Tel: 01394 278441
Fax: 01394 670422

This friendly, personal hotel seeks to meet the needs of both private and business guests, offering unique local character and charm from which to explore the pretty Suffolk coastline and surrounding countryside. The hotel stands just three minutes walk from the seafront with its two miles of gently curving beach. It is within convenient reach of the A45 and has excellent links to both London and the Midlands as well as to the continent via the ferry.

Accommodation throughout offers all the luxuries that one expects from a modern hotel. There are 25 individually decorated suites, including 23 twin/double rooms and two single rooms. Nine of the doubles are classified as executive. Each room is tastefully furnished and has an ensuite bathroom, direct dial telephone, remote control colour television, radio, tea and coffee making facilities. other facilities include a baby listening service, room service and a non-smoking room on request. Special weekend and weekday breaks are specially designed for holidaymakers and are at very competitive prices. The popular Garden Restaurant caters for a variety of tastes with an excellent choice of dishes. There is always a vegetarian alternative and wherever possible, fresh produce is used provided by local fishermen and farmers. The hotel specialises in private functions for dinner dances or receptions and is much in demand for business meetings in the conference rooms, the Deben and the Orwell.

USEFUL INFORMATION

OPEN; All year
CHILDREN; Welcome
CREDIT CARDS; All major cards
LICENSED; Full
ACCOMMODATION; 25 ensuite
GARDEN; Pretty garden. Ample parking

RESTAURANT; Innovative & traditional
BAR MEALS: Not applicable
VEGETARIAN; Always a choice
DISABLED ACCESS; Yes
PETS; By arrangement

SUFFOLK GRANGE HOTEL,
The Havens, Ransomes Europark,
Ipswich   IP39SJ
Tel:01473 272244
Fax: 01473 272484

Recently built, but carefully designed to fit in with the landscape of the Suffolk countryside, this is a hotel which gives you the best in modern comfort and convenience. What it does not omit is the considerate and personal service of the traditional hotel. The management recognise that the staff make a considerable difference to the pleasure of staying in an hotel and their people are friendly, efficient, dedicated and professional. All the sixty bedrooms have en suite bathrooms, hair dryer, trouser press, direct dial telephone, colour TV with free Sky channels, radio and tea/coffee making facilities. There are two suites, the Orwell and the Deben, both beautifully appointed and ideal for a special occasion. A sauna and a solarium are available for residents. Great care and attention is given to the dishes presented by the Chef and his team. The menu is imaginative and innovative but nonetheless never forgets the traditional favourites. The restaurant is comfortable and relaxing and in addition to the excellent food has a skilfully chosen wine list with wines from all over the world - half bottles are not excluded, something which enables many of us to try new wines. The Lounge Bar is a popular meeting place before or after dinner. The Suffolk Grange specialises in looking after business people. There is a friendly and relaxed atmosphere in the comfortable, air-conditioned conference rooms and when it comes to dinners, buffets or wedding receptions - however formal or informal - you may safely leave the arrangements in their capable hands. Ipswich is in the heart of 'Constable'country and the Suffolk Grange is ideally situated for anyone wanting to explore this scenic and historic part of England. To find the hotel travelling east on the A14, once over the Orwell Bridge take the next slip road, signposted Ransomes Europark. The hotel faces you and is accessible via the second exit off the roundabout. Ipswich station is just 4 miles away. Access to and from Northern Europe is via Felixstowe and Harwich. The Suffolk Grange Hotel is a member of the Country Club Hotel Group.

USEFUL INFORMATION

OPEN; All year, 24 hours.
CHILDREN; Welcome
CREDIT CARDS; All major cards
LICENSED; Yes. Fine wine list
ACCOMMODATION; 60 ensuite rooms
RESTAURANT; Excellent food
BAR FOOD; Wide range
VEGETARIAN; Catered for
DISABLED ACCESS; Yes + facilities
PETS; By arrangement

THE MARTELLO COFFEE HOUSE,
Sparrows Nest Gardens,
Whaplode Road,
Lowestoft. NR32 1UX
Tel: 01502 514402

Sparrows Nest Gardens form Britain's most easterly Park overlooking the sea. It is a magical sort of place, much larger than one would suppose and containing the Royal Naval Patrol Service Association Museum, known to thousands of War-time sailors as HMS Europa. The Museum has photographs and models of how 'Harry Tate's Navy' and their 'small ships' played a major part in winning the War at sea, and kept the sea lanes clear of mines. The gardens have Bowling and Putting Greens and Tennis courts, beautiful flowers and well kept lawns. They also house the Sparrow's Nest Bar, the most easterly Public House in Britain. The whole gardens provide a delightful oasis for locals and visitors and there is no doubt this is enhanced by the presence of The Martello Coffee House, a restaurant with a pleasant family atmosphere which serves freshly prepared food throughout the day. There is an excellent choice of food. Few people would not be tempted by the mouth-watering cakes, the home-made scones and the locally baked pastries. The tea and coffe are always piping hot. If you require something more substantial then the extensive menu includes fish, steaks, locally made 'Hutson' sausages, childrens meals and Homemade Daily Specials. To complete a meal there is a delicious selection of desserts or ice creams. The prices are reasonable and the service friendly.

USEFUL INFORMATION

OPEN; Every day except Christmas and Boxing Day. Hours of opening may vary according to the time of year.

CREDIT CARDS; No credit cards.

RESTAURANT; Freshly prepared food All day.

VEGETARIAN; Several dishes

DISABLED ACCESS; Yes

DARSHAM OLD HALL,
Darsham, Saxmundham.
Suffolk
Tel:01728 668514

Reputed to be the oldest house in Suffolk with parts of the building dating back to 1012, this is a house to be savoured and enjoyed for every moment you are within its welcoming portals. Charles I was a guest of Thomas Bedingfield here prior to his trial and subsequent execution. Today the Hall is part of a 227 acre working arable farm. The house is two and a half storeys high and the mix of architectural periods and styles is evident in the high ceilings at the front and the low ceilings elsewhere. A wealth of old beams and timbered doors together with the galleried hall on the upper floor,help to recreate the ambience of a bygone age. The charming bedrooms are spacious, comfortable and furnished and decorated in a manner that pleases the eye and is very restful. Each has good views of the surrounding Suffolk countryside In fact this feeling of tranquillity one gets throughout the house. Having had a peaceful nights sleep you will come down to breakfast which is served in the cheerful and airy pine dining room, ready to enjoy the excellent breakfast freshly cooked by your hostess, Brenda Padfield. Breakfast is the only meal available but with a plethora of good pubs and restaurants in the near vicinity this presents no problem. Darsham Old Hall is very good value for money. It makes an ideal base for anyone wanting to visit Minsmere Bird Sanctuary, Snape Maltings, Norwich and the Suffolk coast. To find Darsham Old Hall you take the roadsignposted Dunwich and Westleton off the A12 just beyond Yoxford in the direction of Southwold. The house is on the left after about half a mile.

USEFUL INFORMATION

OPEN; All year.
CHILDREN; Welcome.
CREDIT CARDS; No credit cards.
DINING ROOM; Breakfast only
VEGETARIAN; Upon request
DISABLED ACCESS No

THE CEDARS HOTEL & RESTAURANT
Stowmarket
Tel: 01449 612668
Fax: 01449 674704

Just outside Stowmarket you will find this delightful hotel. From the A14 you take the A1120 signposted Stowmarket and Needham Market. Turn right at the junction with B1113. Following the signs into Stowmarket. Make a complete circuit Of the roundabout and enter the hotel from the other Carriageway. The Cedars is a privately owned, family-run hotel Which takes pride in offering a warm welcome and personal service To every visitor, holidaymaker and businessman alike. Originally built as a farmhouse in the 16th century it has undergone many changes and extensions but never once has its charm and character been threatened. The effect has been merely To enhance the comfort and facilities of the hotel. Everywhere Is welcoming. You walk into the oak beamed bar with its large Open fireplace and feel totally relaxed and ready for a drink or to enjoy a meal from the varied selection of bar food available. The restaurant which is open to non-residents, offers a wide ranging a la carte menu at reasonable prices with a Comprehensive wine list, expertly chosen. Each of the 24 bedrooms has an ensuite bathroom, radio, and colour television, Telephone, hair dryer and tea and coffee making facilities. Eight of these bedrooms are situated on the ground floor with easy access for disabled or elderly guests. For business people The Cedars has excellent facilities either in The Constable Room which can accommodate up to 20 guests for a Boardroom style meeting, or the Gainsborough Suite which can accommodate 180.Both offering everything needed including Audio/ Visual equipment. The Gainsborough is also ideal for Dinner Dances, Wedding Receptions and Exhibitions. There are a wealth of interesting places to visit closeby such As Aldeburgh and Snape and the beautiful, unspoilt Suffolk coastline,the historic towns of Bury St Edmunds, Colchester And Norwich, Ipswich - the county town of Suffolk and Lavenham - the most famous medieval town in England.. All of these can reached within an hour's drive.

USEFUL INFORMATION

OPEN; All day, all year except 25th December - 1st January
CHILDREN; Welcome
CREDIT CARDS; All major cards
ACCOMMODATION; Ensuite bedrooms, Conference facilities
RESTAURANT; Excellent, reasonable
VEGETARIANS; Catered for
DISABLED ACCESS; Yes. Ground floor bedrooms
LICENSED; Yes

THE CAPTAIN'S TABLE
3, Quay Street,
Woodbridge, Suffolk
Tel: 01394 383145.

For a quarter of a century Tony and Jo Prentice have owned and run this delightful establishment, just one minute from the river and the town centre. Hidden behind a brick wall, the Tudor buildings are painted Suffolk pink, and in summer, the small patio in front of the restaurant is a suntrap protected from the world by the outer brick wall. Once it was a farmhouse with land going down to the River Deben. It has twice been a public house during its long history and most of its superlative timber beams were taken from ships of the King's Fleet when they were built and repaired at Woodbridge. The Captain's Table has gained a deserved reputation throughout Suffolk for the wonderful Seafood it serves. The extensive menu invites you to choose from 'Starters from the Net' including Moules Mariniere, half a dozen Oysters from Butley Creek or a Mousse of Avocado with a fresh tomato and herb dressing. Main courses include local Dover soles, or Scallops tossed in butter with bacon and garlic. There is an alternative selection for those not over keen on fish and seafood, and also a fixed price menu which is both value for money and has excellent choices. because everything is fresh, one saying on the menu is pertinent: 'All dishes are offered subject to wind & tide, fisherman's fancy, farmer's whim and gardener's back'! The complementary wine list has an excellent range, but if all you desire is a bar snack, you will be made equally welcome. You would have to be without soul not to enjoy a meal here.

USEFUL INFORMATION

OPEN; 12-2pm & 6.30-9.30pm (Sat 10pm). **RESTAURANT**; Wonderful seafood
Closed Monday & Sunday. **BAR FOOD**; Delicious snacks
CHILDREN; Welcome **VEGETARIAN**; One dish daily
CREDIT CARDS; Visa/Access/Diners/Amex. **DISABLED ACCESS**; Willing to
LICENSED; Yes assist
GARDEN; Small patio with tables

THE MALT HOUSE,
Palgrave, Nr.Diss
Norfolk IP22 1AE
Tel:01379 642107 Fax:01379 640315.

Marj and Phil Morgan bought this delightfully converted house on their return to this country after 24 years in the Orient. Their intention was to have guests occasionally but because they have entirely the right approach to guesthouse keeping, they have found that their rooms are much in demand. The house is charming, beautifully and interestingly furnished with nice pieces brought from their home in the East - many of them with fascinating stories attached which the Morgans are happy to tell you about. The acre of garden is full of colour and interest and landscaped with many varieties of Conifer, Heather and roses. The large Walled Victorian Kitchen garden provides much of the fruit and vegetables for the table. The garden is a delight to sit in. Phil and Marj have discovered that many of their guests are keen gardeners who have come from far afield to visit the world renowned Bressingham Gardens 2 miles away. The Morgans have made lots of friends with their guests who enjoy swapping hints and tips on 'How to make it grow'! Inside, the house has three deluxe ensuite bedrooms attractively furnished with Interior Designer fabrics. Each room has Colour TV, Radio, and Coffe/Tea making facilities. The beamed Lounge and fireplace makes a splendid venue for coffee and conversation after dinner, a meal that is optional because there are so many good places to eat locally and the Morgans like their guests to be free to do whatever they wish. The house is totally non-smoking, well behaved children over two years are welcome but pets are definitely taboo! Just awarded a 2 Crown de Luxe by the Tourist Board andholding a 'Good Room Award' from Guestaccom, the Morgans are also members of 'A Break with Tradition', a group of people who all have interesting houses in which you can stay.

USEFUL INFORMATION

OPEN; All year except Dec 20th-Jan 3rd.
DINING ROOM; Super food
Dinner upon request
CHILDREN; Over two years
CREDIT CARDS; Most major credit cards.
DISABLED ACCESS; No
LICENSED; No. Guests welcome to bring their own wine.
ACCOMMODATION; 3 de luxe ensuite rooms - A non-smoking house

THE LIMES HOTEL,
Bridge Street,
Fakenham, Norfolk NR21 9AZ

Under the same ownership as Wensum Lodge Hotel also in Bridge Street, The Limes differs totally except for the fact that it is run equally efficiently but catering perhaps for the younger at heart. There are only 3 attractive en-suite bedrooms but the hotel is a centre for many other things. For example it offers excellent value for money bar lunches which are much appreciated by Fakenham's Business and Leisure fraternity. As the evening approaches the large bar becomes an entertainment centre kicking off with half-price cocktails and Happy Hour. Here you can view all the big sports events, enjoy music and out-take videos on the 8ft video screen. The Games Room includes two Pool tables, Pinball and various other current Arcade games. Live bands, Disco's and Karaoke feature Thursday through to Sunday evenings.

USEFUL INFORMATION

OPEN; All year.
CHILDREN; Welcome
CREDIT CARDS; All major cards
LICENSED; Yes
ACCOMMODATION; 3 ensuite rooms
RESTAURANT; Excellent value
BAR FOOD; Super lunches
VEGETARIAN; Catered for
DISABLED ACCESS; Yes

THE WENSUM LODGE HOTEL
Bridge Street,
Fakenham, Norfolk NR21 9AY
Tel: 01328 862100 Fax: 01328 863365.

Known as 'The Country Hotel in Town' Wensum Lodge is delightfully situated. The crystal clear River Wensum glides past this former grain store, close by the old water mill. At the very heart of Norfolk, the hotel is well placed as a base from which to explore all the county's attractions: the superb beaches at Wells-next-the-Sea and Holkham; historical King's Lynn and Norwich (only half an hour away), both with excellent shopping and fast trains to London; the Queen's estate at Sandringham; Thursford's famous Steam Collection; the highly regarded bird sanctuary at Pensthorpe. The sporting enthusiast can fish in the River Wensum, chase divots around the golf course or enjoy a flutter at the horse races, all within a few minutes' walk. There is no doubt that you will be cosseted here. The nine well-appointed en-suite bedrooms each have colour TV, private telephone and tea/coffee making facilities. The oak-beamed ground floor was refurbished sympathetically without loss of character. The Wensum Lodge is beautifully run, the staff welcoming and efficient, the food delicious.

USEFUL INFORMATION

OPEN; All year.
CHILDREN; Welcome
CREDIT CARDS; All major credit cards,
LICENSED; Yes.
ACCOMMODATION; 9 ensuite rooms
GARDEN; Riverside patio and garden with tables.

RESTAURANT; Delicious food
VEGETARIANS; Catered for

DISABLED ACCESS; Yes

CALDECOTT HALL GOLF & LEISURE
Fritton, Gt Yarmouth
Norfolk NR30 9EY
Tel: 01493 488488.

Five miles south of Gt Yarmouth on the A143 is the eleven hundred and fifty acre Caldecott Estate, a rare mix of pinewood, parkland and part working farm. It is set on the edge of the Waveney Valley providing a superb backdrop to the ever developing golf and leisure complex, which incorporates a 9 Hole Main Course, 9 Hole Short Course, Floodlit Driving Range, Pitch and Putt, Large Practice Area, Professional Tuition, Club Hire, Crazy Golf, Adventure Playground and Golf Equipment/Coffee Shop. The unique Equestrian Centre offers many miles of peaceful tracks for Hacking through the 1200 acre Estate where you can ride in complete safety. Qualified Instructors teach beginners and intermediates in the two schooling rings. Caldecott Hall is the estate's centre piece and houses a comfortable bar and two restaurants offering extensive menus to suit all tastes from simple bar food to a full a la carte cuisine. All the dishes are prepared by the Hall's own chefs in modern kitchens, using fresh produce much of which comes from Caldecott Farm . In the fine weather, you can dine in the open air on the patio, and during the summer there are frequent barbecues which are hugely popular. The adjacent Marquee Suite is purpose built to accommodate weddings and parties and also to act as the social centre for corporate days and society golf. The whole complex is set in landscaped grounds featuring lawned areas, patios and gardens, the perfect setting for all occasions.

USEFUL INFORMATION

OPEN; All year, 7 days a week
CHILDREN; Welcome
CREDIT CARDS; All major cards
LICENSED; Yes
ACCOMMODATION; Not applicable
RESTAURANT; Extensive menus
BAR FOOD; Simple menu
VEGETARIAN; Always a choice
DISABLED ACCESS; Yes
GARDEN; Landscaped grounds

BRASTEDS
8-10 St Andrews Hill,
Norwich NR2 1AD
Tel: 01603 625949
Fax: 01603 766445

The customers of this excellent restaurant will tell you that part of the pleasure in going there is to experience the peculiarly welcoming and friendly atmosphere that emits from the ghost who has haunted 8-10 St Andrews Hill since the 17th Century. Your host will be John Brasted who will invite you to enjoy what can only be described as a culinary experience. The Ghost has no desire to leave and once customers have found Brasteds, neither do they. It could not be better situated just three minutes from both the cathedral and the castle. St Andrews Hill is quaintly cobbled and abutts onto the historic old Bridewell Prison, between the main shopping area, London Street, and the classic tourist attraction of Elm Hill. Dishes on the completely new and more extensive menu which is changed regularly include, Tart of Fresh Tomatoes, Filo Pastry Cheese Parcels surrounded by a Home-Made Apple and Thyme Jelly, and Quenelles of Salmon with a rich Lobster Sauce. Main courses of a wonderful Cassoulet, John Brasted's speciality, or Beef Stroganoff are always available and if you are lucky, Braised Lamb Shanks with Lentils will be on offer. To finish, apart from fabulous hot souffles, Chocolate Marquise on a coffee bean cream Sauce is irresistible. Savouries are served as an alternative - a rare treat these days. Maximum use of fresh local produce is evident, treated sympathetically by chef Adrian Clarke. Brasted is a popular place with celebrities and famous personalities who enjoy the welcoming atmosphere of comfort and friendliness created by draped walls and luxurious armchairs on a polished wood floor with Persian rugs, coupled with first class service which avoids uncalled for servility.

USEFUL INFORMATION

OPEN; 12-2pm & 7-9.30pm
No lunch Sat, Closed Sunday
CHILDREN; Welcome
CREDIT CARDS; Visa/Access/Amex /Diners
LICENSED; Fine wine list
ACCOMMODATION; Not applicable

RESTAURANT; Classic European Cuisine
BAR FOOD; Not applicable
VEGETARIAN; A good selection
DISABLED ACCESS; By arrangement
GARDEN; No

CUBITT COTTAGE
Low Street,
Sloley, Norwich NR128HD
Tel: 01692 538295.

The very name 'Sloley' acts as a tranquilliser in this busy world. The pace of the village lives up to its name and within it is Cubitt Cottage the home of Janie Foulkes who delights in having people around her and makes sure everyone feels special. The cottage is surrounded by farm landand quiet lanes. The garden is a joy to behold. Janie specialises in old fashioned roses, clematis and has a collection of perennial geraniums adding to the subtle colours. There is a wild life pond abundant with frogs, newts and dragonflies. Such a peaceful place to sit around and watch nature at work. A bower bedecked with sweet smelling honeysuckle, jasmine and climbing roses and a wildflower area with all the oldfashioned wild flowers completes the picture. On fine mornings breakfast is served in the garden in the company of the many species of birds that nest in the mature trees. Sometimes it is possible to have dinner outside as well and certainly the garden is the place to relax with a pre-dinner drink that you have brought yourself - Cubitt Cottage is not licensed but you are very welcome to bring your own for which no corkage is charged. Inside Cubitt Cottage is as welcoming as your hostess. It has been modernised to a high standard and is furnished with fine antiques. Every room is delightful and has that lived in feeling which only happy homes produce. There is a beamed dining room, a sitting room with wood burning stove, TV, a piano and plenty of books, maps and games for guests' use. The three twin-bedded rooms have wash basins, tea and coffee making facilites and clock radios. One is ensuite, one has a private shower and WC the third has a bathroom adjoining. One room is large enough to accommodate a family of three. A cot and high chair are available. A sumptuous, beautifully cooked breakfast is served every day and a three course evening meal can be provided by prior arrangement using fresh local produce, much of it organically grown fruit and vegetables from the garden. Vegetarians, diabetics, gluten free diets are catered for and packed lunches are available on request. The village of Sloley is situated off the B1150 Norwich/North Walsham road and is a small rural community. Thesurrounding countryside is full of interest. The Norfolk Broads and rivers, unspoilt sandy beaches, bird and wildlife sanctuaries, National Trust Houses and craft centres, are all within easy reach with the Cathedral City of Norwich well worth a day's visit. For those who would rather explore the area at a more leisurely pace there are two bicycles for hire.

USEFUL INFORMATION

OPEN; All year. No credit cards.
CHILDREN; Welcome
CREDIT CARDS; No
LICENSED; No
ACCOMMODATION; 3 twin bedded
DISABLED ACCESS; No

DINING ROOM; Delicious Breakfast. Evening meal by arrangement
VEGETARIAN; Upon request
PETS; No

THE DORMY HOUSE HOTEL
Cromer Road,
West Runton,
Norfolk NR279QA
Telephone and Fax: 01263 837537

This small privately owned Country House Hotel has a deserved reputation for everything that is best in hotel-keeping. Jean, John and James Jarvis own and run Dormy House with an informal professionalism that creates a warm and friendly atmosphere and ensures very high standards. It is one of the few four crown hotels in this part of Norfolk. Standing in its own grounds it is surrounded by beautiful countryside mostly belonging to the National Trust. West Runton is a small coastal village with a wealth of activities for people staying in the area. It is ideal for golfers, horse-riding, fishing or enjoying the beautiful country and coastal walks, and the nearby bird-watching facilities. The beach, only a stone's throw from the hotel, is supremely clean washed by the waters of the North Sea. Close by are facilities for squash, tennis and swimming plus many museums, wildlife parks. The famous North Norfolk Steam Railway station is close to the Hotel.

The fourteen ensuite bedrooms all have scenic views, some overlooking open fields, cliff tops and the sea, while others overlook the golf course. Each room is individually furnished and decorated in a charming, light and airy manner with allfacilities including direct dial telephone, colour TV, trouser press, radio, hair dryer and a hostess tray. The talented chefs produce superb food either on the Table de Hote or A La Carte menus, served in the delightful, intimate candlelit restaurant. Alternatively there is a varied selection of quality bar meals available daily in the comfortable bar and lounge. From here there is a glorious view of the sea, the patio and lawned garden. Staying at the Dormy House Hotel is a memorable experience and one to be repeated.

USEFUL INFORMATION

OPEN; All year
CHILDREN; Over 7 years
CREDIT CARDS; All major cards
LICENSED; Yes
ACCOMMODATION; 14 ensuite rooms
GARDEN; Yes. Car Park
PETS; No

RESTAURANT; Superb Table de Hote & A La Carte
BAR FOOD; Wide choice daily
VEGETARIAN; Always a choice
DISABLED ACCESS; Yes, no special facilities

THE KINGS ARMS
13 Horncastle Road,
Boston,
Lincolnshire
Tel: 01205 364296

On a sunny day to sit on the patio outside the front of the Kings Arms, sipping a drink, is a very pleasant way to pass the time, particularly as it is right alongside the Maude Foster canal and opposite the picturesque windmill of the same name. Inside you will find it a warm and welcoming hostelry serving the excellent ales of Bateman's Brewery and good value Bar Meals. Sunday lunches are a tradition here and deservedly popular, with generous portions at reasonable prices.

Owned by the likeable and energetic Mick Cooper, who also has another pub in Boston, The Roper Arms. Helped by his wife Annette The Kings Arms is totally lacking in formality which makes it a very relaxed place in which to stay. There are six letting bedrooms, most of which are ensuite. The restaurant which seats 36 people is attractive, and so too are the friendly bars. You can take the locals on at Darts, Pool, Cards or Dominoes if you wish but you need to be pretty good! Lingering awhile in historic Boston with its famous Boston Stump is more than worthwhile, and what better place to stay than The Kings Arms.

The Coopers family motto is 'Good Beer, Good Food, Good Company' and this pub certainly lives up to it. You will find everyone welcoming, the food is true pub food with many dishes home-cooked. 'Daily Specials' tempt most palates and if you would prefer to have a snack rather than a full meal then the freshly cut and generously filled sandwiches or Ploughmans will provide the answer. A Children's room has been added in recent years.

USEFUL INFORMATION

OPEN; Mon-Sat: 11-3pm & 5-11pm
Sun: 12-3pm & 7-10.30pm
CHILDREN; Children's Room
CREDIT CARDS; Visa/Access
LICENSED; Full on + Supper Licence
ACCOMMODATION; 6 letting rooms some en-suite

RESTAURANT; Traditional Pub Food
Sunday lunch
BAR FOOD; Wide range pub fare
VEGETARIAN; Yes, 4 dishes daily
DISABLED ACCESS; Sorry, No.
GARDEN; Beer Garden, Benches, tables, Play area

THE RED LION INN
Stickford, Boston
Lincolnshire
Tel: 01205 480488

A fascinating pub in the quiet village of Stickford, just off the A16 Bypass between Boston and Grimsby and right on the edge of the Wolds and Fenlands. The village has an 11th century church and the Allied Forces Military Museum which houses a large private collection Of World War II British, American and post-war vehicles. It is open All the year from 10am-4pm. The Red Lion has served the village for Almost 400 years and its uneven floors and walls, roaring fires and Many other features including a ghost named Ada, who is reputed to Be a camp follower of Cromwell's Officers who were billeted in the 17th century, all add to its charm. The food is good English and French cuisine with local specialities. Philip Constantine, the landlord who originally hails from Cyprus makes a real Greek Moussaka. There are two guest bedrooms complete with tea/coffee making facilities And colour TV. The Lounge Bar is comfortable and frequently there is Very good live music - jazz, piano etc but definitely not rock. Overnight Parking is available for up to five caravans.

USEFUL INFORMATION

OPEN;Every day 9.30am-11pm
CHILDREN;Very welcome
CREDIT CARDS;Access/Master/Visa
LICENSED;Yes
ACCOMMODATION;2 rooms + 5 overnight caravan sites

RESTAURANT;Excellent English & French
BAR FOOD;Wide range, hot & cold
VEGETARIAN;Several dishes
DISABLED ACCESS;Level entrance
GARDEN;Fenced garden with tables And chairs

THE BRACKENBOROUGH ARMS HOTEL

Cordeaux's Corner, Off A16
Brackenborough, Nr Louth,
Lincolnshire LN11 0SZ
Tel: 01507 609169 Fax: 01507 609413

This charming 4 Crowns Highly Commended Hotel is set in the heart of the Lincolnshire Wolds in an area noted for its natural beauty. It is supremely well situated for many purposes. The coastal towns of Mablethorpe, Cleethorpes and Skegness are close, Market Rasen Racecourse, Cadwell Park and historic Lincoln are within an hours drive. You can shop in the pleasant rural atmosphere of Louth, explore the market and the attractive winding streets or the more modern Freshney Place Shopping Complex in Grimsby. There are many local Golf Courses to delight golfers but whatever your reason for coming to this area you cannot do better than to stay or visit the Brackenborough Arms. It has been furnished with great taste, using colour schemes which complement the light rooms perfectly. Every bedroom has all th facilities you could wish for including hair dryers and Mini Bars. Three well appointed and equipped Conference Rooms are available for meetings, seminars and other functions. John and Audrey Lidgard are the owners and it is their careful attention to detail that makes it such a pleasure to come here. In the Lounge you can sit back in comfort and enjoy a tasty home-cooked meal and in the Dining Room, set in the same traditional theme as the Lounge, an A La Carte menu issupplemented by the Chef's Specials which can only be described as first class. The hotel is famous for Grimsby fresh fish every day, and on Sundays the traditional Roast Lunch is a treat. An exceptional establishment with an excellent staff.

USEFUL INFORMATION

OPEN;7-11pm Sun: 8-11pm
CHILDREN;Welcome
CREDIT CARDS;All major cards
LICENSED;Full On
ACCOMMODATION;18 en suite
3 Conference rooms. Weekend breaks.

RESTAURANT;Famous for fresh Grimsby fish
BAR FOOD;Wide range. Chef's specials
VEGETARIAN;Several dishes
DISABLED ACCESS;Yes
GARDEN;Yes

YE OLDE DUN COW INN
Barrier Bank,
Cowbit, Nr Spalding,
Lincolnshire PE12 6AL
Tel: 01406 380543

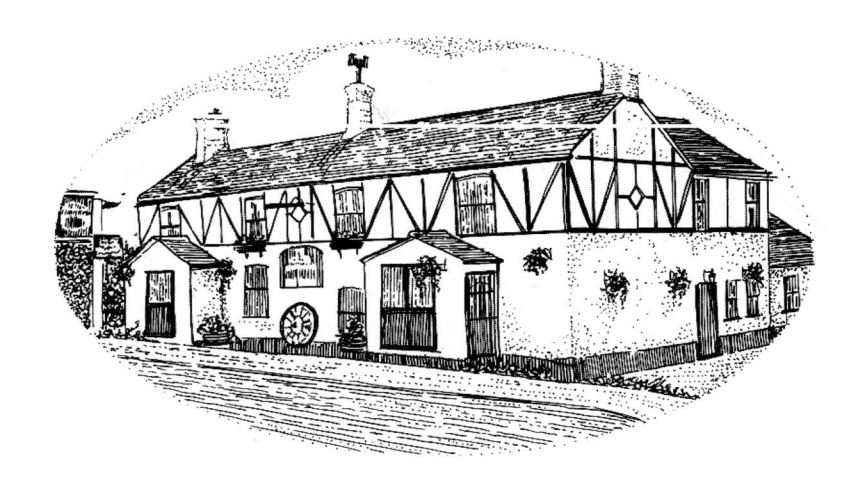

This is a very interesting place situated on the main A1073 Just 4 miles out of Spalding. It is less than 50 years since Cowbit Wash was a flooded area and famous for skating in the Winter months. Inside Ye Olde Dun Cow you can see a collection of Ice Skates, Punt Guns and photographs of wild-fowling and Skating on Cowbit Wash. The husband and wife team, Paul and Lois run this contented pub and both are always to be seen either cooking or to greet you behind the bar. There is a 35 seater restaurant situated in the older part of the building - circa 1700 -. It has a wonderful atmosphere enhanced by old beams, large fireplaces, lots of brass. The menu includes the famous 'Dun Cow Mixed Grill' for the bigger appetite. Steaks and Grills, home-made dishes are all prepared with fresh local ingredients and produce. The wine list covers wines from across the world. There are 7 bitters to choose from, 5 on Traditional Hand Pump plus a good selection of lagers. For those wanting to stay to enjoy the pub and the countryside,there are attractive bedrooms with their own bathrooms also have central heating, TV, tea and coffee making facilities. The price is very reasonable and includes a splendid full English breakfast.

USEFUL INFORMATION

OPEN; 12-3pm & 6.30-11pm
Sun: 12-3pm & 7-10.30pm

RESTAURANT; Renowned for grills Especially 'Dun Cow Mixed Grill Traditional Sunday Lunch

CHILDREN; Welcome.Family room

BAR FOOD; Wide range. Home-cooked

CREDIT CARDS; Visa/Access/Euro

VEGETARIAN; At least 6 dishes

LICENSED; Full On

DISABLED ACCESS; Yes + toilet

ACCOMMODATION; Rooms with bathroom

GARDEN; Beer Garden & Play area

THE MARMION ARMS,
Haltham, Nr. Horncastle
Lincolnshire LN9 6JQ
Tel:01507 568326

Between the Wolds in the North and the Fens in the South of the County nestles the hamlet of Haltham, where the Marmion Arms is situated alongside the A153, midway twixt Horncastle and Coningsby. The pub takes its name from the ancient family of the King's Champion, an honour bestowed on Sir Robert Marmion by William the Conqueror in 1066. The present Queen's Champion, Colonel Sir John Dymoke, still resides on estates close by. The Marmion coat of arms is displayed at the front of the pub, which is believed to be the only timber-framed, wattle and daub, thatched property of its kind in Lincolnshire and possibly the country, dating back to the year of its construction in 1510. The Marmion Arms is ideally situated at the heart of this rural community for a host of outdoor activities. Hunting, shooting, fishing, cycling, and water sports of all kind abound in an area served by a wide variety of self-catering holiday parks with chalets, caravan and camp sites. Ramblers and serious walkers leave and rejoin the Viking Way after refreshment at the Marmion. The disused Horncastle canal provides a great day's sport for fishermen. An a la carte menu using fresh local produce compliments the variety of traditional bar meals available, which includes dishes for discerning vegetarians and children. Quality traditional ales are on tap. The beer garden forms a peaceful suntrap during the summer where you can sit and relax. The Marmion Arms is a friendly, welcoming hostelry run by two professionals, Rob Moon and Maureen Lindley.

USEFUL INFORMATION

OPEN; Mon-Sun.
CHILDREN; Welcome.
CREDIT CARDS; None taken.
LICENSED; Yes
ACCOMMODATION; Not applicable
RESTAURANT; Not applicable
BAR FOOD; Wide range, traditional
VEGETARIAN; Always a choice
DISABLED ACCESS; Yes

THE POACHERS INN

Swineshead Road,
Kirton Holme, Boston
Lincolnshire
Tel: 01205 79310/79443
Fax: 01205 70254

Kirton Holme, four miles distant from historic Boston, has An abundance of history of its own, as well as being one of The most delightful villages in Lincolnshire. Its fine, superbly maintained Topiary Avenue is world renowned. At the heart of the village is The Poachers Inn, purchased by the likeable landlord, John Sail, ten years ago. Throughout his years of incumbency he has striven to improve the standard of comfort and service. The success of what he has achieved is shown by the expansion of thebusiness and the constant awareness that there is always something that can be improved, although when you look round The Poachers, it would be hard to determine. The old inn has parts that date back over 400 years. The bar area was both a stables and cart hovel and there was a small, simply furnished room for the field workers to seek brief respite from their arduous toil. Today, in addition to the bar, with its nooks and crannies, Restaurant areas and garden, there are twelve, spacious, ensuite rooms. All superbly fitted out, five of them are single, six doubles and one equipped for the disabled. It would be hard to find anyone who would not enjoy staying here, especially honeymooners in one of the rooms with a fourposter and whirlpool bath. The Poachers has every amenity including a trim gym and sauna, and a golf course just 200 yards away. Situated as it is so close to Boston and with Grantham 22 miles, and Lincoln and Louth 35 miles, it is an ideal site for conferences and seminars, which can be held in an extremely well set up room. The two restaurants have a good basic menu of grills, fish and poultry. The bar seats 70 and is well served by an economically priced bar snack menu. There is also a sun room leading onto the paved garden area where regular summer barbecues are well supported. Recently John Sail has acquired another hostelry, The Olive Branch, which he is refurbishing and achieving the same sort of success, albeit in a different environment, as he has done with The Poachers. Certainly worth a visit.

USEFUL INFORMATION

OPEN;12-2pm & 7-11pm
CHILDREN;In small garden & Sunroom
CREDIT CARDS;Visa/Access/Master Diners
LICENSED;Full Licence
ACCOMMODATION;12 ensuite 1 disabled
GARDEN;Paved courtyard. Boules

RESTAURANT;Cooked with care, eaten with peace in mind
BAR FOOD;Jaunty & Just.Varied and good value
VEGETARIAN;Several dishes varying
DISABLED ACCESS;Yes + 1 bedroom

THE WHITE HART HOTEL
Cornhill, Market Square,
Spilsby, Lincolnshire
Tel: 01790 752244.

The White Hart is a building that you cannot miss. Its imposing black and white facade has dominated the market place of this ancient town for over 300 years and it, in turn, is gazed upon by the vast, bronze statue of Sir John Franklin, a son of Spilsby, who discovered the North West Passage. The nearby Corn Exchange hosts regular sheep sales and the hotel is a popular meeting place for market-goers. Brian and Sandra Shephard are the hosts of this happy establishment. In addition to the 2 cosy bars, both with coal and log fires, there is a restaurant with 40 covers and a function room which caters for weddings and parties for up to 80 people. Apart from the Pool Room there is also a full size snooker table for anyone who fancies themselves as a Stephen Hendry or Jimmy White. Eight well furnished bedrooms are available, all at a very reasonable price with a traditional English breakfast included. Spilsby is only 10 miles from Skegness and has the Snipedales Nature Reeseve, and the Lincolnshire Aviation Museum closeby. The food served by The White Hart is very popular especially the 4 course Sunday lunch for which booking is advisable. Notice would be appreciated if special catering is required for Vegetarians or Children.

USEFUL INFORMATION

OPEN; 11am-11pm.
CREDIT CARDS; Yes
CHILDREN; Welcome
LICENSED; Yes
ACCOMMODATION; 8 bedrooms

RESTAURANT; Wide range
BAR FOOD; Excellent choice
Book for Sunday lunch
VEGETARIAN; Upon request
DISABLED ACCESS; No

HOTELS, INNS, RESTAURANTS AND COUNTRY HOUSES

… SHORT BREAKS

A GUIDE TO SHORT BREAKS
- COUNTY BY COUNTY

Price band for two people sharing a room with breakfast

A = up to   £30
B =   £35 - £50
C =   £60 - £100
D = over   £100

CAMBRIDGESHIRE

ELY
WHITCHAM HOUSE, Whitcham, Nr Ely.
Tel: 01353 778212.
Delightful Georgian house at the end of the ancient village of Whitcham. Owned by Somerset and Elpie Gibbs who are members of the Wolsey Lodge Consortium. Beautifully furnished, lovely garden, super food and excellent company. Open all year except Christmas, New Year and Easter. Visa. Children over 12. Dogs by special advance arrangement.
Price Band: C

BUCKDEN
THE GEORGE COACHING INN, Great North Road.
Tel: 01480 810307.
Old coaching inn in an historic village. Great hospitality, super food, romantic at night when the bar and restaurant are both candlelit. Garden terrace for summer alfresco eating. 16 en suite rooms. Small pets by arrangement. Open 24 hours throughout the year. All major cards. Well behaved children welcome. Vegetarian dishes on request. 9 Light & Lean dishes.
Price Band: C

CAXTON
CHURCH FARM, Gransden Road.
Tel: 01954 719543.
A member of the Wolsey Lodge Consortium, this is an elegant listed farmhouse which retains original 16th and 17th century features with 19th century additions. A wealth of oak beams, log fires and very comfortable beds add the finishing touches. The owners Peter and Maggie Scott run Heritage Leisure Courses which are very popular. Most of the time is spent visiting historic locations in the informative company of Peter who is a keen amateur historian. Open all year. No credit cards. Children by arrangement with parents. Prior notice for vegetarians.
Price Band: C

HUNTINGDON
PRINCE OF WALES INN, Potton Road, Hilton.
Tel/Fax: 01480 830257.
In a picturesque village one and a half miles south of the new A14 Trunk Road. Everything one would expect of a village inn. No restaurant but good bar food. 4 en suite rooms. Open all year. Visa/Access/Amex. No children under 5. Vegetarians catered for.
Price Band: B

LEIGHTON BUZZARD
GROVE FARM, Grove.
Tel: 01525 372225.
A member of the Wolsey Lodge Consortium, Grove Farm has magnificent views over Dunstable Downs. Extensively modernised 1890 farmhouse which is the family home of Tony and Elizabeth Milhofer and their three grown up sons. Warm, friendly, welcoming. Delicious, imaginative food using home grown organic produce. Open all year. Children welcome. Access/Visa. 3 en suite rooms. Non-smoking house.
Price Band: C

SHELTON
SHELTON HALL, Shelton, Nr Newark.
Tel: 01949 850180/850391.
Delightful Georgian family house owned by Angela and Mike Kimberley. Beautifully furnished with period furniture. Angela is a professional cook. Member of the Wolsey Lodge Consortium. Open all year - closed occasionally. Access/Visa. Not licensed. Bring your own wine. Lovely happy atmosphere, wonderfully relaxed
Priced Band: C

WISBECH
THE FIVE BELLS, 1 New Road, Upwell.
Tel: 01945 772222.
Friendly inn beloved by locals and fisherman. 7 en suite rooms. High standard of cuisine. Flexible hours. Children welcome. All major cards. Vegetarians catered for. The pub has fishing rights on the River Nene.
Price Band: B

SHORT BREAKS

NOTTINGHAMSHIRE

LANGFORD
THE OLD VICARAGE, Langford, Nr Newark
Tel: 01636 705031.
Elegant, comfortable house, owned and run by Jillie and Jeremy Steele whose home it is. Jillie is a brilliant cook and uses much of their own produce in her dishes, mainly English traditional. A much travelled pair they are excellent hosts and good conversationalists. Ideal for a relaxed break and conveniently situated for those who want to explore. Members of the Wolsey Lodge Consortium. Children over 12. Open all year. Visa. Vegetarians catered for on request.
Price Band: B/C

SHROPSHIRE

BISHOPS CASTLE
THE BOARS HEAD HOTEL, Church Street
Tel: 01588 638521.
Granted its first licence in 1642, the inn escaped unscathed in 1645 when, during the Civil War, Royalists plundered the town but thankfully missed the Boars Head. 4 en suite rooms in a converted stable block, some with the original exposed beams, are ideal for anyone wanting to enjoy this beautiful part of Shropshire. Open all year. Children welcome, cots etc. Menu. Vegetarians catered for. All major credit cards.
Price Band: B/C

ELLESMERE
THE BLACK LION, Scotland Street
Tel/Fax: 01691 622418.
Full of charm and old world characteristics, this inn will delight everyone. Only a small number of rooms 2 of which have fourposters. No restaurant but the bar food is good. Open all year. Children welcome. Access/Visa/Master/Switch. Dishes for vegetarians.
Price Band: A/B

LUDLOW
THE WHEATSHEAF INN, Lower Broad Street
Tel: 01584 872980.
5 en suite double rooms are available in this wonderful old pub, first licenced in 1753. It nestles under Ludlow's historic Broad gate, the last of seven town gates built in the 13th century. Good food, friendly people. Children and pets welcome but sadly, because of the age of the building it is not suitable for the disabled. Open all year. Access/Visa/Barclaycard. Vegetarians catered for.
Price Band: B/C

MUCH WENLOCK
THE TALBOT INN, High Street - Tel: 01952 727077.
This town is a treasure trove and where better to stay and enjoy it than this lovely old inn which was already a hostelry in 1361. Good food, a friendly atmosphere, comfortable en suite rooms. Open all year. All major cards. Children over 12 years. Several dishes for vegetarians and one for vegans.
Price Band: B/C

SHIFNAL
THE HUNDRED HOUSE HOTEL, Bridgnorth Road, Norton
Tel: 01952 730353 Fax: 01952 730355.
A very special hotel. Very English but very different. Nine bedrooms in which one can revel in the sensual charms of patchwork drapes, lavender scented sheets, fragrant pot pourris, antique beds and , in some bedrooms even a swing. Described by one visitor as 'An excursion into the past with superb up-to-date food and service'. Delightful beyond description. Open all year. Children welcome. Visa/Master/Amex. Vegetarian dishes.
Price Band: C

WELSHPOOL
GOLFA HALL HOTEL, Llanfair Road, Welshpool, Powys
Tel: 01938 553399 Fax: 01938 554777.
Fine country house hotel standing on a hillside overlooking a delightful wooded valley through which runs the famous Welshpool and Llanfair Steam Light Railway. Beautifully run, the 14 en suite rooms are warm and comfortable, the food is superb in quality and supports a menu which is changed regularly.
Price Band: C

WESTON-UNDER REDCASTLE
THE CITADEL - Tel: 01630 685204.
Splendid castellated dower house, built in the early 19th century by the famous Hill family. It is to be found between Hodnet and Weston on the A49, 12 miles north of Shrewsbury. Delightful house, charming owners. You will be pampered and well fed. Open April-October. No credit cards. Vegetarians with notice. No children.

WHITCHURCH
THE HANMER ARMS, Hanmer
Tel: 1094874 532/640.
Strictly speaking this lovely, typically English village is in Clwyd Wales, but is geographically considered to be part of the 'Shropshire Lake District'. It is one of the most peaceful places you could find and although it is an hotel it never forgets its central role as the village pub. The bedrooms are all en suite and nestle around a cobbled courtyard. Excellent traditional food and a staff who are both courteous and a mine of information, willing to provide a comprehensive list of places to see. Stunning views. Open all day every day. Children welcome. Visa/Access/Amex. Vegetarians catered for. 2 rooms adapted for the disabled.
Price Band: B/C

WHERE TO EAT

GLOUCESTERSHIRE

BIBURY
THE SWAN - Tel: 01285 740695.
17th century Cotswold stone coaching inn. Attractive gardens by the river. Fishing. Beautifully cooked and presented food both at lunch and dinner. Children welcome. All major credit cards. Open all year. Vegetarians catered for.
Price Band: B/C

BOURTON-ON-THE-WATER
THE MOUSETRAP INN, Lansdowne. - Tel: 01451 20579.
This old fashioned pub has a major plus - a car park, something that is like gold dust in Bourton. Good, well kept beer and home-cooked food including the specialities 'Desperate Dans Cow Pie' and Rabbit Pie. Friendly, unpretentious and sensible prices. Bed and Breakfast available. Children welcome. No credit cards. Open: 12-3pm & 6.30-11pm. Vegetarians dishes.
Price Band: A

THE OLDE CHARM, 1, The Chestnuts. - Tel: 01451 20244.
Charming 300 year old restaurant with unobtrusive, friendly service. Food is available all day, the hours depending on the time of the year. Excellent home-made soups, fresh salads, succulent roast meats and a selection of desserts. Cotswold Cream Tea very popular. The bedrooms are beautifully appointed and en suite. Access/Visa/Amex/Diners. Children welcome but no under 5 facilities. Open: approx 10.30am-9.30pm.
Price Band: A/B

CHEDWORTH
THE SEVEN TUNS, Queen Street. - Tel: 01285 720242.
Small 17th century pub - the small lounge bar only seats 16-18. Charming walled water garden. Simple, good pub fare with the emphasis on steaks at night. Great value for money. Open: 12-2.30pm 6.30-11pm. Closed Monday lunch in winter. No credit cards. Well behaved children welcome. Usually 2 dishes for vegetarians.
Price Band: A/B

CHELTENHAM
THE KINGS HEAD, Church Road, Bishops Cleeve, Cheltenham
Tel: 01242 673260.
3 miles from Cheltenham on the A435 Evesham road, this wonderful old thatched 16th century inn is a listed building standing next to a tithe barn and believed to be the oldest inhabited building in the village. No restaurant but delicious 'Daily Specials' and snacks served in the busy bar. Open: 11-2.30pm & 6-11pm. Children not allowed in bar area. Beer garden. No credit cards. 2 dishes for vegetarians.
Price Band: A

HOTELS, INNS, RESTAURANTS AND COUNTRY HOUSES

CHIPPING CAMDEN
THE SEYMOUR HOUSE HOTEL, High Street. - Tel: 01386 840429.
Lovely mellow building, with all sorts of interesting shapes in the beautifully appointed rooms. Delicious food at all times, morning coffee and afternoon tea. Open all year. Children welcome. All major credit cards. Vegetarians catered for.
Price Band: B

FRAMPTON MANSELL
THE CROWN HOTEL, Frampton Mansell, Nr Stroud.
Tel: 01285 760601 Fax: 01285 760681.
Parts of this fascinating building date back to 1595. It is tucked away in the corner of the village looking out over a magnificent valley. You would be difficult to please if you did not enjoy the traditional home-made food which includes Pan Fried Liver and Onions, Gloucester Sausage served with Bubble and Squeak and Poached Fillet of Salmon with Hollandaise Sauce. Bread and Butter Pudding is another favourite with diners. Children welcome. All major cards except AMEX.
Price Band: A/B

GLOUCESTER
FLEECE HOTEL, 19 Westgate Street. - Tel: 01452 522762.
Modernised Tudor coaching inn with 12th century vaulted crypt. Good food, sensible prices. Access/Visa/AMEX. Children welcome. Vegetarians catered for.
Price Band: A

NEWLAND
THE OSTRICH, Nr Coleford. - Tel: 01594 33260.
Charming village pub, no juke boxes, no one armed bandits but superior quality food with normally a choice of ten dishes including local specialities Venison Pie and Game Casserole. Wide choice of bar snacks. Attractive walled garden. Open: Mon-Sat 11.30-
3pm &6-11pm. Sun 12-3pm & 7-10.30pm. Children welcome in the restaurant and garden. No credit cards. Vegetarian dishes.
Price Band: A/B

NORTH NIBLEY
THE BLACK HORSE INN - Tel: 01453 546841 Fax: 01453 547474.
16th century true village inn which opens its welcoming doors with the same friendliness to strangers as it does to those who come in regularly for a pint and a chat, a good meal or a game of dominoes. You will find it on the B4060 midway between the old market towns of Dursley and Wotton-under-Edge. Full of old world charm the pub offers an extensive lunchtime and evening menu from good home-cooked dishes to light bar snacks. Try their home-made mushroom soup - it will be hard to find its equal. Children permitted if eating. All major cards.
Price Band: A/B

STOW-ON-WOLD
OLD STOCKS HOTEL, The Square. - Tel: 01451 830666 Fax: 01451 870014.
A Grade II Listed 16th-17th century building enhanced by the mellow Cotswold

WHERE TO EAT

stone of the period. The restaurant offers a wide variety of dishes including those for vegetarians which will tempt even the most jaded palate. The chef is always happy to produce something special for a child. Good range of bar food. Children welcome. Visa/MasterCard.
Price Band: A/B

THE ROYALIST, Digbeth Street. - Tel: 01457 830470.
The oldest building in Stow and features in the Guinness Book of Records as the oldest inn in England dating from 947AD. It is a Grade II Listed building of botharchitectural and historical interest. The 'Coffee Shop' is open from 10am-5.30pm serving tasty home-made bar food. Children welcome. Visa/MasterCard.
Price Band: A/B

GRAPEVINE HOTEL, Sheep Street. - Tel: 01451 830344 Fax: 01451 832278.
Delightful award winning hotel where nothing is too much trouble. Dinner 7pm-9.30pm, Bar Meals 12-2pm & 7-9pm. Closed Christmas Eve - January 12th. English and French haute cuisine. Daily changing menu. The bar serves a delicious selection of unusual dishes. Children welcome. No dogs. Afternoon teas. No smoking restaurant. All major credit cards. Vegetarian dishes.
Price Band: C

TETBURY
THE TROUBLE HOUSE INN, Cirencester Road. - Tel: 01666 502206.
17th century inn with fascinating history plus a friendly ghost. Traditional and friendly. Serves good casserole and Indian curries at night. No cooked meals on Sundays. Open: 11-2.30pm &6-11pm. Children welcome. Large garden and field to play in. No credit cards. 4 dishes for vegetarians.
Price Band: A/B

UPPER ODDINGTON
THE HORSE AND GROOM, Upper Oddington, Nr Stow-on-the-Wold.
This 16th century inn is as charming inside as it is out. Very much the focal centre of the village - you will find regulars at the bar every day. Everyone is made to feel welcome. Good traditional food comes out of the immaculate kitchen which offers everything from fresh fish to game in season. The bar menu suggests home-cooked Daily Specials as well as the simpler freshly cut sandwich. Children welcome. All major cards except AMEX and Diners.
Price Band: A/B

HEREFORDSHIRE

BISHOPS FROME
THE GREEN DRAGON. - Tel: 01885 490607.
If you are a traditionalist when it comes to pubs, this one you will enjoy. In the heart of hop farming country it has an oddly cosmopolitan air which blends in well with the past traditions of the area. Oak beams, flagstone floors and large fireplaces with roaring fires in winter. Real Ale and home-cooked food, especially

pies. Open: 12-3pm & 5-11pm. Children welcome. Access/Visa. Several dishes for vegetarians.
Price Band: A/B

GLEWSTONE
GLEWSTONE COURT HOTEL, Nr Ross-on-Wye.
Tel: 01989 770367 Fax: 01989 770282.
Spacious, elegant, Listed Country House in 3 acres. Half a mile off the A40 and 3 miles from the centre of Ross-on-Wye. Georgian Restaurant offers food of a very high standard. Bar meals would outshine most restaurants. All major credit cards.
Price Band: B

HEREFORD
GILBIES BISTRO, 4, St Peters Close, Commercial Street. - Tel: 01432 277863.
Modelled in many ways on the kind of Bistro you might find in any of the larger French or Spanish cities, the hours are flexible. Somewhere you can go early for breakfast if it is pre-arranged - have coffee, maybe a snack or a full meal throughout the day. The proprietor describes his food modestly as 'good but not great, at reasonable prices, eaten in a completely relaxed atmosphere'. The menu changes hour by hour and covers all styles of cuisine from steaks to kebabs - from fish to sea-food or simple snacks like bacon sandwiches through to New Zealand mussels. Open: 10am-11pm every day. Good children welcome. Visa/Access. At least 3 vegetarian dishes.
Price Band: A/B

KENTCHURCH
THE BRIDGE INN - TEL: 01981 230408.
Wonderful 400 year old building lying on the banks of the Monnow River with a delightful riverside restaurant and a large beer garden. Nothing pretentious about the menu in the restaurant or the bar, just good, imaginative, home-made fare. Open: 11-2.30pm & 6-11pm. No credit cards. Always 4 dishes for vegetarians. Children welcome.
Price Band: A/B

LEOMINSTER
THE BLACK HORSE COACH HOUSE, 74, South Street
Tel: 01568 611946.
This Listed building has its own brewery attached producing very good Real Ale. Excellent choice of home-made food at very reasonable prices. Open: 11-2.30pm & 6-11pm, Sat 11-11pm. No credit cards. Several dishes for vegetarians. Children welcome.
Price Band: A

MICHAELCHURCH ESCLEY
THE BRIDGE INN - Tel: 01981 23646.
One of those story book places, situated at the foot of the Black Mountains between Hereford and Hay-on-Wye right by Escley Brook, surrounded by fields. In summer,

customers can drink and dine outside watching the trout in the river. Some parts date back to 14th century. Tremendous atmosphere. Home-cooked fare by the owner Jean Draper, who is a talented chef using many of her own recipes, vegetarian ones in particular. Her Leek Croustade is a mega favourite. Open: 12-2.30pm & 7-11pm. Closed Mon lunch. Well behaved children welcome. No credit cards.
Price Band: A

PEMBRIDGE
THE NEW INN, Pembridge, Nr Leominster
13th century, all black and white painted brick on a massive stone base. Enchanting place with uneven stone floors, low beamed ceilings, roaring fires plus two ghosts!. Traditional home-made fare using local produce and as much game as possible in season. Bar food offers a wide range with Daily Specials including vegetarian dishes. No credit cards. Food available lunch and evening everyday.
Price Band: A/B

THE CIDER HOUSE RESTAURANT AT DUNKERTONS, Luntley
Tel: 01544 388161.
Described as 'the best restaurant between Chester and the Channel Islands'. Warm, friendly and beautiful with the emphasis on revival British Cooking. Lunch: everyday except Sunday. Open for coffee, tea, home-made cakes and biscuits, local ice cream and Dunkertons delicious cider and perry on draught. 10am-6pm. Dinner: from 7.30pm Friday andSaturday evenings. Booking for dinner is essential.
Price Band: B

WEOBLEY
YE OLDE SALUTATION INN, Market Pitch - Tel: 01544 318443.
On the outside it is a black and white timber-framed building which dates back over 500 years. Inside it is delightful with a large inglenook fireplace, a comfortable lounge bar leading into 40 seater Oak Room restaurant. The food is of a very high standard and you can stay here in great comfort. Open: 11-3pm & 7-11pm. Children in eating area, lounge conservatory. MasterCard/Visa. 3/4 dishes daily for vegetarians.
Price Band: B

ROSS-ON-WYE
THE CHASE HOTEL, Gloucester Road - Tel: 01989 763161 Fax: 01989 768330.
Handsome Regency Country House standing in own grounds, a few minutes walk from town centre. The chef favours a modern British approach with a continental influence and takes full advantage of the fine local produce. Bar snacks, cold buffet, vegetarian dishes. All major cards.
Price Band: B

HOTELS, INNS, RESTAURANTS AND COUNTRY HOUSES

PHEASANTS RESTAURANT, 52, Edde Cross Street
Tel: 01989 65751.
Once a tiny pub building this has now become an acclaimed restaurant with a Victorian style dining room with no more than a dozen tables, fronted by a dispense bar and a fireside lounge. Intimate dining both at lunch and in the evening on old English recipes makes this special. You can stay here, there are two rooms. A 10% discount on evening meals is offered to those staying. Open: Tues-Sat 12.30-2pm & 7-1-pm. Well behaved children welcome. AMEX/Access/Visa. Vegetarians catered for. Walled courtyard garden with pond in summer.
Price Band: B

CLOISTERS WINE BAR, 24, High Street - Tel: 01989 67717.
This 18th century building stands out in the High Street because of the glory of its stained glass windows. The wealth of exposed beams and nooks and crannies make it a truly secluded and intimate restaurant full of olde worlde charm. The menu is full of gastronomic delights including some unusual fish, such as Parrot Fish, Sweet Lips, Monkfish and Groupa, if you are not adventurous there are steaks of all kinds with or without sauces. Wide selection of wines & beers. Open: Mon-Sun 6-11pm, Sat/Sun lunchtimes. No credit cards. 6 dishes for vegetarians. Difficult for the disabled.
Price Band: A/B

THE CROSS KEYS INN, Goodrich - Tel: 01600 890650/890203.
Traditional village pub complete with a resident ghost. Two friendly bars offering good simple Pub Fare. The pub has 5 double and 2 single rooms, not en suite.
Price Band: A

NORFOLK

BRANCASTER STAITHE
THE LOBSTER POT, Main Road. - Tel: 01485 210262.
Charming fishing village with this very nice pub from which there are stunning views. The restaurant overlooks the harbour, the salt marshes and Scuit Island. Specialises in sea food and fish but there are many other dishes always using fresh produce. Open: Summer 11-3pm & 6.30-11pm, Winter 11-2.30pm & 7-11pm. Children welcome. No credit cards. Several dishes for vegetarians.
Price Band: B

BURNHAM MARKET
FISHES RESTAURANT, Market Place - Tel: 01328 738588.
Standing on the village green this 18th century building is a restaurant of great charm and character. Two simply furnished dining rooms have a vast open fire and bookcases full of the sort of books one might have at home. Specialising in fish, Gillian Cape, the owner, makes one of the best crab soups you will ever taste. It is a very special place. Children welcome. No credits cards. Several dishes for vegetarians.
Price Band: B

WHERE TO EAT

THE LORD NELSON - Tel: 01328 738321.
Friendly pub run by two talented people - Peter Jordan is a keen fungus hunter which provides the pub with some exciting offerings in the autumn when his findings become part to the menu. Valerie Jordan is a skilled artist and regular art exhibitions are held in the stables. Children welcome. Open: Mon-Sat 11.30-3pm & 7-11pm, Sun 12-3pm & 10.30pm. No credit cards.
Price Band: A/B

COLKIRK
THE CROWN, Crown Road,Colkirk, Fakenham - Tel: 01328 862172.
A pub for over 300 years but rebuilt after a fire. Friendly, comfortable and with a reputation for good food. The portions are generous and it is value for money. Open: 11-2.30pm & 6-11pm, Sun 12-2.30pm& 7-10.30pm. Access/Visa. Children welcome. Vegetarian dishes.
Price Band: A

DICKLEBURGH
THE KINGS HEAD, Norwich Road, Nr Diss - Tel: 01379 741481.
Welcoming, unpretentious pub with a ghost!. Three letting rooms. Probably the best Steak and Kidney Pie in the country. Surrounded by open ground which is available for 5 caravans and 10 tents. Open: 12-2pm & 7-10pm. Children welcome. No credit cards. Vegetarian dishes on request.
Price Band: A

GORLESTON
THE CLIFF HOTEL, Cliff Hill - Tel: 01493 662179 Fax: 01493 653617.
Attractive 3 star hotel is open to non-residents and offers good quality traditional dishes. Children welcome. All major cards.
Price Band: B

THE PIER HOTEL, Harbourmouth - Tel:01493 662631 Fax: 01493 440263.
Overlooking sandy beach, open to non-residents. A la carte and table d'hote. Fish a speciality. Wide range of bar meals and for vegetarians. Children welcome, high chairs and childrens menu. All major cards.
Price Band: B

GT RYBURGH
THE BOAR INN, Gt Ryburgh, Fakenham - Tel:01328 829212.
Sitting on the suntrapped patio of the delightful inn looking out on the garden, enjoying a good lunch on a summer's day, is one of life's great pleasures. Inside the 300 year old pub is full of warmth and character. Food of an International flavour is served at lunch and in the evening 7 days a week. Well known locally it has a deserved reputation. Childrens meals. Access/Master/Visa/Barclaycard/ Euro. Always five dishes plus salads for vegetarians.
Price Band: A/B

GT YARMOUTH
THE GALLON POT, 1-2 Market Place - Tel: 01493 842230.
Amusing pub offering good food at sensible prices plus afternoon tea which far exceeds most. Children welcome. No credit cards. Limited dishes for vegetarians.
Price Band: A/B

THE IMPERIAL HOTEL, North Drive
Quite seafront location. The intimate Rambouille Restaurant offers table d'hote and a la carte menus with wide range of dishes to appeal to the gourmet and the more traditional diner. Bar food available for those who want quick service and tasty dishes. All major cards. Children welcome. Dishes for vegetarians.
Price Band: B

HAPPISBURGH
THE HILL HOUSE - Tel: 01692 650004.
Friendly old coaching inn dating back to the 16th century. It was a favourite retreat of Sir Arthur Conan Doyle. Full of character, oak beams, large fireplaces. Here you can relish Real Ales at their best, good home-cooked meals which are substantial and reasonably priced with a sea view thrown in. Children welcome. Visa/Access/AMEX. 2 dishes for vegetarians. Price Band: A/B

HEVINGHAM
THE MARSHAM ARMS HOTEL
Has a newsletter of its own edited by the inn's proprietor, Nigel Bradley. Anyone unfamiliar with this excellent hostelry cannot fail to pick up some of the enthusiasm as you read its humourous message. The food in the bar or in Bradley's Restaurant is excellent with a wide choice and sensibly priced. There are 8 self-contained study bedrooms, all en suite and beautifully furnished. Open: 11-3pm &6-11pm. Children allowed in certain areas. Visa/Access. Many varied vegetarian dishes.
Price Band: B

HORNING
PETERSFIELD HOUSE HOTEL - Tel: 01692 630741 Fax: 01692 630745.
Elegant, comfortable, family run 18 bedroomed hotel, open to non-residents. Impressive restaurant overlooking the garden. High standard of cuisine both a la carte and table d'hote. Saturday night Dinner Dances a major attraction. Children welcome. All major cards. Several dishes for vegetarians.
Price Band: B

KINGS LYNN
THE PARK VIEW HOTEL, Blackfriars Street - Tel: 01553 775146 Fax: 01553 766957.
Unfussy 47 bedroom hotel. The bar is welcoming and serves both traditional ale and good, inexpensive bar snacks and meals. The 52 seater Edwardian restaurant offers a wide range of dishes, beautifully presented and at sensible prices. Children welcome. All major cards. Several dishes for vegetarians.
Price Band: A/B

WHERE TO EAT

THE ROCOCO RESTAURANT, 11 Saturday Market Place
Tel: 01553 771483.
Situated next to the Guildhall, the building is 300 years old and has panache. The food is of the highest quality as are the wines. Comfortable lounge for morning coffee, light lunches and afternoon teas. Dinner is a gastronomic delight. It is not cheap but it is money well spent. Open: Mon Dinner 7pm, Tues-Sat 10-3pm Dinner 7pm, Sun 12-3pm. Booking advisable. Afternoon teas May-September.
Price Band: B

LODDON
THE LODDON SWAN INN, Church Plain - Tel: 01508 20239.
Fascinating history here. Good home-made food. Unpretentious. Book for Sunday lunch - one of the best in Norfolk. Open: 11-3pm & 6.30-11pm, Sun 12-3pm &7-10.30pm. Children welcome. Visa/Access/JCB. 2 dishes for vegetarians.
Price Band: A/B

NEATISHEAD
BARTON ANGLER COUNTRY INN, Irestead Road - Tel: 01693 630740.
500 years old and once a rectory, this is a welcoming, informal establishment. Menu best described as 'English Country House Cuisine with a slight French influence'. It is certainly delicious food. Children welcome. AMEX/Visa/Master. 2 dishes + salads for vegetarians.
Price Band: B

NORTH WALSHAM
SCARBOROUGH HILL HOUSE HOTEL, Old Yarmouth Road
Tel:01692 402151 Fax: 01692 402151.
Open to non-residents and set in a 4 acres of gardens this is a charming spot and within easy reach of The Broads and sandy beaches. The menu is varied and encompasses a range of dishes, mainly English at its best but with a touch of French and the East. Everything is freshly cooked. Bar meals are prepared daily. Vegetarians will find at 2 dishes. Children welcome. Access/Visa/Diners/AMEX.
Price Band: A/B

NORWICH
BEECHES HOTEL & VICTORIAN GARDENS, 4-6 Earlham Road
Tel: 01603 621167 Fax: 01603 620151.
Restaurant offers an interesting menu with an Italian bias but using mostly fresh local produce and cooked to order at modest prices. Children welcome. High Chairs. All major cards. 2 dishes for vegetarians.
Price Band: B

BRASTEDS RESTAURANT, St Andrews Hill
Tel: 01603 625949 Fax: 01603 766445.
Here John Brasted will invite you to enjoy what can only be described as a culinary experience. Customers will tell you that part of the pleasure of eating here is to experience the peculiarly welcoming and friendly atmosphere that emits from the ghost who has haunted 8-10 St. Andrews Hill since the 17th century. Children

welcome. Visa/Access/AMEX/Diners. Good selection for vegetarians. No lunch Saturdays. Closed Sundays.
Price Band: B/C

ST BENEDICTS RESTAURANT, 9 St Benedicts Street
Tel: 01603 765337.
Busy city centre restaurant in a bustling street full of atmosphere. You sit on church pews, choose your food from a blackboard, changed daily which tempts the most jaded palate. Well chosen wine list. All at affordable prices. Closed Sunday & Monday. Children welcome. All major cards. Vegetarian choice.
Price Band: B

REEDHAM
REEDHAM FERRY INN - Tel: 01493 700429.
Well maintained late 16th century inn alongside working car ferry. The pub is full of fascinating memorabilia. Varied menu including game in season, prime meats, fresh produce and home grown herbs. Open: Summer 11-3pm & 6.30-11pm, Sun 12-3pm, Winter 11-2.30pm & 7-10.30pm. Access/Visa. Children in Sun Lounge or restaurant until 9pm. 3 dishes for vegetarians. Wide doorways for the disabled.
Price Band: A/B

WELLS-NEXT-THE-SEA
THE GLOBE INN, The Butlands - Tel: 01328 710206.
Busy, much sought after pub run with efficiency and charm. Steaks are the speciality of the house but there is a good choice. Full bar menu and snacks. Open: 10.30-11pm. No credit cards. Several dishes for vegetarians. Children welcome in Pool room. 4 letting rooms.
Price Band: A

WROXHAM
THE BROADS HOTEL, Station Road - Tel: 01603 782869 Fax: 01603 784066.
Much used by local people, the bars are fun and the a la carte and carvery restaurant is of a very high standard. Children welcome. All major cards. 5 vegetarian dishes daily.
Price Band: A/B

SUFFOLK

ALDEBURGH
NEW AUSTINS HOTEL, 243 High Street - Tel: 01728 453932 Fax: 01728 453668.
Close to the sea, good food both in restaurant and the bar. All major cards except AMEX. Children welcome. Vegetarains catered for. Open all year.
Price Band: B

WHERE TO EAT

BATTISFORD
THE PUNCH BOWL, Bildeston Road - Tel: 01449 612302.
Pretty village with thatched cottages. Pub has oak beams, open fires, plenty of gleaming brass and a wonderful welcome. Simple home-cooked fare. Garden for children. Traditional Sunday lunch. Open: 11-3pm & 7-11pm. No credit cards. 2-3 vegetarian dishes. Children welcome in the restaurant and garden.
Price Band: A

BECCLES
WAVENEY HOUSE HOTEL, Puddingmoor, Beccles
Tel: 01502 712270 Fax: 01502 712660.
Friendly, beautifully run small hotel with excellent restaurant. Riverside frontage & moorings. Lively bar serves good bar food. Children welcome. Access/Visa/AMEX/Diners. 6 dishes for vegetarians. Open all year. Dogs not permitted in bar or restaurant.
Price Band: A/B

BENTLEY
THE CASE IS ALTERED, Caple Road, Nr Ipswich - Tel: 01473 310282.
Nothing pretentious about this oddly named pub but it does offer good home-cooking. The spicy curry and the cauliflower cheese are particularly good. Inexpensive and value for money. Open: 11.30-3pm & 6-11pm, Sat 11-11pm. No credit cards. Dishes for vegetarians. Children welcome.
Price Band: A

BLAXHALL
THE SHIP INN, Nr Woodbridge - Tel: 01728 88316.
If you are a lover of bird life, a rambler or a devotee of music then Blaxhall and this inn are just the place for you. The village is well known to the people who come to the concert hall at Snape, a mile away. 17th century inn much used in BBC productions. Simple pub food at sensible prices. 4 well equipped twin chalets converted from the old stables. Open: 11-3pm & 7-11pm. Not open Monday lunchtime. No credit cards. Children welcome if eating. One or two dishes for vegetarians. Price Band: A

BRANDESTON
THE QUEENS HEAD, The Street, Nr Woodbridge
Tel: 01728 685307.
Set in picturesque countryside near the Deben. Over 400 years old but has been modernised. Letting rooms. Good home-cooked traditional fare is available every day lunch and evenings, except Sunday evenings. Traditional Sunday lunch. Warm and friendly. Certified as camping and Caravan Club accommodaion for 5 touring vans and 15 tents. Open: Mon-Sat 11.30-2.30pm & 5.30-11pm, Sun 12-3pm & 7-10.30pm. Children welcome in restaurant and Family Room. No credit cards. Vegetarian dishes.
Price Band: A

HOTELS, INNS, RESTAURANTS AND COUNTRY HOUSES

BURY ST EDMUNDS
GRILLS AND GILLS, 34, Abbeygate Street - Tel: 01284 706004.
You will find this restaurant as unique in name as it is in its food and Mediterrannean style interior. The food is exciting and beautifully cooked, whether meat or fish. A daily changing Fish Board which also features an extension to the lunch menu with Pies, Cromer Crab, Mussels, Liver and Bacon and a host of other dishes. It is a sister restaurant to 'Somewhere Else' at 1 Langton Place, Hatter Street which is equally good. Open daily. Children welcome. Visa/Access/Master. 10 vegetarian dishes.
Price Band: A

CLAYDON
CLAYDON COUNTRY HOUSE HOTEL, 16-18, Ipswich Road
Tel: 01473 830382.
Small enough to ensure that every guest receives individual attention. Traditional English and French menu. Children welcome. Garden. Visa/Access/AMEX. 5/6 choices for vegetarians. Price Band: B

EAST BERGHOLT
THE RED LION, The Street, Nr Colchester - Tel: 01206 298332.
15th century inn in historic village. Ideal place from which to explore Constable country. First class interesting food. Try Pidgeon in Elderberry Wine or Chicken, Cheese and Mustard Pie. Wide variety of dishes. Bar meals. Children welcome in dining room and garden. 4 letting rooms. No credit cards. Vegetarian choice. Open: 12-3pm & 7-11pm. Price Band: A/B

FELIXSTOWE
THE FERRY BOAT INN, Felixstowe Ferry - Tel: 01394 284203.
Pub dates from 1450. Recently renovated - we have not seen it since. The hospitality is renowned and the food is good home-cooked fare with a blackboard menu that changes regularly. Open: 11-2.30pm & 6-11pm. No food Sunday evening. Access/Visa. Children in dining area only.
Price Band: A/B

GILLINGHAM
THE SWAN MOTEL, Loddon Road - Tel: 01502 712055 Fax: 01502 711786.
78 cover restaurant serving freshly prepared English home-made fare. Blackboard specials and snacks. Children welcome. All major credit cards. Vegetarians catered for. Price Band: A/B

HARKSTEAD
THE BAKERS ARMS, The Street, Nr Ipswich - Tel: 01473 328595.
You will find this friendly pub on the Shotley Peninsula, 6 miles from Ipswich and five minutes walk through fields from the charming tidal River Stour. Amazing value home-cooked food. Just the thing after a walk and no one minds muddy boots, wellies or dogs. Open: 11.30-3pm & 7-11pm. Children welcome in games room. 3-4 dishes for vegetarians. No credit cards.
Price Band: A

WHERE TO EAT

IPSWICH
THE SINGING CHEF, 200, St Helens Street - Tel: 01473 255236.
Not to be missed, this very different and refreshing establishment provides a touch of France. Ken and Cynthia Toye are les patronnes, the food is regional French and quite wonderful. Very much a family restaurant, they close when the customers go. Ken lives up to his name, the 'Singing Chef' and at the end of the evening he sings like an angel. Most customers stay for the whole evening. This is a gastronomic and personal experience to be enjoyed.
Price Band: B

KERSEY
THE BELL INN, The Street, Nr Hadleigh - Tel: 01473 823229.
This 1,000 year old village is almost like a stage set and has been used by film makers time and again. The Bell is a Grade II Listed building, the second oldest in Kersey. You can now stay as well as eat and drink here. Wonderful food produced by an imaginative chef. The bar food is definitely above average. Kersey will put a spell on you and so too will The Bell. Open: Mon-Sat 10.30-2.30pm & 6.30-11pm, Sun 10.30-3pm & 7-10.30pm. Children if well behaved to eat. Visa/Access/Diners/AMEX. Vegetarian choice in bar and restaurant.
Price Band: A/B

KETTLEBURGH
THE CHEQUERS INN, Nr Woodbridge - Tel: 01728 723760.
Super site with a garden that runs down to the banks of the Deben. Good choice of food at realistic prices. Try the Kettleburgh Ploughman with a choice of cheese, ham Mackerel or pate. Childrens menu. Access/Visa. Vegetarian dishes. Open: Mon-Sat 11-2.30pm & 5.30-11pm, Sun 12-3pm & 7-10.30pm.
Price Band: A

LEISTON
THE WHITE HORSE, Station Road - Tel: 01728 830694.
The village dates back before the Norman Conquest. Purpose built in 1770 by the family Gildersleeves, a well known inn-keeping family who supplemented their regular income by a heavy involvement in the smuggling trade. Comfortable hotel providing first class French/English fare in the restaurant and a wide range of food in the bar. Childrens menu. Sunday lunch. Access/Visa. Vegetarian dishes. Open all day weekdays, Sun 12-3pm & 10.30pm.
Price Band: A/B

PIN MILL
THE BUTT AND OYSTER INN, Pin Mill, Chelmondiston - Tel: 01473 780764.
A very special, traditional inn right on the river's edge, with old Thames barges tied up alongside. The ale is superb, the food traditional and interesting, and the company unbeatable. Dick Mainwaring is the jovial landlord whose warmth of character spills over onto all the people he welcomes into this, one of Suffolk's nicest pubs. Children allowed in to eat and in smoke room. No credit cards. Dishes for vegetarians.
Price Band: A/B

HOTELS, INNS, RESTAURANTS AND COUNTRY HOUSES

SAXMUNDHAM
THE BELL HOTEL, High Street - Tel: 01728 602331.
Renovated carefully since 1991, this early 17th century building is comfortable and charming. Good food, good hospitality and well equipped bedrooms. Strong emphasis on Italian cooking and wines. Open: Mon-Sat 11-11pm. Normal Sunday hours. Children welcome. Choice for vegetarians. Access/Visa/Diners.
Price Band: B

THE WHITE HORSE, Darsham Road, Westleton - Tel: 01728 73222.
This is a pretty and well kept village with a thatched church just outside Saxmundham. The partially 16th century inn is on the green. It is cosy with lots of brass and paintings on the walls. Excellent home-cooking using local produce and locally caught fish. Probably the largest Mixed Grill you will ever see. Sunday lunch, Daily Specials, cream teas in the summer plus what is best described as a Scottish High Tea served from 6-7pm, in which for an all inclusive price, you can feast on a main meal, bread and butter, scones, cakes, jam,cream and a pot of tea. Comfortable bedrooms and you will certainly be well fed. Open: winter 12-3pm & 7-11pm, summer 11-3pm & 5.30-11pm. Children welcome. No credit cards. Vegetarian choice.
Price Band: A/B

SOUTHWOLD
THE RED LION INN & RESTAURANT, 2 South Green - Tel: 01502 722385.
Good, sensibly priced food in a pleasant atmosphere. Open all year.
Price Band: A

STOKE-BY-NAYLAND
THE ANGEL INN - Tel: 01206 263245.
All fresh international cuisine. Welcoming, beamed bars, nice atmosphere. All major cards. No children. Open all year. Vegetarians catered for.
Price Band: A/B

WOODBRIDGE
THE CAPTAIN'S TABLE, 3Quay Street - Tel: 01394 383145.
For 25 years Tony and Jo Prentice have owned and run this excellent restaurant in what was once a farmhouse with land going down to the Deben. The Tudor buildings are painted Suffolk pink, and in summer the small patio in front of the restaurant is a suntrap protected from the world by the outer brick wall. The extensive menu specialises in fish and sea food. 'Starters from the Net' include Moules Mariniere, have a dozen oysters from Bentley Creek or a Mousse of Avocado with a fresh tomato and herb dressing. Main courses maybe local Dover soles, or Scallops tossed in butter with bacon and garlic. There is an alternative selection for those not keen on seafood. A fixed price menu which is value for money. 'All dishes are offered subject to wind and tide, fisherman's fancy, farmer's whim and gardener's back'!. If you only desire a bar snack you will still be very welcome.
Price Band: B

WHERE TO EAT

WARWICKSHIRE

KENILWORTH
CLARENDON HOUSE, Old High Street - Tel: 01926 57668.
Old building in the heart of Kenilworth. Full of atmosphere. Cromwells bistro restaurant, partially housed in the original kitchen of the Elizabethan Castle Tavern, offers an extensive menu of fine foods and wines in a relaxed and informal setting. Royalist Retreat Bar has an extensive range of bar snacks available at lunchtime. Open all year. Children allowed. Visa/Access/Switch. Vegetarian dishes.
Price Band: A/B

SHIPTON-ON-STOUR
GEORGE HOTEL, High Street - Tel: 01608 661453.
In historic small town, this delightful inn dates back to the 15th century. Has an unbelievable air of the past. Delicious food in the restaurant and a varied and exciting bar menu. Open all year 10.30-11pm. Children welcome, special space. Visa/AMEX. Vegetarians catered for.
Price Band: A/B

STRATFORD-UPON-AVON
THE FALCON, Chapel Street - Tel: 01789 205777 Fax: 01789 414260.
16th century inn beautifully extended. Restaurant renowned for its friendly service and the culinary skills of the chef and his team. Good food in the lounge and Oak Bars. Coffee or afternoon tea in the 'covered walkway' overlooking the garden. Open all day, all year. Children welcome. All major credit cards. Vegetarians catered for. Price Band: A/B/C

ETTINGTON PARK, Aldminster - Tel: 10789 450123 Fax: 01789 450472.
There can be few hotels in this country more grand or beautiful that Ettington Park. Dine here in the spectacular Oak Room on the very finest of English and French cuisine and it will be never forgotten. Everything about the hotel is superb.
Price Band: C

WORCESTERSHIRE

ARLEY
THE NEW INN, Pound Green
Arley is three and a half miles from the historic riverside town of Bewdley. A pub in which Acoustic Musicians are especially welcome - the landlord Malcolm Gee publishes the international magazine 'The Accordion News' and runs high profile accordion concerts. The pub is essentially a 'conventional' one and caters for families although children are not allowed to roam the lounges. The 40 cover restaurant is presided over by a Head Chef who has an excellent reputation for good traditional food, generous portions and modest prices. Good bar food is available. Several vegetarian dishes. No credit cards.
Price Band: A

ECKINGTON
THE ANCHOR INN & RESTAURANT, Cotheridge Lane
Tel/Fax: 01386 750356.
On the edge of the Cotswolds, Eckington, close to Pershore, is a quiet village dating back to Saxon times. The 18th century Anchor Inn, full of character is famous for the excellence of its restaurant. Fish and Steaks are the speciality but there is an excellent, varied menu which includes dishes for vegetarians as well as Daily Specials. The bar food is exciting and home-made. Children welcome. All major cards within Cardnet.
Price Band: A

LITTLE MALVERN
HOLDFAST COTTAGE HOTEL - Tel: 01684 310288 Fax: 01684 311117.
This is a charming 17th century hotel set in its own grounds surrounded by orchards and open farmland; far removed from traffic noise although it is less than 15 minutes drive from the M5 and M50 and only 4 miles from Malvern and Upton-Upon-Severn, offers dinner to non-residents. The delicious food is cooked by the owners Stephen and Jane Knowles whose love of food is reflected in the varied choice and the delicate use of herbs from the hotel's Victorian Herb Garden. Visa/Access/Master/Euro.   Licensed.
Price Band: B

MALVERN WELLS
THE COTTAGE IN THE WOOD HOTEL, Holywell Road
Tel: 01684 575859 Fax: 01684 560662.
Excellent hotel with stunning views perched high onthe Malvern Hills. The Daily Mail calls it 'The best view in England'. Delightful restaurant open to non-residents. At lunchtime choose from the Light Bite menu which reflects the modern trend for healthy eating. Dinner is a gastronomic dream, essentially English at heart, but influenced by styles and flavours of the world. Children and vegetarians welcome.   Access/Visa/Amex/Switch.
Price Band: B

FLYFORD FLAVELL
THE RED HART INN, Kington, Flyford Flavell - Tel: 01386 792221.
Over 400 years old and much of the original black and white building remains. You will find it on the A422 halfway between Worcester and Stratford-upon-Avon. Over the years it has become known as the 'Sportsmans Pub' because of its great cricketing connections. A la carte restaurant serving traditional food. Sunday carvery lunch. Good bar meals. From Easter to September breakfast and a super afternoon tea are available. Open: Sat 11-2.30pm & 6-11pm, Sun 12-3pm & 7-10.30pm, longer Easter-Sept. Price Band: A/B

PERSHORE
THE OLD CHESTNUT TREE, Manor Road, Lower Moor
Tel: 01386 860380.
This Grade II Listed building has a gently flowing river behind it, along whose banks is a delightful walk. Black and white with ancient leaded windows, it was

WHERE TO EAT

built in 1547 as a Granary for the Manor House. Heavy beams, open fireplaces, ghosts!. Good, traditional food at reasonable prices. 2 letting rooms not en suite. Open: Mon-Fri 11-2.30pm & 6-11pm, Sat 11-11pm, Sun 12-3pm & 7-10.30pm. Children welcome. No credit cards. Vegetarians catered for.
Price Band: A

THE ANGEL INN & POSTING HOUSE, High Street - Tel: 01386 552046.
In the heart of the town, welcoming, family run. Extensive bar food. Imaginative meals. Price Band: A

ST MICHAELS
CADMORE LODGE - Tel/Fax: 01584 810044.
Situated 2 miles west of the market town Tenbury Wells, and lying in its own secluded valley with 60 acres of woodland with a nine hole golf course and 2 shimmering lakes. The skilled chefs offer a tempting menu whether it is the set price dinner, dishes taken from the a la carte selection or the good value bar food. Vegetarians catered for. Children welcome. Access/Visa/Master.
Price Band: B

SEVERN STOKES
THE OLD SCHOOL HOUSE HOTEL & RESTAURANT
is only 35 miles from the centre of Birmingham and is a popular venue for diners who come to enjoy 'School Dinners' - gastronomic feasts that bear no resemblance to those we remember!. The only similarity is the superb range of old fashioned steamed puddings with custard. The menu is imaginative, beautifully presented and the price is reasonable. Snacks and Daily Specials are available served in the Study. During the summer one can enjoy drinks and meals on the terrace overlooking the garden with its swimming pool and marvellous views of the Severn Vale. Vegetarians & children welcome. All major cards.
Price Band: B

UPTON-ON-SEVERN
THE WHITE LION HOTEL, High Street
Tel/Fax: 01684 592551. Famous old inn on banks of the River Severn, in the centre of this historic Tudor town. Surrounded by a wonderful pastoral landscape leading to the majestic Malvern Hills. Charming restaurant serving interesting English fare with a French influence. Busy bar offering good meals with an emphasis on fresh fish. Open all year. Access/Visa/Amex/Diners. Vegetarians catered for.
Price Band: B

HOTELS, INNS, RESTAURANTS AND COUNTRY HOUSES

GUIDE TO CONFERENCE VENUES

GLOUCESTERSHIRE

STOW-ON-THE-WOLD
THE OLD STOCKS HOTEL, The Square. - Tel: 01451830666 Fax: 01451 870014. Small 16th-17th century hotel has rooms which can be used for meetings. Worth discussing your needs with the owner, Alan Rose.

LINCOLNSHIRE

WOODHALL SPA
EAGLE LODGE HOTEL, The Broadway - Tel:01526 353231 Fax:01526 352797. For business men or companies looking for something different, the Falcon Room provides corporate facilities and a private area for meetings and conferences from 5-50 delegates. Expert advise, efficient staff always available to assist.

NORFOLK

GORLESTON
THE CLIFF HOTEL, Cliff Hill. - Tel:01493 662179 Fax:01493 653617. This attractive AA & RAC 3 star hotel with a superb position overlooking the harbour on the quieter side of Gt. Yarmouth, provides a quiet and relaxing environment for the business man either for a small one day seminar or a larger residential conference. There are two conference rooms equipped with everything from a Flip Chart to a Projection screen. There is a special all in rate for delegates. Well stocked bars, good food, fine wine list and 40 en suite bedrooms. Open all year. Vegetarians catered for.

GT YARMOUTH
THE IMPERIAL HOTEL, North Drive. - Tel:01493 851113 Fax:01493 852229. Quiet, seafront location overlooking the Venetian waterways and tennis courts. 39 en suite bedrooms. Conference suites, fax and photocopying services. Intimate Rambouillet Restaurant. Open all year.

HORNING
PETERSFIELD HOUSE HOTEL - Tel:01692 630741 Fax: 01692 630745. Elegant and comfortable hotel with a high standard of accommodation and cuisine, discreetly tucked away in a riverside setting. Ideal for seminars, conferences, wedding receptions or private parties. Open all year.

KINGS LYNN
PARK VIEW HOTEL, Blackfriars Street. - Tel:01553 775146 Fax:01553 766957. Originally the stagecoach stop between London and Lincoln, The hotel still retains the balconied courtyard and many original features. Comfortable, friendly with excellent service it offers conference facilities for up to 100. Open all year.

SHERINGHAM
SOUTHLANDS HOTEL, 3 South Street. - Tel/Fax:01263 822679.
Open residentially from Easter until the end of October, the hotelremains open all year for Functions, Wedding Receptions, Conferences Golfing and Bowls Parties. 16 en suite rooms. Within 3 minutes walk of the town, golf.

NOTTINGHAMSHIRE

LANGAR
LANGAR HALL, Langar, Nottinghamshire, NG13 9HG.
Tel: 01949 860559 Fax: 01949 861045.
The Indian Room built in 1993 for conferences and meetings, looks out onto the church and herb garden. Catches the morning sun. Available for meetings for up to 20 people with the use of conference equipment, telephone, fax and service throughout the day. Every booking is exclusive to ensure that your business can continue in privacy and without disturbance. Rates for conferences vary according to individual requirements.

NOTTINGHAM
WALTON'S HOTEL AND RESTAURANT, 2, North Road, The Park.
Tel: 01159 475215 Fax: 01159 475053.
This elegant 19th century hunting lodge is close to the city centre and convenient for motorway access. An ideal venue for business meetings and conferences. Secure parking.

SHROPSHIRE

LUDLOW
DINHAM HALL, By the Castle. - Tel: 01584 876464 Fax: 01584 876019.
Delightfully appointed hotel in the heart of Ludlow. The Merchant Suite offers complete private dining or meeting facilities for small numbers. Delicious, award winning, creative food. Open all year.

WELSHPOOL
GOLFA HALL HOTEL, Llanfair Road, Welshpool, Powys, SY21 9AF.
Tel: 01938 553399 Fax: 01938 554777.
Fine country house hotel. Excellent service and food, and very comfortable. Private parties of up to 20 can be held in the Drawing Room whilst the Conifer Suite accommodates 120 for seminars and functions of all kinds.

SUFFOLK

ALDEBURGH
NEW AUSTINS HOTEL, 234 High Street. - Tel: 01728 453923 Fax: 01728 453668.
Comfortable hotel close to the sea. Experienced hotelier able to provide good facilities for meetings, conferences and wedding receptions.

IPSWICH
CLAYDON COUNTRY HOUSE HOTEL, 16-18 Ipswich Road, Claydon.
Tel: 01473 830382.
Charming house with the ability to cater for all manner of functions from wedding receptions to conferences and meetings. First class cuisine. 14 en suite rooms. Open all year.

BECCLES
THE WAVENEY HOUSE HOTEL, Puddingmoor. - Tel: 01502 712270 Fax: 01502 712660.
Delightful hotel with frontage onto the River Waveney. 15 bedrooms (13 en suite). Ballroom can seat 100 boardroom or 140 buffet style. Very efficient and willing to work with you to ensure success whatever the occasion.

WARWICKSHIRE

KENILWORTH
CLARENDON HOUSE, Old High Street.
Tel: 01926 57668 Fax: 01926 50669 Reservations: 0800616883.
Perfect venue for business. The Fieldgate Suite has conference facilities for up to 120 delegates whilst the Latimer Suite is ideal for private board meetings for up to 18 people. Open all year.

STRATFORD-UPON-AVON
THE FALCON HOTEL, Chapel Street.
Tel: 01789 205777 Fax: 01789 414260 Telex: 312522.
Whether for 2 or 200 delegates The Falcon is a first class venue for residential or non-residential conferences, exhibitions, training courses and meetings with a choice of several equipped rooms. The beautifully furnished function suites make impressive venues for weddings, dinner dances or any special private functions offering a wide choice of imaginative menus and wines.

ETTINGTON PARK,
Alderminster, Stratford-upon-Avon. - Tel: 01789 450123 Fax: 01789 450472.
Magnificent Victorian Gothic mansion in 40 acres of landscaped gardens on the banks of the River Stour. The Long Gallery is one of the leading meeting rooms for country house retreats and has hosted many of the world's most prestigious corporations. Discreetly located under the high Gothic roof it is the choice of the discerning business visitor who requires the very best of hotelkeeping for his company, the elegant Little Drawing Room, 14th Century chapel, Oval Room and South Room - once a ballroom of the Victorian house - are also available for the small board meeting or private dinner party.

WORCESTERSHIRE

LITTLE MALVERN
HOLDFAST COTTAGE HOTEL, - Tel: 01684 310228 Fax: 01684 311117.
Charming, peaceful setting with pretty garden. Mainly 17th Century. Warm and comfortable. Excellent for small business meetings, wedding receptions etc. 8 en suite bedrooms. The hotel is owned and run by Stephen and Jane Knowles in the friendliest but most efficient manner. Food is excellent. 15 minutes drive from both the M5 and M50 and 4 miles from Malvern and Upton-upon-Severn.

MALVERN
THE COTTAGE IN THE WOOD HOTEL, Holywell Road.
Tel: 01684 575859 Fax: 01684 560662.
A popular venue for business meetings this charming hotel with 20 en suite rooms is ideal. Perched high on the Malvern Hills its magnificent vista unfolds across 30 miles of the Severn Vale to Bredon Hill and beyond to the Cotswold Hills, which form the horizon. The food and wines are exceptional. Contact the owner, John Pattin for more details.

ST. MICHAELS
CADMORE LODGE, St. Michaels, Tenbury Wells.
Tel: 01684 310288 Fax: 01684 311117.
Comparatively new hotel offering excellent sporting opportunities, good food, well appointed accommodation and conference and function facilities. The function room overlooking the lake seats 150 and is ideal for a conference of private functions. Has its own bar. Cadmore Lodge is 2 miles west of Tenbury Wells and lies in its own secluded valley with 60 acres of woodland, a nine hole golf course and 2 shimmering lakes. In addition to golf there is good fishing on the estate lakes and streams. The River Teme offers salmon, grayling and coarse fishing. Ludlow is 7 miles away and within 20 miles are the cathedral cities of Hereford and Worcester. 8 double en suite. Old Mill which is self-contained sleeps 4/6.

SEVERN STOKE
THE OLD SCHOOL HOUSE HOTEL - Tel: 01905 371368 Fax: 01905 371591.
A 17th Century barn in the corner of the garden has been converted into a function/conference suite which can seat 100 theatre style and is equipped with every modern business need. Much sought after for weddings. During the summer months guests can enjoy drinks and meals on the terrace overlooking the garden with its swimmingpool and marvellous views of the Severn Vale. The hotel dating back to 1620 was the village school until the 1960s. Full of character and mementos of the past, it has 14 well appointed bedrooms. 'School Dinners' are served in the Restaurant whilst Daily Specials are served in the Study at lunch time only. Just 35 miles from Birmingham this has to be ideal for business people. Please ring or write for further details.

VISITOR ATTRACTIONS

BEDFORDSHIRE

BEDFORD DISCOVER THE BEDFORDSHIRE COUNTRYSIDE
Tel: 01234 228671
Discover the wonderful landscape and varied heritage by taking a family day out to visit one of the many country parks and cyclewalks that Bedfordshire has to offer. Throughout the year there is plenty to do. Visitor Centres and Country Parks are open all the year round.

BEDFORD MUSEUM
Tel: 01234 353232
This lively museum is set in attractive surroundings close to the River Great Ouse. Excellent displays interpret the human and natural history of the region. Open Tues-Sat 11-5pm Sun & Bank Holidays 2-5pm. Closed Mondays. Admission free.

CECIL HIGGINS ART GALLERY & MUSEUM
Tel: 01234 211222
A Victorian mansion, original home of the Higgins family, is furnished in authentic style, with an adjoining modern gallery displaying fine collections of watercolours, prints, drawings, ceramics, glass and lace. Open all year Tues-Sat 11-5pm Sun & Bank Holidays 2-5pm. Admission free.

THE BUNYAN MEETING FREE CHURCH & MUSEUM
Tel:01234 358870
Scenes from The Pilgrim's Progress are depicted on the bronze entrance doors, presented to the church in 1876 by the 10th Duke of Bedford, and on the five stained glass windows. The museum contains most of the known possessions of John Bunyan, many editions of his 60 recognised works, including The Pilgrims Progress in 168 foreign languages. Open Apr-Oct Tues-Sat 2-4pm & July-Sept 10.30-12.30pm

BROMHAM MILL
Tel: 01234 824330.
Built in 1695, Bromham Mill is an attracive stone building set by the River Great Ouse. Now restored to its former working glory, the enormous revolving water wheel is the focal point .

DUNSTABLE WHIPSNADE ANIMAL PARK
Tel: 01582 872171
Location: 20 miles from the M25 junction 21 following elephant signs from Dunstable. Europe's largest conservation centres offering 2,500 rare and endangered species in 600 acres of beautiful parkland, including all the family favourites - elephants, tigers, penguins, bears, rhinos and many more. Free daily demonstrations of Elephant Encounters, Californian Sea Lions and free flying Birds of the World will keep all the family entertained. Open daily 10-6pm.

HARROLD ODELL COUNTRY PARK
Tel: 01234 720016
Tufted duck, great crested grebe, Canada and greylag geese, coots, moorhens, swans, mallards and kingfishers are just some of the birds that visit the landscaped lake of this 144 acre country park. Open Apr-Sept Tues-Sat 1-4.30pm Sun & Bank Holidays 1-6pm. Oct-Mar Sat Sun & Bank Hols 1-4pm.

LEIGHTON BUZZARD RAILWAY
Page's Park Station, Billington Road (A4146)
Tel: 01525 373888
This is one of England's foremostnarrow gauge preservation sites; home to over fifty engines. It provides a great day out. Page's Park Station is situated alongside a large public recreational area offering grassy open space, children's play equipment and sports facilities. The station has a souvenir shop and buffet serving hot and cold snacks and refreshments at most times when trains are running. There is a picnic area, free car parking and space for coaches. The five and a half mile return journey by historic steam train takes just over an hour.
A museum project display is open to visitors and much of the railway's historic locomotive and wagon fleet is based here. Steam locomotive viewing, a working quarry display and the demonstration sand trains are planned throughout the year. Industry Train Displays are live demonstrations of authentic locomotives and wagons which represent the major industries served by narrow gauge railways. Another form of heritage transport can be enjoyed on your day out to the railway. Cruises on the 19th century Grand Union Canal can be combined with your historic steam train ride. Ring or write for details. Although the trains mainly operate on Sundays from April-October, there are Festive Specials in December complete with Father Christmas, mince pies etc.

LEIGHTON BUZZARD GREBE CANAL CRUISES
Pitstone Wharf, Pitstone, Nr Leighton Buzzard LU79AD
Tel: 01296 661920.
Rod and Margaret Saunders founded this business some 20 years ago and operate passenger vessels on the Grand Union Canal on a most beautiful length of the Canal where it climbs up the Chiltern escarpment from the Vale of Aylesbury into the Chilterns themselves. Built 200 years ago, the passage of time has seen the canal mellow into the beautiful countryside, it's quaint hump-back bridges and locks complimenting the scene.
The fleet of passenger vessels operate from the purpose built base, Pitstone wharf, near to the village of Cheddington (of 'great train robbery fame') and there is a regular service of one and a half hour trips run during the peak summer months via the Chiltern Summit level of the canal at Tring, the highest point of the waterway, 396 feet above sea level. Passengers have the opportunity to leave the boat in the lock flight and view Marsworth reservoirs and nature reserve and to picnic ashore if they wish. The boats are mainly wide-beam, offer all weather protection, and provide considerable comfort for the passengers.
There are bars on all the boats and for pre-booked parties meals can be served while cruising - try the very popular afternoon cream teas. At Pitstone Wharf the Saunders have developed a boat yard which is open to everyone, where the non-

boat owner can come and enjoy the canal and if so wished, can hire a self-steer boat, from a single day hire to a week or fortnight's holiday. Tuition is available for the beginner. Superbly run, with efficient professional crews, you can relax aboard and enjoy Grebe Canal Cruises.

LUTON   WOODSIDE FARM & WILD FOWL PARK
Tel: 01582 841044.
At Woodside Farm Shop and Wild Fowl Park, there are over 160 different breeds of animals and birds to see and feed with special feed from the Farm Shop. Large picnic areas, pony rides, tarzan trails, birds of prey displays and daily tractor and trailer rides are available. Open all year round Mon-Sat 8-5.30pm. Closed Sunday.

THE WERNHER COLLECTION
Tel: 01582 22955
The works of the Russian Court Jeweller, Carl Faberge are part of the finest private art collection in Great Britain. There are many paintings, costumes and other personal possessions of the Russian Imperial Family Romanov. Treasures include old master paintings, magnificent tapestries, English and French porcelain, sculpture, bronzes and renaissance jewellery. Open to the public 29th Mar-16th October Fri-Sun 1.30-5pm.

SANDY RSPB NATURE RESERVE & GARDENS
Tel: 01767 680551
Enjoy a day out and discover a wealth of wildlife when you visit The Lodge Nature Reserve set in the beautiful Bedfordshire countryside. A great day out will include woodland walks and nature trails, observation hides and wildlife garden and picnic area. Open all year round 9-9pm.

SILSOE WREST PARK HOUSE AND GARDENS
Tel: 01525 860152
The history of English gardening from 1700-1850 is set out in acres of stunning delights at Wrest Park. In the Great Garden, water catches the eye in every direction, while intersecting alleys provide splendid vistas of the many garden buildings and ornaments.
West Park House was inspired by an 18th century French chateaux. the delightful intricate French Garden, with statues and fountains, enhances any view of the house from The Great Garden. Open 1st April-30th Sept weekends & Bank Holidays only 10-6pm.

OLD WARDEN THE SWISS GARDEN
Tel: 01767 627666
Regarded as one of the top ten gardens in the country, though still under restoration, the secret of The Swiss Garden's romantic charm lies in its unique landscape design of the early 19th century. Shrubberies and ponds, intricate ironwork bridges, an award winning fernery and grotto, in a variety of follies and tiny, Thatched Swiss Cottage are all contained within just ten acres. Open Mar-July & Sept, Sat, Sun & Bank Holidays 10-6pm Oct-Jan & Feb Sun 11-4pm.

HOTELS, INNS, RESTAURANTS AND COUNTRY HOUSES

WOBURN
Tel: 01525 290666

Home of the Dukes of Bedford for over 350 years, Woburn Abbey is now lived in by the Duke's heir, the Marquess of Tavistock and his family. The house contains one of the most important collections and works of art in the world and is surrounded by a 3,000 acre deer park with nine species of deer. Open 1st Jan-26 Mar weekends only 27th Mar-30th October everyday.

WOBURN SAFARI PARK
Tel: 01525 290407.

Britain's largest drive through safari park with lions, tigers, rhinos, wolves, bears, hippos, monkeys and many more are all part of the attractions which make the safari park a great family attraction. New attractions include: The Adventure Ark, Penguin World and Great Woburn Railway. Open 5 Mar-30 October everyday.

BUCKINGHAMSHIRE

AYLESBURY   AYLESBURY BREWERY COMPANY
Tel: 01296 395000

Thecompany has been part of Buckinghamshire since 1895. It has some 200 Public houses most of them in the county, but you can see the ABC sign in parts of neighbouring Bedfordshire and Oxfordshire too. In addition to its own wide range of beers and lagers, you'll find a number of outstanding products from several other breweries. Visit Aylesbury and sample for yourself.

THE CHILTERN BREWERY
Tel: 01296 613647
Location: A413 Aylesbury.

The ancient and revered art of the English Brewer can still be discovered flourishing in the beautiful countryside of Buckinghamshire. Completely independent and family run since its inception in 1980, this unique small brewery specialises in the production of high quality, traditionally brewed English beers with a real local flavour. Included in the large selection of home brewed ales is a 300 year old ale available in imperial pint bottles. Open Mon-Sat 9-5pm.

BUCKS RAILWAY CENTRE
Tel 01296 75440

Home to the private collection of steam locomotives. The centre boasts vintage carriages, signal box, station and gift shop. Throughout the year the centre holds special events and steaming days including regular visits by Thomas the Tank Engine, steam train rides and the extremely popular Victorian afternoon cream teas.

VISITOR ATTRACTIONS

BUCKINGHAMSHIRE RAILWAY CENTRE
Tel 01296 75720
The centre's 25 acre site is at Quainton Road station and exchange sidings, the last remaining Metropolitan Railway county station. On display is one of the country's largest collection of historic steam and diesel locomotives as well as a comprehensive collection of coaching and freight rolling stock. Open 11-6pm daily.

BEACONSFIELD BEKONSCOT MODEL VILLAGE
Tel: 01494 672919
The oldest model village in the world is a charming minature covering over one and a half acres. Included in the many things to see are beautifully landscaped gardens, miniature houses, castles, churches, shops and railway stations, through which runs the finest outdoor model railway (Gauge One) open to the public in the United Kingdom. The 'country' of Bekonscot is planted with 8,000 conifers, 2,000 minature shrubs, and 200 tonnes of stone used for the rockeries alone. There are no less than one hundred and sixty buildings icluding churches, hotels, shops and private houses constituting Bekonscot and the outlying villages. Souvenir Shop. Refreshment Kiosks, 2 Picnic Areas, Childrens Playground, Miniature Tramway and many other scenes. It is a paradise for photographers, a fascination for model-makers, an admiration for gardeners, 'Heaven' for small children. In fact a must for the whole family. OPEN; Every day from 10am-5pm from 17th February to 3rd November.

BUCKINGHAM SILVERSTONE MOTOR RACING CIRCUIT
Tel: 01327 857271
Home of the internationally famous British Grand Prix, Silverstone is the centre of the British motor racing industry. Throughout the year there are regular national and international race meetings featuring all shapes and forms of motor vehicles.

STOWE LANDSCAPE GARDENS
Tel: 01208 822850 These beautiful gardens are placed in an impressive 18th century mansion set in over 500 acres of landscaped gardens inspired by William Kent and Capability Brown. The gardens feature a multitude of follies, ornate lakes, temples and monuments. Once home of the Dukes of Buckingham it is now home to one of the nation's premier independent schools, whose old boys include jazz singer George Melly and entrepreneur Richard Branson. During the summer months a series of musical events are regularly organised including music and fireworks concerts and the famous Stowe Opera.

CLAYDON HOUSE
Tel: 01296 730349
Famous as the home of the Verney Family and a house which Florence Nightingale often visited, Claydon House has impressive rococo state rooms, and a Chinese tea-room. Florence Nightingale's bedroom and a museum of her nursing work from the Crimean Wars are also open to the public

WADDESDON MANOR
Nr Aylesbury HP18 OJH Recorded information
Tel: 01296 651211 Enquiries 01296 651282 Fax: 01296 651293

Open after five years of restoration to celebrate the Centenary of the National Trust, this is one of the most exciting houses and gardens to visit in England. On a cold December day in 1874 Baron Ferdinand de Rothschild and his sister Alice took their cousin Constance, Lady Battersea to view the site that Ferdinand had chosen for his new home. Standing on a windy hill top in Buckinghamshire, Constance can hardly have imagined how completely it would be transformed in the space of a few years. In her memoirs she describes toiling up the hill only to be rather disappointed by the view at the top. She was certainly more indulgent of Ferdinand's aspirations than some of his other relatives, but not even she anticipated the magnificence of the fairytale chateau and its splendid garden that he was planning to create. Today we are invited to revel in the restored beauty of the manor and its gardens as well as to explore the superb wine cellars. We can see the exquisitely carved 18th century panelling from Paris rescued by Baron Ferdinand, feast our eyes on the Waddesdon collection which icludes 18th century portraits by Gainsborough and Reynolds. There is the French royal furniture and superb Savonnerie carpets. On the first floor there is a new suite of grand reception rooms, as well as bedrooms which have been restored. Waddesdon's important collection of Sevres porcelain is magnificently displayed in six rooms. It includes the three-hundred piece dinner service presented by Louis XV to the Austrian ambassador in 1766. Bakst illustrated the fairytale of Sleeping Beauty with members of the Rothschild family as characters. The painting are exhibited for the first time.

The Wine Cellars have been opened as part of the centenary restoration of the Manor, in recognition of the Rothschild family's long wine-making tradition. Beneath the west wing of the house, lie the Cellars, modelled on private 'caves' of distinguished Bordelais vineyards. With the co-operation of Baron Eric de Rothschild at Chateau Lafite-Rothschild and Baroness Philippine de Rothschild at Chateau Mouton-Rothschild, one of the finest 'libraries' of Rothschild wines in the world has been assembled. Over fifteen thousand bottles lie in three brick vaults; their lighting, temperature and humidity have been carefully studied and are maintained constant at prescribed levels. Adjacent rooms house estate maps and land deeds of the various vineyard properties as well as photograps of the 'Chai2000' recently designed by Ricardo Bofill at Lafite and of the 'Grand Chai' at Mouton. The tower room designed for dining and wine tasting, houses historic bottles. A collection of wine-related works of art is on display, including a pair of 17th century marble reliefs carved by Kerricx the Elder for the guild of coopers in Antwerp.

The decision in 1989 to begin an extensive restoration of Waddesdon Manor inevitably begged the question as to whether the gardens should also be restored. It quickly became clear that the work in the grounds could only reflect rather than reproduce Victorian horticulture, because many of the species of plants and flowers used in the Baron's garden are now unobtainable. Instead there has been a match of colours of modern flowers to the 19th century strains which have now vanished. The technique of ribbon bedding in order to restore the Parterre on the Terrace has been highly successful although there are some features that it has not been practical to reinstate. The magnificent Waddesdon glasshouses are gone for ever, but the Aviary continues to be open to the public and the restored Victorian Water Garden is open for special visits. OPENING HOURS; The Garden, Aviary, Shops and Restaurant are open from March 1st-22nd December - Wednesday to Sunday 11am-6pm (5pm when the house is closed to the public). The House is open from the 28th March-15th October Thursday to Saturday 12.30-6.30pm Sundays, Good Friday and Bank Holiday Mondays 11am-6pm. Wednesdays in July and August only, 1pm-6pm (Last admission 5-15pm) TIMED TICKETS Entry to the house by timed ticket only; these may sell out early on busy days. Sold from 11am (10.30 Sundays, Good Friday and Bank Holiday Mondays) on a first come, first served basis. Garden, Restaurant, Shop. Connoisseur Days for groups by arrangement.

HADDENHAM   OAK FARM RARE BREEDS PARK
Tel: 01296 415709.
Aylesbury is perhaps best known for its association with ducks. In the 18th century and 19th century many people in the town kept the distinctive pure white ducks considered to be a delicacy by the rich and famous in London. The ducks became known as the Aylesbury. By the 20th century tastes changed and duck breeding died out in Aylesbury. Nowadays, one of the few remaining breeds can be seen at Oak Farm Rare Breeds Park at Broughton. The park which opened in 1993 is a traditional livestock farm featuring a variety of farm animals including sheep, goats, cattle, pigs and poultry, many of which are rare breeds.

CHALFONT SHIRE HORSE CENTRE
Model Farm, Gorelands Lane, Chalfont St Giles.
Tel: 01494 872304.
You will find a very warm welcome awaiting you at this home of the majestic Shire Horses. Brigadier is a magnificent black and white shire whose harness and accoutrements are fittingly splendid. Guardsman and Drayman pull the Chalfont show dray. All the horses bred at the centre are allowed to mature. Very little is done with them until they reach four years old but there are always plenty

of horses for you to see. It is an education to watch Harold Sherfield, one of the best heavy-horsemen in the country at work. Watch him braid and see how expertly it is done. There are as many as five generations of heavy horse-men in Harold's family. There is a fascinating collection of carriages including some old hearses, a Picture Gallery, Go-karting, a Souvenir Shop and a largetearoom where you will always get a good cup of tea. Cast your eyes to the ceiling whilst you wait for your meal and you will see a display of over 600 jugs above you. It is a thrilling day out for all the family. OPEN; 5 days a week from Mid-March until the end of September, Wednesdays-Sundays plus Bank Holidays 10am-4.30pm. During school holidays the centre is open 7 days a week. Special rates are available for coach parties. Visitors are asked to park in the free car parks provided and not on the approach roads or in front of private residential property.

HIGH WYCOMBE ODDS FARM PARK
Wooburn Common, High Wycombe, HP10 0LG
Tel:01628 520188
With easy access from the M40 and M4 and tourist signs to guide you on approach roads, Odds Farm Park is somewhere for all ages although the park has been created particularly with children in mind. There are opportunities for them to observe the animals closely and safely, to make comparisons between the old and the new, to learn about feeding methods, animal life cycles and the history behind some of the rarer breeds. Detailed information on each of the breeds is displayed on the individual pens. This is a large, well-run farm with a variety of animals including many rare breeds of cows, pigs, sheep, poultry and goats. You are invited to meet 'Prince Charles', the Wensleydale sheep and 'Clarence' the Angora Goat as well as many guinea pigs, rabbits, ducks and chickens, Food is available to feed the animals. Various special events are held including Shire horse demonstrations, Falconry and Pottery. Take part in the seasonal farm activity and feed the lambs, tend the chickens, or milk the goats. There is a pets corner, craft shop, childrens play area and hot and cold food available. OPEN; Daily, April-mid September 10-5pm. Mid-Sept to March Thursdays, Fridays, Saturdays and Sundays 10am-4pm.

BUCKS GOAT CENTRE
Layby Farm, Old Risborough Road, Stoke Mandeville HP22 5XJ
Tel: 01296 612983 Fax: 01296 613063
Goats galore! Is an apt description of this busy centre. There are more than a dozen different breeds on display including Anglo Nubian, British Alpine, Golden Guernsey, British Saanen, British Toggenburg, Friesian, Boer, Angora, Cashmere, English, Pigmy and Bagot. Most of the goats are both named and numbered, and details of their breeds are indicated on notices in the goat house. In addition to goats, other farm livestock are also on display. They include examples of domestic poultry including rare breed bantams, guinea fowl, quail, geese, ducks and turkey. You should also look out for Ho-Chi-Min, the Vietnamese pot belly pig and the small flock of Ryeland sheep.
Rabbits and guinea pigs can be seen in the Pets Corner. Sometimes there is a surplus of young rabbits and guinea pigs, and occasionally poultry for sale. The livestock collection is completed by Bambi, the 13 year old Shetland pony and by

two female donkeys, Jenny and Penny. One of them is usually available for rides on weekend afternoons, weather permitting. You are asked not to feed Bambi. He can bite, and is kept indoors or in a bare ground paddock on a strict grass-free diet to control the horse ailment, laminitis. Bags of feed for the goats are usually on sale in the Farm and Gift Shop. Please do not bring any other animal feed into the Goat Centre. The shop also sells a range of goat produce including milk, mohair, cheese, ice cream and fudge. It also leads into the plant sales area. Capricorn Nurseries, which stocks a range of popular and unusual plants and shrubs. For anyone interested in keeping goats it is possible to buy some of the kids that are born here each Spring. Please ask the Farm Manager for further information.

You are welcome to bring picnics into the Centre, or to enjoy hot and cold drinks, meals and snacks from the Naughty Nanny tea room situated just outside the entrance on the way in to the Silkwood Pine Furniture Showroom. It should be noted that after touching animals hands shoud be washed before eating. Pregnant lady visitors should also steer clear of ewes and lambs. There are only two ewes so that should not be difficult! OPEN; 10am-5pm Tuesday to Sunday. All attractions closed on Mondays (except Bank Holidays).

GRAND UNION CANAL
Tel: 01296 661920

A branch of the Grand Union Canal connects into Aylesbury offering a variety of waterside walks and excellent course fishing. Picnic sites can be found beside the canal at Pitstone Wharf and at the three Locks of Soulbury. Grebe Canal Cruises run regular scheduled services into the Chiltern Hills from Pitstone Wharf.

ST GILES   CHILTERN OPEN AIR MUSEUM
Tel: 01494 871117.

Many wonderful aircraft to be seen which would otherwise have been destroyed. These have been rescued, re-erected in 45 acres of countryside. The buildings illustrate everyday life and work of planes in the Chiltern region. Open 2-6pm 1st April-31st October.

CAMBRIDGESHIRE

CAMBRIDGE   OLIVER CROMWELL HOUSE
Tel: 01353 662062.
Standing almost in the shadows of Ely Cathedral this was the home of Oliver Cromwell and his family for some ten years. Several rooms have been refurbished in Cromwellian style to show features of the house which Cromwell would have known in his time. Displays tell the story of the house's history, for although Cromwell was still the most famous occupant, the house itself has medieval origins and a fascinating past. Built in the early 14th century for the collection of tithes, it was used as a brewery and inn during the 19th century. Open 1st Apr-30th Sept 10-6pm daily including Sat, Sun and Bank Holidays 1st October-30th April 10-5.15pm.

DUXFORD AEROPLANE MUSEUM
Tel: 01223 833376
Location: Duxford is next to junction 10 off the M11 motorway, 48 miles from London. A day at Duxford is a day you'll never forget. You'll find Europe's biggest collection of historic aircraft, over 130, displayed in the giant exhibition hangers. Flimsy biplanes that fought over the trenches of the First World War through to Gulf Jets are on show at this preserved wartime airfield. See the legendary Spitfire, Lancaster and B-17 Flying Fortress. Marvel at the U-2 Spyplane that flew on the edge of space and climbaboard Concorde. Look at the only F-111 supersonic swing-wing bomber on show in Europe and be amazed by the Harrier jump-jet. Open everyday except 24,25 & 26 December. Summer 26-Mar-16 October 10-6pm. Winter 10-4pm.

ELY CATHEDRAL
Tel: 01353 667735.
Location: A10 from Cambridge. In 673 St Ethelreda, Queen of Northumbria, founded a monastery in the centre of the Fens on the Isle of Ely where she was Abbess until her death in 679. Some 400 years later in 1081, work on the present building was begun, under the guidance of Abbot Simeon. It was completed in 1189 and the cathedral now stands as a remarkable example of Romanesque architecture. Undoubtedly, the most outstanding feature of the cathedral is the octagon, built to replace the Norman tower which collapsed in 1322. The regular free guided tours will help you appreciate all that is special about the cathedral. The Cathedral Shop in the High street offers an imaginative selection of beautiful greetings cards, pottery, glassware, and jewellery. Open daily all year round. Summer 7-7pm and in the winter 7.30-6.30pm. Sun 5pm.

LINTON ZOO
Tel 01223 891308
Llocation: Ten miles east of Cambridge on the B1052 just off the A460. All set in 16 acres of beautifully landscaped gardens. Find time to visit the zoo and you will find lots to interest the whole family from Sumatran Tigers, African Lions, Snow Leopards, Lynx, Wallabies and Toucans and many exciting and unusual wildlife

to be found at Cambridgeshire's Wildlife Breeding Centre. The zoo is continually expanding as more of the world's threatened species are taken on board. Open all year round every day including Bank Holidays.

HINCHINGBROOKE COUNTRY PARK
Tel: 01480 451568.
At Hinchingbrooke Country Park you can wander freely through beautiful, unspoilt Cambridgeshire countryside, through woodland glades and meadows or along river banks and lakesides. Set in 156 acres of woodland, there is a natural habitat home to a suprising variety of wildlife. Here you can see herons, woodpeckers, snipe, foxes and even deer, especially on a peaceful early morning walk. Terns and dragonflies hunt over the lakes in the summer and butterflies drift effortlessly over the meadows. As dusk falls bats emerge and you may even hear a nightingale sing. Open all the year round.

THE OLD HUNTINGDON CAR TRAIL
Tel 01480 425831
This wonderful car trail has been designed to allow motorists or cyclists to join at any point, journeying around until you return to your starting point. Travelling through all parts of Cambridgeshire taking in all the major sights and attractions, the trail is a great way to travel. Open throughout the year Mon-Fri 9.30-5.30pm Sat 9-5pm. Closed Bank Holiday Mondays.

HAMERTON WILDLIFE PARK
Hamerton, Huntingdon, PE17 5RE
Tel: 01832 293362
The Centre has been successfully breeding many rare and endangered species for several years. As the collection has grown so the owners, Andrew and Sally Swales, have moved towards creating a wildlife sanctuary that was open to the public. Thiswas achieved in 1990. Many new animals have been added since then and there is a continuous programme of building and development to house these and a number of others planned to arrive in the near future. What you won't see here are pets and other domestic animals but the many species that might have disappeared from the wild if this dedicated couple had not set about their task. What you will see are Ring-tailed Lemurs, the spectacular Ruffed Lemur and the Black Lemur. The tiny, colourful Marmosets and Tamarins from the dense rain-forests of Amazonia are fascinating. Gibbons and Bushbabies add to the Primates. Wallabis, Meerkats, Otters, Rodents, Sloths and the small Reeve's Muntjac deer, native to Eastern China form the Mammal section. There are over 100 different birds from around the world including the East African Crowned Crane, considered by some to be the most beautiful bird in the world. A whole world of Geese cackle away and the popular, gaudy Parrots make their presence felt. With Game Birds and Owls there is always something delightful to catch the eye and enrich the mind. You are asked not to feed the animals or birds and please respect the animals in their homes. OPEN; Every day except Christmas Day 10.30am-6pm in Summer and 4pm in Winter. A free car and coach park is available. No dogs or ets allowed inside the Centre. Coffee Shop, Picnic Area. Children's Play Area.

BUCKDEN TOWERS
Tel: 01480 811868
Former Palace of the Bishops of Lincoln. Splendid 15th century gatehouse and tower, Catherine of Aragon was imprisoned here. Open Wed 1.30-5.30pm. Thurs-Sat 9-5pm Sun 9-12.30pm. Admission free.

GRAYS HONEY FARM
Cross Drove, Warboys, Huntingdon PE17 2UQ
Tel: 01354 693798

A great place to visit. In the pleasantest of surroundings an exhibition allows you to learn all you want to know about the hard working and mysterious Honey Bee. A subject few know about and yet one that is exciting and rewarding. Here you can browse around taking in the displays and watching the bees at work. The expression ' busy as a bee' immediately assumes great relevance! If you have questions you want answered the friendly and knowledgeable staff are more than willing to help. Do bees talk to each other? Find out for yourselves using the Black Forest model railway. Have you ever made a candle? Now is the opportunity to make your own beeswax candle and take it home as a souvenir.
The shop set amid an attractive garden is very well stocked. You will find a wide range of quality honeys, honey marmalade and honey mustard. Royal Jelly, Propolis and other alternative health products are available at very reasonable prices. If your conscience does not allow you to use ordinary toiletries you will find a cruelty free range as well as perfumes made with honey, beeswax, plant oils and other natural ingredients. Beeswax polishes for fine antique furniture and leather are also there for purchase. Beeswax candles - natural, coloured and perfumed, Honey Ice Cream and confectionery complete the list. If you cannot come here in person do send for the comprehensive mail order catalogue.
There are excellent refreshments available with wonderful home-made cakes, many of them made with honey. Sandwiches are made toorder and there are snacks, tea, coffee, soft drinks, and the speciality Honey Ice Cream. If you prefer to eat alfresco there is an attractive picnic area. Try a Honeycomb Bear Ice Cream Special and take a Gray's Honey Farm mug home FREE. OPEN; Exhibition: 31st March-24th December, Monday-Saturday 10.30am-6.00pm. Closed Sundays. Winter Shop Opening: As well as the normal exhibition opening times the shop will also be open from: 4th January-31st March Tuesday-Saturday 10.30am-5.00pm. Closed Sunday and Monday.

VISITOR ATTRACTIONS

GLOUCESTERSHIRE

BERKELEY   BERKELEY CASTLE
off A38 Tel: 01453 810332
Perfectly preserved 800 year old castle. Keep, dungeons, staterooms, Great Hall kitchen, tapestries, furniture, silver. Ornamental gardens and Butterfly house. Open Apr-Sept Tues-Sun. October Sundays only.

BIBURY   BIBURY TROUT FARM
Tel: 01285 740215
A working farm which breeds Rainbow trout. Visitors can see developing trout in 20 ponds and may feed the fish. Gift shop, picnic area, fishing. Open all year daily.

BOURTON ON THE WATER   COTSWOLD MOTOR MUSEUM
Tel: 01451 21255.
30 motor vehicles and the largest collection of vintage advertising signs in Britain. Also Village Life exhibition. Open daily Feb-Nov.

BIRDLAND
Rissington Road.
Tel: 01451 20689   Bird garden on the banks of the River Windrush. Penguins, waterfowl, tropical and sub tropical birds, many at liberty. Open daily all year.

BOURTON-ON-THE-WATER THE MODEL VILLAGE
Situated behind the Old New Inn, this is an incredible piece of work which delights and intrigues people of all ages from childhood upwards. The idea of building came from the late Mr C.A.Morris, landlord of the inn who in 1935 decided to turn his vegetable garden into something more decorative. It was not his intention to build a miniature model village but gradually the idea evolved and the model village was born. Every building and every feature of the landscape was built carefully to a scale of one ninth of the original and everything was erected exactly in position with the sole exception of the Church of St Lawrence, which stands at the far end of the model from the inn. One of the most fascinating aspects of the village is the miniature River Windrush, which is an artifical stream about three feet wide flowing from the working model of the mill through the whole length of the village. It is spanned by five little stone bridges, all of which are precise replicas of the famous bridges of Bourton. Now that the Model Village has been standing for some years the Cotswold stone of which all the buildings are constructed has begun to mellow. Each year it looks more and more like the original. OPEN; Summer 9-6pm. Winter 10-dusk. Not Christmas Day. Pets on leads. No access for disabled.

FOLLY FARM WATERFOWL
Off A436 near Bourton-on-the-Water.
Tel:01451 20285.
Collection of rare poultry breeds and waterfowl including endangered species, in natural Cotswold farm surroundings. Open daily all year.

HOTELS, INNS, RESTAURANTS AND COUNTRY HOUSES

BROADWAY   SNOWSHILL MANOR
Tel: 01386 852410.
Location: 3 miles south west of Broadway off A44.
The Cotswold manor house is full to the brim with Charles Wade's collection of craftsmanship from all over the world. Each room has a theme from Samurai armour to navigation, from musical instruments to carts and bicycles. The cottage garden is charming. Open Easter Sat, Sun and Mon 1-6pm. Closed Good Friday. April-October; Sat and Sun 1-5pm. May to end September: daily except Tues 1-6pm. National Trust.

CHELTENHAM CHEDWORTH ROMAN VILLA
Yarnworth. Tel: 01242 890256
Location: 10 miles south east of Cheltenham.
One of the best exposed Romano-British villas in Britain. Open March-end October Tues-Sun and Bank Holiday Monday 10-5.30pm Closed Good Friday. 2nd November -4th December: Wed-Sun 11-4pm. National Trust.

CHELTENHAM ART GALLERY & MUSEUM
Clarence Street.
Tel: 01242 237431.
Important arts and crafts collection, including furniture, pottery and silver inspired by William Morris. Also local history and archaeology, rare Oriental porcelain and Dutch and British paintings. Admission free. Open all year. Mon-Sat plus Sunday afternoons in summer.

HOLST BIRTHPLACE MUSEUM
4 Clarence Road.
Tel: 01242 524846
Regency house where the composer of 'The Planets' was born. Showing 'upstairs-downstairs' way of life in Victorian and Edwardian times. Admission free. Open Tues-Sat. Closed Bank Holidays. Open all year.

PITTVILLE PUMP ROOM MUSEUM
Pittville Park
Tel: 01242 512470
Housed in the magnificent Pump Room overlooking its own beautiful lake and gardens, the museum imaginatively uses original costumes to bring to life the history of Cheltenham from its Regency heyday to the Swinging Sixties, Jewellery showing changing taste and fashion from Regency to Art Noveau, and a spectacular collection of tiaras are also included. Open end of May-September Tues-Sat 10-4.20pm. Sunday 11-4.20pm. Bank Holiday Monday 11-4.20pm

CHIPPING CAMDEN   HIDCOTE MANOR GARDENS
Hidcote Bartrim
Tel: 01386 438333
Location: 4 miles east of Chipping Camden off B4632, Internationally renowned, this memorable garden is, in reality, a series of smaller gardens. Each has its own special atmosphere and leads on to the next surprise. Open: April to end of Oct

daily except Tues and Fri. 11-7pm. Closed Good Friday. Shop. Restaurant. Plant Sales Centre. National Trust.

WOOLSTAPLERS HALL MUSEUM
High Street
Tel: 01386 840289
Constructed in 1340 for merchants to buy the staples of Cotswold fleece; the Hall with its superb roof carving, is now a museum. It houses an interesting collection of town and country bygones.
Open: Daily 1st April-31st October 11-6pm.

RIFTSGATE COURT GARDENS
Tel: 01386 438777.
A magnificentlysituated house with fine views and trees. The garden, created over three generations, has many unusual shrubs and a good collection of old fashioned and specie roses including RosaFilipes Kiftgate, the largest rose in England.
Open: Wed, Thurs and Sun 2-6pm. Also Bank Holiday Mondays and Saturdays in June and July 2-6pm. 1st April-30th Sept.

CINDERFORD DEAN HERITAGE CENTRE
Camp Mill, Soudley on B4227.
Tel: 01594 822170.
The museum of the Royal Forest of Dean interpreting the natural and man-made environment. Nature trails, shop, picnic/barbecue sites, art and craft exhibitions. Open daily all year.

CIRENCESTER CORINIUM MUSEUM P
ark Street.
Tel: 01285 655611
One of the finest collections of antiquities from Roman Britain. Full scale reconstruction of kitchen, dining room and mosaic craftsman's workshop bring Corinium (Roman Cirencester) to life. New Cotswold pre-history gallery. Special exhibitions of local history and archaelogy. Award winning museum and one of the Good Museums Guide 'Top Twenty'.
Open: Daily all year. Sunday afternoons and all Bank Holidays. Closed Mondays from November to March and Christmas. Facilities for the disabled.

BREWERY COURT
Tel: 01285 657181.
The Cirencester Workshops and the Niccol Centre are housed in a converted Victorian brewery and comprise a specialist craft centre where 20 professional craftworkers run their businesses, a shop selling the best of British craft work, a theatre, studios where courses are held in a wide variety of disciplines, a gallery showing exhibitions in applied and fine art and a wholefood Coffee house.
Open: Cirencester Workshops - Mon-Sat 10-5pm Niccol Centre Mon-Fri 9.30-5.30pm and Sat 9.30-1pm. Admission free. Open all year.

HOTELS, INNS, RESTAURANTS AND COUNTRY HOUSES

COTSWOLD WATER PARK
Tel: 01285 861459.
It lies to the south of Cirencester and offers exciting and varied activities based on a network of lakes formed as a result of 60 years gravel extraction. In addition to the variety of water-based activities including angling, windsurfing, sailing, water, skiing and power boat racing, there are lakeside walks and picnic sites provided at two country Parks. The area is recognised as being nationally important for nature conservation. A number of public and private nature reserves provide an opportunity to study the enormous variety of its wetland flora and fauna. Open all the year. Facilities for the disabled.

BARNSLEY HOUSE GARDEN
The Close
Tel: 01285 740281
Spring bulbs, autumn colours. Mixed borders, climbing and wall shrubs. Knot garden, herb garden, laburnum walk (early June). Decorative vegetable potage. 18th century summer houses. House (not open) 1697. Interesting plants for sale. Carpark. Pub lunches available in Barnsley at the village pub.

COLEFORD   CLEARWELL CAVES
Royal Forest of Dean
Tel: 01594 32535
Superb caverns and tunnels stretching far under the Forest of Dean. Worked for iron over 2,000 years until 1945. Open daily Mar-Oct. 1-24 December Christmas fantasy.

PUZZLEWOOD
Lower Perrygrove Farm on B4228.
Tel: 01594 33187.
OpenRoman iron mines in 14 acre woodland setting. Paths arranged in a puzzle landscaped in 1800s. Open Easter-October. Tues-Sun and Bank Holidays.

GLOUCESTER   GLOUCESTER CITY MUSEUM
Brunswick Road
Tel: 01452 524131
Famous Iron Age mirror, Roman sculptures and mosaics. Also Georgian silver, barometers, furniture and exhibitions. Admission free. Open Mon-Sat & Bank Holiday Mondays all year.

HOUSE OF THE TAILOR OF GLOUCESTER
9 College Court.
Tel: 01452 422856.
The building chosen by Beatrix Potter to illustrate her famous story. Now a gift shop and exhibition. Admission free. Open Mon-Sat all year.

NATURE IN ART
On A38 2 miles north of Gloucester.
Tel: 01452 713422.

Unique collection of wildlife art from all parts of the world and all periods. Specially commended in National Heritage Museum of the year awards. Nature gardens and outdoor sculptures. Full programme of artists in residence.
Open Tues-Sun and Bank Holidays all year.

REGIMENTS OF GLOUCESTERSHIRE MUSEUM
The Docks,
Tel: 01452 522682
Museum of the Year Award for the Best Small Museum 1991. New displays tell the story of Gloucestershire's soldiers in peace and war. Gift shop.
Open Tues-Sun & Bank Holidays all year.

ROBERT OPIE COLLECTION MUSEUM OF ADVERTISING AND PACKAGING
Albert Warehouse, Gloucester Docks.
Tel: 01452 302309
Memories of childhood brought to life. Goods which since Victorian times have crowded the shelves of Britain's grocers, confectioners, chemists, tobacconists, pubs and corner shops. Vintage TV Commercials.
Open all year but closed winter Mondays.

GLOUCESTER SKI CENTRE
Robinswood Hill,
Tel: 01452 414300.
240m 200m nursery slopes. Full length ski lifts. Beginners to experts. Full tuition and equipment. Ski shop.
Open daily all year.

GLOUCESTER ANTIQUES CENTRE
Severn Road, Gloucester Docks
Tel: 01452 529716
Collections of all kinds of antiques taking up four floors of a magnificent restored warehouse. Admission free.
Open daily all year.

CRICKLEY HILL COUNTRY PARK
6 miles east of Gloucester on B4070.
Tel: 01452 863170.
145 acres of grassland, woodland and parkland with panoramic views. Site of archaeological interest. Visitor Centre and 5 self-guided trails. Admission free.
Open daily all year.

ROBINSWOOD HILL COUNTRY PARK
2 miles south of Gloucester.
Tel: 01452 412029.
250 acres of countryside with walks and views. Waymarked trails. Visitor Centre. Gloucestershire Trust for Nature Conservation Centre. Admission free. Open daily all year.

GUITING POWER   COTSWOLD FARM PARK RARE BREEDS CENTRE
Off B4077
Tel: 01451 850307. The country's most comprehensive collection of rare breeds of farm animals. Adventure playground, farm trails, pets corner. Open daily Easter -September.

MORETON-IN-MARSH   BATSFORD ARBORETUM,
Batsford
Tel: 01608 50722.
Fifty acres of garden containing over 1200 different species of trees, many rare, with superb views over the Vale of Evenlode. Springtime carpets of bulbs, magnificent magnolias, flowering cherries and a spectacular 'Handkerchief' tree. Later in the year the large collection of maples and sorbus provide wonderful autumnal colours. Refreshments. Open 1 March- early November 10am-5pm daily.

LECHLADE   COTSWOLD WOOLLEN WEAVERS
Filkins.
Tel: 01367 860491.
Working woollen mill showing traditional skills in 18th century buildings. Permanent exhibition areas. Large mill shop. Admission free. Open Mon-Fri and Sat am. Restricted opening Christmas, Easter, Bank Holidays.

NEWENT   THE NATIONAL BIRDS OF PREY CENTRE
Tel: 10531 820286.
A full day out for the family is offered plus the chance to experience Birds of Prey at close quarters. The Daily Flying Demonstrations are undoubtedly the highlight of the day but there is so much more to see and do. Coffee-shop. Book and Gift Shop. Children's Play Area and Picnic sites. No pets. Free parking. Open: 7 days a week 10.30-5.30pm Closed December-January. Facilities for the disabled.

THE SHAMBLES
16-20 Church Street.
Tel: 01531 822144.
A staggeringly large collection laid out as a complete Victorian town of shops, cobbled streets, gas lamps and alleyways, rural and town trades and crafts. All approached through a fully furnished four storey house, in an unexpectedly spacious location behind the main streets of this attractive market town. Open: 10-6pm mid March-December Tues-Sun and Bank Holiday Mondays. Facilities for the disabled.

THREE CHOIRS VINEYARD
Welsh House Lane.
Tel: 01531 890555
Production of English Wine reviving the ancient tradition of Gloucestershire wine making. Admission free (Charge for tours)
Open daily all year.

VISITOR ATTRACTIONS

NEWENT BUTTERFLY & NATURAL WORLD CENTRE,
Birches Lane off B4215
Tel: 01531 821800
Tropical Butterfly house, Nature Exhibition, Menagerie and Water Life. Spiders, snakes, rabbits, guinea pigs, rare breed fowl, waterfowl, pheasants, peacocks, parakeets and other small birds. Open daily Easter-October.

LYDNEY   DEAN FOREST RAILWAY
Norchard Steam Centre B4234 Nr. Lydney.
Tel: 01594 843423.
Full size railway engines, coaches and wagons. Admission free to site. Open daily all year. Admission charge for steam rides (certain days throughout the year).

NORTHLEACH   COTSWOLD COUNTRYSIDE COLLECTION
Tel: 01451 60715.
Fine collection of agricultural history. Set in former 'House of Correction' Restored cells and courtroom. Special exhibitions. Open daily Apr-Oct.

KEITH HARDING'S WORLD OF MECHANICAL MUSIC,
Oak House.
Tel: 01451 60181.
A museum of antique clocks, musical boxes, automata and mechanical musical instruments in an old wool merchant's house. Restorers of clocks and musical boxes. Gift shop. Open daily allyear.

PAINSWICK   PAINSWICK ROCOCO GARDEN,
The Stables, Painswick House.
Tel: 01452 813204
18th century, 6 acre Rococo garden with garden buildings. Vistas and woodland paths. Open Feb-mid Dec. Wed- Sun.

PRINKNASH ABBEY
Nr. Painswick. On A46.
Tel: 01452 812455.
Benedictine Abbey with world famous pottery worked by local craftsmen. Adjoined by Bird Park. Open daily all year.

SLIMBRIDGE   THE WILDFOWL AND WETLANDS TRUST.
Off A38 Tel: 01453 890065.
World's largest collection of wildfowl in 73 acres of grounds. Tropical house. Permanent exhibition. Open all year. Closed Dec 24th & 25th.

STANWAY   STANWAY HOUSE,
Near Cheltenham.
Tel: 01386 73469
The jewel of Cotswold manor houses is very much a home rather than a museum. The mellow Jacobean architecture, the typical squire's family portraits, the exquisite Gate House, the old Brewery and medieval Tithe Barn, the extensive

pleasure grounds and formal landscape contribute to the timeless charm of what Arthur Negus considered one of the most beautiful and romantic manor houses in England. Open: June, July, August Tuesdays and Thursdays 2-5pm.

TETBURY   CHAVENAGE
Tel: 01666 502329
Elizabethan manor house (1576). Tapestry rooms, furniture and relics of Cromwellian period. Chapel and Edwardian wing. Personal tours by the owner. Spacious gardens for visitors to the house to enjoy. See where Agatha Christie's 'Hercule Poirot' was filmed. Open: May-Sept, Thurs, Sun, Bank Holidays 2-5pm. Also Easter Sunday and Monday.

WESTONBIRT ARBORETUM
On the A43 nr Tetbury
Tel: 0166 880220. 600 acres containing one of the finest collections of temperate trees and shrubs in the world. Open all year. Visitor Centre open daily Easter-Mid-November.

WESTBURY
Tel: 01452 760461
Location: 9 miles south west of Gloucester on A48.
Laid out between 1696 and 1705, this formal Dutch water garden is a rare survival of its type in England. Historical varieties of apple, pear, plum, along with many other species of plants introduced to England before 1700, make this a fascinating study for any gardener.
Open: April-end October: Wed to Sun and Bank Holiday Monday 11-6pm. Closed Good Friday. National Trust.

WINCHCOMBE   HAILES ABBEY
Tel: 01242 602398
Location: 10 miles north east of Cheltenham off B4632.
Picturesque ruins of great Cistercian Abbey and centre of pilgrimage. English Heritage. Open: April 1st- end September daily 10-6pm. Oct-March Tues-Sun 10am-4pm. Closed 24-26 December and New Year Bank Holiday. Museum may be closed on certain days from October-end of March for staffing reasons. Ring first.

SUDELEY CASTLE AND GARDENS
Tel: 01242 602308.
Once the residence of Queen Katherine Parr, Sudeley is now the charming home of Lord and Lady Ashcombe. Sudeley houses many fineantiques, civil war relics and old-master paintings.
The gardens with the Queen's garden as their centrepiece, are quite magnificent and are complemented by 'Sudeley Castle Roses' a specialist plant centre. Also available: craft workshops, adventure playground, castle shop, licensed restaurant. Calendar of special events throughout the year. OPEN: Apr 1st-31st October. Grounds 11am-5.30pm. Castle apartments 12 noon - 5pm. Sudeley Castle Roses; 10am-5.30pm. Free parking for cars and coaches.

GLOUCESTERSHIRE - WARWICKSHIRE RAILWAY,

Toddington, at intersection of B4632/A438. Tel: 01242 621405. Restored GWR Station. Mainline steam rides. 8 miles round trip. Large rail complex, rolling stock under restoration. Admission free to site. Open daily. Admission charge for steam rides (Easter-October Sat, Sun & Bank Holidays) Open all year.

HEREFORD AND WORCESTERSHIRE

DROITWICH HANBURY HALL
Tel: 01527 821214
Location: Off M5 Junction 5 to Droitwich, 4 miles east of Droitwich off B4090. William and Mary style brick house, notable for the famous Thornhill staircase. Fine collection of porcelain. Re-creation of formal 18th century garden. Open: Easter to end October; Sat, Sun and Mon 2-6pm. Closed Good Friday. Aug: also open Tues and Wed 2-6pm. Shop, Tearoom, National Trust.

HEREFORD CITY MUSEUM & ART GALLERY,
Broad Street. Full of interest.
Open: Tues, Wed, Fri 10am-6pm. Thurs & Sat 10-5pm 10-4pm in winter. Sunday May-September 10-4pm. Open Bank Holiday Mondays.

THE OLD HOUSE
17th Century Museum. Open: Monday 10-1pm Tues-Sat 10-1pm & 2.5.30pm. Sat (winter) 10-1pm. Sunday May-September 10-4pm. Open Bank Holiday Mondays.

DINMORE MANOR AND THE COMMANDERY OF THE KNIGHTS HOSPITALLERS OF ST JOHN OF JERUSALEM
6 miles north of Hereford on A49
Tel: 01432 830322.
Spectacular hillside location. A range of impressive architecture dating from the 12th-20th century. Chapel, Cloisters, Great Hall (Music Room) and extensive roof walk giving panoramic views of the countryside and beautiful gardens below. Large collection of stained glass. Open 9.30am daily all year. Refreshments available most afternoons during summer.

LEDBURY EASTNOR CASTLE
Tel: 01531 633160.
Splendid Georgian Castle in fairytale setting with Deer Park, lake and arboretum. Inside this family home tapestries, fine art, armour and furniture from the Italianate and Gothic in richly decorated interiors, many recently restored to critical acclaim. Home-made cream teas and ice cream. Open Sundays Easter to end September, Bank Holiday Mondays. Sunday to Friday during August 12 noon-5pm.

HOTELS, INNS, RESTAURANTS AND COUNTRY HOUSES

LEOMINSTER BERRINGTON HALL
Nr. Leominster.
Tel: 01586 780246
Location: 3 miles north of Leominster.
Signposted off A49. A classical elegant 18th century mansion by Henry Holland, set in a gracefully landscaped park by 'Capability' Brown. Park walk open July to end October only. Open Easter to end September; Wed-Sun (open Bank Holiday Mon. closed Good Friday) 1.30-5.30pm. October Wed-Sun 1.30-4.30. Grounds open from 12.30pm. Shop. Licensed restaurant. Dogs on leads in car park only. National Trust.

CROFT CASTLE
Tel: 01586 780246
Location : 5 miles north west of Leominster.
Signposted off A49 and A4110. Just 5 miles from Berrington Hall, this Marcher Castle has been the home of the Croft family since Domesday (with a short break of 170 years). Ancient walls and castellated turrets house an interior shown as it was in the 18th century with fine ceilings and Gothic staircase. The surrounding parkland is open all year. Open: Easter Sat, Sun & Mon 2-6pm. Closed Good Friday. April and October Sat & Sun 2-5pm. May to end Sept: Wed-Sun and Bank Holiday Monday 2-6pm. National Trust.

LYDE RENCHESTER WATER GARDEN
Church Road,
Tel: 01432 270981.
Largest and perhaps best stocked aquatic centre in the South Midlands. More than two hundred tropical fish tanks, fresh and saltwater, are filled with some of the most fascinating , colourful and eye-catching sea and fresh water creatures. The best view of the beautiful gardens is from the Tea Rooms. On the A49 Hereford to Leominster Road - two miles north of Hereford. Free admission. Carpark. Disabled access.
Open every day of the week.

BRINGSTY LOWER BROCKHAMPTON
Tel: 01885 488099
Location: 2 miles east of Bromyard on A44.
A 14th century half timbered moated farmhouse with a very unusual gatehouse. Only the medieval hall and parlour are shown.
Open: House; April-end September; Wed-Sun and Bank Holiday Monday. 10-5pm. Closed Good Friday. Oct: Wed-Sun 10am-4pm. Estate open all year.

ROSS-ON-WYE THE BUTTON MUSEUM
Kyrle Street.
Tel: 01989 566089
Unique award winnng Museum of Dress and Uniform Buttons, worn by ladies and gentlemen over the last two hundred years. Museum shop.
Open 7 days a week 1st April-31st October 10-5pm.

VISITOR ATTRACTIONS

SWAINSHILL   THE WEIR
Location: 5 miles west of Hereford on A438. Fine views of the River Wye and the Welsh Hills from a steep bank studded with trees, shrubs and plants. Beautiful, particularly in springtime, with drifts of flowering bulbs. Open: Mid-February to end October; Wed to Sun (including Good Friday) and Bank Holiday Monday 11am-6pm. National Trust.

WELLINGTON QUEENSWOOD GARDEN CENTRE
Wellington HR4 8BB
Tel: 01432 830880. Fax: 01432 830833.
The Milne Family - Tony, Frank, Kathleen, Eric and Alexi own and operate this attractive garden centre which is far more than somewhere one comes just to buy plants. It is an outing that is thoroughly enjoyable and one from which you can gain gardening advice from an expert and helpful staff. The plants are second to none. The company offers all its customers a unique plant and gardening equipment ' finder service'. If they do not have a product in stock they will makeevery attempt to source it for their customers to collect or have sent to them by post. To help gardeners and those interested in horticulture a joint venture with Pershore College of Horticulture has been set up resulting in Pershore setting up a lecture hall at Queenswood and offering courses/qualifications to local people. All of this demonstrates how dedicated the Milne family and their staff are to the centre. A large pet shop on the site offering small domestic pets such as rabbits and guinea pigs and a huge selection of tropical and cold water fish attracts many people. Here too advice is top notch from PTIA trained staff. The Tea House is a favourite place for customers. Not only does it serve excellent tea but lunches and evening meals are available including cakes and specialities made on the premises. OPEN; Mon-Sat 1st April-30th June & 1st Dec-23rd Dec. 9am-8pm. 27th Dec-31st March & 1st July -30th Nov 9am-6pm. Sundays. Teahouse & Outdoor Plant Area 9am-5pm. Main Building and Pet Shop 11am-5pm. Easy parking - 500 spaces. Coaches welcome.

WHITNEY-ON-WYE   CWMMAU FARMHOUSE,
Brilley.
Tel: 01497 831251.
Location: 4 miles south west of Kington between A4111 and A438. Attractive early 17th century timber-framed and stone-tiled farmhouse. Open: Easter, May, Spring and Summer Bank Holiday weekends only and Weds in August 2-6pm. National Trust.

WORCESTER   THE GREYFRIARS,
Friar Street.
Tel: 01905 23571
Still surviving in the heart of Worcester, this medieval timber-framed house has been carefully restored. Delightful walled garden. Open: April-end October. Wed, Thurs and Bank Holiday Monday 2-5.30pm. National Trust.

HOTELS, INNS, RESTAURANTS AND COUNTRY HOUSES

HERTFORDSHIRE

BARNET   BARNET RIDING CENTRE
Tel: 0181 449 3531.
Location: Situated only 25 miles from Central London ideally situated off the A1 and on the border of Hertfordshire junction 23 off the M25. Away from the hustle and bustle of inner-city life children and adults alike can take time off to spend some time amongst nature and take horse riding lessons. Amateurs and professionals can spend one hour or more learning how to ride and hack through the Hertfordshire countryside. Open Tues-Sat all year including Bank Holidays.

BROXBOURNE   PARADISE WILDLIFE PARK
White Stubbs Lane, Broxbourne EN10 7QA
Tel: 01992 468001.
Paradise Wildlife Park is unique! As Britain's most interactive Wildlife Park it is an ideal place to touch, feed and meet many animals - both domestic and exotic. You can learn a great deal during the 'meet the animals' session where experienced keepers impart information about the wonderful creatures and answer visitors questions. The 'Meet the Animals' experience includes: foxes, birds of prey, reptiles, chinchilla, camels, llamas and zebras.
There are many other daily events including Dr Do and Dr Little amazing animal facts show, the Sweetie man, the feeding of the lions and tigers and lion and tiger cub talks. The friendly family run Park is very compact and is set in the wonderful backdrop of Broxbourne woods. Other attractions on the sitecomprise a Woodland Railway, Crazy Golf, Children's rides and Tractor Trailer rides for which there is a fee of 50p per ride. FREE facilities include 3 superb adventure playgrounds, Fantasy Land, Adventureland and Fun Land plus a woodland walk. There is a wide range of catering from Mannings Snack Cabin, The Pembridge Cafeteria to a Barbecue and Bar area and The Pembridge Restaurant. There are also ample picnic areas spread across the park.
Paradise Wildlife Park also offers the public the chance to meet their lion or tiger cubs. This is literally the opportunity of a lifetime and is available outside the normal opening hours of the park. The money raised goes to Project Life Lion, a registered charity which helpe to save African lions in the Serengeti from Canine Distemper. The sessions last up to 30 minutes and are for a group of up to 4 people. Priced at forty pounds a session - numbers are strictly limited. For further details or to book ring 01992 470490.
The Park is located 6 miles from Junction 25 off the M25. Brown and White tourist signs direct you to the Park from the A10 at the Broxbourne/Turnford Junction. Admission prices are as at January 1996 #4.50adults, #4.00 senior citizens and #3.50 children (3-15_. Opening times are 10am-6pm (Summer) and 10am-dusk (Winter). Paradise Wildlife opens every day of the year. Information line 01992 468001. Paradise Wildlife Park is a truly wonderful place with something for everyone - whatever your age!

HATFIELD   MILL GREEN MUSEUM
Tel: 01707 271362.
This local museum is housed in what was for centuries the home of the millers

who worked in the adjoining water mill. Mill Green Museum has two permanent galleries where local items from Roman times to the present day are on show - everything from pottery and craft tools to underwear and school certificates. Open throughout the year Tues-Fri 10-5pm and Sat,Sun and Bank Holidays 2-5pm Admission free.

MILL GREEN MILL
Tel: 01707 271362.
Adjoining the museum is the water mill which has been restored to its full working order, as it would have been during the 18th and 19th century. Visitors can take a look at how a mill used to work, with the reconstruction of a new water wheel. Mill Green Flour freshly ground from organically grown wheat is on sale. Open throughout the year Tues-Fri 10-5pm and Sat, Sun and Bank Holidays 2-5pm. Admission free.

WELWYN ROMAN BATHS
Tel: 01707 271362
Preserved under the A1(M) in a steel vault, Welwyn Roman Baths are the remains of a bathing suite which was originally part of a country villa. The site was excavated during the 1960s and early 70s by the Welwyn Archaeological Society and the vault installed to save the bathing suite from deconstruction when the motorway was built. The layout of cold room, warm room, hot room cold and hot baths and furnace room can be clearly seen together with the remains of the hypocaust. Also on show are related archaeological finds from the Welwyn area and an explanatory exhibition on Roman baths and the history of the site. The site is open on Thurs-Sun and Bank Holidays from 2-5pm.

HATFIELD HOUSE;
Tel: 01707 262823.
Location: 21 miles north of London on the Great North Road (A1), seven miles from M25. This celebrated Jacobean house, which stands in its own great park, was built between 1607 and 1611 by Robert Cecil, the first Earl of Salisbury and Chief Minister to King James I. It has been the family home of the Cecils ever since. The State Rooms are rich in world famous paintings, fine furniture, rare tapestries and historic armour. The beautiful stained glass in the chapel is original. Within the delightful gardens stands the surviving wing of the Royal Palace of Hatfield (1497) where Elizabeth I spent much of her childhood. Open 25th Mar-9th October weekdays from 12-4pm, Sun 1.30-5pm.

HATFIELD GARDEN
Tel: 01707 262823
Connected to Hatfield House, the West Gardens date back to the late 15th century when the Palace of Hatfield was built. Keeping in line with the manner of the garden of the 17th century, the garden has been planted with a great variety of sweet smelling flowers, bulbs, trees and shrubs for every season of the year. Although the West Garden is planted with mainly herbaceous plants, roses, irises and peonies, with a considerable number of rare and unusual plants. The West Gardens are open daily except Good Friday 11-6pm.

HOTELS, INNS, RESTAURANTS AND COUNTRY HOUSES

THE OLD PALACE, HATFIELD PARK
Tel: 01707 262055
Location: 31 miles north of London AI (M) junction 4.
Take an exciting trip back to Elizabethan times by visiting The Old Palace for an authentic Banquet. Set in the Great Hall people enjoy a magnificent five course meal of royal proportions including red or white wine and mead. From the moment you take your seat you are under the spell of a troop of costumed minstrels and players. Singing songs from the period, performing some of the picturesque ceremonies and customs of the Elizabethan era, they move from table to table serenading you as you dine. The authentic setting, the cuisine, the atmosphere and spectacle combine to make this not just a feast of entertainment but an unforgettable experience too. The Banquets are held every Tues, Thurs, Fri and Sat evenings.

KNEBWORTH   KNEBWORTH HOUSE & GARDENS
Tel: 01438 812661
Location: entrance direct from Junction 7 of the AI (M) at Stevenage. Hours of fun can be had by all the family at the historic home of the Lytton family since 1490. The house contains many beautiful rooms, and magnificent paintings, fine furniture and objects d'art. As well as a visit to the historic house children can enjoy hours of fun at the giant Adventure Playground which includes a fort, suspension slide, bouncy castle and miniature railway, or a trip around the 250 acres of Parkland to see the herds of Red and Sika deer. Open daily 26th March-17th April and 28thy May-4th September. 11-5.30pm.

ROYSTON   WILLERS MILL WILD ANIMAL SANCTUARY
Tel: 01763 262226
Moulded out of a wilderness of nettles, rubbish, and an old deserted cottage, between the railway line and the village cricket pitch of Shepreth, Terry and Gill Willers have created a wonderful setting for their animal sanctuary. Here between a duck pond and in a totally enclosed environment, young children are able to come into direct contact with a variety of animals, often for the first time, and are able to touch and handle allspecies, much to their obvious enjoyment. It is a place for unwanted or injured animals to live in safety and to be well cared for, just as homes exist for unwanted cats and dogs. The animals come from a variety of sources, such as road, gun and gassing casualties, unwanted pets, research centres, zoos, safari parks and meat markets. Some even arrive by themselves! The majority of the animals have the run of the sanctuary and can indeed leave at any time if they wish to. However, some have to be kept in enclosures for their own protection as their injuries prevent them from leading a normal life. The more exotic species require special diets and a heated environment to keep them healthy. Willers Wildlife Park receives no form of government grant or other help. Entrance fees are its sole source of revenue so please do go and visit. OPEN; Summer 10am-6pm every day. Winter: 1st Nov-28th Feb 10-5pm every day. Closed Christmas Day.

ST ALBANS   BOWMANS OPEN FARM
Tel: 01462 424055.
Bowmans Farm is open daily throughout the year and provides both an

entertaining and educational day out for the whole family. It will allow you to see both the livestock and arable enterprises, see the herd of pedigree Freisian cows being milked every afternoon, see the new born piglets and calves, visit the pets corner and take a stroll around the lake to observe the nature and wildlife. Or why not visit the farm shop and restaurant and sample a wide selection of fresh vegetables, home-made yoghurt and award winning ice-cream. Open throughout the year 9-5.30pm.

STEVENAGE   STEVENAGE MUSEUM
Tel: 01438 354292.
When you step inside you enter another world. Fascinating collections of everyday objects tell the story of Stevenage from pre-history to the present. There are hundreds of objects for you to see including a 1950s living room, a perfect 1930s dolls house, gas masks, old farm tools and a Roman silver coin hoard. Open Mon-Sat 10-5pm. Free admission.

ROGER HARVEY GARDEN WORLD
Tel: 01438 814687.
A 400 year old complex of farm buildings has been converted into a Garden Centre. Seasonal displays of plants, bulbs and Christmas Wonderland decorations means that there is something special for everyone including tropical fish, children's adventure playground, pets corner, gift hall and houseplant conservatory. Open daily 9.30-5.30pm Admission free.

WELWYN GARDEN CITY   PANSHANGER GOLF COMPLEX
Tel: 01707 333350.
Set in some of Hertfordshire's most delightful countryside this offers one of the most popular 'Pay as you Play' courses in the country. The Herts Golf Academy offers men, women and children of all ages the opportunity to learn to play golf or improve their skills. The golf course offers a scenic and challenging eighteen hole par 72 golf course, nine hole pitch and putt, putting green and cafe open from 9am providing excellent refreshments. Open daily.

WHITEWELL   WATERHALL FARM & CRAFT CENTRE
Tel: 01438 871256.
Open all year round this farm and craft centre offers adults and children the opportunity to take a step back to nature to see how many farm animals live today. A wide range of quality gifts and souvenirs is always available from the craft shop includingantiques, bric-a-brac and pine furniture. A visit can also be made to the tea-room which serves a selection of light lunches, delicious cream teas and home-made cakes. Open Wed-Sun 10-5pm March-October and all Bank Holidays.

HUMBERSIDE

SCUNTHORPE   ELSHAM HALL COUNTRY PARK
Tel: 01652 688698.
Elsham Country Park was opened in 1970 by Captain and Mrs Elwes because they wanted visitors to enjoy the Park and appreciate wildlife, Rural Crafts and Arts. The award-winning facilities now include the Granary Restaurant and Tea-Rooms, the 'Haybarn Centre', the new Garden Centre; Monk's Wood Arboretun; Children's Animal Farm and Pets Corner. There are also many special events and Arts Exhibitions throughout the year. Why not take a look for yourself. Open Easter Sat- mid Sept 11-5pm and mid-Sept-Easter Sun 11-4pm. Closed Good Friday and Winter Bank Holidays.

LEICESTERSHIRE

ASHBY   THE FERRERS CENTRE FOR ARTS & CRAFTS
Tel: 01332 863337
Fourteen craft workshops around a magnificent Georgian courtyard. Skills include pottery, woodworking, handweaving, quilt making, automata making, china restoration and sign designs. The tea-room serves morning coffee, a variety of home-cooked lunches and cream teas. Open daily throughout the year 10.30-5pm in summer and 10.30-4.30pm in winter. Admission free.

CASTLE DONNINGTON   AEROPARK AND VISITOR CENTRE
Tel: 01332 810621
See the action from this 12 acre park next to the taxiway at the eastern end of the airport. Aircraft exhibitions in the Aeropark include a Lightning jet fighter, Vulcan bomber, Canberra bomber, Argosy freighter and Whirlwind helicopter. There is also a viewing mound, themed children's play area and picnic tables. Open Easter-October Mon-Fri 10-5pm Sat 11-4pm Sun 11-6pm.

COALVILLE   SNIBSTON DISCOVERY PARK
Tel: 01530 510851
Built on the 100 acre site of a former colliery, Snibston Discovery Park is Leicestershire's largest attraction where finding out is a great day out for everyone. The Exhibition Hall contains five galleries exploring the Industrial Heritage of Leicestershire including transport, engineering, extractive industries, textiles and fashion. Follow fashion through the ages, travel through time from 1600 until the present day or see what it was like for a miner in the mid 19th century. Open daily all year round from 10-6pm.

HINCKLEY   ASHBY CANAL
Tel: 01455 232789
The Ashby-de-la-Zouch Canal was a relative latecomer being completed in 1804 but had many of the attributes of the earliest navigations. It follows the contours of surrounding countryside and has no locks throughout its lengths. The Canal is

home to a wonderful variety of creatures and plants, including ducks, fish, dragonflies, waterlilies, kingfisher and many more. Open daily it is a great escape from the hustle and bustle of everyday life.

LEICESTER   THE JEWRY WALL & MUSEUM
Tel: 01533 473021
The Jewry Wall is the largest Roman Civil building to survive in Britain. It forms part of the Roman public baths, the foundations of which are also visible. The Museum houses a range of prehistoric, Roman, Anglo-Saxon and Medieval exhibits. Open Mon-Sat 10-5.30p, Sun 2-5pm.

GURU NANAK SIKH TEMPLE
Tel: 01533 628606
A former hosiery factory has been transformed into an impressive Gurdwara - Sikh Temple. Dramatic paintings and models allow you to see the history of Sikhism and the sacrifice and devotion of its followers. Open to visitors on Thursdays only.

WYGSTON'S HOUSE
Tel: 01533 473056
One of the oldest buildings in Leicester this 15th century dwelling was home to Roger Wygston, one of Leicester's famous wool merchants and benefactors. It now houses the Museum of Costume with displays of 18th century to 20th century fashions and reconstruction of 1920's shops. Open Mon-Sat 10-5.30pm Sunday 2-5.30pm.

THE GUILDHALL
Tel: 01533 532569
The Guildhall is within five minutes walk of the City Centre. From the Clock Tower, turn into East Gate, and turn left onto Silver St. The Guildhall is on Guildhall Lane, the continuation of Silver St. It is a unique Grade I listed building and has been the scene of many significant events in Leicester's history. The Building comprises the following rooms: THE GREAT HALL: The timber framed Great Hall is the original Guildhall of the Gild of Corpus Christi dating back to c1390 and evokes a wonderful sense of space and time. As well as direct promotions, the Hall, outside museum hours, is available for public hire. THE MAYOR'S PARLOUR; The ground floor of the West Wing c1490 contains the Mayor's Parlour, a smaller civic room, remodelled in 1563. The room is oak panelled with a beautifully carved and painted overmantle above the fireplace.
THE JURY ROOM; The west wing also contains The Jury Room, above the Mayor's Parlour and was originally the retiring room for the Jury after Quarter Sessions. It now houses the Library of the Leicestershire Archeological and Historical Society founded in 1855. The room is available as a study and meeting room and seats 30 people. THE LIBRARY; The upper floor of the East Wing houses the Town Library. The Library is the third oldest public library in the country and was established in 1632. THE POLICE STATION; Leicester's first police force was established in 1836 and is the third oldest in Great Britain. The Borough Police Force was based at the Guildhall, and originally had 3 cells. The Cells have 2 replica criminals based on real criminals of the Victorian period. THE RECORDER'S BEDROOM;

The office of Recorder was established in 1464 and the Recorder was required to visit the borough at least 4 times a year to preside over the Quarter Sessions. A bedroom was granted to the Recorder and it's fitting out is recorded in the Chamberlain's records for 1581-82. THE CONSTABLE'S HOUSE: The brick built house off the side of the courtyard was built in 1836 for Leicester's first Chief Constable and is now the administrative base of the Guildhall and will shortly be converted into a new exhibition hall.
GUIDED TOURS; Available on request. PUBLIC HIRE; Available for both community and commercial hire. PERFORMANCES AND CONCERTS; Magical atmosphere with its audience capacity of 100 people. SPECIAL EVENTS;Throughout the year. OPEN; Mon-Sat: 10am-5.30pm Sundays:2-5.30pm. Admission Free.

THE CATHEDRAL
Tel: 01533 625294
The Church of St Martin's was one of six parish churches recorded in Leicester in 1086. Extended in the 14th and 15th centuries and restored in the 19th century it was hallowed as the Cathedral of Leicester in 1927. Visitors are invited to tour the building and see its impressive roof, stained glass windows and stone and wood carvings. Inside the chancel is a memorial to King Richard III. Outside the graveyard has been laid out as a garden containing many interesting slate headstones. Open every day.

THE JAIN CENTRE
Tel: 01533 543091
A 19th century Congregational chapel was converted in the 1980's into a magnificent Jain Centre; the only one of its kind in the western world. The centre boasts a white marble frontage, 52 hand carved marble and stone pillars, hand carved ceilings and domes, mirror mosaic walls and stained glass windows. Visitors can view by appointment.

NEWARKE HOUSE MUSEUM
Tel: 01533 473222
The Museum of the Social History of Leicestershire is contained within two 16th century houses; the Chantry House of 1511 and Skeffington House 1570. The Museum contains displays and artefacts dating from 1500 to the present day and includes a 17th century panelled room with period furniture, a 19th century street scene and collections of toys and games. Open Mon-Sat 10-5.30pm.

CASTLE GARDENS & CASTLE MOTTE
This used to be a low-flying marshy area of reeds and willows. At the end of the 19th century the land was drained and used for allotments before being opened as public gardens in 1926. The Motte is a man-made mound built by Leicester's first Norman Lord in about 1070. It may originally have been several metres higher and would have had timber fortification on the top. The Motte is open to the public and in the gardens is the statue of Richard III which commemorates his links with Leicestershire. Garden open daily during daylight hours.

VISITOR ATTRACTIONS

ST MARY DE CASTRO
Tel: 10533 628727

St Mary's was founded in 1107 and is still in regular use. It has excellent examples of Norman work, especially the chancel, stained glass, stone and wood carving and interesting tombstones. Geoffrey Chaucer was probably married here and King Henry VI was knighted in the church in 1426. Open with guides on Sat & Bank Holiday afternoons from Easter to end of October.

RIVERSIDE PARK

This eight mile stretch of footpaths along the banks of the River Soar and Grand Union Canal passes through Castle Park and allows an insight into Leicester's early industrial history. The dominant Pex Building was originally a worsted spinning factory providing yarn for the knitting trade. Goods were brought to and from the City by the major waterway network. Flood alleviation work to the river in the late 19th century formed the 'Mile straight' on which rowing regattas are held annually. The line of the Great Central Railway has now been developed as a pedestrian walk and cycleway.

FARMWORLD
Stoughton Farm Park, Gartree Road, Leicester LE22FB.
Tel:01162 710355

This is an exciting day out for every age group. You will find it 3 miles SE of Leicester City Centre and 6 miles off the M1/M69 Junction 21. Follow the southerly ring road. Signposted 'Farm Park' from A6 and A47. It is a real working Dairy Farm with acres of Parkland for pleasure and play. There are Shire horses and cart rides, rare farm animals, lakeside and woodland walks, a picnic area, Toy Tractor park and indoor sandpit. A special Children's Farmyard and Playground. You are invited to the Milking Parlour to watch the herd being milked and to try your hand at operating a milking machine. The Craft workshops are fascinating and quite frequently there are demonstrations. Add to this lots of lovable pets, an Edwardian Ale House, Audio Visual Theatre and Exhibitions and displays featuring the countryside at work and it becomes very clear why Farmworld is so popular. In keeping with Leicester's innovative and go ahead thinking, Farmworld also offers a unique Conference venue. It is housed in beautifully restored and converted 18th century farm buildings and equipped with a wide range of modern facilities to provide for every business requirement. For further details please ring 01162 710355 or Fax: 01162 713211

FARMWORLD IS OPEN; Daily 10am-5.30pm (Winter 5pm) except December 25th &26th and January 1st. Dogs cannot be admitted. (Except Guide dogs) Disabled access. Gift Shop. Wheatsheaf Cafe.

LOUGHBOROUGH STONEHURST FAMILY FARM & MUSEUM
Tel: 01509 413216

All the family will enjoy visiting Priscilla Pig, Dink the Donkey and their friends on a walk around the farm. Small animals can be held and stroked in 'Cuddle Corner'. On the farm there is an old blacksmiths forge, also a Motor Museum with vintage cars, motorbikes and memorabilia. Open 10-5pm daily except Wed.

MARKET BOSWORTH TWYCROSS ZOO
Tel: 01827 880250
This is an ideal day out. There is a wide variety of animals including gorillas, chimps, orangutans, gibbons, elephants, lions and giraffes. There is also an adventure playground, pets corner and penguin pool. Open daily from 10-6pm all the year round.

OADBY FARM WORLD
Tel 01533 710355   A day in the country can provide a wonderful and exciting experience for children and adults so enter the fascinating world of farm life here and have fun. Shire horses and cartrides, rare farm animals, lakeside and woodland walks and a working dairy farm are all part of the fun. Open daily throughout the year 10-5.30pm summer and 10-5pm in the winter.

OAKHAM   RUTLAND FARM PARK
Tel: 01572 756789
In 18 acres of beautiful parkland Rutland Park Farm has a wonderful selection of farm animals, goats, poultry and wildfowl for the whole family to see. Apart from visiting the animals and old farm vehicles why not stroll through the countryside and look at the fern, bamboo and wildflower meadow. Open 3rd April-18th Sept 10-5pm.

RUTLAND WATER ANGLIAN WATER BIRD WATCHING CENTRE AND RUTLAND WATER NATURE RESERVE
Egleton, Oakham, Rutland, Leicestershire LE15 8BT
Tel: 01572 770651
Rutland Water has become one of the most importnt wildfowl sanctuaries in Great Britain, regularly holding in excess of 10,000 waterfowl of up to 28 species. It is a Site of Special Scientific Interest and has received recognition of itsinternational importance by the European Community and has been designated as a globally important wetland. It covers an area of 450 acres and the wide variety of habitats ensures that many species of birds are present throughout the year, but the reserve is best known for the thousands of wildfowl which flock to spend the winter on the lagoons and open water. Gadwall shoveler, teal, tufted duck, pochard and shelduck are present all year round; in winter they are joined by pintail, goldeneye, goosander, wigeon and other, rarer ducks, such as smew, red-breasted merganser and long-tailed duck. Rare grebes and divers are frequent visitors. In summer common terns and cormorants breed communally on the lagoons. During spring passage, little gulls, Arctic terns and black terns pass through, often in their hundreds, while rare Caspian and white-winged black terns have been recorded. Wader passage may bring up to 19 species in a single day. Birds of prey include breeding kestrel and sparrowhawk; osprey and harriers during migration; regular sightings of peregrine and merlin in winter; and spectaculr views of hobbies in summer as they feed on insects over the lagoons. Three lagoons and 9 miles of shore and open water are overlooked by a total of 17 hides. Other attractive wildlife habitats contain species rare elsewhere; wildflowers, butterflies and dragon flies. Old hay meadows, rough grassland, hedges, plantations and woodland invite wildlife and visitor alike. On both reserves, trails lead to the hides through all

these habitats. Car parking is provided free to reserve visitors at Egleton and Lyndon. There are toilets in both reserves. Disabled facilities at Egleton. Dogs not allowed at Egleton. At Lyndon they must be on a lead. Disabled visitors access is available at Egleton at the Anglian Birdwatching Centre and Shoveler hide and at Lyndon Centre using Teal and Swan hides.

LINCOLNSHIRE

GRANTHAM   BELVOIR CASTLE
Tel: 01476 870262
Location: Near Grantham signposted off A607. Home of the Duke and Duchess of Rutland, Belvoir Castle is superbly situated overlooking the Vale of Belvoir. The house has magnificent staterooms, containing notable pictures, tapestries and fine furniture. The Queen's Royal Lancers Museum is also situated within the Castle. Open April 1st -29th Sept. Tue, Thurs, Sat, Sun & Bank Holidays 11-5pm.

LINCOLN LINCOLN CATHEDRAL is one of the largest in England and has many attractive features including the magnificent open nave, St Hugh's Choir, the Angel Choir and beautiful stained glass windows including the 14th century 'Bishop's Eye'. The Chapter House Cloisters, Wren Library and Treasury are other interesting features and all visitors are invited to seek out the Lincoln importance... Services are held daily and there are generally guided tours and tower tours.

LINCOLN CASTLE is on the site of the original Roman fortress and the present castle dates back to 1068. Interesting architectural features include the keep known as the Lucy Tower, Cobb Hall which was the site of the public gallows, and the Observastory tower which offers tremendous views of the cathedral and city as a whole. The Victorian prison includes a unique prison chapel with separate pews like upright coffins. This building alsohouses an original version of the famous Magna Carta from 1215, and an exhibition interpreting the history of this document and its importance to modern freedoms and democracy. Guided tours and wall walks are available.

NORFOLK

AYLSHAM BLICKLING HALL
One and a half miles west of Aylsham on the B1354, signposted off the A140 Cromer Road. Tel: 01263 733084. One of the most spectacular Country Houses in East Anglia. 17th century red brick house, extensive colourful garden, surrounded by wonderful parkland and woodland. National Trust. Open: Easter to end October Tues/Wed/Fri/Sat/Sun & Bank Holiday Mondays 1-5pm. Closed Good Friday. Garden same as Hall and also open daily in July and August.

BURE VALLEY RAILWAY
Tel: 01263 733858.
Travel in style through 9 miles of beautiful Norfolk countryside as the Bure Valley Railway takes you from the historic market town of Aylsham to Wroxham. Regular services run most days from Easter to October. There is a unique Boat-train service that combines a trip on the train and a cruise on the Broads.

BANHAM   BANHAM ZOO
Tel: 01953 887771
A great day out in a zoo which has just celebrated its 25th year. Open daily from 10am except Christmas and Boxing Day.

HOLT NATURAL SURROUNDINGS,
Bayfield, Holt, Norfolk NR25 7JN
Tel: 01263 711091.
The full name of this beautiful and exciting place is 'The Natural Surroundings centre for Wildlife Gardening and Conservation. Opened in June 1989 you will find within the eight acres of ground a combination of natural and man-made habitats and gardens all designed to encourage our native wildlife. You are free to wander at will - there is no set route. Bayfield was mentioned in the Domesday Book and originally comprised a village of 24 houses. Now all that remains is a ruined Saxon church in which a service is held once a year and the private Elizabethan Bayfield Hall which was converted in the mid 18th century, Victorianised in 1880 and restored to its Georgian facade in 1947-1963. The lake is comparatively recent and has a tiled bottom whilst the river Glaven is tunnelled in the valley side. Natural Surroundings was set up as a wildlife garden design and consultancy service in 1987 but it soon became apparent that not only was specialist advice required, but also the seeds, plants, shrubs, trees and other items needed to create wildlife habitats in gardens and larger areas. Space was needed for the growing of plants and for illustrating habitat creation and management. Mr and Mrs Combe, the Bayfield estate owners, offered the ideal site here and the new Natural Surroundings Centre was born. Obviously the gardens and other man-made habitats are still young but already they are full of wildlife and it is hoped they will inspire you to 'have a go' at wildlife gardening. The site has the added bonus of several natural habitats which are managed purely for their wildlife value. The Show Garden illustrates some of the features for attracting wildlife that can be easily incorporated into any of an design. A

Pond is essential which is instantly accepted by a vast range animal life. You will see newts and many aquatic wet meadow plants which are quite rare but with a pond and a marsh garden you can grow some of these beautiful wildflowers - all native to Britain. The Flower Border is made up of a variety of cottage garden flowers, wild flowers and herbs all of which benefit wildlife, especially insects. The Shrub Bed has a variety of bird and insect attracting non-native species, while the Woodland Corner is made up of native trees and shrubs particularly suited to a small/medium garden. Surround the garden on two sides is a mature Wildlife Hedge with a mix of native species - Hawthorn, Field Maple, Dogwood, Blackthorn, Crab Apple and Hazel. All these components make a 'living' but also a usable garden. As you walk around you will find so much to see, please the eye and the nostril and at the same time learn so much about the wonders of our wildflowers and wildlife. There is everything from a Stumpary and Scrub Garden, Wildlife Hedge, two acre Woodland, Wildflower Meadow, Wildlife Pond to the gently flowing River Glaven which is a good example of an unpolluted lowland stream and it supports a wide range of species. It is one of the very few Norfolk streams that can still support a breeding population of Brown Trout. What is so wonderful about Natural Surroundings apart from its flowers, plants, shrubs is the wealth of flying insects - Dragonflies and Damselflies. Then there are our native butterfliesattracted by the wild flowers, shrubs and trees. Beautiful and colourful. An excellent way to spend a day. You will find Natural Surroundings on the B1156 Letheringsett to Blakeney road, off the A148. **OPEN**; Easter-September Tues-Sun 10am-5.30pm October-Easter Thurs-Sun 10-4pm. Always open on Bank Holidays

BRANCASTER   The National Trust's property at Brancaster includes four and a half miles of tidal foreshore comprising just under 2,200 acres of beach, sand dunes, marsh and saltings including Brancaster Staithe harbour and the site of the Roman shore fort of Branodunum. Most of the area is designated as a Grade I Site of Special Scientific Interest. The North Norfolk coast footpath runs through the Trust property. Guided walks from April-October. Meet at NT Information Centre, the Harbour, Brancaster Staithe. Toilets and Car parking. Walks 4 hours with 3 stops. Bring a picnic and wear Wellingtons (or remove footwear to cross shallow creeks at end of walk. Short walk of 2 hours with 2 stops. Wellingtons not essential.

BURGH ST MARGARET   THE VILLAGE,
Fleggburgh,Burgh St Margaret,
NR GT YARMOUTH
NR29 3AE Tel: 01493 369770.
Here is somewhere for the whole family at a sensible price. It is an idyllic sight to stumble upon on the A1064 between Acle and Caister.It is a quaint English village, the way we all imagine such a place should be. Here is the traditional village green with its pond surrounded by a sprinkling of houses and shops, school and chapel, an atmospheric old inn and an old-fashioned tea shoppe where you can stop for a refreshing drink or snack. For the younger visitors there is plenty of entertainment; the fairground, adventure play area, 2ft narrow gauge railway, the 97 year old gallopers, farm animals, not to mention entertainment throughout the day. There are three shows, in season, which offer as much fun for adults as

for children. In the school house the ever popular school show is an hilarious 25 minutes of comedy not to be missed by anyone. Inthe village hall Zodiac puppets perform an unusual show that includes living marionette puppetry. In the Regent Concert Hall, The Village's own 500 seat theatre, the Great Compton-Christie organ is played daily by the resident organist (in main season) which includes the showing of a silent film.
The Vintage Vehicle Barn houses an Austin 7, an original Reliant a 1934 Sunbeam Dawn 1627cc amongst others. There is a Motorcycle Barn and a great display of fire engines. Working steam is a focal point of The Village with up to 3 engines in steam daily (during main season). Christmas is a very special time in The Village. In the Regent Concert Hall there are regular seasonal concerts complete with traditional carols.Christmas concert meals before and after the concerts are very popular.Indeed the Village has several eating places.

CROMER   CARTING ACTION SPORTS,
The Avenue, Northrepps, Nr Cromer. Off A 149 opposite Aldis Service Station. Tel: 01931 111819.
If you are aged 12 and over and have ever wanted to be a Formula One or Rally Driver, Grass Carting can satisfy your ambitions. Its fast, fun and above all affordable. Whether you are a novice or an accomplished driver you are bound to gain both experience and pleasure from this sport. Wise to book in advance.

NORFOLK SHIRE HORSE CENTRE AND COUNTRYSIDE COLLECTION
West Runton Stables, West Runton.
Tel: 01263 837339.
See Heavy Horses bred, preserved and protected. Show Itinerary every day. Indoor Area for wet weather demonstrations. Museum of farm equipment and bygones. Picnic area, cafe. Open 10-5pm. Easter to end October. Closed Saturdays unless Bank Holiday weekends.

FELBRIGG HALL
2 miles south west of Cromer off B1436. Signposted off A148 and A140 at Roughton
Tel: 01263 837444.
17th century house built on site of an existing medieval Hall. Bequeathed to National Trust in 1969. 27 rooms to visit. Superb collection 18th century furniture, pictures, and an outstanding Library. Walled garden, Dovehouse, Woodlands, Park and Lake.Turret Tea Room. Park Restaurant and Shop.

BRESSINGHAM
2.5 miles west of Diss on A1066. Tel: 01379 88382.
See Alan Bloom's world famous Dell Garden. Adrian Bloom's 'Foggy Bottom' Garden, Bressingham Plant Centre, Historic locomotives. Three train rides. Victorian Steam Gallopers. Historic fire engines. Steam traction engines and wagons. Restaurant, shop, picnic and play areas.
Open April 1st-30th September. Tuesday-Sunday and Bank Holiday Mondays. Sundays only in October apart from School Half term. Phone for details of 'Gardeners' Days'.

VISITOR ATTRACTIONS

EARSHAM   THE OTTER TRUST
A unique wonderland of waterfowl, Otters, Night Herons and Muntjac Deer, on the banks of the River Waveney. The worlds largest collection of otters in natural enclosures where the British Otter is bred for re-introduction to the wild.
Open daily 1st April-31st October 10.30-6pm.

FAKENHAM   PENSTHORPE WILDLIFE CENTRE
One mile south-east of Fakenham, clearly signposted off the A1067 Norwich road.
Tel: 01328 851465.
In two hundred acres of beautiful reserve, Pensthorpe brings visitors and wildlife close together. Outside the visitor centre explore waterside walks and nature trails. There are excellent access facilities for the elderly and disabled, quiet picnic areas and plentiful seating. Courtyard Restaurant. Children's Adventure Playground, wildlife, brass rubbing centre and discovery areas.
Open 7 days a week (except Christmas Day) from mid-March to beginning of January. Weekends only January, February to mid-March. Dogs not allowed (Guide dogs excepted).

MILL FARM RARE BREEDS
Hindringham.
Tel: 01328 878560.
Over 50 breeds of rare and minority farm animals on display. Pets Corner. Nature Trail. Adventure Playground. Tea Rooms.
Open Tues-Sun 10-5pm Easter-September 30th.

THURSFORD
Thursford Green, Thursford.
Tel: 01328 878477.
Wonderful, exciting collection and constant live musical shows. Christmas is especially magical.
Open daily April-May-Sept-Oct 1pm-5pm. June-July-August 11am-5pm. Off the A148 Fakenham to Holt road.

GREAT YARMOUTH   THRIGBY HALL WILDLIFE GARDENS,
Filby.
Tel: 01493 369477.
6 miles from Norwich. A family outing with acres of marvellous grounds and many animals from Asia. Open every day of the year from 10am.

THE LIVING JUNGLE,
Central Sea Front, Marine Parade.
Tel: 01493 842202.
The Genesis Experience takes you back to the beginning before mankind, to give you an insight into what heaven must be like. You will see a lush tropical jungle garden, butterflies, birds and fish. You will hear the sound of the garden's creatures and the gentle trickle of warm waters.
Open daily March to end October 10am.

NORFOLK RARE BREED CENTRE AND FARM MUSEUM,
Decoy Farm House, Ormesby St Michael.
Tel 01493 732990.
14 breeds of sheep, 9 rare breeds of cattle and all 9 rare breeds of pigs plus 70 varieties of poultry. Shire Horse and Clydesdales, Shetlands, donkeys and goats. Picnic on the 17 acre site. Parking is free. Open daily 11-5pm Good Friday until end of September and Sundays all year. Closed Saturdays.

STRUMPSHAW OLD HALL STEAM MUSEUM
AND FARM MACHINERY COLLECTION.
Follow brown tourist signs, off A47 between Gt Yarmouth and Norwich.
Tel: Norwich 712339.
Beam Engines, Mechanical Organs, Narrow Gauge Railway, Steam Rally, Working Toy Train layout for children. 10,000 sq ft filled with Steam Engines and working Beam Engines. Picnic in park. Free Parking. Open: Easter, Spring Bank Holiday weekend, 14th July-2nd October 11-4pm everyday except Saturday.

GRESSENHALL
NORFOLK RURAL LIFE MUSEUM AND UNION FARM.
Union Farm is a working 1920's farm with rare breeds of horses, sheep, cattle, pigs and poultry. There is a nature trail. The Museum is housed in an imposing 18th century workhouse, has thousands of exhibits. Tea Room. Gressenhall is 2 miles from East Dereham on the B1146. Open Easter-30th October. Tues-Sat 10-5pm. Sun 12-5.30pm Bank Holiday Mondays 10-5pm.

HEACHAM   NORFOLK LAVENDER,
Caley Mill.
Tel: 01485 70384.
England's working Lavender Farm and the home of the National Collection of Lavenders. Excellent cream teas and home-made cakes. Shops selling lavender products + plants and herbs, gifts. Free Admission and Car Parking. Open daily 10-5pm (Closed for 2 weeks at Christmas). On A149 3 miles south of Hunstanton. Guided tours from end of May to end of September.

KINGS LYNN   CAITHNESS CRYSTAL
Paxman Road, (off Hansa Road) Hardwick
Industrial Estate, King's Lynn PE30 4NE Tel: 01553 765111
The A47 Bypass comes to a big roundabout and here you turn onto the A149 Hardwick Road and shortly afterwards the right handturn will take you into Hansa Road and so to Caithness Crystal. This is one of the friendliest and most welcoming places in Norfolk. Everyone in the company looks forward to welcoming you to the Visitor Centre and the factory. It is an enthralling experience in which you are invited to go on a self-conducted tour to watch the centuries old craft of glass blowing at close quarters. When you see exquisite pieces of glass taking shape before your eyes, it is with an awesome sense of inadequacy that one acknowledges that the art of the craftsmen is way beyond ones own abilities. Having watched the Glassmakers at work then it is time to visit the Factory Shop which sells an extensive selection of giftware, glass animals,

tableware and paperweights, all factory seconds and discontinued line, with superb bargains all year. If you have Christmas shopping in mind then there is an annual blockbusting sale in November and December - well worth a visit. Having chosen a piece it may be possible to get the Resident Glass Engraver to engrave your purchase, if she has time. You will certainly be able to watch her delicate art as she works in wording and pictures on an extensive range of glassware for all occasions. The Restaurant which seats 70 comfortably, may well be your next stop. Here you will find a wide selection of light refreshments and lunches. Try the home-made fruit pies which are a house speciality.
OPEN: All Year 6 days a week (also Sundays Easter to Christmas) Open Bank Holidays. Factory Shop Mon-Sat 9-5pm. Sundays (Easter to Christmas) 11-4.30pm Glassmaking demonstration Mon-Fri 9.15-4.00pm throughout the year. Also Saturdays and Sundays (end of May to mid Sept) 11-4pm.

THE OLD GAOL HOUSE,
Saturday Market Place.
Tel: 01553 763044.
Let your imagination run riot as your personal stereo guide takes you through King's Lynn 1930's Police Station and into the cells beyond. Open daily Easter and Spring Bank Holiday until the end of September 10-5pm. Closed Wednesdays and Thursdays October-Easter.

BIRCHAM WINDMILL
6 miles from Sandringham. Tel: 01485 23393
Bakery, Tea Rooms, Cycle Hire, Free Parking. Open daily Easter-30th September 10-6pm (Tea Rooms and Bakery closed Saturdays).

ENGLISH HERITAGE IN NORFOLK
Tel: 01604 730320.
Climb the steep flights of stone stairs inside the Keep of the aptly named Castle Rising Castle. Look down into the shell of the Great Hall and imagine medieval festivities when the castle played host to a succession of English Kings. Castle Rising lies north east of King's Lynn from where it is a short journey to the tranquil setting of Castle Acre Priory. Open: 1st April-31st October daily 10-6pm Sept 1st-31st March, Wed-Sun 10-4pm. Closed 24-26 Dec and Jan 1st. Small admission charge.

LANGHAM   LANGHAM HAND-MADE CRYSTAL,
The Long Barn, North Street, Nr Holt
Tel: 01328 830511.
Glassmaking Mon-Fri Nov-March. Sun-Friday April-October 10-5pm. Free parking. Live Glass Making Museum. Adventure Playground. Restaurant/Cafe.

HOLT   LETHERINGSETT WATERMILL,
Riverside Road, Letheringsett, Holt NR25 7YD
Tel: 01263 713153.
Voted the top tourist attraction in North Norfolk for four years consecutively in the nineties, this is a fascinating place to visit. It is a step back in time and

somewhere that both delights and amazes. It is a fully water powered Flour Mill generally accepted to be the onlyproducing one in Norfolk. You are invited to visit this outstanding part of working Norfolk history. The Norfolk red brick Mill was built in 1802 on a Doomsday site but in the early part of this century it began to fall into disrepair until 1982 when restoration work was started. The miller and his staff would like to welcome you to see their skills of making flour using this traditional method on their demonstration days which are normally between 2-4.30pm on Tuesday, Wednesday, Thursday and Friday also on Bank Holiday Sundays and Mondays from 2-4.30pm, or whenever flour is required. During the demonstration the miller gives an informative and often humourous running commentary. At other times you are more than welcome to visit even if it is standing idle. You will no doubt have a lot of questions to ask which are readily answered by the staff who are keen to share their interest, knowledge and enthusiasm with you. Before you leave do visit the shop where you can purchase flour or the Gift Shop which is full of attractive and tempting goods. Eager Ducks patrol the property outside always on the look out for food; they seem to have an insatiable appetite! You will find the pretty village of Letheringsett just off the A148 Cromer to Fakenham Road. OPEN; Tuesday-Saturday 9-1pm & 2-5pm. Tues, Weds, Thurs, Fri Demonstrations 2pm-4.30pm. Also open Bank Holiday Sundays and Mondays. Sundays school summer holidays only. There is an excellent small book available for purchase which tells you all about the history of the watermill which was mentioned in the Domesday Book.

VISITOR ATTRACTIONS

LONG STRATTON   GREENACRES FARM,
Woodgreen, Long Stratton, Norwich NR15 2RR
Tel: 01508 530261.
This 17th-century farmhouse is full of character with exposed beams, an inglenook fireplace and the atmosphere that only comes about for tworeasons, firstly age and secondly the happiness that has permeated the lives of all who have lived here. Joanna Douglas who owns and runs Greenacres ensures that all her guests feel welcome and comfortable, and there is no doubt that they will be well fed. Breakfast is a truly English meal although lighter breakfasts are available and in the evening Joanna cooks homely, two course farmhouse meals in which she always uses fresh produce. There are 2 double and 1 twin bedded room, both ensuite with tea/coffee making facilities and TV. The attractive sittingroom has colour TV. There is a snooker room and an all weather tennis court. A Car is essential if you are to enjoy the neighbourhood. Greenacres is situated on the edge of a 30 acre common with ponds and ancient woods. It is just one and a half miles from Long Stratton with its variety of shops, public houses, sports centre. Golfing, riding, fishing, swimming facilities are nearby. The fascinating cathedral City of Norwich is easily reached and there is no difficulty in taking in The Broads and the coast or going in the other direction to find Suffolk and Constable country. OPEN; All year. No credit cards. Large Garden. No access for Disabled. Not licensed. Pets welcome. 3 ensuite rooms. Children welcome.

LONG SUTTON   BUTTERFLY AND FALCONRY PARK
signposted off A17 Kings Lynn-Seaford road.
Tel: 01406 363833
Stroll through one of the largest tropical Butterfly Houses in Britain. A wealth of tropical, Mediterranean and temperate flowers and foliage set around ponds, streams and waterfalls adds to the enjoyment. A small insectarium contains scorpions, tarantulas and giant stick insects all safely housed behind glass. In the Falconry Centre watch the stunning flying displays. Tea Room and Tea Garden. Adventure playground. Animal Centre & Nature trail. Mouse house. Picnic area. Open mid-March-October 31st daily 10-6pm Sept & Oct 10-5pm.

NORWICH   THE MUSTARD SHOP
3 Bridewell Alley Tel: 01603 627889
Trace the history of Colman's Mustard over 150 years. Buy a sample of the extensive range of mustards or browse through the kitchen ware and other items in the shop. Open: Mon-Sat 9.30-5pm. Closed all day Sunday and Bank Holidays.

KENNINGHALL THE POTTERY,
Church Street, Kenninghall, NR16 2EN
Tel: 01953 888476.
Kenninghall is a delightful conservation village with a lovely old market place. The Pottery is in quaint Church Street. Built in 1807 it was formerly the Particular Baptist Chapel which accounts for the name of the Pottery. It is both the workshop and the home of potter, **David Walters** and his family. In addition it provides a superb gallery environment for the work of many of East Anglia's finest crafts people. In creating a home, some changes were inevitable but the result is exciting. David works exclusively in Porcelain, creating hand-thrown bowls of all sizes, as well as large platters, vases and urns. OPEN: Tuesday to Saturday 9am-5pm. Also Bank Holiday Weekends. If the family are there on Sundays, they are usually open. Please ring first to be sure or take pot luck! Off street parking. Disabled access. Affordable workshop prices. Visa, Access and American Express welcome. Children should be accompanied by an adult.

REDWING HORSE SANCTUARY
Hill Top Farm, Hall Lane, Frettenham
Tel: 01603 737432
6 miles out of Norwich on the North Walsham Road (B1150) Founded in 1984 to provide a caring and permanent home for horses, ponies, donkeys and mules, rescued from neglect and slaughter. Visitors are welcome every Sunday and Bank Holiday Mondays from 1-5pm from Easter-mid December. Also open every Monday afternoon from 1-5pm during July and August.

THE FAIRHAVEN GARDEN TRUST
Woodland and Water Garden, South Walsham
Tel: 01603 270449
9 miles north east of Norwich on B1140. Delightful natural woodland and water gardens set in the heart of Broadland. Enjoy the Rhododendrons, Primulas, Azaleas Giant Lilies, rare Shrubs and plants, Native Wild Flowers and the 900 year old King Oak. 'The Lady Beatrice' a vintage style river boat runs trips every half hour from within the gardens on all open days. Open: 11-6pm weekdays and Sundays 2-6pm. Saturdays 2-6pm. Easter week daily. Wednesday-Sundays and Bank Holidays from May-September.

NORFOLK WILDLIFE CENTRE & COUNTRY PARK
Gt Witchingham. On A1067
Europe's mammals and waterfowl in 40 acres beautiful parkland. Rare and unusual trees and flowering shrubs. Command and Adventure Play area. Woodland Steam Railway. No dogs. Open daily April 1st-31st October.

VISITOR ATTRACTIONS

CASTLE MUSEUM houses one of the country's finest regional collections of natural history, archaeology and art. Busy programme of temporary exhibitions and free talks, tours and activities for all the family. Open: Mon-Sat 10-5pm Sun 2-5pm.

NORWICH & BROADS CRUISES
Southern River Steamers from Elm Hill Quay and Foundry Bridge Quay.
Tel: 01603 624051.
Enjoy a cruise to Surlingham Broad through historic Norwich. Either cruise to Surlingham Broad via Brundall or take a trip under Norwich Bridges, daily throughout the season. Ring for times.

OXBROUGH   OXBURGH HALL,
7 miles south west of Swaffham on the Stoke Ferry Road. Signposted from Swaffham and A134. A moated house, built in 1482 by the Bedingfield family. Its rooms show the development from medieval austerity to Victorian comfort. Massive Tudor Gatehouse. The chapel in the grounds is open to the public and contains a magnificent altarpiece. Beautiful and colourful garden, an orchard, a Victorian wilderness garden and a charming woodland walk. Shop and Restaurant. Open: Easter-Sat-Wed 1-5pm Bank Holiday Monday Monday 11-5pm. Garden: Easter - 30th October Sat-Wed 12-5.30pm. Dogs only in the car park.

SANDRINGHAM SANDRINGHAM HOUSE, GARDENS AND MUSEUM
Tel: 01553 772675
The private country retreat of Her Majesty the Queen is at the heart of the beautiful estate which has been owned by four generations of Monarchs. All the main rooms used by the Royal Family are open to the public. The Museum contains fascinating displays of Royal memorabilia ranging from photographs to vintage Daimlers and an exhibition of the Sandringham Fire Brigade. Sandringham Country Park is open daily all year 10.30-5pm. House, Grounds and Museum open daily from Good Friday until the beginning of October with certain exceptions. Grounds 10.30-5pm House and Museum 11-4.45pm. Dogs except Guide Dogs not permitted in Grounds. Sandringham Visitor Centre open daily Easter to end of October.

SHERINGHAM NORTH NORFOLK RAILWAY
The Station
Tel: 01263 822045
Runs regularly from Sheringham to Holt. Climb aboard for an historical ride back in time and relive memories of a bygone age. Ring for details.

SNETTISHAM   SNETTISHAM PARK FARM
Nr. King's Lynn off A149 in Snettisham.
Tel: 01485 542425
Deer safari. Sheep centre. Giant Adventure Playground. Horse and Pony rides. Childrens Farmyard. Tea Room. Theatre and Information Room. Free Parking.

WELLS-NEXT-THE SEA HOLKHAM HALL
Tel: 01328 710227.
One of Britain's most majestic stately homes, situated in a deer park. This classic

18th century Palladian style mansion is a living treasure house of artistic and architectural history. Apart from a tour of this stunning house with its superb alabaster entrance hall, there are Bygones Museum, Pottery, 18th century Walled Garden. Deer Park & Lake and a sandy beach. Open daily (except Fridays and Saturdays) from the beginning of June to end of September 1.30-5pm, also Easter, May, Spring and Summer Bank Holiday Sundays and Mondays 11.30-5pm.

WALSINGHAM AND WELLS LIGHT RAILWAY
Tel: 01328 856506.
Visit the longest 10 1/4 inch narrow gauge steam railway in the world. See the unique Garratt Locomotive 'Norfolk Hero' which was specially built for the four mile journey between the seasidetown of Wells and the pilgrimage town of Walsingham. Open daily from Easter - 30th September. Free parking. Follow the Brown Tourist signs on the A149 coast road.

WEYBOURNE   THE MUCKLEBURGH COLLECTION
Weybourne Military Camp.
Tel: 0126 370210
On the coast road A149 between Sheringham and Blakeney. Exciting collection. Britain's largest private Military Collection 1759-1991. Whatever the weather this is a great day out. All the exhibitions are under cover. Open: Easter- end of October 10am-5pm

WROXHAM   NORFOLK DRIED FLOWER CENTRE
Willow Farm, Cangate, Neatishead.
Tel: 01603 783588
A dazzling display of dozens of varieties and colours. Flower arranging classes and demonstrations. Free admission and parking. Two miles east of Wroxham just off the A1151 and follow the Brown Tourist signs on the A149 coast road.

WROXHAM BARNS
Tunstead Road off B1354.
Tel: 01603 783762
Discover the finest rural centre of craftsmanship in East Anglia. See resident craftsmen at work producing original and exclusive gifts. Enjoy browsing in the Gallery Craft Shop, offering unusual gifts and stylish clothing. Junior Farm is a farmyard full of friendly animals sure to delight children and adults. Open: 7 days a week all year round. Parking and admission is free except to the Junior Farm.

BROADS TOURS
The Bridge
Tel: 01603 782207
Enjoy a relaxing trip on the Norfolk Broads on luxurious passenger boats. Ring for details.

VISITOR ATTRACTIONS

NORTHAMPTONSHIRE

NORTHAMPTON FLAMINGO GARDENS & ZOOLOGICAL PARK
Tel: 01234 711451

This has been built over the last three decades by its owner, Mr Christopher Marler, into one of the finest bird collections in the country. In lovely natural surroundings thegardens are situated in the peaceful stone village of Weston Underwood, one mile from the market town of Olney. The flowers and blossom in the spring and autumn make the gardens an attractive alternative to the avian beauty; but the breathtaking colour of the Flamingos must surely make a lasting impression on the visitor. Open: Good Friday & Bank Holiday Mondays, Sat,Sun,Wed & Thurs until end of June. Every day except Mondays in July & August. Opening hours 2-7pm.

ST GILES
CHILTERN OPEN AR MUSEUM
Tel: 01494 871117

Many wonderful aircraft to be seen which would otherwise have been destroyed. These have been re-erected in 45 acres of countryside. The buildings illustrate everyday life and work of planes in the Chiltern region. Open 2-6pm 1st April-31st October.

OXFORDSHIRE

BANBURY   EDGEHILL COUNTRY PARK,
Turnpike Cottage, Warmington
Tel: 01295 690528

This is an unspoilt little corner of Middle England. The spring on the site drains into the valley and via the Cherwell to the Thames and the English Channel. The spring in the next field drains into the Avon and out through the Severn to the Atlantic Ocean. The B4086 which runs past the gate was part of the Jurassic way, which stretched from Bath to the Humber in iron age times. The Iron Age Nadbury camp is just 100 metres away. After the Norman Conquest the land was owned by French monks who developed the wool trade with France. Cavaliers camped here the night before the Battle of Edgehill. It is easy to imagine them watering their horses at the ponds before going off to battle. More recently drovers brought Welsh cattle by here on their long walk from the mountains of North Wales to London.From the parking area at the top of the site, which is on Jurassic ironstone, the site tumbles over the Edgehill escarpment through a remnant of ancient Broadleaved woodland. A spring line emerges below the woodland, feeding ponds and watering the ancient meadowland which overlies Warwickshire clay. Because these meadows have never been farmed using modern farming methods they are rich in herbs and wild flowers. These in turn support a wide range of butterflies and moths. Within the woodland area sympathetic replanting is maintaining the diversity of trees and shrubs that are native to this area including Wild Cherry, and the Midland Thorn. It cannot be guaranteed that visitors will see all the wild creatures that make this site their home. However, the evidence of rabbits and badgers is quite clear. Ask and you will be shown their tracks. Muntjack deer are often found grazing the site at dawn and dusk but are shy and hide up when the park is busy. The woodland and hedges provide homes for a wide variety of birds and the woodpeckers can often be heard creating new homes in the spring! The ponds abound with insect life, in the early summer they are home to damsel and dragonflies. OPEN; Weekends + Bank Holidays from 11am. Strictly no dogs. Group bookings 01295 690704. Ample Parking. Picnic areas. Adventure play equipment. Toilets. Shop. Special Family Ticket (2 adults and up to 4 children) £5

BURFORD COTSWOLD WILDLIFE PARK
Burford OX18 4JW
Tel: 01993 823006

On 27th March 1970 the Cotswold Wildlife Park opened its gates to the public for the first time and since that date many thousands of visitors have been to the Park, many of them returning time and time again. Twenty five years on the original concept of the Park remains unchanged, the animals are still the main attraction and their care and well-being the top priority for their keepers. The Park is set in approximately 50 hectares of gardens and parkland around an old English Manor House and the collection includes mammals, birds, reptiles, fish and invertebrates from all over the world in spacious and landscaped enclosures which take full advantage of the beautiful rural setting. In the Manor House itself the old dining-room is now a brass-rubbing centre and the drawing-room is used for meetings and lectures. One area of the Park which is extremely popular with visitors is the Walled Garden. This was originally the large kitchen garden where fruit and vegetables were grown for the family at the Manor. The garden is surrounded by high walls and these give valuable protection from the winds to the many delicate tropical mammals and birds exhibited there. Within the Walled Garden particular attention is given to a complementary blend of animal and plant exhibits. The flower beds are replanted every spring and summer and the many trees and shrubs include some of the old apple trees from the original garden. This is also a charming area in which to sit and rest, and seating is provided for this purpose. Within the Walled Garden is the Tropical House. The first tropical house at the Park utilised the the original glasshouse, which was in fact one of the oldest in Oxfordshire but as time went by and the number of visitors to the Park increased, it became necessary to replace this. In 1981 the present house was designed and this is now a most attractive and ever-changing exhibit of luxuriant foliage and flowers with tropical birds flitting through the leaves alongside the rhinoceros iguana and a number of fish. Visitors wander through the Park at their leisure, taking time to stop and observe those animals which interest them most. It may be the massive white rhinos (three of the original residents) which can sometimes be seen running from one end of their five-acre enclosure to the other in the company of the Chapman's zebras: or the dainty, inquisitive meerkats, sunbathing under their heat lamp on dull days, or the shy, rare red panda from the Himalayas. There are many animals, too numerous to mention, but they include monkeys, lemurs, ostriches, emus, rheas, penguins, waterfowl, flamingoes, cranes, Bengal tigers, leopards, birds of prey and a fine collection of owls. During the twenty five years that the Park has been open to the public facilities have continued to improve to give visitors an enjoyable and trouble-free day out. There are landscaped picnic areas, a large cafeteria and bar, toilet facilities, including a purpose built toilet block for the disabled and plenty of free parking. The narrow-gauge railway is operational from April to October inclusive and youngsters enjoy being able to have close contact with the animals in the farmyard area and also the Adventure Playground. Birds of prey demonstrations take place during the summer months as well as Snake Days and car rallies. The Park is easily accessible on the A361, two miles south of its junction with the A40. It is about 22 miles east of Cheltenham, 20 miles west of Oxford and 18 miles north of Swindon. It is also within easy reach of Stratford and the many lovely old towns in the Cotswolds. The Park is open daily throughout the year, except for Christmas Day, from 10am. Last admissions are 6pm or dusk, which ever is the earlier. Group rates are available and there are special rates for school parties and parties of disabled.

OXFORD
THE OXFORD STORY
6 Broad Street
Tel: 01865 790055
Created by Oxford University and the people behind York's 'Jorvik' Viking Centre, this is an extraordinary exhibition about Oxford's 800 years past. Now recognised as the best short introduction to Oxford. The Oxford Story uses a ride through the streets from the past, from medieval Oxford to Inspector Morse Magnus Magnusson or Timothy Mallett (for children) provide the commentary.
Open: April-October 9.30-5pm. July-August 9.30-7pm. Nov-March 10-4pm. Closed Christmas Day.

WITNEY
COGGES MANOR FARM MUSEUM
Church Lane.
Tel: 01993 772602
A working museum of Victorian rural Life on a 20 acre site, close to Witney town centre. The historic site includes the manor house with room displays, walled garden, orchard, riverside walks, farm buildings housing traditional breeds of animals, exhibitions in the barns, daily demonstrations of cooking on the kitchen range and special weekends and activities. Buttery serving light lunches and teas, gift shop and car park. Open: April-end October, Tues-Friday abd Bank Holiday Mondays 10.30-5.30pm. Saturday and Sunday 12 noon- 5.30pm.

WOODSTOCK   BLENHEIM PALACE
Tel: 01993 811091
Home of the 11th Duke of Marlborough, birthplace of Sir Winston Churchill. A visit to Blenheim is a wonderful way to spend a day. An inclusive ticket covers the Palace tour, park and Gardens, Butterfly House, Motor Launch, Train, Adventure Play Area and Nature trail. Optional are the Marlborough Maze and Rowing Boat hire on Queen Pool. Car parking is free for Palace visitors. Shops, Cafeterias and Restaurant. Special events include the Blenheim Audi International Horse Trials. Mid- March- 31st October daily 10.30-5.30pm.

HOTELS, INNS, RESTAURANTS AND COUNTRY HOUSES

SHROPSHIRE

BRIDGNORTH RAYS COUNTRY PARK
Tel: 01299 841255.
Enjoy a warm welcome at this farm set in the heart of unspoilt Shropshire countryside and spend a relaxing day delighting in the many varieties of animals at this traditional English farm A great selection of unusual animals include Martha, the famous pot-bellied pig and Sebastian the Llama, along with Rufus the Red Deer Stag, or why not take a stroll around the farm and look at the many attractions, or take a woodland walk strolling along the well marked paths past many different varieties of trees, shrubs and wild flowers. Open every day 10-6pm.

ONBRIDGE JACKFIELD THE MUSEUM
Tel: 01952 433522
One of the several museum sites within the famous Ironbridge Gorge which no one should miss. . Within the Gorge you will find hours of pleasure and fascinating features to absorb. Jackfield the Museum was a world centre of the decorative tile industry. The museum houses an impressive collection of wall and floor tiles ranging from the Victorian era, through the art deco periods, to a range of attractive silk-screened designs from the 1950s. Open daily all year round.

IRONBRIDGE TOY MUSEUM
Tel: 01952 433926
Overflowing with toys, games and childhood memorabilia from magic lanterns to Bayko building sets, clockwork trains to Rupert Bear can all be seen at this wonderful museum. See how toys reflect our lifestyle from houses, cars, fashion and TV culture. Also visit the well-stocked shop selling high quality traditional toys, collectors' models, dolls and teddies, children's books and greeting cards. Open daily from 10am.

IRONBRIDGE
Tel: 01952 433522
This is one of Britain's 11 World Heritage Sites, where the modern world began over 250 years ago. This was the birthplace of the Industrial Revolution, and here were made the first iron railing the first iron wheels and even the first high pressure steam locomotive. Today the Ironbridge Gorge Museum shows 20th century visitors how and why these events took place and how people lived during those momentous years. Open daily through the year 10-5pm.

MUCH WENLOCK   MUCH WENLOCK MUSEUM
Tel: 01952 727773
Interesting local museum, housed in former market hall. It contains new displays on the geology and natural history of Wenlock Edge, local history, exhibits including the Wenlock Olympics and information about Wenlock Priory. Open Apr-Sept Mon-Sat.

VISITOR ATTRACTIONS

WENLOCK PRIORY
Tel: 01952 727466

Much Wenlock is a picturesque market town lying between Wenlock Edge and the Ironbridge Gorge in some of the most attractive countryside in Shropshire. Set amongst smooth lawns and ornamental topiary, are the magnificentremains of Wenlock Priory. A prosperous and powerful monastery in its time and a place of pilgrimage, Wenlock is an inspiring place to visit. There is plenty to explore and the Priory church still dominates the scene. The Norman Chapter House has some superb decorative arcading and you can also see the remains of the Cloister, once the bustling hub of daily life. Open daily 1st April-31st October 10-6pm 1st November-31st March Sun & Wed 10-4pm

BENTHALL HALL
Tel: 01952 882159

An attractive mullion-windowed stone house with an impressive carved oak staircase and elaborate plaster ceiling. Family collections of furniture, ceramics and paintings are on display with a carefully restored plantsman's garden to visit at the rear of the house. Open Apr-Sept Wed, Sun and Bank Holidays 1.30-5.30pm.

WESTON PARK
Tel 01952 76207

This wonderfully and elaborately designed 17th century house contains a wealth of period furniture and art treasures collected by the Bradford family over the centuries. The formal gardens have been restored and the parkland designed by 'Capability' Brown. Apart from strolling around the house, take a trip to the adventure playground, pets corner and museum. Open Apr-Sept.

THE AEROSPACE MUSEUM
Tel: 01902 374112

Locaton: On A41 just one mile from junction 3 on the M54.

One of the largest aviation collections in the UK with over 70 aircraft on display, including many unique examples, together with missiles, engines, uniforms and aviation memorabilia.
Open all year round.

SEVERN VALLEY COUNTRY PARK
Tel: 01746 781192.

The Severn Valley Country Park which covers both banks of the Severn near Highley and Alveley, about six miles south of Bridgnorth, contains some of the finest scenery in the Severn Valley. There is a visitors centre with education, display and information facilities as well as a car park. Open daily throughout the year.

WYRE FOREST
Tel: 01299 266302

This magnificent 6000 acre forest nature reserve is home to a variety of wildlife, including deer, butterflies and wild flowers. A visitor centre includes forest information, exhibitions and a shop and cafe. Explore the forest on a range of way-marked paths, including a special wheelchair route. Open daily all year round. Visitor Centre open 11-4pm.

CHURCH STRETTON   ACTON SCOTT WORKING FARM
Tel: 01694 781306.

A visit to Acton Scott will enable visitors to experience life on an upland farm at the turn of the century. The waggoner and his team of shire horses work the land with vintage farm machines.

Daily demonstrations of rural crafts complete the picture of estate life 100 years ago. There are weekly visits from the wheelwright, farrier and blacksmith and children will love the cows, pigs, poultry and sheep in the farmyard and fields. Open 29th Mar-3oth Oct Tues-Sat 10-5pm Sun and Bank Holidays 10-6pm.

MARKET DRAYTON   HODNET HALL GARDENS
Tel: 01630 685202

Over 60 acres of brilliantly coloured flowers, magnificent forest trees, sweeping lawns and a chain of ornamental pools which runtranquilly along the cultivated garden valley to provide a natural habitat for waterfowl and other wildlife are just some of the many attractions on offer. No matter what the season, visitors will always find something fresh and interesting to ensure a full and enjoyable days outing. Open from 1st April-end September Mon-Sat 2-5pm. Sun & Bank Holidays 12-5.30pm.

KIDDERMINSTER   WYRE FOREST NATURE RESERVE
Tel: 01562 827800

The Wyre Forest Area offers many excellent examples of nature and man-made habitats for everyone to enjoy. Whether you want to picnic with the family, take a gentle stroll or enjoy a nature ramble, there are plenty of locations to visit including the Springfield Nature Reserve which is an important habitat for many species of plants and wildlife.

Or why not visit Burlish Top Heathland Nature Reserve which gives you an excellent opportunity to enjoy a habitat which is now scarce both nationally and internationally. Open daily throughout the year.

SHREWSBURY ATTINGHAM PARK
Tel: 01743 709203.

Attingham Park is one of the finest houses in the country, set in its own grounds of 250 acres, and offers the whole family a wealth of things to see and do. Explore the landscaped park, take a gentle stroll by the river or through the woods, discover the estate history at the Bothy exhibition, enjoy the elegant house and its beautiful furnishings, learn about the Berwick family and end your visit with home-made refreshments in the tea-room or purchasing a gift or souvenir from the shop. The Park and House are open throughout the year from the end of March until the end of September. 1.30-5pm, last admission 4.30pm.

HAUGHMOND ABBEY
Tel: 01743 709661.

Just three miles north-east of Shrewsbury stand the evocative ruins of this 12th century abbey. A flourishing religious community in the reign of Henry II, the abbey was dissolved under Henry VIII.

The church was demolished and the abbots lodging, Great Hall and kitchens were converted into a private house. Indeed, the first impression given by the grey stone tiles, with their large and airy bay windows is of a gracious country house. A peaceful place, it is amongst pleasant wooded countryside. Open 1st April-30th September Wed & Sun 10-6pm.

BUILDWAS ABBEY
Tel:01952 433274
Founded in the 12th century Buildwas Abbey was largely untouched by the great events of history though periodically attacked by raiders from across the Welsh border. Its simple, sturdy buildings give a powerful impression of both grandeur and the austerity of monastic life, with its fine vaulted roof and unusual medieval floor tiles, depicting birds and animals. Open 1st April-30th September 10-6pm daily.

WROXETER ROMAN CITY
Tel: 01743 761330
To visit Wroxeter today is to step back in time to the heyday of Roman Britain. The centrepiece is the remains of the extensive bath complex, one of the best preserved in England. The enormous hill which divided the baths from the exercise area still stands, and whilst walking around you can recreate the everyday activities of the thriving Roman City.
Open; April 1st - 31st October 10-6pm.

TELFORD   BOSCOBEL HOUSE
Tel: 01902 850244.
A visit to Boscobel House will take you to the scene of one of the most romantic stories in English history. King Charles II sought refuge in an oak tree at Boscobel House when he was chased by Cromwell's soldiers after the Battle of Worcester in 1651. The Royal Oak can be seen to this day painted on signs outside countless pubs all over the country, and you can still see a direct descendant of the famous oak itself now nearly 300 years old, in fields surrounding the house. A visit to the house will show that it has retained its romantic character.
There are panelled rooms and hiding places, including the 'sacred hole' in the attic where Charles is said to have stayed at night.
Open daily from 1st April-31st October 10-6pm. 1st Nov- 31st Dec & 1st Feb - 31st March Wed 7 Sun 10-4pm.

IRONBRIDGE
THE IRONBRIDGE GORGE MUSEUM,
Ironbridge, Telford TF8 7AW
Tel: 01952 433522 (weekdays) 432166 (weekends)
Fax: 01952 432204

The heart of the Industrial Revolution was forged in the spectacularly beautiful Ironbridge Gorge in Shropshire. The word 'Museum' in this instance encompasses virtually all there is to see in this green and tranquil valley with the world's first Iron Bridge as its centrepiece. The whole is awe inspiring and the sense of the changes which took place here 250years ago, awesome. It is one of Britain's 14 World Heritage Sites. The Ironbridge Gorge Museum shows how and why the area is so significant, and brings its momentous past vividly back to life. An exciting programme of special events is organised all year round. Please contact the museum or pick up a leaflet for details. You are invited to take 'Nine Steps Back in Time' whilst you cover each different section. **THE MUSEUM OF THE RIVER AND VISITOR CENTRE** is housed in The Coalbrookdale Company's 1840's warehouse and is home to a 40ft model of the Gorge in 1796, plus displays about the River today. Time needed: one hour. Leave car here when walking to the Iron Bridge. The nearby Merrythought Teddy Bear Shop and Museum salutes a more recent industry in the Gorge, dating from the 1930s. Time needed 30 minutes. **MUSEUM OF IRON, AND DARBY FURNACE** Visit the furnace where, in 1709 Abraham Darby first smelted iron ore with coke, turning this valley into the most important iron making area in the world in the 18th century. The Museum and Gallery highlight the history and achievements of the ironmakers. Free parking. Time needed:90 minutes. **ROSEHILL AND DALE HOUSE.** The former homes of the Quaker Ironmasters. Rosehill House completed in the 1830s, is now set out to display the possessions and lifestyle of its mid-nineteenth century occupants. Dale House is being restored. Limited parking for the disabled, otherwise free parking at Museum of Iron. Time needed: one hour. Open summer season only.
THE IRON BRIDGE AND TOLLHOUSE The dramatic Iron Bridge, the first of its kind, was cast in 1779. Incidentally parking in central Ironbridge is 'pay & display'. The Tollhouse contains an exhibition about the building of the Bridge. Time needed:30 minutes. **BLISTS HILL OPEN AIR MUSEUM** A 50 acre reconstruction of town life at the turn of the century, with shops, offices, workshops, machinery, pigsties and railway sidings. Change modern currency into Victorian pennies to buy butcher's pies, real beer, candles and newspapers. Free parking. Time needed: at least 2 1/2 hours. **THE TAR TUNNEL** Don a hard hat and go underground to see bitumen still oozing from the walls of this natural phenomenon discovered in 1786. Free parking at Coalport. Time needed: 20 minutes. **BEDLAM FURNACES** Built in 1757, the subject of Philip de Loutherbourg's famous 'Coalbrookdale by Night' painting. Free parking. Time needed: 10 minutes.**COALPORT CHINA MUSEUM** The works where decorative Coalport china was manufactured until 1926. Now restored to show manufacturing techniques and Coalport products - today's range is on sale in the Museum shop. Free parking. Time needed: 90 minutes. **JACKFIELD TILE MUSEUM** Two of the world's largest decorative tile works were based at Jackfield in the late 19th century. One of them, Craven Dunnill,is now a museum and conservation workshop. See a kaleidoscopic variety

of colourful tiles produced locally up until the 1960s, as well as modern production today. Free parking. Time needed: 90 minutes.

Today, the nine sites of the Ironbridge Gorge Museum, spread over some six square miles, provide a window on a world which shaped our modern age. OPEN: Most sites are open every day except December 24th & 25th 10-4 in winter, 10-5 from 1st April- 5th November, and 10-6 in July and August. Some sites close November-April. Check before visiting. A Passport Ticket is available which admits you to all the Museums.

HODNET
HODNET HALL GARDENS,
Hodnet, Market Drayton TF9 3NN
Tel: 01630 685202 Fax: 01630 685853

Hodnet is a garden that proudly recognises its own beauty, knows silence, serenity and tranquillity. In the dark glades there is only the occasional muted sound of a fish at the surface of the water or a twig snapping underfoot. Each pool is an enclosed world of deep reflection. There is a sense of timelessness everywhere. A truly wonderful place to be. The gardens were started in 1922 and planned and developed by the late Brigadier A.G.W. Heber-Percy with a staff of only three; their maintenance and development are continued today by a staff of four under the direction of the late Brigadier's son, Mr A.E.H. Heber-Percy. There is a chain of seven lakes and pools and woodland walks planted with rare trees and shrubs. Rhododendrons and camellias thrive in the acid soil; iris, candelabra primulas and bog plants enjoy the fairly high rainfall of the area and their position around the pools. Daffodils, blossom and bluebells flourish in early Spring, followed by a burst of colour from rhododendrons, azaleas, laburnums and lilac; summer borders are full of the colour of hydrangeas, roses and other summer shrubs. The autumn brings an abundance of foliage tints and berries.OPEN; April-Sept Tues-Sat 2-5pm (closed Monds) Suns & Bank Holiday Mondays 12-5.30pm Free car and coach park. Tea-rooms open during Garden opening hours. Dogs allowed but must be kept on leads.

SHREWSBURY
ATTINGHAM PARK,
Shrewsbury SY4 4TP
Tel: 01743 709203
Fax: 01743 709352

Located in Atcham on the B4380, 4 miles south east of Shrewsbury. The nearest railway station is 5 miles away at Shrewsbury. The extensive neo-classical facade of this great house is a fitting climax to the approach, through Nash's imposing screen in the village of Atcham and across Repton's deceptively spacious landscape. This vast mansion was designed for the 1st Lord Berwick in 1783 by George Steuart. His distinctive plan, with masculine and feminine wings, is enhanced by the interiordecoration and the fine plaster-work ceilings. The rich collections of furniture, paintings and silver which now furnish these splendid rooms represent the taste of two brothers, the 2nd and 3rd Lords Berwick, and together form one of the most complete representations of Regency taste to survive. So extensive were the purchases of the 2nd Lord Berwick that he commissioned Nash to make the only major alteration to Steuart's original palladian scheme, adding a top-lit central picture gallery. Still decorated in its original Pompeiian red, this and the circular painted boudoir are among the most important country house interiors to survive unaltered. The 8th Lord Berwick, who inherited in 1897 and bequeathed the house and estate to the National Trust in 1947, devoted his life to restoring and enhancing this great Shropshire house.

That task is being continued by the National Trust, with recent restoration work in the picture gallery and in the 18th century orangery. Special guided tours may be booked Saturday to Wednesday starting at 12 noon or 4.30pm. The tour lasts approximately one and a half hours. Special evening tours can also be booked. Guided tours can also be arranged for the park, landscaped by Humphry Repton but revealing evidence of earlier medieval and Roman usage.

Visitors with disabilities are requested to contact the house before arrival. A lift is available, for which special access arrangements are made. Wheelchairs can be borrowed. The Tearoom is up 5 steps, but there are picnic tables outside. Home made light lunches and traditional teas are offered Saturday to Wednesday in the Stewards Room. A Shop sells Attingham souvenirs and a full range of National Trust merchandise.

OPEN; 1st April-27th September Saturday to Wednesday 1.30pm-5pm.(last admissions 4.30pm) Bank Holiday Monday 11am-5pm. October:Saturday and Sunday only 1.30pm-5pm. Park and Grounds open daily 8am-8pm (5pm in winter) (Except Christmas Day).

VISITOR ATTRACTIONS

STAFFORDSHIRE

BARTON UNDER NEEDWOOD
THE SHOULDER OF MUTTON
16 Main Street, Barton under Needwood
Tel: 01283 712568   Fax: 01283 716349

Barton-under-Needwood is a charming village in the heart of the Staffordshire countryside, just off the A38 and near to the canal. In its midst is The Shoulder of Mutton, a much loved village inn, used regularly by the locals. Owned and run by Robert and June Spurrier, it is a welcoming place in which strangers are rapidly made to feel at home. The building is old, dating back to the 17th century and it is full of character.

Oak beams, old pictures and memorabilia decorate the walls. It is comfortable and unpretentious; somewhere to relax, enjoy a pint of real ale or select a glass of wine from the wine list, have some good conversation and tuck into a delicious meal that will delight your taste buds and do no harm to your bank balance.

This is a pub to visit all the year round, but in summer the children occupy themselves safely in the new Smugglers Cove play area, whilst you relish a glass of chilled white wine. The menu has many familiar dishes and you can eat here seven days a week either at lunchtimes or in the evenings (except Sunday evenings). The chef changes the menu monthly and there are always two or three dishes on the daily special board.

All the dishes are served with fresh vegetables and prepared to order. Vegetarian dishes are included in the menu, there is also a children's menu. OPEN; Mon-Thurs 11-3pm & 5.30-11pm. Fri/Sat 11-11pm. Sun: 12-3pm & 7-10. 30pm. Skittle alley. No credit cards. No accommodation. Disabled access. Garden with tables, chair/benches.

BARTON-UNDER-NEEDWOOD
THE SHOULDER OF MUTTON -SMUGGLERS COVE PLAY AREA

Smugglers Cove is a newly built play area. It has a large grassed area surrounded by high fencing and separated from the car park by a ranch style fence. The entrance is through an archway from the car park.

The main feature of the play area is a Galleon complete with ships wheel, walk the plank, mast and sail, all set into the Quay with its Treasure Chest full of coins and jewellery, and an adjoining sand pit. The Galleon was converted from an old canal barge.

A competition was held to choose a name for the galleon with the name of 'The Magic Mutton' being chosen from over 50 entries.

There is also a Toddlers Tavern which is a small building containing a soft play area and Ball Pool. There is also a swing, slide and seesaw. The whole area is surrounded by planted areas and rockery containing trees, shrubs and plants. Seating areas make it a delightful place to enjoy a meal and watch your children play.

OPEN; The same hours as The Shoulder of Mutton.

TAMWORTH
TAMWORTH CASTLE & MUSEUM,
Holloway, Tamworth B79 7LR
Tel: 01827 63563.

A visit to this magnificent English showpiece is rewarding in every way. It is a Castle 'reborn' and the result is spell binding, described succinctly by one visitor 'England at its best'. People from all over the world have enthused about the major three-phased programme of refurbishment and re-interpretation which was carried out between the autumns of 1989 and 1991 at a total cost of £345,000. The Castle is blessed with apartments from almost every century from the twelfth to the twentieth and is open to visitors all year round. It has had, for many years, a fine collection of 16th-19th century furniture on loan from the Victoria and Albert Museum in London. Now there are fifteen rooms opento visitors including a permanent exhibition on Norman Castles, a dungeon and haunted bedroom. Indeed Tamworth Castle is reputed to have not one, but two ghosts! For many the most exciting features are the Living Images also known as 'Talking Heads'. These high-tech figures have been skilfully incorporated into the overall interpretation of the Grade I listed building which also boasts a fascinating collection of original artefacts in fully furnished period room settings. The Tamworth Story exhibition is scheduled to open in April 1996. Set in an attractive park with magnificent floral terraces with a garden for blind and disabled people, the Castle dominates the centre of Tamworth. Within sight of the shopping centre, the Castle Pleasure Grounds extend for a considerable distance along the banks of the Rivers Anker and Tame. There is a special Swan Walk along the banks of the River Anker where at certain times herd numbers of these beautiful birds can reach over 100. Guided Tours can be arranged for groups of at least 10 adults (20 outside normal daytime opening hours). Coach and car parking is provided adjacent to the Jolly Sailor public house, 400m from the castle.
OPEN; 10-17.30 Mon-Saturday. 14.00-1730 Sunday. Last admission 16.30 hours. Daily all year, except December 24, 25, & 26.Ground floor only accessible to those in wheelchairs. No catering but there are several restaurants and cafes close by.

SUFFOLK

ALDEBURGH
MOOT HALL
Sea Front.
Town history and maritime affairs including prints, paintings, relics of Snape Anglo Saxon ship burial. In 16th century timbered town hall.
April, May: Sat & Sun 2.30-5pm. June-Sept: daily 2.30-5pm. July, August: daily 10-12.30pm & 2.30-5.30pm.

ILKETSHALL ST LAWRENCE
THE CIDER PLACE
Cherry Tree Farm, Ilketshall St Lawrence, Near Beccles NR34 8LB
Tel: 01986 781353.
You will find The Cider Place on the main Bungay-Halesworth Road A144. Cider, the word deriving from the Anglo-Saxon word Selder, has been in Suffolk for over six hundred years, since 1300 and was a common drink for all that time. The introduction of Beer in the 18th century was responsible for the decline in Cider. In the 19th and early 20th centuries, Ciders were being made on the farms for the farmworkers to drink in the summer whilst working in the hay and harvest fields - sadly this tradition completely died out after the wars. The Cider Place is a family run concern in which they have revived the art of making Farm Ciders, putting Suffolk back on the map by producing a range of four traditional Ciders for the true Cider drinker at the farm.

All the Ciders and Apple Juices are produced using only original wooden Grinding-mills and Presses dating from 1864, which crush over a ton of apples at a time. They crush most Saturdays during the Apple Season (September-November). All the Cider is matured in Oak Barrels for over two years.

The Cider Place also produces a range of four different types of Apple Juice, all non alcholic, which make a refreshing and thirst quenching drink that is also suitable for diabetics, as they contain no sweetener or preservatives - just as it comes from the apple. Apple Juice for wine-making can be obtained from the press during the Apple Season. Mead (Honey Wine) is also brewed and a small and varied selection of well matured country wines is grown and produced.

Cider Vinegar for culinary and medicinal use. There is a selection of local home-made 'Garden of Suffolk' Jams, Pickles and Chutneys as well as a selection of Suffolk & Norfolk Honeys. OPEN; Daily all the year round from 9am-1pm and 2-6pm.

BRUISYARD
BRUISYARD VINEYARD & HERB CENTRE,
Church Road, Bruisyard
Tel: 01728 638281.
Producers of the award-winning Bruisyard St Peter English wine, and herbs, the Vineyard provides a fascinating exploration. There is a 10 acre vineyard and adjoining winery which you can discover aided by a 40 minute Sony Walkman cassette. You are then invited to enjoy a little wine tasting accompanied by a light hearted video. The shop will tempt you to browse and in the tranquil beauty of the picturesque herb and water gardens most people find peace.

You can relax in the delightful restaurant and tea shop, or even bring your own picnic and use the wooded picnic area. Children will always be happy in the specially designed play area.

Follow Brown Tourist Signs from A12/B1119 Saxmundham Bypass. A1120/B1120 Badingham. B119/B1120 Framlingham Road.
OPEN: All year except 25th Dec-15th January 10.30am-5pm.

BURY ST EDMUNDS
MANOR HOUSE MUSEUM
Honey Hill.
Tel: 01284 757072.
A new museum of art and horology in refurbished Georgian Mansion. Collection of clocks, watches, paintings, furniture, costumes and ceramics. 'Hands on' Gallery. Cafe & Shop. Open all year. Mon-Sat 10-5pm. Sun: 2-5pm. Closed Good Friday, Christmas Day and Boxing Day.

REDE FARM PARK,
Rede, Bury St Edmunds IP2940G
Tel: 01284 850695
DIRECTIONS; The Farm Park is situated on the A143 Bury St Edmunds to Haverhill Road. Do not go the village of Rede because there is no access from that direction. This is a working farm based on the agricultural life of the 1930's-1950's including working Suffolk Horses, use of agricultural implements, waggons and woodland management. Young English oxen being trainedto farm work and forestry. Poultry including game fowl, guinea fowl and peafowl are given free range access to the whole farm. Some livestock can be handled by children. Farm walks comprising of a small lake and conservation area, new woodland and meadowland containing East Anglian breeds of livestock. You can see management of cattle and sheep of the era, a working farrier shop, a Cafeteria and gift shop. Childrens play and picnic area, nature trail and cart rides. Bygones and working displays of seasonal activities. School and coach parties are welcome by appointment.
OPEN: Daily 10-5.30pm 1st April-30th September.
Admission Adults 3.00 Children 1.50. Over sixties 1.75

SUFFOLK REGIMENTAL MUSEUM
The Keep, Gibraltar Barracks, Out Risbygate.
Tel: 01284 752394 ext 6
Military uniforms, weapons, medals, photographs, drums etc, illustrating history of the Suffolk and Cambridgeshire regiments from 17th century.
Open all year. Mon-Fri 10-12 & 2-4pm. Closed Bank Holidays. Admission free.

ST EDMUNDSBURY CATHEDRAL
Angel Hill. 11th century Mother church of Suffolk with fine hammer beam roof and a display of 1,000 embroidered kneelers.
Open June-Aug 8.30-8pm Sept-May 8.30-6pm. Exhibitions in the Cloisters.

BURY ST EDMUNDS ABBEY
Ruins of St Edmunds Abbey church. 12th century Norman Tower and magnificently restored Abbey Gate. Set in attractive gardens. Guide from TIC. Open daily. Admission free.

EUSTON HALL Tel 01842 766366 18th century house, set in Evelyn and Kent landscaped park. Paintings by Lely, Van Dyck and Stubbs. 17th century with Wren style interior. June-September Thursdays 2.30-5pm. TeaRoom.

CHARSFIELD
AKENFIELD
1 Park Lane.
Half an acre cottage garden in village made famous by Ronald Blythe's book. Orchard/picnic area. Mid April-October 1st daily 10.30-dusk

COTTON
COTTON MECHANICAL MUSEUM
off B1113 south of Diss.
Tel: 01449 613876.
Extensive collection, includes organs, street pianos, polyphones, gramophones, music boxes, musical dolls, fruit bowls and even a musical chair. Also the mighty Wurlitzer Theatre Pipe Organ in specially reconstructed cinema. Open; June-September.

DUNWICH
DUNWICH MUSEUM
St James St.
Tel: 0171 873796.
History of the town of Dunwich from Roman times, chronicling its disappearnce into the sea over the centuries. Open: March Sat &Sun 2-4.30pm. Good Friday-September 30th daily 11.30-4.30pm. October daily 12-4pm. Admission free.

EAST BERGHOLT
BRIDGE COTTAGE,
Flatford
Tel: 01206 298260
16th century cottage in Dedham Vale close to Flatford Mill (Mill not open to public) Easter, Apr, May, Oct: Wed-Sun. June-Sept daily 11-5.30pm Free, but fee for car park. National Trust.

EAST BERGHOLT CHURCH
Impressive perpendicular exterior. Tower never completed. Unique 16th century timber framed bell cage. Open in daylight.

FELIXSTOWE
FELIXSTOWE MUSEUM,
Landguard Point, Viewpoint Road, Felixstowe Tel: 01394 286403. This increasingly popular independent museum adjoins the 18th century Languard Fort at Landguard Point, Felixstowe in Suffolk. Ten display rooms consist of artefacts, models, uniforms, maps and photographs of local and military interest. Well worth a visit. Schools and out of hours groups welcome OPEN:2-5pm Wednesday and Sunday afternoons also Thursday afternoons during the School Summer holidays only.

FLIXTON NORFOLK & SUFFOLK AVIATION MUSEUM
On B 1062 Homersfield Road.
17 historic aircraft; other aviation material. 446th Bomb Group Museum. Royal

Observer Corps Museum. Open: April- October Sundays and Bank Holidays 10-5pm. Also summer school holidays. Tues, Wed & Thurs 10-5pm Free.

FRAMLINGHAM
FRAMLINGHAM CASTLE
Tel: 01728 724189
Built in 12th century by the Bigod family. One of the finest examples of a curtain walled castle. Open: April-30th September daily 10-6pm Oct 1st-March 31st daily but closed Mondays, Dec 24-26 and Jan 1st. 10-4pm. English Heritage.

FRAMLINGHAM CHURCH
Outstanding hammer beam roof, monuments. Open in daytime.

HARTEST
GIFFORD'S HALL
Tel: 01284 830464
'A small country living', 33 acres with vineyard/winery (free tastings), wild flower meadows, organic vegetables, rare breeds,sheep, chickens. Flowers, Rose Garden. Shop & Tea Room. Children's pet and play areas. Open: Easter -Sept 30th daily 12-6pm.

HELMINGHAM
OTLEY HALL
Tel: 01473 890264
Outstanding latemedieval moated hall. Historical associations. Open: Easter, Spring & August Bank Holidays. Guided tours by arrangement all year.

ILKETSHALL ST LAWRENCE   THE CIDER PLACE.
Cherry tree farm on A144. Tel: 01986 781353. Traditional farm-brewed ciders, apple juices, country wines, mead and preserves. Tastings. All year. 9-1pm & 2-6pm. No admission charge.

IPSWICH
CHRISTCHURCH MANSION & PARK,
Christchurch Park, Ipswich IP2 2BE
Tel: 01473 253246.

Christchurch lies just beyond the old town walls and North Gate of Ipswich. The estate was established by the Augustinian Priory of the Holy Trinity (also known as Christchurch) which was founded in the twelfth century. Although the Priory housed only six to twenty monks, it was extremely wealthy with 643 acres of farmland and fish ponds attached to the estate, as well as lands and rents in several other parishes. In addition to their own Trinity Church (later demolished) in the Priory grounds, the monks, were responsible for St Margaret's Church. Today's Round and Wilderness ponds, which draw from natural springs, seem to have survived from monastic times. In 1677 John Evelyn recorded ' The stewes for fish succeed one another and feed one the other...' and in 1711 Sir James Thornhill remarked upon the 'very good fish ponds, one of which has a brace of carp..' By the 1870's the Wilderness Pond contained 'Carp up to seven and eight pounds, also tench, roach and gudgeon..' Pond water used to overflow down Dairy Lane to Northgate Street and Brook Street, giving the latter its name and so the history of Christchurch continued. It became the family home of the Fonnereaus who lived there until 1892. The story then becomes very interesting showing how the mansion and park were saved for the people of Ipswich. From 1847 the Upper Arboretum had been leased to the Corporation of Ipswich to convert into pleasure grounds for the poorer classes. In addition to the fields used as a vast playground and cricket pitch by the children of the town, the Corporation laid out the grounds with beds of flowers and shrubs, gravel paths and fixed seats. Although in 1892 William Neale Fonnereau offered the complete site to the Corporation for 50,000 pounds, it was rejected and a property syndicate bought it and part of the land was immediately sold and built upon. However Felix Thornley Cobbold, a member of the syndicate, then presented Christchurch Mansion to the town as a gift on the condition that the main structure of the house 'be preserved in its integrity.' and that the Corporation purchased the remainder of the park. The gift and the conditions were accepted and on the 12th April 1895 the Park was opened free to the public and a year later so too was the Mansion. Over the year so much has been added for the pleasure of the public including a purpose built Art Gallery. At the centre of the Park is a children's Wild West theme play area. Adults and children enjoy visiting the Wilderness Pond to watch and feed the interesting selection of ornamental and wild fowl. There are two bowling greens let to local clubs and a putting green for public use. The Christchurch Park and Arboreta of today comprise sixty-seven acres. Inside the Mansion there is a superb reconstructed Tudor Hall, some wonderful bedrooms including one with an oak bed with carved and panelled headboard and tester, all from the early to mid-17th century. Magnificent panelling constantly catches the eye. The collection of early oak furniture and carving is particularly rich. The Hawstead Panels which were originally in the 'painted closet' at Hawstead Place, near Bury St Edmunds, date back to the early 17th century. Brilliant portraits, fine statues, ceramics and so much more makes Christchurch Mansion a must on any visitor's list.
OPEN; Monday to Saturday 10am-5pm Sunday 2.30-4.30pm (Closes at dusk in winter) Closed Good Friday and 24th-26th December inclusive.

TOLLY COBBOLD BREWERY & BREWERY TAP
Cliff Road.
Tel: 01473 281508.
Taste the malt, smell the hops and enjoy a complimentary glass of beer at one of the country's oldest breweries. A must for those interested in beer, heritage and history. Artefacts from 1723. Guided Tours: Easter & May-Sept; daily 12 noon (extra tours weekends). Oct-Apr: Fri, Sat Sun, 12 noon. Min age 14. Public Bar. Food.

KEDDINGTON
KEDDINGTON CHURCH
Fine roof, delightful interior with superb wood carvings, monuments, screen, pulpit, box pews. Saxon crucifix. Easter-end September: Weekends and Bank Holidays 2-4pm.

LAVENHAM
THE GUILDHALL OF CORPUS CHRISTI
Tel: 01787 247646
History of the wool, cloth and horsehair industries, historic Lavenham and its timber-framed Guildhall. Open Easter-October 31st daily 10-5pm. Closed Good Friday.

LITTLE HALL
15th century 'hall' house with crown post roof. Rooms furnished with Gayer-Anderson collection of furniture, pictures, sculptures and ceramics. Walled garden. April-October Wed, Thurs, Sat, Sun, Bank Holidays 2.30-5.30pm. See Pakenham Water Mill

THE PRIORY
Tel: 01787 247003.
14th-16th century timber-framed house. paintings. herb garden. Gift shop. Restaurant. Easter. October daily 10.30-5.30pm

LAVENHAM CHURCH - outstanding 'Cloth' church. Richly carved screens. Fine tower. 10-5.30pm in summer. 10-3.30pm in winter.

LAXFIELD
BIRDS OF PREY CONSERVATION CENTRE
St Jacobs Hall
Tel: 01986 798844.
On B1117 from the A140 Stowmarket-Norwich road. The Centre is in the heart of rural Suffolk just one and a half miles from the delightful village of Laxfield. You can spend time studying a wide variety of Birds of Prey in their large aviaries, or walking amongst the newly planted woodland trees covering around 4 acres of the 12 acre site. there are 3 flying displays every day, at 11.30, 2.00pm amd 4.00pm. Open all year 10.30am-5.30pm every day.

VISITOR ATTRACTIONS

LEISTON
THE LONG SHOP MUSEUM
Main Street.
Tel: 01728 832189
Award winning steam and industrial musuem. History of Richard Garrett Engineering Works and Leiston town featuring original machinery and memorabilia. In restored 1853 Grade II Listed factory. One of the earliest examples of assembly line production of steam engines. Open April 1st-Oct 31st daily 10-5pm except Sun: 11-5pm.

ALDRINGHAM CRAFT MARKET,
Aldringham, Near Leiston, IP16 4PY
Tel: 01728 830397
Within minutes of entering any of the three galleries or coffee shop, the first-time visitor becomes aware that this is a well-established business that is genuinely founded on goodwill towards its visitors: in short, it is devoted to meeting their needs and expectations.
The sentiment is achieved by offering high quality products at sensible prices, in a friendly and relaxed environment. This welcoming atmosphere is naturally engendered by the proprietors and staff, but never obtrusively, for they appreciate that people frequently wish only to browse in an unhurried manner without feeling obliged to make a purchase. It is clear that the proprietors - who live close by - precisely understand the style of retailing they pursue. And, as it has remained constant since the foundation of the business in 1958 -and the business is obviously in sound health despite the recent recession - there can be no doubt about the success of their policies. The name 'market' is misleading as visitors will find a retailing establishment comprising three large and substantial galleries, a coffee shop, a children's play area with a slide and see-saw, and an ample car park.

The galleries are always stocked to their maximum capacity. Indeed, the owners often find difficulty in accommodating new items that they cannot resist acquiring. Products stocked in depth include: studio ceramics; domestic and garden pottery; etchings, and oil, gouache and watercolour paintings, notably of East Anglia; prints; turned wood; studio and domestic glass; jewellery; corn dollies; ladies' cotton clothes and knitwear; sheepskin slippers; toiletries; kitchenware. In addition, many items of giftware are offered including children's toys, dolls, kites, games, books, maps,

HOTELS, INNS, RESTAURANTS AND COUNTRY HOUSES

leather; locally made preserves, chocolate and honey, cards and stationery. And this list is far from complete!
OPEN; 7 days Mon-Sat 10.00-5.30pm Sunday 2.00-5pm (all year) 10.00-12.00 Spring and Summer. Children welcome. Master/Access/Visa/Connect. Evening party visits by prior arrangement. Location: at B1353/B1122 crossroads, 3 miles north of Aldeburgh. Selina's Coffee Shop throughout Spring, Summer & early Autumn offers fresh-ground coffee, tea, soft drinks and home-made cakes. Exhibitions of paintings and craft work held each year. Collectors are advised by mailing list, apply for details if interested. Christmas Fayre in November to start the celebrations - complementary hot mince pies, coffee and drinks express the owners thanks to their customers for their support.

LITTLE BLAKENHAM
BLAKENHAM WOODLAND GARDEN
March 1st-June 30th; daily except Sat:1-5pm.

LONG MELFORD
MELFORD HALL
Tel: 01787 880286
Turreted brick Tudor mansion. Rooms in various styles. Chinese porcelain collection. Gardens. Apr: Sat, Sun & Bank Holidays, May-Sept 30th Wed, Thurs, Sat, Sun & Bank Holidays. Oct: Sat, Sun 2.5.30pm. National Trust.

KENTWELL HALL.
Elizabethan Manor House with moat and gardens. Unique mosaic Tudor Rose Maze. Rare breeds farm animals in park. Home-made teas. House, Moat House, Gardens and Farm open 12-5pm (except for re-creations).
Late March-mid-June and October: Sundays only and Bank Holiday weekends. Mid-July-end Sept. Daily. Ring for details of Re-Creations and other times.
Tel: 01787 310207.

LONG MELFORD CHURCH
Outstanding 'cloth'church in fine setting of parkland and historic buildings. Fine medieval glass. Good brass rubbings. Open in daytime.

LOWESTOFT
EAST ANGLIA TRANSPORT MUSEUM
Chapel Road, Carlton Colville. On B1384. Working trams, trolley buses in reconstructed 1930's street scene. Also narrow gauge railway, battery powered vehicles, commercial vehicles, steam rollers etc.
Open Easter Sun & Monday, other Bank Holidays and Sundays from May to end of September 11-5pm. Saturdays: First week in June to end of September. Weekdays: Mid-July beginning of September 2-4pm.

LOWESTOFT
SOMERLEYTON HALL,
Somerleyton, Lowestoft NR32 5QQ
Tel: 01502 730224 Fax: 01502 732143

This is a perfect example of a house built to show off the wealth of the new Victorian aristocracy. The house was remodelled from a modest 17th Century Manor House by the prolific railway builder Sir Morton Peto. When he was declared bankrupt in 1863, his extravagant concoction of red brick, white stone and lavish interiors was sold to another hugely successful businessman, carpet manufacturer Sir Francis Crossley. The present owner Lord Somerleyton, is his great-grandson. Somerleyton is the home of the family and everything about its great beauty is enhanced by the fact that it is lived in and cherished. No expense was spared in the building or fittings. Stone was brought from Caen and Aubigny and the magnificent carved stonework created by John Thomas (who worked on the houses of Parliament) has recently been restored. In the State Rooms there are paintings by Landseer, Wright of Derby and Stanfield, together with fine wood carvings by Willcox of Warwick and from the earlier house, Grinling Gibbons. The Oak Room retains its carved oak panelling and Stuart atmosphere; the rest is lavishly Victorian. Grandest of all is the Ballroom with its crimson damask walls reflected in rows of long white and gilt mirrors. The 12 acres of gardens are justly renowned and contain a wide variety of beautiful plants, trees and Victorian greenhouses which provide many attractive flower displays. The highlight of the garden is the 1846 yew hedge maze, one of the few surviving Victorian mazes in Britain. The stable tower clock by Vuilliamy made in 1847 is the original model for a great clock to serve as the Tower Clock in the new Houses of Parliament, now world famous as Big Ben. Colour is added to the gardens by rhododendrons, azaleas and a long pergola trailing mauve, pink and white wisteria. The Loggia Tea Room serves delicious home-baked food including light lunches and the ever popular cream teas. The Miniature railway runs from 3pm on Sundays, Thursdays, Bank Holidays and other days when available. The house and gardens can be booked for private functions, special events and private tours of the house and gardens with luncheon, arranged. School party visits are welcome and a Conference room with catering is available for Corporate functions. One of the special facilities is the Evening Garden Walks with ploughman's supper and shop visit. Lord and Lady Somerleyton hope that you will enjoy your day here and also that you will pay a visit to Fritton Lake Countryworld, part of the

Somerleyton Estate which is only a 10 minute drive away and is open from 10am every day during the season. Somerleyton Hall is open Easter Sunday through to the end of September. Gardens Open and Light Lunches from 12.30pm House Open from 2-5pm. Opening Days April, May,June and September; Sundays, Thursdays and Bank Holidays. July and August: Sundays, Tuesdays, Wednesdays, Thursdays and Bank Holiday.

SUFFOLK WILDLIFE PARK, KESSINGLAND
Tel: 01502 740291.
The African Wildlife experience set in over 100 acres. Take the Safari Road-train or enjoy a leisurely walk to discover the many rare and endangered animals. Gnus and visitors shelters with interesting animal facts. Children's play area, cafeteria, shop. Open daily: 10a, except Dec25/26. Telephone for admission charges.

ST MARGARETS CHURCH
Oulton Road. Fine 'flushwork'. memorials to Lowestoft's seafarers. Open June-Sept weekdays 10-4pm.

NEWMARKET
NEWMARKET NATIONAL HORSE RACING MUSEUM
High Street.
Tel: 01638 667333.
Story of the development of horse racing over 300 years, housed in Regency Subscription Rooms. Arts, bronzes, development of the rules, institutions and the great men of the sport. Also British Sporting Art Trust Vestey Gallery. April-end November Tues-Sat 10-5pm. Sun 2-5pm except July, Aug 12-5pm. Also Bank Holiday Mondays and July, August Mondays 10-5pm. Various guided tours of the gallops, training grounds. National Stud, Jockey Club, Museum and Historic town by prior arrangement.

ORFORD
ORFORD CASTLE
Tel: 01394 450472
Built in 12th century for coastal defence by Henry II. Near perfect example of Norman Keep with panoramic views. Opening times as Framlingham Castle.

ORFORD CRAFTS,
Front Street, Orford IP12 2LN
Tel: 01394 450678
Stuart Bacon who owns Orford Crafts is a highly respected marine archaeologist and writer specialising in everything to do with the Suffolk coast. Here you may buy his many books, all of which will give you a fascinating insight into the chosen subject. It is also the homeof Suffolk Underwater Studies which has evolved from the Dunwich project and covers the whole of the Suffolk shoreline and 12 miles offshore.It was established in November 1985 to study the coastal and nearshore area using divers and beach observers. The information gleaned is used to build up a picture of the coastal process. The study includes seabed movement, marine

archaeology, coastal erosion, deposition and the recording of wrecks and archaeological sites on the seabed. Orford Crafts houses The Dunwich Exhibition designed to give an insight into underwater exploration off the Suffolk coast. There are other small displays on various subjects all linked to underwater exploration of the North Sea including Orford and Orford Ness, Aldeburgh and Slaughden (1953 floods), Coastal erosion, The Spanish Armada and the East coast, The Roman Shore Forts, The Battle of Sole Bay 1672 (Dutch Wars) and Cannon recovered from the seabed. OPEN: Daily from 11-5pm.

PAKENHAM
PAKENHAM WATER MILL,
Grimstone End, Pakenham, Bury St Edmunds
Tel: 01359 270570. 01787 247179
This fascinating place was saved by The Suffolk Preservation Society and is owned by The Suffolk Building Preservation Trust, both charitable organisations. It is run by a volunteer group of about 50 people who not only have restored it but also continue the never ending task of maintenance. It is their love and dedication which has made it possible for the many visitors to enjoy and appreciate this old building. Excavations of the foundations of the Mill recently revealed the remains of a Tudor mill which was replaced by the present building in the late 18th century. The Suffolk Preservation Society became concerned about the future of the Mill when it ceased to work in 1974 and in 1978, with the aid of a substantial anonymous donation, bought it from the late Mr Brian Marriage. The restoration won the Society a prestigious Europa Nostra Diploma in 1985.

The parish of Pakenham is now unique in Britain in having both a working windmill and watermill. The Domesday Survey records that there was a watermill on the site of the present building in 1086; thus corn has been ground here for at least 900 years. All this history and much more information is available from the volunteer guides who will take you round and explain much to you. The power to work the Mill, for example comes from a tributary stream of the Blackbourn, flowing gently down from Pakenham Fen to join the main river at Ixworth. The great iron waterwheel was made by Peck of Bury St Edmunds about 1900. Water drives the three pairs of millstones and the flow of grain and meal in the Mill depends on gravity, so first the grain must be taken up into storage bins on the top of the bin floor. This is just the start and you can see its progress until it becomes meal on the ground floor where a sack is waiting. It is an intriguing process and in recent years with the increasing demand for stone ground wholemeal flour, the mill is able to make money from its sale of flour to help defray the very high overheads of maintenance and insurance. Don't miss this opportunity to see an old craft which is very much part of the present. OPEN;To General Public from Good Friday 1996 until the end of September on Wednesdays, Saturdays, Sundays and Bank Holiday Mondays 2-5.30pm. Schools, Clubs and organised coach parties welcome all the year round. Please book in advance. Why not enjoy a famous hot Pakenham Pie Lunch or Supper at the Fox Inn, High street, Pakenham when in the area.

LITTLE HALL,
Market Place, Lavenham, Suffolk CO10 9QZ
Tel: 01787 247179 Fax: 01787 248341

Lavenham is full of superb buildings from the time when it flourished proudly in the fourteenth to sixteenth centuries as one of the foremost wool and cloth making centres in England, famed for itsblue broadcloth. The medieval and Tudor structures have lasted and none is more beautiful than Little Hall which began life as a fifteenth century clothier's hall. The Little Hall later became cottages housing as many as 20 inhabitants. In 1924 the Great house next door was bought together with the six cottages by the Gayer-Anderson brothers to house their collection of books, pictures, china and antiques - many of them on display there today. The brothers were twins who after service in the army, retired to Lavenham and worked for twelve years on the restoration of Little Hall and its conversion back to a single dwelling. Lifelong collectors they drew, painted and sculpted well. They bequeathed Little Hall to Surrey County Council as a hostel for art students. Reginald Brill, a well-known artist and friend of the twins, then head of Kingston School of Art became warden from 1960 until his death in 1974. By that time Surrey County Council with changing boundaries, a lack of funds to sustain Little Hall, closed it and offered the house and its contents to the Suffolk Building Preservation Trust. It is now their headquarters and the public are invited to tour this delightful timber-framed building with its wide entrance door and little personal door wicket within, its dining room whose ceiling contains massive timbers as used in the larger Lavenham Tudor houses. The room is graced with an oak dresser made by Colonel Gayer Anderson and other interesting pieces of furniture as well as paintings. The Inner hall, the Library and the Panelled Room furnished as a study, the Dormitory and the Solar demand attention. Visitors are welcome to visit the terrace and English garden. OPEN: Easter to end of October on Wednesday, Thursday, Saturday,Sunday and Bank Holidays 2.30-5.30pm.Parties by appointment at other times. School parties are welcome and find much of relevance to National Curriculum studies.

SNAPE MALTINGS
SNAPE MALTINGS
Converted Maltings beside River Alde, Home of the world famous Aldeburgh festival in June and other concerts/master classes during the year.

Tel: 01728 452935.
Riverside Centre includes six unusual shops and galleries, teashop, pub and restaurant. Open all year daily 10-6pm (5pm in winter). River trips in summer. Tel: 01728 688303/5

STOKE BY NAYLAND
Tower brasses, tombs. Open in daytime but closed on wet days.

STOWMARKET
MUSEUM OF EAST ANGLIAN LIFE
Iliffe Way.
Tel: 01449 612229
Fine collection of East Anglia's rural past on attractive 70 acre site. Displays of gypsy caravansm domestic life, farming etc. Working watermill and wind pump. Craft workshops smithy, tithe bar etc. Suffolk Punch horses. An exciting outing. Refreshments, picnic area. Open April, May, October Tues-Sun and Bank Holiday Mondays June-Sept daily 10-5pm.

HAUGHLEY PARK
Tel: 01359 240205
Jacobean Manor house, gardens and woods. May-Sept Tues 3-6pm

SUDBURY
GAINSBOROUGH'S HOUSE
Gainsborough St.
Tel: 01787 372958
Birthplace of Thomas Gainsborough RA 1717-88 Georgian fronted town house with attractive walled garden. Displays more of the artist's work than any other British Gallery. 18th century furniture and memorabilia. Open; Easter-October Tues-Sat 10-5pm Sun & Bank Holiday Monday 2-5pm. Nov-Easter Tues-Sat 10-4. Sun 2-4pm Closed between Christmas and New Year. Good Friday.

SUTTON HOO
SUTTON HOO archaeological site, burial grounds of Anglo Saxon Kings of East Anglia. Access by foot from B1083 at Hollesley turn. Open: Easter, Sat, Sun, Mon. May-early Sept Sat, Sun & Bank Holidays. Guided Tours at 2pm & 3pm.

WEST STOW
WEST STOW ANGLO SAXON VILLAGE
6 buildings reconstructed on original sites. Open daily 10-4.15pm. Access via Visitor Centre in West Stow Country Park.

WOODBRIDGE
FRAMLINGHAM CASTLE,
Framlingham IP13 9BT
Tel: 01728 724189
This Norman castle built by the Bigod earls of Norfolk has today only the outer walls and towers remaining but like another Norman castle, Orford, just thirteen

miles away and built by Henry II, the impressive remains give you an understanding of the conditions in which great men - and even the king himself - lived in the twelfth century, and of the defences put up as part of the struggle for local control between the Crown and the baronage during the Middle Ages. Framlingham Castle lies to the north of the town, beyond the parish church. The castle has thirteen towers linked together with high curtain walls - you can walk safely all the way round the battlements. Within the walls are an attractive group of flint and brick buildings built as a school and poorhouse but now housing displays of local history and a shop. If you buy a guide you are likely to do so from the Poorhouse and it is here that your recommended tour starts. Built long after the castle had fallen into ruin, the Poorhouse was for children only at first. It was rebuilt in 1729 for up to a hundred adult paupers. Now for the Wall Walk which is reached by climbing the spiral staircase next to the shop. These stairs are unusual because most castle stairs corkscrew up the other way so that an attacker climbing the stairs could not wield a sword properly in his right hand. But at Framlingham this was the only permanent access to the wall walk, and it would be more likely to be defenders, rushing to man the wall walk and towers who would be climbing the stairs rather than attackers. As you reach the top of the stairs, notice the light timber-framed back wall of the tower. All thirteen towers are very similar, usually with open backs and wooden gangways across the gaps they made in the wall walk. These gangways could be removed by the defenders when any attackers had succeeded in getting on to the battlements. Then the attacker could neither fight their way right round the wall walk, nor dominate the interior of the castle. Each tower is interesting and provides the visitor with an insight into castle life and wonderful views.

Everywhere you look you will find something to excite the imagination or be stirred by the events of the past. English Heritage have the care of Framlingham Castle and apart from preserving the ruins they also maintain the beautiful grass swards within the walls and courtyards. This must be one of the most interesting castles in Suffolk not only for its ruins but also for the distinguished families who have lived here over the centuries.

Opening times 1st April-30th September: daily 10am-6pm, 1st October-31st March: daily 10am-4pm. Credit cards taken except Switch. Dogs and cats on leads permitted. Disabled access to grounds and ground floor only.

FRAMLINGHAM
SHAWSGATE VINEYARD,
Badingham Road, Framlingham
Tel: 01728 724060 Fax: 01728 723232

You will find this well established vineyard just one mile from Framlingham on the left hand side of the B1120. With a wealth of Gold, Silver and Bronze medals for the quality of the wine made here, visitors can see what has been achieved to reach this standard. Established in 1973, the 17 acre vineyard wasbought in 1985 by Ian Hutcheson and is managed by Rob and Penny Hemphill. It has undergone major restoration - new post and wirework has been constructed, natural windbreaks have been planted and artificial windbreaks installed. The majority of grapes are Muller Thurgau but they have introduced Bacchus, Reichensteiner and Seyval Blanc which all produce white wine. A new frost resistant red grape

called Amurensis has also been planted which makes a red wine. The grapes are hand picked in October and processed immediately. Visitors are invited to taste a selection of the wines either at the vineyard shop or at the second shop in Walberswick near Southwold on the coast. In addition to a well stocked shop selling a range of wine accessories, pottery, books and local produce including various alcohol free beverages, vines of different varieties are also for sale. The Winery built in 1987 is fabulous. It has been fully equipped with stainless steel winemaking equipment including a one tonne press, grape trailer, bottling line and tanks used for the fermentation and storage of the wine.
OPEN; 10.30am-5pm daily. TOURS: Easter to end October. Group visits by appointment. Picnic Area. Childrens Play Area. Coach and Car Park. Teas and Coffees.

WARWICKSHIRE

STRATFORD-UPON-AVON
STRATFORD-UPON-AVON BUTTERFLY FARM,
Tramway Walk, Swan's Nest Lane, Stratford-upon-Avon CV37 7LS
Tel: 01789 299288
This Butterfly Farm was opened in 1985 and provides a truly spectacular day out in an exotic setting. It is housed in a large glasshouse which is landscaped with waterfalls, ponds and a wide variety of unusual tropical plants. Butterflies from all over the world fly freely around in this area. Visitors can walk throughout and observe behaviour and life-cycles at first hand. By providing correct caterpillar food-plants they are breeding most of the species on display. Exotic insects, such as leaf-cutting ants, praying mantis, stick insects and giant beetles can be seen in Insect City. On display in Arachnoland are spiders and scorpions, including the deadly Black Widow and the worlds largest species of spider; the Goliath bird eater. The whole concept of the exhibition is to show live insects behaving as naturally as possible, rather than cases of dead specimens. Stratford Butterfly Farm is the largest and most comprehensive attraction of its type in Europe.
OPEN; Every day except Christmas Day. Summer: 10am-6pm Winter: 10am-dusk. Last admission is 30 minutes before closing time. Group visits by arrangement. HOW TO FIND IT Five minutes walk from the centre of town, just over River Avon footbridge, opposite the Royal Shakespeare Theatre. Gift Shop. Disabled access.

HOTELS, INNS, RESTAURANTS AND COUNTRY HOUSES

WEST MIDLANDS

BINLEY
COOMBE ABBEY PARK COUNTRY FAIR
Tel: 01336 411285
Location: Brinklow Road, Binley, Nr Coventry.
Coombe Abbey Park is a major new outdoor events and entertainment centre for the Midlands. Already famous for its beautiful parkland and teeming wildlife, Coombe Abbey Park is the ideal place for a Country Fair which brings the past to life and explores the wayforward. Open all year round 10-6pm.

COOMBE ABBEY PARK FOLK FESTIVAL
Tel: 01336 411285
A non stop weekend of first class folk music in an idyllic setting takes place in September each year. Two performance marquees plus tents for dancers, singers and musicians will ensure non-stop music and entertainment from Friday evening to Saturday afternoon.

COOMBE ABBEY COUNTRY PARK
Tel: 01203 453720
Come and explore the splendid beauty of Coombe Abbey Country Park with its beautiful gardens, woodland and lakeside walks and drink in the historic surroundings. There are plants, animals and birds in abundance and everyone has the chance to get close to nature. Most of the parkland is classified as a Site of Special Scientific Interest in recognition of its importance to wildlife. Country Park open every day 7.30dusk.

COVENTRY
GODIVA CITY
Tel: 01203 832630
Location: the Herbert Art Gallery and Museum. Godiva City is an exciting new exhibitions of over one thousand years of history. The exhibition looks at Lady Godiva as a real person who had huge influence in the Midlands through her wealth and estates. The exhibition discovers the 'real' Lady Godiva, but gives people the opportunity to also find out how she was marketed as a tourist attraction over 300 years ago! Admission free. Open Mon-Sat 10-5.30pm Sun 2-5pm.

KENILWORTH CASTLE
Tel: 01926 52078
Location: Off the M40 near Warwick. Great and gaunt against the Warwickshire sky, Kenilworth Castle rises up to dominate the surrounding town and peaceful countryside. Kenilworth is the finest and most extensive castle ruin in Britain. As you survey the soaring walls of the Great Hall and the elegance of the Earl of Leicester's additions to the castle for the visit of Queen Elizabeth I in 1575, you can almost recreate the pomp and pageantry of life here in the past. Open 1st April-31st October 10-6pm. 1st November-31st March 10-4pm.

MUSIC HALL ABBEY GATE
Tel: 01203 452406
The Abbeygate Empire proudly present its own evening of contentment and conviviality. Come and listen to the songs and humour of an apocalyptic era, join lustily in the chorus and refrains and partake in a mouth-watering three course supper.

LUNT ROMAN FORT
Tel: 01203 832381
In AD60, seventeen years after the Roman invasion, the Britains rebelled against foreign rule. It took more than a year for the Roman Army to put down the revolt by the East Anglian Iceni tribe. As a result forts were rebuilt, and the army moved to new strategic locations. The Lunt is the only reconstructed Roman Fort of this type in Britain and provides valuable evidence about life in a Roman Cavalry fortification. Situated on a spur of high ground overlooking the River Sowe, the Lunt was in an ideal location, typical of rural Roman forts. Museum shop, free parking, picnic area and toilets. Open: April-30th October 10-5pm and everyday from mid-July to 31st August inclusive.

RYTON ORGANIC GARDENS
Tel: 01203 303517
Location: off the A45, five miles south of Coventry. There's something for all the family here. Ten acres of beautiful grounds with formal rose gardens, ornamentals, alpine banks, colourful flower beds, not to mention the wonderful array of vegetables - many of them rare or unusual - and a top and soft fruit collection. Open every day except during Christmas week 10-5.30pm. Last admission to the garden is at 5pm.

SHOPMOBILITY
Tel: 01203 832020
Location: Upper Precinct, Coventry. Shopmobility is a service which provides powered and unpowered wheelchairs and scooters for people who have either permanent or temporary limited mobility. It will allow them greater independence to use the pedestrianised shopping areas in the City Centre. The opening hours are Mon-Sat 9-5pm.

CATHEDRAL LANES SHOPPING CENTRE
Tel: 01203 632532.
Cathedral Lane provides an ideal setting for shopping, meeting and eating in the heart of Coventry. Browse in a wide range of shops selling books, fashion, beauty, sportswear, gifts and much, much more. Relax over a drink or meal in the light airy brasserie, or just sit and watch the regular, fun entertainment.

THE GUILDHALL OF ST MARY
Tel: 01203 832381.
Location: High Street, Coventry. The Guildhall of St Mary has a long and glorious history reflecting the changes in Coventry's fortunes as well as changes in our society. It has been a feasting hall for Kings and Queens, a soup kitchen for

unemployed weavers during the slump period of 1858 to 1865, a fish market in the 16th century, damaged by 18th century rioting and 20th century bombing, but lovingly restored to its former glory. However, the Guildhall's main purpose has been to act as a centre of civic life in Coventry. Open to the public May-Sept. Closed over the winter period.

MUSEUM OF BRITISH ROAD TRANSPORT
Tel: 01203 832425.
At the Museum you'll delight in the largest display of British made road transport in the world, all under one roof. With more than 150 cars, 75 motor cycles and 200 cycles, the Museum tells the fascinating story of Coventry's contribution to Britain's road transport history, as seen through the famous Marques of Alvis, Daimler, Hillman, Jaguar, Riley, Rover, Standard, Triumph and many more. Open daily all year round from 10-5pm.

WARWICK ARTS CENTRE
Tel: 01203 524524.
Warwick Arts Centre - a resource provided by the University of Warwick - attracts over 250,000 visitors a year to the artistic programme, and provides a vital link between the local and regional community. Entertainment facilities include the arts, dance, exhibitions and a selection of International Celebrity Concerts. Open daily throughout the year.

THE HERBERT ART GALLERY & MUSEUM
Tel: 01203 832381
Introduction to Weaving is a Crafts Council exhibition which takes an intriguing and delightful look at woven textiles from the Crafts Council Collection, with weaving bylocal maker Susan Wright. Admission free. Mon-Sat 10-5.30pm. Sun 2-5pm.

VISITOR ATTRACTIONS

WALES

BEDDGELERT   SYGUN COPPER MINE,
Beddgelert, LL55 4NE
Tel: 01766 890595
24 hour info/line: 01766 890564.
Sygun is one mile from the village of Beddgelert on the A498 road to Capel Curig. Sygun Copper Mine is one of the wonders of Wales - a remarkable and impressive example of how part of our precious industrial heritage can be reclaimed, restored and transformed into an outstanding family attraction. The mine provides an excellent and informative experience of the underground world of the Victorian miner.The mine, a unique modern day reminder of 19th century methods of ore extraction and processing is situated in the glorious Gwynant Valley - the heart of the stunning Snowdonia National Park - and on probably the most popular tourist route in Wales. The incomparable scenery captured the imagination of movie-makers, who turned the mountainside surrounding Sygun into a Chinese village in 1958 for the filming of 'The Inn of the Sixth Happiness' which starred the late Ingrid Bergman. Sygun offers a rare opportunity for those with a sense of adventure and curiosity, from the young to the elderly, to discover for themselves the wonders it still shelters after being abandoned in 1903. Audiovisual tours allow you to explore the old workings on foot in complete safety. there are winding tunnels and large chambers, magnificent stalactite and stalagmite formations and copper ore veins which contain traces of gold, silver and other precious metals. It usually takes about 40 minutes to complete the quarter mile route which rises140feet via stairways to emerge at the Victoria level for a breathtaking view of the Gwynant Valley and surrounding Snowdonia mountain range. A shorter, less demanding tour can be arranged. Refreshments and a wide range of souvenirs are available in the visitors centre. **OPEN**; All year. Oct, Nov, Feb, March 10.30am-4pm. (11am Sunday) Dec, Jan 11-3.30pm. Main season: Easter or late March - Sept inc. 10am-5pm (11am Sun. & 4pm Sat.) Visa/ Access/Switch. Flat soled shoes advisable. Dogs not permitted underground.

BLAENAU FFESTINIOG   LLECHWEDD SLATE CAVERNS,
Blaenau Ffestiniog,LL41 3NB
Tel: 01766 830306 Fax:01766 831260.
This is a day out to remember. Winner of all Britain's top tourism awards, Llechwedd Slate Caverns have been visited by five million people, including Edward VIII when he was Prince of Wales, the Princess Margaret, the Duchess of Gloucester and the Crown Prince of Japan. The spectacular underground lake has been used for a Walt Disney film set. Other sites have endeavoured, unsuccessfully, to copy the magic of Llechwedd - where the tourist operation has the benefit of historic authenticity while also remaining part of the biggest working slate mine in Wales. Here you can take two quite different rides, one exploring the complexities of old slate mining skills, the other the triumph, humour, religious fervour, and the pathos of the Victorian miner. Visitors are at liberty to take either or both. Add to that an exploration of the Victorian Village, and some refreshment at one of the wide selection of catering facilities, and there is no reluctance to

spend at least a day at Llechwedd. A very interesting and informative little book about Llechwedd written by Ivor Wynne Jones, a Director, is well worth acquiring. Not only does it tell you about the mine but also about the history of slate, and relates Llechwedd Slate Caverns' unexpected contribution to the conservation of Wales' endangered wild life. Choughs' Cavern which visitors see while riding the Miners' Tramway, was named after the shy crow-like birds which nested there for many years returning in 1969, disappearing in the 1970s but rediscovering the same unlikely spot in 1991, since when annual nesting has been re-established. On the surface hovering kestrels are a common sight and buzzards nest on the northern rock face. One of nature's most beautiful contributions is rhododendron ponticum which bursts into flower each spring. An interesting highlight of a visit to Llechwedd is the facility for spending Victorian coins, at Victorian prices, in the village shops and the ever popular Miners Arms. This journey back in time begins at the Old Bank of Greenway & Greaves. This is a banking museum, preserving the appearance of a small country branch early in the last century. The Llechwedd 'bank' has a shop counter where five pre-decimal coins may be purchased. They show correct designs on the reverse, but with modern dating. All prices in the Victorian Village -Pentre Llechwedd - are shown in old and new currencies, enabling such experiences as buying a 'pennorth' of sweets or a 3d pint at the Miners' Arms.In 1972 when a half-mile level section of the Miners' Tramway was opened to the world revealing the vast workings, it was immediately given the top awards of both the British Tourist Authority and the Wales Tourist Board. Boarding a train in a corner of the original slate slabbing mill of 1852, visitors now ride into an 1846 tunnel, hauled by battery-electric locomotives. Entering through the side of the mountain, this journey into the early Victorian past remains on the level, and traverses some spectacular caverns. Passengers alight at various points to learn something of the strange skills needed to extract slate. There is a sound and light tableaux deep underground and guides describe the other chambers. **OPEN:** Daily 10am including Sundays. (Closed on Christmas Day, Boxing Day and New Year's Day) Last tours into mines: 5.15pm March to September 4.15pm October to February. Access, Visa, Switch. Special terms for parties of 20 or more. Free car parking, free surface exhibitions. Dogs not allowed on either ride. Separate cafe. Victorian Pub and Licensed restaurant.

CAERNARFON   CAERNARFON AIR WORLD,
Museum and Pleasure Flights
Caernarfon Airport, Dinas Dinlle, Nr Caernarfon, Gwynedd   LL545TP
Tel: 01286 830800.
In the great hangar here you can see planes and helicopters in landscaped settings, aircraft engines, ejector seats and over two hundred model aircraft. If you enjoy the history and nostalgia associated with planes and flying, this is the place for you and it is 'Hands On'. You can sit in cockpits, take the controls in the Varsity Trainer and wander round full size planes. There are also exhibitions featuring Local Aviation History, the story of the Dambusters, Welsh Flying V.C's, the first RAF Mountain Rescue Service, fascinating wartime newspapers and historic First Day Covers. There is a cinema where you can watch aviation shorts and full length films. The well stocked museum shop has been extended, and for small children there is a themed adventure playground, built around a Dragonfly helicopter.

Pleasure Flights will provide you with a unique experience in North Wales. Take a bird's eye view of mountains, castles and coastline in a Cessna or the Vintage de Havilland Dragon Rapide. There are three standard flights, but you can always plan your own. The first is a ten minute flight over the Menai Strait around the 13th century Caernarfon Castle and back over the 18th century Fort Belan. The second flight is a breathtaking 25 minute experience flying over the mountains of Snowdonia, over the summit of Snowdon, the highest peak in England and Wales, over Crib Coch and the Llanberis Pass, then back to the airport taking in Caernarfon Castle and Fort Belan. The third is another 25 minute flight that is offered if weather conditions do not favour a mountain trip. This one flies over the Menai Strait and the lovely island of Anglesey, taking in the foothills of Snowdonia and Caernarfon Castle on the return journey.

OPEN; MUSEUM Daily 1st March -31st October 9am-5.30pm.
PLEASURE FLIGHTS Daily, weather permitting throughout the year. Check by phone prior to visit. RESTAURANT Open daily all year. Coffee Shop open from Easter to 31st October.

COLWYN BAY EIRIAS PARK,
Colwyn Leisure Centre, Colwyn Bay LL29 8HG
Tel: 01492 533223

Here you will find something for all the family. With over half a million visitors annually to Eirias Park its popularity as a tourist and recreational attraction cannot be questioned. Set in 50 acres of beautiful parkland, the facilities on offer provide a unique recreational experience and offer an outstanding day out for all ages. Facilities available all year round include: Leisure Pool/Waterchute, Sports Halls, Squash Courts, Sauna/Solarium Suite, Function Room, Fitness Room, Lounge Bar/Cafe, Athletics Stadium, Indoor/Outdoor Tennis Courts and Synthetic Pitch. Facilities available throughout the summer season include: Crown Green Bowling Greens, Boating Lake with small and large pedaloes, Model Yacht Pond, Mini Golf Par Putting, Children's Play Area, Picnic Areas and Dinosaur World. From a promotional point of view, the facilities within Eirias Park, serve as an ideal location for the hosting of a corporate day and last year such days were organised on behalf of the Inland Revenue for Wales and the Post Office, North West. Simply choose from the available facilities or allow the competent, friendly staff to arrange a programme of activities to suit your company's personal needs. To complement the days activities, the Catering Manageress will be delighted to arrange a buffet with a wide selection of menus to choose from. From its commanding position overlooking the promenade and beach, the park is easily accessible by road via the A55 Expressway which links North Wales with the UK Motorway network and by rail with regular inter-city services from all parts of Britain. Easy access for the disabled. Free Car Parking.

CWMBRAN   GREENMEADOW COMMUNITY FARM,
Green Force Way, Cwmbran NP44 5AJ
Tel: 01633 862202

In the early 1980's a group of local people formed an action committee in a bid to protect one of the last green spaces in Cwmbran from further development. The group came up with the exciting prospect of establishing a Community Farm.

Today, the original, fully refurbished c17th farmstead with 150 acres of land throughout Cwmbran, offers a magnificent rural retreat in an urban setting. It is a place full of excitement where you will see traditional farm animals and Rare Breeds, a well-stocked aviary, an Exhibition Barn with ever changing exhibits. On the woodland trails you will see a surprising variety of wildlife and the Pets Corner is a place in which children have a chance to make friends with the smaller animals. All visitors are encouraged to feed and handle selected farm animals. The Farm House Tea Room offers traditional home-made fare. The Sheep Dip Bar is open every evening and the 16th century Cordell's Restaurant is ideal for an intimate meal. It opens every evening 7-10pm and for Sunday lunch. Special events are organised throughout the year. OPEN; All year except Christmas Day Summer 10-6pm Winter 10-4.30pm. Disabled people welcome. Pets allowed. Licensed. Conference facilities.

DOLGELLAU GWYNBFYNYDD GOLD MINE,

The Marian, Dolgellau, Gwynedd LL40 1UU
Tel: 01341 423332 Fax: 01341 423737

To get to the mine take the courtesy bus from Welsh Gold in Dolgellau and enjoy the short guided journey through some of the most beautiful countryside in Wales. Here you will see the place where a huge bonanza of gold was found a century ago: worth £5 million if found today. As far as one can tell Gwynfynydd Gold mine is the only working gold mine open to the public. Gold ore is mined daily but actual gold is very rare ; the mine yields about 25g per month on the whole but most times it can be less. 8 full time miners work here with additional staff to guide people through the mine during the summer season. Once you arrive at the mine you are presented with protective clothing whichinclude a hard hat, waterproof jacket and boots. (It is advisable to take a sweater with you as it can be quite cold underground.) On the tour itself you can experience the roar and thunder of modern machinery, the blast of explosions, and take away your own free sample of a Welsh Goldmine ore. You will also see how they mined in the olden days, by candle light. After being underground for around one hour you will see the Gold Smelting room, where gold is melted down to a small gold bullion. At the end of your tour you may pan for gold, should you find any, which is normally found in small pieces of rocks, you may take it home!! The retail shop sells Welsh Gold Jewellery which is displayed amongst other crafts from Wales. It is advisable to book in advance for tours throughout the year. The gold centre is open throughout the year 9.30am until 5.00pm, later on some occasions in the summer. It is open 7 days from Easter to September and closed on Sundays during the winter.

HOLYWELL HOLYWELL LEISURE CENTRE

Fron Park, Holywell CH8 7UZ

An exciting Leisure Centre offering something for every age. The 6 lane swimming pool incorporates broad shallow steps for easy access. Contained within the pool hall is a small shallow water area where toddlers can play in safety and a splash pool which provides a safe landing area to the 42 metre corkscrew water slide. The swimmng pool is open from 10am each day but closes each weekday between 3.45pm and 5.15pm for junior swimming classes. Indeed there is a whole range of classes for swimmers of all ages and all stages. The Silhouette Fitness Centre and the Silhouettes Health Suite are both excellent for anyone and supervised by an experienced and caring staff. Both open from 10am-10pm seven days a week. The Sports Hall has five a side football, basketball, volleyball and four badminton courts, bookable from 10am-10pm each day. The Dance Studio has a comprehensive range of dance classes and some popular aerobic and step aerobic sessions. This multi use area is excellent for small theatrical productions, drama workshops, film shows, seminars and training courses. The Hall is also used for Karate, Thai Boxing, Kung Fu, 50+ Exercise classes and children's birthday parties. Open from 10am-10pm seven days a week. The Snooker Room has 6 tables. For Bowling, two crown greens, one of which is floodlit are available for casual use from the beginning of April to the end of October. There is an Outdoor Area, two floodlit tennis courts, and a Synthetic Pitch for soccer. The Cafeteria is open from 9.30am-9.30pm each day and there is a comfortable lounge bar which opens from 7.30pm each evening. For further details please ring 01352 712027.

LLANDRINDOD WELLS
THE RADNORSHIRE MUSEUM,
Temple Street, Llandrindod Wells, LD1 5LD
Tel: 01597 824 513
Situated in the centre of Llandrindod Wells, the museum houses exhibits relating to the history of the old mid-Wales county of Radnorshire. Displays illustrate the largely rural farming lifestyle of the area as well as the development of Llandrindod Wells as a country Spa Resort during the Victorian and Edwardian Era. The museum also displays material relating to Fine Art, costume and the Prehistoric, Roman and Medieval history of the area: including the Roman Fort of Castell Collen. New for 1995 was the Red Kite Centre: set on the museums first floor, this exhibition highlights the lifestyle and successful fight back from the edge of extinction of Britons most beautiful bird of prey. The exhibition also includes a thirty minute video on the Red Kite and computer information station on the birds of Europe. **OPEN**; 10-12.30 and 2-4.30. Closed Wednesday (all year) and Saturday afternoon and Sunday (winter only).

TEIFI VALLEY RAILWAY,
Henllan Station, Henllan, Nr Newcastle, Emlyn SA44 5TD
Tel/Fax: 01559 371077
The only Famous Little Trains of Wales in West Wales gives hours of pleasure to people of all ages. A 40 minute train ride experience for which you pay once and ride all day (if seats available). Facilities include Woodland Theatre (Phone for details), Woodland Trails, Cafe. Shop, Pictorial Museum, Crazy Golf/Quoits/ Skittles, Childrens' Play Areas, Picnic and Barbeque Areas. W.C's, large Car Park, Coaches Welcome. Usual Coach Driver Facilities.
OPEN; Easter-Oct inc 10.30am-6pm. Closed: Saturdays. Apr 13/20/27 May 4/11/ 18 Oct 5/12/19.
TRAINS: Apr. May. June Oct. 10.30, 11.30, 12.30, 2pm, 3pm, 4pm. July, Aug-Sept Last train 5pm + Bank Holidays.
SPECIAL EVENTS: April 6th, Aug 17th, 25th and 26th, Oct 26th, December - SANTA SPECIALS Entrance/Parking 50p (Adults) £3.50 (Children) £1.50 (OAP) £3 Dogs 50p. Opending hours: daily Easter -26th October.

LLANGOLLEN
MODEL RAILWAY WORLD & DR WHO EXHIBITION,
Lower Dee Mill Llangollen LL20 8SE
Tel: 01978 860584. These two exciting attractions opened in the summer of 1995 and rapidly drew attention from visitors to the area as well as curious locals! The Model Railway World Museum is based around the original Hornby Dublo Factory from Binns Road, Liverpool. You will see 24 large superb layouts with 1000s of models on display. You can try shunting in the hands-on section and watch and talk to experts about building these models. Fascinating and educational. Dapol Ltd design and manufacture precision model railways and a wide range of toys including Dr Who models. The move to Lower Mill not only enabled Dapol to improve its manufacturing but also to realise the life-long dream of its Managing Director, David Boyle - to establish a National Model Railway Museum. Over the years David has ,amassed a huge collection of model railway artefacts and memorabilia including the original design drawings, art work, photographs, lathes, jigs, etc from Hornby, Dublo, Mainline,Wrenn. Airfix. All these are displayed together with the working layouts resulting in a unique exhibition relating to the history of model railways from the very beginning to the present day. The DR WHO exhibition adds yet another fascinating dimension at Lower Dee Mill. It was opened by former Dr Who actor, Colin Baker on the 17th June 1995 and has been mounted in association with the BBC who have provided the original costumes, Daleks, Cybermen monsters, visual effects (many of which are priceless).In consultation with BBC Dr Who producer, John Nathan-Turner the exhibition, covering three huge rooms, has been designed more as an experience than an exhibition with a full size working TARDIS and original sound effects give a fascinating insight into how the longest running science fiction series in the world was made for television.
Please ring 01978 860584 for opening times.

LLANGOLLEN
LLANGOLLEN HORSE DRAWN BOAT TRIPS
Llangollen Wharf, Llangollen
Tel: 01978 860702 for general enquiries. 0169 175322 for Group bookings, Day Boats and Holiday Hire.
To take a trip on one of these boats eases you back to the days of leisure as you glide noislessly through the spectacular scenery of the Vale of Llangollen. You may find yourself being pulled along by one of five horses who are all friendly and have names. Spot is the old boy who only works occasionally and then there is Fred, Sam, Stan and Arthur. They seem to enjoy their work as they go slowly along the towpath. In this timeless setting, the horse-drawn canal trips are as relaxing today as they were when the first pleasure boats slipped away from the Wharf in 1884. On the Wharf, you will find the Canal Exhibition Centre, telling the Canal Story with words, pictures and models. It is good to wander among the gaily painted canal ware in the gift shop and delightful to take tea on the terrace overlooking the town. Llangollen Wharf is a fascinating place for a day out. The popular cruise on the luxury narrowbat Thomas Telfrod includes a crossing of the Pontcysllte Aqueduct. **OPEN**; Daily for 45 minute horse-drawn boat trips andexhibition visits from Easter to September with limited opening in October.

VISITOR ATTRACTIONS

LLANGOLLEN
LLANGOLLEN RAILWAY,
Abbey road, Llangollen LL208SN
Tel:01978 860979
Llangollen is at the junction of the A5 and A539. The railway station is by the bridge over the River Dee. The nearest car parks are in Market Street in the town and at Lower Dee Mill on the A539 approaching from Ruabon. The nearst British Rail station is 5 miles away at Ruabon. Bryn Melyn buses operate hourly to Llangollen from Wrexham and Ruabon, two hourly on Sundays. The Llangollen Railway Society rescued this delightful line and have spent years bringing the track, the station and the trains back to their original beauty and splendour. The Railway you see at Llangollen today is a direct result of the dreams and aspirations of the former Flint and Deeside Railway. The work has been done mainly by volunteer enthusiasts who removed masses of undergrowth and rubble from the trackbed and vandalised buildings without water or supplies to be restored. The journey in the restored carriages through the countryside with the River Dee appearing constantly, is both beautiful, exciting and relaxing. Thrilling for youngsters and an outstanding experience for steam railway enthusiasts. There are opportunities for people to spend two hours on the footplate on 14 miles of firing and driving. Full hot meals for the trainee and light refreshments for up to six guests. Try the Llangollen Steam Driving Course - something you will never forget or regret. There are special dining opportunities and Sunday Lunches aboard the Berwyn Belle. Friends of Thomas Events, Santa Specials and much more.
Ring for further information 01978 860979.

COWBRIDGE
TASKFORCE PAINTBALL GAMES
147 Ynysddu, Pontyclun CF7 9UB
Tel:01443 227715 Fax:01443 225803
Situated just off the A48 west of Cowbridge, part of a large three and a half thousand acre estate at Penllyn. With easy access from the M4, just 10 minutes away, it can be reached with ease from most of the south west's major towns via the motorway network. Task Force is set in 30 acres of woodland within a deep undulating valley. It has been a venue for Paintball games since 1989 and during this period has had many special features added to it to create an exciting and varied site to play. Amongst its many varied features and scenarios are numerous bunkers, dugouts, a helicopter, bridges and a HUGE 'woodland village'. Your day will begin with a comprehensive briefing, followed by the issuing of all the equipment you will need for the day. Then once you are all kitted up and have had a practice on the firing range, you are ready for battle to commence. During the day you will play approximately 12 games. You do not need a special amount of players to book. There is an excellent Junior Paintball Game exclusively for 11-16 year olds.
OPEN; Saturday and Sunday or during the week if you have a group of 15 or more people. Credit Cards: Visa/Delta/Access/Master .

LLANDYSUL
TY HEN FARM
Llwyndafydd, Nr New Quay, Llandysul SA44 6BZ West Wales.
Tel: 01545 560346

Approached by a bumpy lane and set on a sheep farm in peaceful countryside closeto the Cardigan coast, near Cwmtudu, this attractive Guest House which also offers delightful, converted self-catering cottages is wonderful for people who want to relax, be well cared for and within easy reach of a whole host of exciting places. The main house has well appointed en suite bedrooms, the self-catering cottages and apartments are around the farmyard and so too is The Pits Centre which houses the restaurant and leisure facilities which comprise an indoor heated pool, well equipped gymnasium, sunbed, sauna, changing rooms, toilets, bowls/skittle alley, coin operated washing machine and drier. Good food is part of the reason this excellent place was awarded 3 Crowns and the farm-house award.
OPEN; Mid-Feb - Mid-Nov. Residential & Table Licence. Pets by prior arrangement. Disabled Access. Visa/Mastercard. Children welcome

MACHYNLLETH
KING ARTHUR'S LABYRINTH
Corris, Machynlleth, SY20 9RF
Tel: 01654 761584   Fax: 01654 761575

King Arthur's Labyrinth is a fairly recent visitor attraction which has delighted people since it opened in 1994. An underground boat takes visitors deep into the spectacular caverns under the Braichgoch mountain at Corris. As visitors walk through the caverns, Welsh tales of King Arthur are told with tableaux and stunning sound and light effects.

The journey ends with a return trip along the beautiful subterranean river into the grounds of the Corris Craft Centre. This exciting centre is the starting point for King Arthur's Labyrinth and home to six craft workshops at which visitors are invited to see at first hand the skills of the craft workers and, if they wish, to buy from the displays of woodcraft, toy making, jewellery, leather work and hand-made candles, while the Labyrinth shop provides a range of souvenirs, books and gifts on the Celtic Arthurian theme.

The Crwbyr Restaurant provides full meals, teas and refreshments throughout the day. There is also a picnic area in the gardens and an extensive children's play area. Visitors to the Labyrinth are advised to wear warm clothing as the underground caverns are cool. The 45 minute tour of the caverns involves a walk of about half a mile along level gravel paths unsuitable only for the very frail. However the variety of craft shops, gardens and refreshments within the Corris Craft Centre and the stunning scenery of the Corris valley provide ample enjoyment for everyone. Group bookings are welcome.
OPEN; 10-5pm daily from April to October.

MACHYNLLETH
MEIRION MILL,
Dinas Mawddwy, Nr Machynlleth SY20 9LS
Tel: 01650 531311

In a wonderful setting in the mountains of the Snowdonia National Park, shopping becomes a sheer delight when you see what wonderful goods, clothing, crafts and gifts are on offer. There is a tremendous range of wool products all under one roof: traditionally woven tweeds and rugs, skirt lengths, wool jackets, knitwear from black sheep, warm jumpers, subtle blended colours in ties and hats, sheepskin slippers, hats and gloves and of course, sheepskin rugs. The shelves are full of locally produced honey and jams, slate gifts, Celtic jewellery, lovespoons, jumping sheep and small items for children to collect. They also stock Portmeirion Pottery. Meirion Mill has everything going for it parking couldn't be simpler nor the access easier. The Old Station Coffee Shop has a restaurant licence and serves delicious home-cooked fare. There is a level entrance to the shop and all areas are accessible by wheelchair. You will find Meirion Mill situated on the Powys/Gwynedd border at the southern end of the National Park.

The Mill site was originally the terminus for the old Mawddwy railway which ran for six miles down the valley to join the main railway at Cemmaes Road. The double arched Pack Horse Bridge spans the river Dyfi next to the entrance gate. Heavily laden donkeys were led across this narrow bridge transporting bolts of flannel to be sold over the border.

OPEN: Daily early March to late November. Mon-Sat 10am-5pm. Sun: 10.30am-5pm. Times do vary in the early and late season. Current times can be obtained by phoning 01650 531311. Normally closed during winter months. Amex/Visa/Access/Mastercard/Delta/Switch. Childrens Play Area. Picnic area. Dogs not allowed in play area, shop or coffee shop.

CENARTH
THE NATIONAL CORACLE CENTRE,
Cenarth Falls, Newcastle Emlyn

NEWCASTLE
EMLYN
SA389JL
Tel: 01239 710980

Rescued from decay by Mr and Mrs Martin Fowler in 1983, Cenarth Mill was re-roofed in 1991 and the National Coracle Centre stands in the grounds of the 17th century flour mill where the mill pig stys and workshops once were. The mill is included in your visit here. An organised tour of the Centre takes you back to one of the earliest forms of transport, and presents a unique display of Coracles from many parts of the world. As well as nine varieties of Welsh Coracle and those from other British rivers, you can see examples from Iraq, Vietnam, India and North America. The workshop is an important part of the Centre and the ancient craft of Coracle making is displayed here. Coracles can be seen on the river during the summer holidays, and trips in one can sometimes be arranged. Viewing areas and pathways allow easy access for disabled people and provide wonderful views of the falls, salmon leap and 200 year old bridge.

OPEN; Easter-October Sunday to Friday 10.30am-5.30pm and other times by appointment. Gift Shop. Tea rooms.

HOTELS, INNS, RESTAURANTS AND COUNTRY HOUSES

PORT DINORWIC Y FELINHELI
THE GREENWOOD CENTRE
Tel: 01248 671493 Fax: 01248 670069
Indoors and outdoors the Award Winning Greenwood Centre is all about discovering the fascinating World of Trees. It is an enjoyable and educational experience for all ages. You can find out how trees work, how they clean the air, visit the Rainforest and hear its sounds, see a banana plant and find stick insects. Try out your sense of smell at the scent boxes and see if you can identify the fragrances. Find out about the history of forestry in Wales. Explore the rhododendron maze, tree nursery, root circle. See the wildlife pond and make friends with the rabbits in pets corner, and in the main holiday season, watch forest craft demonstrations and try out a Welsh Longbow from May to September. Enjoy a picnic outdoors or sample some of the tasty snacks and light lunches in the Tea Room.
OPEN; Daily   10am-5.30pm March to October inclusive. Winter visits by arrangement. Dogs on leads welcome. Free car & coach park. Disabled and baby changing facilities.

PORTMEIRION,
Gwynedd LL48 6ET   - Tel: 01766 770228
One single word, Portmeirion, conjures up a magical place, somewhere that everyone should visit at least once in a lifetime. It is the realisation of a dream by its creator Sir Clough Williams-Ellis who had long nurtured the idea of one day building his own ideal village on some romantic coast. Eventually he was offered the Aber la peninsula, only five miles from his ancestral home- a perfect place to prove that the development of a naturally beautiful site need not necessarily lead to its defilement. Work began when he ws 42 in 1925 and when Sir Clough died in 1978 at the age of 95 he was content in the knowledge that his dream had become a reality. For people like myself the sheer beauty, colour and charm of Portmeirion is enough to make me want to just stand and stare. There are different vistas at every turn and each one you think cannot be more beautiful than the last, but it always is. Portmeirion is a world apart and you may come here as a day visitor - not the best way because you cannot see and absorb all it has to offer. Portmeirion has six different shops including the Seconds Warehouse, which is theonly place in Wales selling second quality Portmeirion Pottery, designed by Susan Williams-Ellis. The Ship Shop sells best quality Portmeirion Pottery plus a wide range of design led gifts for all ages. There is also a Papur a Phensal for cards, the Golden Dragon bookshop, and Pot Jam selling Portmeirion preserves and confectionery. The Six of One shop specialises in The Prisoner TV series. The village has a licensed self-service restaurant with a pleasant terrace for meals outside. There is an ice-cream parlour and several ice-cream kiosks. The Hotel restaurant on the quayside welcomes non-residents and provides reasonably priced two and three course lunches.

RHAYADER
WELSH ROYAL CRYSTAL,
5 Brynberth, Rhayader LD6 5EN   - Tel: 01597 811005
Winner of Wales Tourism Awards 1995 'Highly Commended' Welsh Royal Crystal is the Principality's own complete manufacturer of hand-crafted lead crystal

products in tableware, stemware, presentation trophies and gift items. All production processes are undertaken on the one manufacturing site situated in Rhayader in the heartlands of Wales. Welsh Royal Crystal melts glass containing a lead content in excess of 30% (known as Full Lead Crystal) which is considered to be the best quality glass from which fine quality crystal glass products are made - weight and feel, definition of cutting and polishing brilliance are very much enhanced. Welsh Royal Crystal's range of products is traditional and the decoration combines classic florals (intaglio) with straight diamond cuts. A unique range of Celtic themes reflecting the design images of the Welsh Celtic heritage has been successfully introduced. The design and supply of presentation trophies and gifts is an expanding area of the Company's business. Welsh Royal Crystal can number within its customer portfolio important corporate customers in Wales and is pleased to be associated with the Cardiff Singer of the World Competition sponsored by British Petroleum, the Young Welsh Singer Competition sponsored by the Midland Bank and more recently, the Welsh Women of the Year sponsored by the Western Mail and HTV. In addition to supplying our fine Welsh crystal to over 100 retail accounts in Wales, sales are increasing across the borders of thePrincipality into England, Scotland, Saudi Arabia, North America, Australia and Canada. Time spent in the Welsh Royal Crystal Visitor Centre provides an opportunity to see the **WELSH MASTERS OF FIRE AND GLASS** handcraft full lead crystal products to the finest quality. A visit to the Welsh Crystal Shop presents an enviable opportunity to purchase quality crystal manufactured in Wales, whether it be a valuable centre piece or small gift item. **OPEN**; All year round 9am-12.30pm and 1.30-4.30pm. Glass blowing demonstrations may not be available on some weekdays, Saturdays and Sundays.

MUMBLES
THE LOVESPOON GALLERY
492 Mumbles Road, Mumbles, Swansea SA348X
Tel: 01792 360132.
You will find this unique gallery located on the right opposite the 1st Car Park just before the mini-roundabout in Mumbles. Do not miss the opportunity of visiting The Lovespoon Gallery. It is the world's first gallery devoted entirely to Welsh Lovespoons. Until you have seen the astonishing range you will have no idea that there are literally hundreds of designs made by some of the very best carvers in Wales. The Lovespoon has a well earned reputation for having only genuine carved Lovespoons and is known world wide. A Lovespoon makes a wonderful gift for special occasions like weddings, anniversaries christenings, birthdays and any important event. For 400 years this has been a Welsh tradition which is another good reason for buying one. When you examine the spoons you will see what wonderful artistry is employed when they are carved. They are certainly collectors' items.
OPEN: 10am-6pm Sunday opening in August. Children welcome. Credit cards: Visa.Mastercard. Suitable for the disabled, just one small step. Assistance given. Amex and Diners.

A-Z, GLOSSARY & INDEX

INDEX TO PLACES AND VENUES

A
Aberaeron 26
Aberdaron 8
Aberdovey 20
    Preswylfa Guest House 47
Abergavenny 46
    Three Salmons Inn 48
Abergele 14
Abergynolwyn 20
Aberporth 27
Abersoch 8
Aberystwyth 23
Abingdon
    200 Abingdon Lodge 200
Aldeburgh 238
Alstonfield 116
    The George 171
Amersham 217
Amlwch 12
Ampney Crucis 201
    The Crown of Crucis 201
Anglesey Abbey 12
Anglesey 6, 12
Ashby de la Zouch 157
Aylesbury 217

B
Bakewell 172
    Renaissance 172
    Pack Horse Inn 173
Bala 11
Banbury 198
Bangor 6
Bangor-on-Dee 17
Banham 230
Bardsey Island 7
Barmouth 11
    Llwyndu Farmhouse 58
Barnwell 174
    Montagu Arms 174
Barry 40
Barton-under-Needwood 129
    Shoulder of Mutton 129
Battisford 238
Beaumaris 12
Beaconsfield 217
Beaulagh 231
Beccles 238
Beddgelert 9
Bedford 215
Belbroughton 130
    Freshmans Restaurant 130
Bentley 239
Bethesda 6
Bethleham 33

Betws-y-coed	18
Fron Heulog	49
Bewdley	12
Bibury	196
Bildeston	239
Billingford	230
Birmingham	125
Bishops Frome	91
Bishopston	35
Blaenau Ffestiniog	8
Bledington	196
Blickling	230
Blockley	195
The Crown Hotel	202
Blythburgh	243
Bodelwyddan	14
Bontddu	11
Borth	23
Boston	266/7
Kings Arms	266
Red Lion	267
Boughton	169
Bourton-on-the-Hill	194
Bourton-on-the-Water	196, 203
Lansdowne Villa	203
The Old New Inn	204
Brackenborough	268
Brackenborough Arms Hotel	268
Bradenham	216
Bramford	239
Brancaster Staithe	230
Brandeston	239
Brecon	42
Breedon-on-the-Hill	158
Bressingham	231
Bridgend	39,40
Bridgnorth	108
Broadway	195
Bromsgrove	123
Bromyard	91
Bronabar Rhiw Goch Hotel	82
Broseley	107
Bryncroes	8
Brynford	15
Buckden	246
Buckenden	231
Buckingham	205
Buckingham Lodge Hotel	205
Builth Wells	26
The White Horse	50
Bungay	252
Outney Meadow Caravan Park	252
Burford	196
Elm House Hotel	206
Burgh-next-Aylsham	231
Burnham Norton	231
Burnham Deepdale	231
Burnham Market	231

A-Z, GLOSSARY & INDEX

Burnham Overy 231
Bourton-in-the-Wolds 175
    Greyhound Inn 175
Bury St Edmunds 239
Buxhall 239

C

Caerleon 44
Caernarfon 7
Caerphilly 43
Caerwent 44
Caldicot 44
Cambridge 245
Cannock Chase 115
Cannop 192
Cardiff 41, 42
Cardigan 27
Carew 30
Carey 136
    Cottage of Content 132
Carmarthen 32
Carreg Cennen 33
Castle Ashby 167
    Falcon Inn 176
Castle Donnington 157
Cavendish 240
Caxton 246
Chaddesley Corbett 123
Chalfont St Giles 217
Charlbury 207
    The Bull at Charlbury 207
Cheltenham 191
Chepstow 45
Cheriton 36
Chipping Norton 198
Chipping Camden 195
Chirk 17, 111
Church Stretton 109
    Longmynd Hotel 131
Cilgerran 27
Cinderford 192
Cirencester 197
Clarach 23
Clare 240
Claverley 132
    The Plough 132
Clifton 198
Clwyd 16
Coalville 157
Coleford 192
Colkirk 231
Coltishall 231
Colwyn Bay 14
Conwy 9
Corris Uchaf 20
Corris 20
Coventry 26
Cowbit 269

387

HOTELS, INNS, RESTAURANTS AND COUNTRY HOUSES

Ye Old Dun Cow	269
Craswall	94
Crick	17
Cromer	231
Crynant	38
Cwyn-yr-Eglwys	29

D

Daventry	170
Deddington	198
Denbigh	19
Denham	217
Devil's Bridge	23
Dickleburgh	232
Din Lligwy	12
Dinas Head	29
Dinfwr	32
Dolcaucothi	33
Dolgellau	11, 19
The Ivy House	55
Droitwich	123
Dryslwyn	32
Dudley	125
Dunstable	216
Dunwich	240
Duxford	246
Dyserth	15

E

Eardisland	95
East Bergholt	240
Eccleshall	113
Edington	232
Edith Weston	162
Eglwysfach	23
Eglwyswrw	28
Ellesmere	110/111
Elstow	215
Ely	247
Empingham	162
Eton215 The Christopher Hotel	223
Evesham	99
Eyam	165

F

Fairford	197
Fakenham	232
Limes Hotel	260
Wensum Lodge	261
Farndon	17
Felixstowe	241, 253
Brook Hotel	253
Ferryside	37
Fishguard	29
Flash	116
Flint	16
Flyford Flavell	133
The Red Hart Inn	133

A-Z, GLOSSARY & INDEX

Forncett St Mary 232
Fotheringay 168
Framlington 241
Fritton 232

G

Geddington 169
Glan Conwy The Old Rectory 56
Glanwydden 14
Glasbury The Maesllwch Country Hotel 57
Glaston 160
    Monkton Arms 177
Gloucester 189
Glyndyfrydwy 18
Gnosall 11
Goodrich 91
Gorleston-by-Sea 232
Grafton Underwood 169
Great Malvern 102
Great Snoring 233
Great Yarmouth 233 262
    Caldecott Hall Golf & Leisure 262
Great Ryburgh 233
Grimley 104
Guiting Power 194
Gwalchmai 13

H

Haltham 270
    The Marmion Arms 270
Hampton-in-Arden 126
Hanley .... 134 II
    Mago 134
Hanmer 17
Happisburgh 233
Hardingstone 169
Harlech 10
Haverfordwest 30
Hay Bluff 94
Hay-on-Wye 95
Hayfield 178
    The Skillet 178
Herringfleet 92
Hevingham 233
Higham Ferrers 170
Hinxton 248
Hodnet 112
Holdenby 167
Holt 17
    Holt Lodge 73
Holyhead 13
Holywell 15,16
Horning 233
Hughenden 216
Hundred House Village 25
    Hundred House Inn 60
Huntingdon 247/8

I

Ingworth	233
Inkberrow	137
Bulls Head	137
Inslip	169
Ipswich	238
Suffolk Grange Hotel	254
Irthlingbrough	170
Iver	217

K

Kedington	241
Kegworth	158
Kempsey	138
Walter de Cantelupe	138
Kenilworth	120
Kersey	241
Kidderminster	123
Kidwelly	36
Kilpeck	93
Kingston Bagpuize	198
Fallowfields Hotel	198
Kirton Holme	271
The Poachers	271
King's Lynn	234
Knowle	126

L

Langley	234
Lavenham	241
Lechlade	197
Ledbury	91
Leicester	179
Weavers Wine Bar	179
Leighton Buzzard	216 219
Grove Farm	219
Leiston	23
Leominster	92
Letton	139
The Swan Inn	139
Lillingstone Daynell	217
Litcham	234
Little Malvern	102
Little Stretton	109
Llanasa	15
Llanberis	6
Llanddeusant	12
Llanddewi Brefi	24
Llandeilo	33
Llandewi	36
Llandiloes	24
Llandovery	26
Llandrindod Wells	25
Guidfa House	59
The Llanerch 16th Century Inn	61
Llandudno	10,13
Bryn-Y-Bia Lodge	62
Southcliffe Hotel	63

A-Z, GLOSSARY & INDEX

Llandudno Junction 10
    Queens Head 64
Llaneilian 13
Llangammarch Wells, Lake Country House 65
Llangedwyn 22
Llangian 8
    Tafarn Pantydderwen 51
Llangollen 18
Llangrannog 27
Llangwnnadl 8
Llannefydd 53
    The Hawk and Buckle Inn 53
Llanrhaedr-ym-Mochnant 22
Llanrhidian 36
Llanrhystud Penhros Golf and Country Club 66
Llanrwst 10
Llantwit Major 40
Loddon 244
Long Itchington 140
Long Melford 241
Longnor 116
Lound 234
Lower Slaughter 194
Lowestoft 255
    Martello Coffee House 255
Lubenham 158
Ludlow 109
    The Merchant House 109
Lyddington 160

M

Machynlleth 20
    The Dolbrodmaeth Inn 67
Maidenhead 215
Malvern Link 102
Malvern Wells 102
Market Rasen 250
Market Deeping 249
Market Harborough 158
    The Three Swans Hotel 180
Market Bosworth 158
Market Drayton 110/111
Melbourn 247
Melton Mowbray 159
Melton Constable 236
Merthyr-Mawr 39
Michaelchurch Escley 94
Milford Haven 31
Moelfre 12
Moira 157
Mold 16
Monmouth 45
Montgomery 21
Moreton-in-Marsh 195 208
    White Hart Royal Hotel 208
Moulton 242
Much Marcle 91
Much Wenlock 107 Wheatland Fox 141

N

Mumbles	34
Mundesley	234
Nant Gwernot	20
Nantwich	111
Neath	38
Neatishead	235
Nefyn	7
Nevern	28
New Bolingbroke	250
Newark	164, 181
The New Ferry Restaurant	181
Newbury	215
The Ibex Inn	220
The Lord Lyon	221
Newcastle-under-Lyme	117
Newmarket	242
Newport	28
The Golden Lion	68
Newport (Shrops)	105
Newquay	26
Newtown	21
North Elmham	235
North Malvern	102
North Walsham	235
Northampton	166
Northleach	196
Northwold	235
Norwich	221, 263
Brasteds	263
Cubitt Cottage	264
Nottingham	163

O

Oakham	162
Orford	242
Oswestry 110 Restaurant Sebastian	142
Otley	242
Oulton Broad	235
Oundle	170
Overstrand	235
Overton	17
Oxford	199
Oxnead	234
Oxwich	35
Oystermouth	34

P

Palgrave	259
The Malt House	259
Pantasaph	15
Pembridge	95
Pembroke	30
Penarth	40
Penbryn	27
Pendclawdd	36

Penhow 44
Penley 17
Penmaenpool 11
    Penmaenuchaf Hall Hotel 11, 54
Penn 217
Pensarn 14
Pentraeth 12
Pin Mill 242
Plas Newydd 13
Pontrhydfendigaid 24
Pontypool The Lower New Inn 69
Pontarfynach (Devil's Bridge) 23, 24
Port Einon 35
Porthcawl 39
Porthkerry Egerton Grey Country House Hotel 70
Porthmadog 8
Porthoer 7
Portmeirion 9, 71
Portskewett 44
Prestatyn 15
Pumsaint 33
Puzzlewood 192

Q
Quorn 182
    Quorn Grange 182

R
Reedham 235
Resolven 39
Reynoldston 36
Rhayader 25
Rhos-on-Sea 14
Rhossli 35
Rhuddlan 15
Rhyl 15
    Barratts Restaurant 72
Rossett The Alyn 74
Rockingham 168
Ross-on-Wye 90
    The Loughpool 143
Rowen Gwern Borter Country Manor 52
Royal Leamington Spa 121
Ruthin 19
    Ye Old Anchor Inn 75
Rutland 160
Rugby 144
    Sheaf and Sickle 144

S
Sale 235
Sandringham 235
Sawston 246
Saxmundham 242
    Darsham Old Hall 256
Saxtead 242
Shebdon 113

Sheringham	236
Shipston-on-Stour	121
Shrewsbury	109/110
Skomer Island	30
Sloley,	264
Cubitt Cottage	264
Slough	222
The Copthorne Hotel	222
Snape	243
Snowshill	194
South Thoresby	250
Southwell	165
Spilsby	272
The White Hart Hotel	272
St Albans	217
St Asaph	15
St Clears The Old Mill	76
St Davids	29
St Nons Hotel	77
Ramsey House	78
St Dogmaels	28
Stafford	114
Stamford	249
Stody	236
Stoke Bruerne	168
Stoke-by-Nayland	243
Stoke-on-Trent	117
Stone	114
Granvilles	145
The Wheatsheaf	146
Stourport-on-Severn	124
Stow-cum-Quy	246
Stow-in-the-Wold	196
Stow Lodge Hotel	209
Stowmarket	243
Cedars Hotel & Restaurant	247
Stratford-upon-Avon	118
The College Arms	147
Stratton Strawless	233
Sudbury	243
Surlingham	236
Swaffham	236
Swansea	34,37
Symonds Yat West	90

T

Talgarth The New Inn	79
Talsarnau Hotel Maes-y-Nevadd	80
Talybont The Ysgethin Inn	81
Tamworth	127
Taplow	215
Telford	105
Temple Balsall	126
Temple Guiting	194
Tenbury Wells	92
Tenby	31
Tetbury	197
Tewkesbury	191

Thorncliffe 148
    The Red Lion 148
Thorngrove 104
Thrapston 169 183
    The Woolpack Hotel 183
Thursford 232
Tibberton 149
    The Sutherland Hotel 149
Tiger Bay 41
Tintern 45
Tinwell 161
Tong 106
Towcester 184
    The Pickwick Restaurant 184
Trapp 34
Trearddur Bay 13
Trecastle Castle Coaching Inn 83
Tregaron 24
Tresaith 27
Trwyn 20
Twywell 185 The Old Friar 185

U
Upper Slaughter 194
Upper Oddington 196
Uppingham 160
Upton 30
Upton-upon-Severn 101
Usk 45
Uttoxeter 115
    The Roebuck 150

V
Valley 13

W
Waddesdon 217
Waen 15
Walberswick 243
Wall-under-Heywood 151
    The Plough 151
Walsall 125
Waltham 169
Wantage 198
Water Stratford 217
Waterbeach 246
Wells-next-the-Sea 236
Welney 247
Welsh Newton 93
Welshpool 21
    Golfa Hall Hotel 84
    Peppers Restaurant 85
Wem 110
Weobley 95
West Malvern 102
West Runton 236
    The Dormy House 265
Westleton 243

Weston Turville	287
Weston-under-Lizard	105
Whitchurch	110
Whittington	111
The Narrowboat Inn	152
Whitwell	162
Wichenford	104
Wilbarton	186
The Fox Inn	186
Willersey	153
The Old Rectory	153
Windsor	223
Christopher Hotel	223
Wing	160
Wisbech	247
Witney	210
Witney Lodge Hotel	210
Wolverton	236
Woodbridge	243
The Captains Tabe	258
Woodhall Spa	250
Wootton	167
Worcester	98
Worstead	237
Worthing	237
Wrexham	16
Erddig	86
Llwyn Onn Hall	87
Wroxham	237

Y

Yoxford	244

A-Z, GLOSSARY & INDEX

HOTELS, INNS, RESTAURANTS AND COUNTRY HOUSES

A-Z, GLOSSARY & INDEX

HOTELS, INNS, RESTAURANTS AND COUNTRY HOUSES

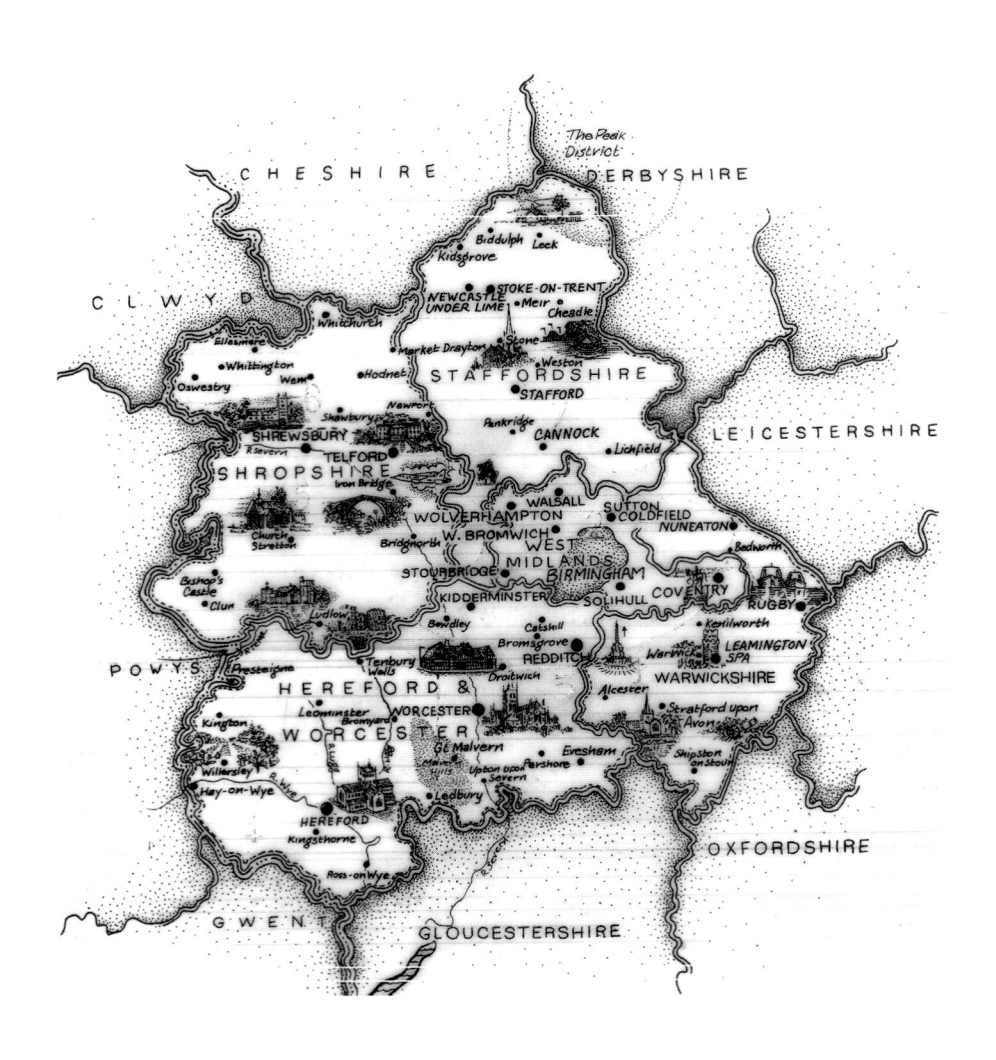

THE WELSH ALPHABET; PRONUNCIATION

b,d,h,l,m,n,p, and t are sounded as in English

c, as in king	ch, as in loch
dd, as in this	f, as in vowel
ff, as in fall	g, as in great
r, well trilled	s, as in sugar
ng, as in long	ph, as in phrase
rh tilled with h	th, as in thorough

ll is more easily learnt when hearing it used

Welsh vowels, a,e,i,o,u,w,y, can be pronounced long AND short for example:

a, as in harm and man;
e, as in gate and pet;
i, as in feel and hit;
o, as in moor and hot;
u, as long as 'i';
w, as in cool and hood;
y, as in sun and sit.

Words of two syllables and over in Welsh, usually have the emphasis on the last but one syllable.

GLOSSARY

Aber	1. a small stream
	2. a confluence of a river or stream
	3. mouth of the river (usually followed by its name)
Aberaeron	mouth of river Aeron (name of goddess)
Abergavenny	mouth of river Gavenny (from gof-smith)
afon	a river
allt(or gallt)	hillside or wood
Banc	mound, bank or hillock
bedd	a grave
blaen	source of river; head of valley
bont (pont)	a bridge
bron	a hillside
bryn	a hill
Bryn-mawr	big hill
Bwlch	pass
caeau	fields
Cardigan (Ceredigion)	
	land of Ceredig (persons name)
carreg	a rock
castell	a castle
Cefn	ridges
Cemais	river bend
cil	a nook; source of stream
Clwyd	a hurdle
Clynnog	place of holly
Coed	wood
Conwy	name of river (full and flowing)
dan	below, under
dol	a meadow; a river meadow
Dolau	meadows
Dolgellau	meadow of the monk's cells
Dwygyfylchi	round forts; Dwy = two
Dyfed	name of old tribal land
Dyffryn	a valley
esgair	a mountain ridge
fach	small
fawr	big
Felin	mill
Felin-gwm	valley of the mill
Foel	a bare-topped hill
Fron	a hillside
Ffestiniog	land of Ffestin (persons name)
Ffridd	mountain pasture
Ffynnon	a well or spring

Garn	a heap of stones or cairn
Garreg	a rock or cliff
Gelli	a small wood
Gilfach	small recess
Glan	a river bank
Glyn	a glen
graig	a rock or crag
Gwern	marsh or alder trees
Gwynedd	land of Venedotae (a tribe)
Hafan	haven
Hafod	summer dwelling and pasture
Halkyn (Helygen)	willow tree
Hen	old
Hendre	winter dwelling
heol	a road
hir	long
llan	originally an enclosure, now 'church' usually followed by name of saint, although spelling is not always certain. eg. Llanidloes or Llanfyllin
Llanaber	church of the stream's mouth
Llanbedr	St Peter's Church
Llandovery (Llanymddyfri)	church among the waters
Llandrindod	Church of the Trinity
Llanfairpwllgwyngyllgogerychwyrndrobwllllantysiliogogogoch	-meaning St Mary's Church of the pool of the white hazel near the rushing whirlpool, St Tysylio's church, near the red cave!
Llanerch	a glade or clearing
Llanystumdwy (goddess)	llan-church, ystum-bend, Dwy-name of river
llech	a flat stone
Lluest	small hill farm; a hut
Llwyn	a bush or grove
Llyn	a lake or pool
llys	court or mansion
Machynlleth	the plain of Cynllaith (persons name)
Maen	a rock
Maes	a field (originally unenclosed)
Melin	a mill
Merthyr	a martyr; a martyr's grave
Moel	bare hilltop or hill
mynydd	a mountain
Nant	a stream, small valley containing water
Nantgaredig	nant-stream; caredig-kind
Neuadd	a hall or mansion

Pant	a hollow or valley
Pen	head
Pen-dre	end of top of town or homestead
Pen-maen	head of rock
Penmaen-mawr	head of the big rock
Pentre	village
Plas	a mansion
pont	a bridge
Powys	a Tribal name; pau- a country
Pwl	a pit or pool
Pwllheli	salt-water pool
Rhiw	a hillside
Rhos	moorland
rhyd	a ford or stream
Rhuddlan	red bank
Rhyl	prob. the hill
tal	end: front
Tan	below
tir	land
tre	a homestead; a home; a town
Tudweiliog	land of Tudway (person's name)
ty	a house
tyn (tyddyn)	a small farm or cottage
Uwch	above
Waun (gwaum)	moorland or meadow
y	the (before consonants)
Yr	the (before vowels)

A-Z, GLOSSARY & INDEX

JOINING FORM

TITLE...INITIALS...

SURNAME...

SEX   M.....................   F.....................

NATIONALITY...

AGE GROUP   18-30.................. 31-49.................. 50+..................

ADDRESS...

TOWN..

COUNTY..

POSTCODE..

HOW MANY HOLIDAYS DO YOU TAKE A YEAR?.........................

HOW MANY OF THESE IN THE UK?............ EUROPE..............

OTHER..

HOW MANY OF THESE ARE:

SHORT BREAKS? .... W/ENDS...............................

PLEASE STATE YOUR INTERESTS

i.e. Fishing, Golf, antiques etc ....

DO YOU NORMALLY BOOK IN ADVANCE?...................Y................N

WHICH OF THESE DO YOU NORMALLY STAY IN?

HOTEL .... INNS .... COUNTRY HOUSE ....

HOW DO YOU SETTLE YOUR ACCOUNT?

CREDIT CARD - CHEQUE - CASH

HOW OFTEN FO YOU EAT OUT?..

WHERE DID YOU BUY THIS BOOK?

....

SIGNATURE..

DATE..

Please note that this is not a credit card and is provided for the use of the applicant only at the venues included in the quarterly list which will be sent to you. The publishers cannot be held responsible for any changes in the offers made by establishments. Information is sent out in good faith and is believed to be correct at the time issued to Advantage Club members.

Please return your application form to: JOY DAVID'S ADVANTAGE CARD, FREEPOST, 4a St. Andrews Street, Plymouth, and allow 28 days for delivery.

HOTELS, INNS, RESTAURANTS AND COUNTRY HOUSES

JOY DAVID'S CHOICE

If you would like to have any of the other titles currently available in this series, please complete the coupon and send to:

JOY DAVID'S CHOICE
4, St. Andrews Street, Plymouth,
Tel: 01752 220774

I would like to receive the following (please tick as appropriate):

☐	An Invitation to Plymouth	£12.00 inc p&p
☐	An Invitation to Dartmoor	£6.20 inc p&p
☐	Joy David's Choice - England	£12.00 inc p&p
☐	*Joy David's Choice - Wales, Central England & East Anglia	£12.00 inc p&p
☐	*Joy David's Choice - Scotland	£12.00 inc p&p
☐	Joy David's Choice - Selected Bed & Breakfast	£16.25 inc p&p
☐	Self Catering in Britain	£12.95 inc p&p
☐	Joy Davids Choice - Eat Out, Eat Well in Britain	£12.95 inc p&p

Due out in 1996

Please tick to receive more information about future titles ☐

NAME..
ADDRESS..
....
....
Tel. No. (Daytime) ....

Please make cheques payable to 'Joy David's Choice'

JOY DAVID'S CHOICE

4, St Andrews Street, Plymouth
Tel: (01752) 220774

Dear Reader,

I hope you have enjoyed my choice of places of all kinds, I have certainly enjoyed researching them in order to write this book.

It would make the next edition much easier if you would help by suggesting places that could be included and your comments on any establishment or attraction you have visited, would be much appreciated.

I enjoy corresponding with my readers and look forward to hearing from you.

Yours sincerely,

Joy David